To Petersbı
Army of tl

To Petersburg with the Army of the Potomac

The Civil War Letters of Levi Bird Duff, 105th Pennsylvania Volunteers

LEVI BIRD DUFF

Edited by
Jonathan E. Helmreich

McFarland & Company, Inc., Publishers
Jefferson, North Carolina, and London

Portions of this book appeared in "Levi Bird Duff: Political Views of a Union Soldier," by Jonathan E. Helmreich, *Western Pennsylvania History*, 91, no. 3 (Fall 2008), 24–35, and are reprinted by permission.

Frontispiece: Levi Bird Duff, from an oil portrait most likely painted after he left the army (courtesy Allegheny College).

LIBRARY OF CONGRESS CATALOGUING-IN-PUBLICATION DATA

Duff, Levi Bird, b. 1837.
To Petersburg with the Army of the Potomac : the Civil War letters of Levi Bird Duff, 105th Pennsylvania Volunteers / Levi Bird Duff ; edited by Jonathan E. Helmreich.
p.   cm.
Includes bibliographical references and index.

ISBN 978-0-7864-4430-4
softcover: 50# alkaline paper ∞

1. Duff, Levi Bird, b. 1837 — Correspondence.   2. United States. Army. Pennsylvania Infantry Regiment, 105th (1861–1865)   3. United States — History — Civil War, 1861–1865 — Regimental histories.   4. Pennsylvania — History — Civil War, 1861–1865 — Regimental histories.   5. United States — History — Civil War, 1861–1865 — Personal narratives.   6. Pennsylvania — History — Civil War, 1861–1865 — Personal narratives.   7. Soldiers — United States — Correspondence.   I. Helmreich, Jonathan E.   II. Title.
E527.5105th.D84   2009
973.7'81 — dc22   2009015748

British Library cataloguing data are available

Cover images: Portraits of Levi Bird Duff and Harriet Nixon Duff; portion of a letter from Harriet; flower sent by Levi to Harriet from "Drainsville," December 1861 (all images courtesy Allegheny College)

Manufactured in the United States of America

McFarland & Company, Inc., Publishers
Box 611, Jefferson, North Carolina 28640
www.mcfarlandpub.com

For
Audrey, Evie, Maggie, and Will

Acknowledgments

First and foremost, my thanks both personally and on behalf of Allegheny College are extended to the descendants of Levi Bird Duff, who donated his papers to his alma mater. In particular, these thanks are directed to the heirs of Agnes Eccles "Nan" Duff, the great-granddaughter of the Civil War soldier. The generosity of Ms. Duff's nephews Roger and Tom Duff and niece Jane Lea Beuyukian is highly appreciated.

Several persons had much to do with the transfer of the papers to the college. Judge Thomas D. Gladden (Allegheny College Class of 1954) made us aware of the papers. William M. Kline III kept them in safekeeping for Agnes Duff and safely brought them to the college in horrendous weather. Wendy Denton Heleen, Esquire, supervised legal matters, and Joseph Fetcko aided with college arrangements. I am grateful for their effective assistance.

My thanks are also extended to *Western Pennsylvania History*, which kindly granted permission to use here portions of my article originally published in that magazine.

Numerous colleagues facilitated the transcription and editing of the Duff letters. Encouragement and support from Dr. Richard J. Cook and Dr. James H. Mullen, presidents of Allegheny College, have been significant for all aspects of the college and especially for the effort to document and rediscover its history. The friendship and help of the staff of Pelletier library have been wonderful. Special thanks are due Linda Bills, librarian; Ruth Ash, archivist; and to Alan Bartlett, Helen McCullough, Jane Westenfeld, Suzanne Williams, Don Vrabel, and Nancy Brenot. Don Covill Skinner offered the benefit of his careful eye and understanding of the Civil War. William N. Owen provided skilled photography.

I would like here also to remember my friend, neighbor, and office-mate from the first half of my career at Allegheny, the late M. Jay Luvaas. It was Jay who led me (sometimes through battlefield poison ivy) to take interest in the Civil War, even though at the time I was more deeply immersed in the diplomacy of Europe.

As always, I am indebted to my wife, Nancy, for her support and much, much more. I also gratefully give thanks for our extended family and all their hopes and joys. Finally, it seems appropriate to offer thanks to two unusual people who suffered much and gave much: Levi and Harriet.

Contents

Introduction: Levi and Harriet

"Flowers for my <u>good</u>, <u>good</u> wife." As he traveled from battlefield to battlefield of the Civil War in the United States, Levi Bird Duff sent mementos to his friend, then fiancée, then bride, Harriet Howard Nixon. In the summer these took the form of flowers; in fall or winter leaves or twigs might serve. Each traveled to Allegheny City, now part of Pittsburgh, laden with kisses and enclosed in letters of love. In all, Levi wrote about ten score letters. The remarkably supportive Hattie sent 221, usually unparagraphed, epistles. The two cherished and preserved these paper and flower evidences of love, loyalty, and relationship. Indeed they had few other ways to make their union seem real. Levi kept Harriet's missives in a black oilcloth toilet kit she made for him, rereading her letters, as she did his, to bolster spirits on dark days and lonely evenings. To the best of their, and the family's knowledge, perhaps only one or two of these communications was lost or destroyed.

At first awkward and studiedly courteous, Levi's correspondence became increasingly frequent, extensive, and informal as his relationship with Harriet deepened. Because the Army of the Potomac spent most of the war fairly close to Washington, D.C., which city had good connections with Pittsburgh, the letters for the most part traveled quickly. Though all Levi's notes did not follow the same pattern, generally they began with a report regarding which of Harriet's messages had arrived, expression of the joy they brought to him, followed by admonitions to keep the letters coming. Levi next might scribe a lengthy paragraph or two expressing his private feelings of love and admiration for Harriet. A chronicle of events in the army and a commentary on the Union's military fortunes and leadership would follow. A closing paragraph returned to the theme of love and fidelity, ending with the sending of love to all and kisses to Harriet. His salutary, after only the first

Harriet Nixon Duff, from an oil portrait (courtesy Allegheny College).

1

few messages, was invariably "Dearest Harriet." Levi's valedictory in the first letters was "Yours sincerely," but it soon graduated to "Adieu, <u>Bird</u>." Later, it became "Your own" or "Your husband <u>Levi</u>."

The collection, now in the keeping of Allegheny College, presents a picture of life in the Army of the Potomac that is unusual for the literacy of its pages, the frequency and continuity of reports, the forthrightness of Levi's observations, the strength of his opinions, and their source: a volunteer private who rose to the rank of lieutenant colonel and thus was a witness of the army at several levels. Written only for the eyes of Harriet and often jotted in haste at the end of a long day, the messages carry an immediacy of thought and genuineness that add piquancy.

Like scores of other combatants, Levi eschewed description of the gory details of battle. They were too horrible to allow relish in the telling, and Levi recognized that such information would only exacerbate the worry afflicting Harriet's fragile nerves. Moreover, as time passed Levi himself became increasingly inured to loss in battle. There is no mistaking his reasons for fighting against what he always termed the "Slaveholders' Rebellion." Yet his wish to support the cause of freedom and justice for all men was severely challenged by desire to be home with Harriet. The contest between the two motivations swayed back and forth just as did the fortunes of the war.

Challenges posed by weather and lack of regiment reinforcements are made clear. So too are some of the organizational, leadership, and morale problems that plagued the Union troops in the first years of the contest. The growing confidence of the soldiers in future victory, in President Abraham Lincoln, and in General Ulysses S. Grant that produced the "soldier vote" that assured Honest Abe's reelection in 1864 is firmly detailed.

Princeton historian James M. McPherson has described the avidity with which troops read the surprisingly available newspapers.[1] That interest is well evidenced in Duff's letters, as is the rank and file's cynicism regarding the accuracy and motives of the media. An almost day by day, sometimes hourly, account of weather encountered by his regiment over months in a row could be assembled from Duff's correspondence, for some mention of climatic conditions appears in nearly every note. So also can be discerned the peevishness and restlessness that develops in long encampments without forward movement. The effect of alcohol is chronicled as is the amazing speed with which veteran soldiers could build — and take pleasure in remaining in — relatively comfortable quarters. The age-old army experience of "hurry-up and wait" is described. The frequency and scope of rumors is shown as well, although for reasons of space a portion of Levi's discussion of these must be here omitted.

Samuel Duff, Levi's father, shown about 45 years of age, was a successful entrepreneur in the iron business. His opinions were sought and respected by Levi (courtesy Allegheny College).

Courage, perseverance, sense of duty, longing, stoicism in the face of horrors and danger all emerge from Duff's letters. So too does the personality of a self-disciplined man who held to his independence and his principles in a manner that took but slight account of the weaknesses of human nature, which he scorned. The letters also hold the story of a love that grew and deepened as pen and pencil brought two lives closer together. Levi's disquisitions on his possessive care for Harriet and hers for him are too lengthy and involved to countenance full inclusion in this reproduction of his letters. But enough has been transcribed for readers to perceive a truly romantic journey of heart and mind. The coy, clever, intelligent, and religiously inspired epistles sent by Harriet to her lover and husband are only briefly quoted, yet still reveal her character, emotions, and capacity for endurance.

Who were Levi and Harriet? They were born on the same day, September 18, 1837. Levi was the fourth of eight children of Samuel Duff, whose great-grandfather came to Pennsylvania from Scotland before the Revolutionary War.[2] Among the siblings, Levi appears to have been closest to his brother Firman, who was older by five and a half years. Their mother, Catherine Eckerberger Duff, was of Pennsylvania Dutch heritage. Born in a log house on Standing Stone Creek, Barre Township in Huntingdon County, Pennsylvania, Levi moved with his family by Conestoga wagon at the age of three to the village of Clarion in the far western region of the state. Samuel Duff entered the iron business, and in 1845 the family again relocated to a house on Fiddler's Run near Pike Furnace.

Levi studied in local schools, showing sufficient aptitude that in the summer of 1853 his father sent him to Reimersburg to an establishment run by a Mr. Lyon. His performance there led Samuel to enroll his son that November in Eldersridge Academy to prepare for college. Levi entered Allegheny College in Meadville, Pennsylvania, performed well, became a member of both the Philo-Franklin Literary Society and the recently formed Phi Kappa Psi social fraternity, and graduated in 1857. He and six other classmates in his twenty-four member senior class developed a close friendship that resulted in what they called the "Society of Seven." They took themselves, their character, their behavior, and their performance seriously, discussing their lots and their futures and how best to shape these. It was their sworn agreement that each would write to the others once a year, critically assessing their personal activities and revealing their plans to improve themselves. It was also their plan to meet every seven years. Such sabbatical gatherings of all seven did not take place, for sadly some of their number did not survive even seven years past graduation. But some did, and Levi held a fifty-year reunion with at least two of his fellow society mem-

Catherine Eckerberger Duff, Levi's mother. He mentioned her rarely in his correspondence (courtesy Allegheny College).

bers, Bishop James Mills Thoburn, the famous missionary of Methodism to India, and Harvey Henderson, a noted lawyer in Meadville and a key trustee of Allegheny College.

In his first "statement of my shortcomings" sent to colleagues in the Society of Seven in May 1858, Levi reported studying law at home until the previous December, when he entered the office of George S. Seldon for further training and study. "Of money I have made none, but spent a good deal. Of fame I have acquired none, either good or bad. I am in a community where I am little known, and all that I have heard said, for or against me, is that I am a diligent student. This is certainly as much as I could ask, and as much as I want. The way to gain a lasting impression anywhere is to keep back the weak and shove out the strong points, so that, when men do get to know you, they may know you only for good."[3]

Duff applied for admission to the Bar in Pittsburgh in 1860. In his first appearance before the Board of Examiners, he failed to pass—in his mind not because he did not know the law but because the older men wished to hold the confident young man back. Discouraged, he returned to Clarion where his family urged him to reapply. Advised by Seldon to appear to take a month or so for further study, he took examination again in April and succeeded easily. Levi then opened an office in Pittsburgh, his chief and somewhat limited legal work consisting of routine matters directed to him by his businessman father. At the time of his enlistment in the Pittsburgh Rifles on May 1, 1861, he was 23 years and seven and a half months old, making him very close to the average age at enlistment of Union soldiers.[4] Today, his letters read as if written by a man of more mature years. As Harriet wrote on their twenty-fourth birthday, "you are young, yet the times in which we live require young men to be old in wisdom."[5]

When Levi began his legal career he took board and lodging just outside of Pittsburgh proper in Allegheny City, a middle class town that has long since become a portion of the larger metropolis. At nearby Craig (later Cremo) Street dwelled Roseanna Nixon, the widow of Hezekiah Nixon, former mayor of Allegheny City and a prominent contractor. Living with their mother were her five children, the oldest of which was Harriet.

The young lady, in addition to helping with the younger children (Tom was just ten years old), taught in the Allegheny City Public High School. She was used to fulfilling a role of responsibility within the family, for as her parents' previous children had died in infancy, Harriet in her youth became the close companion of her father. When his eyesight began to fail when she was about fourteen, she kept his business books and conducted his correspondence until his death in December 1858. Bright, with a fine command of English at an early age, Harriet's progress in her schooling was such that at the age of sixteen she was qualified to teach and at age seventeen began to do so.

Financial reverses initiated by fire at Hezekiah's mill and lumber yard sharply

Duff as a student at Allegheny College, where he sought out acquaintanceship with other leading students (courtesy Allegheny College).

reduced his estate in his last years. To augment family income the Nixon family took in board-ers. Most were theological students, for the Nixons were active and prominent members of the First and later the Third Presbyterian Church of Allegheny City. Their home had long been a meeting place for religious and educated people; conversations were animated and well augmented by Harriet's way with words and wide-ranging familiarity with the best of liter-ature. Acquaintances brought friends to tea, and soon lawyer Duff made regular appearance.

Levi stood out among the young men because of his education, his drive, good charac-ter, and seriousness of purpose. He also was handsome. At five feet ten inches in height, he was taller than average for his time. Young and trim, he weighed about 160 pounds; his waist was 33 inches in circumference and he took a size 37 shirt. Levi's erect posture, graceful bear-ing, and broad shoulders, joined with blue eyes, sandy-brown hair, ruddy complexion, and red beard grown after college graduation all made him noticeable.

Harriet nearly matched Levi in height, standing five feet eight inches tall and well pro-portioned (she weighed 130 pounds). Her legs, arms, and hands were long and slender. She wore her dark brown hair in curls, though soon she would pull it back somewhat severely. Harriet's voice was strong and of medium pitch. Her eyes were hazel blue, and her complex-ion was reported both as "olive" and as "fair" with delicate coloring. Whatever the case, what people most noted was not beauty of appearance but her vivaciousness and the richness, both in content and form of expression, of her conversation.

She and Levi seemed a natural match, both mentally and physically. Each stood out in their circle of mutual acquaintances. Each took life seriously—Harriet may have had more of a sense of humor than Levi, who appears to have had little leaning in that direction. Both were safely of the middle class, their families' position won by the ingenuity and hard work of fathers who came up from the ranks of commoners. Their ancestries (English and German for Levi, English and Scot for Harriet) not antithetical. Alas, there was one major problem. Hezekiah and Roseanna Nixon came from Covenanter families. Later deeply active in the Pres-byterian Church, they and Harriet considered themselves confessing Christians firmly con-vinced of an afterlife won only by faith and surrender to Jesus of Nazareth as Savior and Master. Equally real were the machinations of Satan. Repentance of sin was seen as the only path to salvation.

Levi, however, took a different posture on religious matters. His mother was a Methodist, he attended that church, and he had studied at a college patronized by the Methodist Epis-copal Church. He associated with persons of religious persuasion such as Thoburn and Har-riet's friends. But, like his ancestors on his father's side, he was not a church member. He could show respect for the religious views of others, yet believed that one must be responsi-ble for one's own conscience, successes or failings, "rather than blame a personal Devil for misfortune, or expect happiness to be procured by daily confession of sins and reliance on a supernatural power to be reached only through the dogmatic practice of so called revealed religion," to use the words of Levi's son.[6]

Could it be possible for persons of such differing views on such an important matter to live happily together? Levi feared that any attempt to carry their relationship beyond friend-ship would be repulsed. Harriet worried that God would not bless such a union. Concern over this matter and her view of Levi's need for salvation caused Harriet deep anxiety. Yet the two shared much: they detested slavery; they supported the Republican cause (on this Levi differed from his father, who was a Democrat); they favored the election of Abraham Lin-coln; *volens-nolens* they enjoyed each other's presence, conversation, patterns of thinking; and they simply were attracted to each other. The religious issue was overcome—or set aside. Yet it remained a leitmotif in their correspondence. The letters reveal the accommodation achieved, one that pivoted less on the saving personal sacrifice of Jesus than on consideration of the role of God, or what the classicists might have called the fates, in history and personal lives.

Levi Bird Duff participated in more than twenty battle engagements during his enlistment in the Army of the Potomac, from that at Dranesville in 1861 to the conflict at Petersburg in 1864. At times his survival was more than problematic, yet survive he did to live a lengthy life and produce a family. One son, Samuel Eckerberger Duff, in 1934 undertook the writing of a family history for the benefit of his own young son, Levi Bird Duff III. In that history, the son quotes extensively, yet judiciously, from his father's Civil War letters. Passages critical of leading personalities or which revealed a wavering of Levi's hopes for the Union cause were generally omitted, and Samuel introduced his own spelling corrections and paragraphing. The account, especially of the early and later events of Levi's life, has been of great help in the preparation of the present compilation.

An additional source of value on Duff's military career is Kate M. Scott's *History of the One Hundred and Fifth Regiment of Pennsylvania Volunteers*, published in 1877, a copy of which Duff donated to his college in the same year.[7] In December 1861, disease struck the 105th, the regiment in which Duff was enrolled, as it lay at Camp Jameson in Virginia. An appeal for nurses brought response from four young women. Kate Scott was among them and remained a regimental nurse until the 105th was posted to the Peninsula with no provision for nurses to accompany it. Deeply attached to the "boys" she cared for, Scott closely followed the fate of the regiment and, when later asked to write the history of the regiment, again answered the call. Her acquaintance with its members and survivors enabled her to garner much information from letters, diaries, and regimental papers. She was in correspondence with Duff, with whom she later discussed plans for a revised second edition of her work that never appeared. The close parallel of some of her paragraphs describing maneuvers with the wording of Levi's letters to Harriet suggest that Levi drew upon those letters in providing information to Scott. In addition, she occasionally quotes Duff's postwar accounts of military events. Although written in hagiographic style, Scott's history nevertheless presents an accurate rehearsal of maneuvers and battle events.

The letters Levi wrote to Harriet were most often set down by candlelight late in the evening after a long day. When in camp Duff habitually woke before dawn. The first half hour of his day was perhaps the most enjoyable, for he would lie in his bunk and imagine Harriet beside him with her head on his chest, softly conversing and occasionally kissing his cheek. Then Duff was off to drill, picket duty, or other assignment until evening. He seems to have been relatively adept at navigating the army system, learning how to find free time

Duff as a young lawyer in Pittsburgh, where he at first had only limited business (courtesy Allegheny College).

and how to establish a comfortable tent. His personal discipline regarding alcohol, tobacco, and profane language distanced him from his fellow soldiers; the time he did not spend with them he shared with Harriet. As Duff rose in rank, he gained the assistance of what might be termed a batman, a black contraband who Levi dubbed "Doctor" Melton. The latter would stay with the Duff family as a paid servant for about fifteen years until late in life his mind failed and he had to be placed in an asylum.

Picket duty or regimental movement often required night marches, and Levi would snatch whatever moment was available to write Harriet that he was still safe and what he was doing. Consequently many of his letters were hurriedly scribed when he was dog-tired, by failing light or guttering candle in a cold tent or even in the open, with little opportunity to reread or correct what he had first written. It is not surprising that word omissions and spelling, capitalization, and punctuation vagaries slipped into his messages. These have been left uncorrected, though occasionally an omitted word has been editorially inserted in brackets for ease of reading.

Where Levi's normally legible handwriting leaves doubt, the transcription employs presently accepted spelling and punctuation. For reasons of space and to reduce redundancy, his salutations ("Dearest Harriet") and valedictions ("Your husband") have been omitted, even though their absence lessens the reader's sense of the personal nature of the lovers' correspondence. These features remain in the correspondence of others. For the same reasons, the header indicating the location where the letter was written is shown only when it differs from the location of the previous message.

A portion of most letters has been omitted from the transcriptions. The lacunae include many of the ample sections wherein Levi expressed his respect and love for Harriet and commented on their relationship, short passages about relatives or acquaintances, sections that essentially duplicate information provided in other letters, a few listings of the order of deployment of regiments, and some observations regarding rumors of military movements and comments on politics in Clarion County, Pennsylvania. In other words, what follows are excerpts. To ease their reading and to avoid filling each page with a myriad of dots, ellipses are used only when words are omitted from a sentence or sentences from paragraphs. But they are not used to indicate omission of beginning words in the first paragraph of a letter or of paragraphs in their entirety. This is done even though such omissions may lend more prominence to a given observation than it holds in a rambling, perhaps hastily, written letter where the comment was jotted as a thought in passing or to fill out a page. Yet often it is these that are the most revealing.

It is time now for Levi, with occasional assists from Harriet, his father, and a few others, to tell of his experiences.

1

In Defense of Washington, D.C.

The April 12, 1861, attack by Southern forces on Federal Fort Sumter in the harbor of Charleston, South Carolina, brought quick response from patriots in the North. In her journal entry of April 13, Harriet wrote:*

[D]isagreeable rainy day. report of yesterday confirmed great excitement all the volunteer companies are filling up their numbers. The President calls for 75000 men and proclaims his intention of retaking all the property of the USA. His proclamation is well received party feeling giving place to patriotism....

I confess that at times my timid heart shrinks from the prospect that now forms before us. But when I remember that the wise and good of all parties have endeavored by all means to prevent this collision it seems that it is God's purpose now that a great battle should be fought. Let us then accept the honor of battling in the cause of humanity — precious blood will be spilled lives of those near and dear alas! must be given[1]

On May 1, Levi Duff enlisted in the Pittsburgh Rifles for three months' service. Eight days later, Harriet wrote of watching him drill:

Visited <u>Camp Williams</u> today [May 9]. As this is the first pleasant day we have had this week every body seemed anxious to visit the soldiers— upon entering we met the Pittsburg Rifles drilling they were soon dismissed however when friends Todd Wallace & Duff joined our party.[2] We strolled around watching the various companies drilling. The Erie soldiers wear uniforms of blue jacket and trouwsers with yellow trimming also yellow flannel shirts. They are a hardy looking set of men — noted a company of <u>Germans</u> (from the city) in excellent drill. The orders were given in German — The Iron City Rifles dress in Gray with black trimming. The Pittsburg Rifles in like manner excepting a silver band on the cap. We returned to the P R quarters found them comfortable but <u>not elegant</u> our friend seemed in good spirits. — Treated us to <u>turtle soup</u> and crackers. We enjoyed it very much....

Two days later on Saturday Harriet recorded:

Up early. Busily engaged in home worked until ten o'clock when L. B. D. came he looked well in his uniform is it right that such an educated mind should be lost as we know not but his life will be. Oh how hard it is to look forward with calmness to the approaching conflict, it will be a sanguinary contest. Thousands must die, whose precious ones will they be? Suffered from nervous headache the rest of the day....

Stationed in Pittsburgh where he could continue to visit Harriet on a regular basis, Levi did not often have to resort to letters to maintain their relationship. It is apparent, however, that as in his private life he had worked to advance his career, he held hope of doing similarly so in the military.

---

*Throughout the text, comments by the editor are in italics.

The Pittsburgh Rifles. Recruited from the Pittsburgh area, the Rifles constituted Company A of the 9th Pennsylvania Reserve Volunteer Corps (courtesy Allegheny College).

Camp Wright
June 13th, 1861.

We will leave here in two or three days for Chambersburg. I cannot tell certainly what day. We go in the Erie Regiment & will be mustered into the United States' service "for three years or during the war." Some five or six members of the company have resigned but the rest will go. We had the privilege of going into the United States' service or state service for three years & we chose the former. I am already tired of state service & so are many other members of the company.

Clarion,
June 23rd 1861

Dear Son

I am sorry to see that you have not been successful. I fear your application [for appointment to the regular army] went in too late.... The appointment in this case are like all others it goes by favour and an applicant must have some influential friend or he cannot cause it as the say is. I suppose your chance for preferment is very slim and I hope you will reconcile your self to your fate and make your self as comfortable you can and if you live to be discharged that it may be an honorable one....

Your aft. Father

On June 28 the Pittsburgh Rifles and Private Duff were mustered into the service of the State of Pennsylvania as Company A of the 9th Pennsylvania Reserves (later designated the 38th Regiment Pennsylvania Volunteers) for three years' service.

Excerpts from the journal of Harriet Nixon:

July 4th. Grand parade of Home Guards 3000 fine soldierly men met with Capt. Glass and Lieut. Tyler of [Daniel E.] Sickles Brigade.... Mr. Duff and Messrs Sloan from Camp Wright took tea with us. Had a long talk with Mr. D. on the subject of religion. O thou great God of Hosts from Thee alone cometh light. For Jesus sake send forth thy light and truth.

July 9th At six o'clock Mr. Duff came in.... Worked at my silk quilt whilst Mr. D. drew me an accurate pattern, a party of serenaders in the vicinity made <u>sweet discord</u>, In our own hearts, how little do we know of them? With a most vivid presentiment that Levi once started to war <u>will not return</u> I must school myself to bid "good bye" as though it were for an hour, which I feel that it is—but I cannot think of the future. Will the God of all grace strengthen me.

July 22nd. Oh sad day. Our army has been routed [at Bull Run] ... and just when most horrified we are to part with dear friends all the soldiers encamped here leave to morrow. With a smile on my lips I have said "good bye" when I felt it was a "farewell forever."—at such a moment what is the whole world to us. Yet in <u>firm unswerving faith</u> I lean on God's promises. He is a God of love and <u>will</u> give grace and strength.

On July 23 Duff's regiment left Pittsburgh for Harrisburg and then Washington where it was posted to defend Washington from an expected attack by Confederate forces.

Camp Curtin
Near Harrisburg
July 24th, 1861

We left Pittsburg yesterday morning at 8 o'clock ... & had a pleasant ride to this place where we arrived about eleven o'clock last night. We got out of the cars, the regiment was formed & we were marched to Camp Curtin, where after an annoying delay of an hour, we were assigned quarters on the Parade ground. About twelve o'clock we unrolled our blankets & laid down. I went to sleep in a moment (for you may know that I was sleepy) & slept till 5 o'clock this morning. I woke feeling much refreshed. We had furnished to us some port & hard bread for breakfast which were very good, but to make my breakfast really good I went to the market house & had some coffee & bread & butter.

Afterwards I walked around the Capitol Grounds.... We are here now awaiting orders to go to Baltimore....

Camp Jackson
(near) Washington D.C.
July 29th 1861

We left Harrisburg on Wednesday evening for Baltimore, but lay over all night within sight of the town. The next morning at daylight we got under way & arrived at Baltimore about noon. We laid there idle all day but were not allowed to leave the place where we halted — an open common west of the city. Just at dark we left that city and at daylight the next morning we arrived in Washington, & halted on an open common north of the capitol. We lay here idle all day as usual & late in the evening we were marched to our present encampment.

Ever since then we have been fixing up our tents & have them now pretty well arranged. Our tents, however are small & crowded. They would suit well enough for cool weather, but in warm weather they are a little unpleasant. We have good water here, but our rations are not the best. I can, notwithstanding, to get along very comfortably; am well....

...The drum is now calling for regimental drill & I must close....

It was at Washington on July 28 that Duff was mustered into the service of the United States as 6th Corporal of Company A of the 38th Regiment Pennsylvania Volunteers.

Aug. 5th, 1861

Never were letters more welcome.... Your forethought in sending it as soon as you ascertained my whereabouts shows me plainly that you feel interested in my welfare & are ever following me with kind wishes & kind offices....

...We received orders yesterday evening to move from here to some camp near Georgetown, & of course we must lay aside every thing & obey the order. The camp is about five miles distant from here, & we are obliged to march, and if they do not haul our knapsacks, our journey will not be pleasant. I am confident, however, that I can endure it for I am growing stronger every day. I have never enjoyed better health, & have never felt stronger than I do to-day. I feel sure that if nothing untoward happens [to] me I will be greatly improved by campaigning....

I believe that all our men would prefer to remain here. We thought when we first came here that we had a bad camp, but we have since been convinced we were mistaken, & we are now as loath to leave as we were to stay at first. As a general thing we know very little about camp life, we will learn more by & by.

Our food has been very poor since we came here — altogether the fault of our officers. They know very little of their duties & are neglectful besides, & you may imagine that we are poorly cared for. Our company, however, suffers much less than others. We all have a little money & know how to take care of ourselves, others are not so fortunate.

All the boys are packing up & I will soon have to join in. We may remain here nearly all day & may move in a very few minutes. We must be prepared to go whenever the baggage wagons arrive & not knowing when that will be we are obliged to hold ourselves in readiness all the time....

Camp Tenally
Aug. 8th, 1861

I wrote you a letter on Monday morning just before we left our camp near Washington. I had scarcely finished writing when the order came to strike tents, which we did in a very short time. We got under way for this camp about 10 o'clock & arrived here at 3 in the afternoon, having made three stops on the way. We marched about seven & a half miles, under the most terrible sun I ever felt. The first five miles we marched with arms in position & without a rest. We had not gone far until the men began to drop out overcome by the heat. But one of our men dropped out but when we halted one of them named Bailey fell down almost dead & was restored with difficulty, in fact he is not well yet. I stood it pretty well but I became convinced, that I would have to become inured to the heat before I could make many such marches.[3]

We are now encamped some six miles from the city, on what is called the Fredricksburg Turnpike. We have a fine field for our tents, but our water is bad & very scarce.

On Tuesday evening nine companies of our regiment were ordered to march three miles from here in the direction of Harpers Ferry to stand Picket Guard. Although we started late in the afternoon — 4 o'clock — the heat fatigued us a good deal though none gave out. We reached the place, however, in good time, and as our company was posted as a Reserve to give aid to the Pickets in case of attack, we had an opportunity to lie down & rest. We unrolled our blankets & lay down for the night in a stubble field with nothing but the heavens above us for a covering. The night was clear & pleasant, but the morning dew was heavy enough to wet our blankets & make us a little uncomfortable. On Wednesday morning, twenty four of our company including myself, were sent out on a scout. We scoured the country for three or four miles in front of our Pickets but returned without finding anything. We were relieved from picket duty yesterday evening, & returned to our camp, coming into camp about 11 o'clock, somewhat fatigued with our long turn on duty. On our return to camp we learned that some very wild & improbable rumors had been circulated concerning us during the day. I fear that those rumors have reached Pittsburg, & if so will create a great deal of anxiety in the community. It was rumored that our regiment had been attacked by the secessionist[s] & "cut to pieces["], & that the Pittsburg Rifles alone had lost thirty five men. This of course was entirely false & the man who concocted it deserves no better fate than the gallows. There was an alarm on Tuesday night, which called out the 10th & 11th regiments, but what it arose from we are not permitted to know. As soon as we came in last night we were ordered to hold ourselves in readiness to march at a moments notice. We are still under these orders, but have not yet been required to march. Last night several batteries of artillery passed here on the road leading towards Harpers Ferry, but halted a short distance beyond here. There is a movement now making in this direction, but of course I can tell you nothing about it, not knowing any thing about it.

Harriet, we are all safe yet, but it will not be long until some of us must go down. We are here in the advance, & every thing seems to indicate that a pitch battle will take place here soon. I must caution you however not to believe any reports of single regiments being "cut to pieces." Such a thing is not likely to happen; but a general battle is not improbable, & you & I must accept the result.... Give my love to all. You know I cannot <u>send</u> my love to you.

Aug. 13th 1861

We do not hear too frequently from Pittsburg & consequently a letter from you is never out of place. There are other reason[s] why a letter from you should be welcome at all times, but I need not mention them here, it will suffice to hint at them.

We have just come in from regimental drill of one hour in the rain. The boys are all complaining of the colonel — not because he drilled us in the rain but because he had the impudence to wear an India rubber coat when he well knew that the privates could not afford such a covering.[4] He is fast getting the ill-will of all the men in the regiment, & judging from the progress of this feeling within the last few days, in a week he will be as little respected as Col. [Irvin] McDowell.

It may be truthfully affirmed that [he] cares nothing about his men — at least he never looks to their comfort in any respect. We might starve, drown or die by any other mode & he would never know it, until on going into the field for regimental drill, he would not find his regiment. All this could be overlooked at least by me for I can take care of myself but in addition to this he is trifling & unaccomodating. The other day I went to him & ask[ed] permission to visit the tenth regiment which is encamped about a hundred yards from us across the turnpike & he ... refused it. I at once set him down a fool & shall continue to think him such until he proves himself something else. Others can get out of camp by running past the sentinels, but I cannot stoop to that, so I have to stay in. I can tell him that he will never gain anything by acting so towards his men.

These things have already had their legitimate effect upon the men. Some days when we go out on regimental drill the men do just as they please. This annoys him so much that he can scarcely sit on his horse, & he never ceases to sweat while he is on the field, which conclusively proves to all men that he is unfit for the position he holds. A man who cannot govern his own temper, cannot govern a regiment of a thousand men. If the committee which was authorized by Congress to inquire into the qualifications of the volunteer officers, is ever appointed & does its work thoroughly, we may have some hope of losing him soon, otherwise we will be bothered with him until we go into battle some time, when I have no doubt he will be summarily disposed of.

Aug. 19th, 1861

For twenty four hours previous to the receipt of [your letter] I had been acting as corporal of the Guard—for be it known that I am a corporal—& was a good deal fatigued for the duty is an arduous one. Your kind words, however revived my drooping spirits, so much so that after reading your letter I felt like a new man....

...I know I shall never be able to repay your love, but I will make every effort to render you contented & happy....

...The Sabbath to you & to me are not the same. But although I do not religiously observe the Sabbath I love the peace & quiet which it always brings when I am at home. Here in the army it is not taken into account at all. We are obliged to drill & parade on Sunday the same as on any other day & we hardly know when it comes, except that on that day in addition to ordinary duties we have a review & inspection....

I thank you for the faith which you have that I will be preserved & return to you safe. Your faith is not stronger than mine. I know that I will see you again, but ... it will not be long. It is reported that Gen. [Winfield] Scott [general-in-chief of the Union armies] said a few days ago that we would be home by Christmas ... but if the old Gen said so I must doubt the fulfillment of his prophecy. I have not changed my opinion since I left you. I still believe that we will not be sent home for a year.

Was I not fortunate in enlisting early? By this I have avoided your patriotic indignation, which has burst furiously upon the heads of the "cravens." I have not heard anything about drafting. I think the fears of the few "cravens" who remain at home have given rise to the report. I should be sorry if this should have to be resorted to. Although those who remain at home & consider volunteering beneath their notice should by some means be impressed into the service—not for any benefit that they would be to it, for men who have not their hearts in it are not fit to fight in a cause like this—but to punish them for not responding to the call of their country in time of need. If we are obliged to impress men into service to fill up our army to the necessary complement, it will produce a bad impression, not only in Europe but also in the South & would dampen the ardor of the few union men who remain there. I hope that every other expedient will be exhausted before this is resorted to.

...Our line of pickets now extends from the Potomac in the neighborhood of the Chain bridge to Harpers Ferry. A few evenings since a picket at Harpers Ferry called out "Five o'clock & all is well" which call was repeated by every picket from that place to the chain bridge. It reached here at twenty minutes past five, so that in twenty minutes we can learn the condition of our line. Every thing is very quiet here now....

We are now having very dismal weather here. We have not seen the sun for eight days. For that length of time it has rained constantly.... Nearly all of our boys have the horrors, & say that the rain is about "played out."... Our camp ground was a beautiful green sod, when we encamped on it, ... [but the rain and a thousand men] have converted the sod into mud. The mud in the shallowest place is about three inches deep. I have not attempted to fathom it in the deepest places. The floor of our camp is just like the road. Our shoes & every thing on the floor collect mould, & all our clothes have a rotten smell. Just imagine me seated in a small tent on an India rubber blanket spread on the floor, & leaning on a pile of woolen blankets on which are placed my paper & eating utensils, & which serves for a table. Before me dimly burns a candle which is stuck into a bottle to elevate high enough to throw the light on my table. The rain falls on the tent constantly & runs in at the front & forms a puddle in the middle of it. To the left of me sit four of five men smoking & cursing the weather. Imagine all this, & you will have a faint picture of *your* soldier writing you a letter....

Aug. 20th, 1861

Our col. for the last two or three days has been more respectful to his men when on the field than usual. We got along very smoothly this morning; & if he would only keep cool & not open his mouth except in giving commands we would never have any trouble.

Our captain has been sick ever since we arrived in Washington.[5] He went home yesterday but expects to return again in about ten days. We will be in a bad fix if we should happen to loose him. Our Lieutenants are of no account at all. Instead of improving as men would ordinarily under such circumstances, they are getting worse every day, at least it seems so. They have lost the confidence of every member in the company. Some of the men talk very freely & loud about them, but I take care to keep my mouth closed, well knowing that talk will not better the matter, but on the other hand increase the discontent in the company....

Aug. 28th, 1861

Did I not consider it a patriotic duty to remain here & help to fight the battles of my country I should hasten home. So strong is the temptation, that I verily believe that no other consideration would restrain me from doing so. Though separated, Harriet, I feel that our acquaintance still grows....

If you failed to open your heart to me when present (& I think you did, at least some times) you have not neglected to do so in your letters.... I know that to me you are a firm support, holding me up when I would falter, encouraging me & enabling me to do my duty manfully, when I might be lukewarm & fail, & shielding me from evil in my present exposed and trying situation. If any thing assails me, the memory of your love .... [is] alone sufficient to protect me.... I ask no other lot than to be permitted to live with you — whatever fate may befall us.

Since I last wrote to you we have been on Picket, though we had a very quiet time. Part of the time it rained, & of course it was a little unpleasant, but as a general thing we enjoyed ourselves more than if we had remained in camp. We went out on Thursday evening last & returned on Friday evening. We were posted on a road about 3 miles North of this—a road running East from the Harper's Ferry road. We were not the outside picket as we were when out first, but were posted as a sort of police to keep down the Maryland secessionist, who are plenty in Montgomery county. We left camp about five o'clock & marching very fast, reached our front a half an hour afterwards. Our company was divided into squads, & the squads were posted along the road, extending about a mile. I was stationed as chief of a squad of five at a point where a by-road entered the main road from the South, & instructed to overhaul every thing passing along the road.

After we had been assigned our station we ate our supper & immediately began to fix up for the night. The men who had been there before us had built a sort of covering for themselves with branches & leaves; but on examination it was found to be a poor protection from rain. As there was a heavy rain storm coming up in the Southwest, we shrugged our shoulders in anticipation of a "good soaking" & a disagreeable night. On the side of the road opposite to the poor covering which had fallen to our lot, was a thick wild grape vine, which had run up a small oak & spread out making a fine shelter, but too small to accommodate more than one. Seeing this I told the men that I would lie there and that they might have the shelter on the other side of the road to themselves. As it had already begun to rain the men soon crawled under their shelter, to avoid as much of the rain as possible. I put my India rubber blanket round my shoulders, crossed the road & sat down under the grape-vine, both to keep a vigilant eye on the road & to await the "coming storm." The storm came on, but the fury of it passed over us without bursting, & we were favored only with a clever shower of rain against which we were well enough protected. About eight o'clock the rain ceased, & as it was part of my duty to keep a man posted in the road during night, I brought one of the men out and stationed him on a high place in the road which happened to be just alongside the grape-vine — very convenient for me. I also ordered the whole squad to load their pieces to be pre-pared for any emergency, though I apprehended no danger. Having made these arrangements I concluded to lie down & sleep. In order not to be disturbed too often I gave a watch to the man who was standing guard & directed him to wake up another man in two hours, & to relieve each other every two hours thereafter during the night. My sentinel was standing near the grape vine where he could awake me without leaving his post, so I congratulated myself on my situation expecting to have a night's sleep.

The first thing in order was to make my bed, which I did in this wise: Laying two rails parallel to each other & about a foot & a half apart, I filled the space between them with fine brush not to make my bed soft, but to elevate it slightly from the ground. On top of the rails & the brush I spread my India rubber blanket. On this I lay down, my gun by my side loaded, & pulled my woolen blanket over me. I felt snug, & soon went asleep. I slept very soundly for about two hours, when it began to rain hard, & after continuing to rain a short time it soaked through the grape-vine & fell down in my face. I got rid of this annoyance by pulling the blanket over my head & again slept on undisturbed. In about an hour I was awakened again by one of my men who told me that an alarm had been fired by a scouting party which had been sent out in the evening, & that word had been sent along the line for us to be on the alert. I told him to lie down & not mind it for I felt certain that the alarm was false, & we immediately resumed our accustomed quiet. But the alarm, though unheeded by us, was not unheeded by a brigade of volunteers from the Eastern states which was encamped on our right. The drums beat the regiments to arms & four turned out & stood in readiness for sev-eral hours until it was ascertained that the alarm was false.

The scouting party to which I referred above was composed partly of our company, & partly of some Massachusetts volunteers who were in the brigade above mentioned. They went out to search an old house which was situated about three miles from our lines, & as it was unoccupied was supposed to be a place of rendezvous for the secessionists. They approached the house through the woods of course, & when near it one of the Mass. Volun-teers fell & accidentally discharged his gun, & it was this discharge that caused the alarm of which I have first told you. Our men & the Mass men were not together, but were approach-ing the house in different directions, & when the piece went off our men supposing they were fired upon lay down & kept still until they had discovered what it was. There are various sto-ries told of the courage displayed by our men when they supposed that they were attacked. It is well ascertained I believe that some of them were frightened.... The whole party, how-ever, charged on the house carried it, but found it empty, & having accomplished their object returned to camp, or rather to the line of pickets.

I was very little disturbed during the remainder of the night.... I got along very quietly during the day, having to stop only <u>one</u> wagon, which was found to contain nothing....

Well, Harriet, camp-life is just as monotonous as ever. We are generally very busy; but it is very seldom that we do any thing but drill. Yesterday we had a little variety, having been detailed to work on a fort which they are building just beyond Tennallytown. I worked all day very hard, too hard in the afternoon, for when I came home I was not able to eat any supper. I have the satisfaction of knowing that I have given some of my strength to the defense of Washington....

Yesterday evening we were ordered to pack our knapsacks & put two days rations into our haversacks & be ready to march at a moments notice. We prepared accordingly but have remained in quarters ever since. Just a moment ago we received another order to have three days rations in our haversacks & to be prepared to march forthwith. The men declare that they have been fooled so often that they will not prepare until they get an order to fall in....

Harriet Nixon. The young school teacher was physically frail but possessed gritty determination, an active mind, and a pleasing demeanor (courtesy Allegheny College).

> Allegheny City
> Sept. 2nd 1861

My dear Bird:

Coming home this evening, very tired for I had much extra labor I heard all the bad news I could bear. Hope trailed her shining wings until better thoughts came. "The darkest hour is just before day." I determined that I <u>would not</u> despond since, "come what there may, to stand in the way, the <u>Might</u>, with the <u>Right</u> and the <u>Truth</u>, shall be." Away! this trembling fear, our cause is just and *must* prevail. An hour ago I wished for wings that just once more I might meet you e're the battle's smoke closed around you; now I know that whilst you do your duty in battle, mine to pray submit and trust must also be performed. I give up all to God.... Levi let me remind you, as I would my own heart, <u>death might come. Be ready</u>.... You said to me (and I shall never forget the words) "Some men <u>must die</u> for the Country" if yours is to be one — what words do I write, alas! What thoughts must I think.... I must be a woman worthy of a soldier's love, <u>trusting, hoping</u>....

> Harriet

> Camp Tenally
> Sept. 4th, 1861

Last night about twelve o'clock we were roused up & marched to the chain-bridge, about two & half miles it being alleged that the Rebels were advancing in that direction.... We were halted on the river-bank, & ordered to be on the look out during the night, but all of the men felt so confident that no enemy was coming that they unrolled their blankets & lay down & slept. I among them. No enemy came & this morning just at day-light we were aroused washed ourselves, breakfasted as well as we could which was very poorly, for we had left camp in such a hurry that most of us got nothing but bread. We were posted behind a breast-work which has been thrown up ... to prevent the enemy should he cross the river, from marching on Washington. The 6th Wisconsin regt. came to our relief & we were marched back to camp....

To-day the 7th P. R. C was fired upon by the Rebels at Great Falls.... The rebels approached on the Virginia side [of the river] & fired upon them with four rifled cannon. It has not been ascertained whether any were killed. The 7th had no rifled cannon & could not reply effec-

tively to the rebels, but the 8th has been sent to its assistance with rifled cannon. It is probable that we are destined for some dangerous post to-night.... The enemy is getting very bold
on the other side of the river.... I think they will soon have to yield to us. There are now
in Washington about two hundred thousand troops & as soon they are furnished with wagons for transportation such an advance will be made on Manassas as will clear the rebels
out....

Allow me to thank you for your kind letters & for the love which you extend to me constantly.... I know not how to honor you more than by performing my duty manfully here, &
I feel certain that as long as I continue to do so, you will love me.

> Headquarters 9th Regt. P.R.C.
> Camp "Starvation" Co. A,
> Great Falls
> Sept. 11th, 1861

We were waked up early on Monday morning.... We reached our present camp at about
half past two o'clock, but our company was compelled to march six miles further to do picket
duty. Our colonel too, hurried us off before the baggage trains came up, & we were obliged
to [go] without our overcoats & blankets, the need of which was sorely felt before morning. We arrived at our post at a little after four o'clock, having marched since nine o'clock
eighteen miles. We were tired, our feet were wet, we had nothing to put over us, no dry socks
to put on, in fact nothing to make us comfortable but every thing to make us uncomfortable. In addition to this there was a night guard in prospect, & we grumbled not a little at
Col. Jackson's carelessness in sending us out to such an inhospitable place without our knapsacks.

...In the afternoon I went down to the falls where the secessionist are just on the opposite side of the river.... I skulked around among the rocks for about two hours but saw nothing.... They have scouts posted on the other side of the river to fire on our men whenever they
get an opportunity. We have to keep a sharp look out, & dare not be seen on the river shore.

...Harriet, I can love you — you can love me, & what else do we need to make us happy...

> Camp Tenally
> Sept. 17th, 1861

We are shifted about so much that it is impossible for me to write to you regularly. You
probably have no idea of the manner in which we are knocked about at present, to check here
there & everywhere the movements of the enemy....

Our twenty fourth birthday has come & gone.... I was happy in the thought that I was
the possessor of your love & your watchful care.... Oh! what a joyous life spread out before
me. I thought that our *life* would be all happiness, yet I know it must be tempered with sor-
rows. But it is in our hands in a great measure to make our *life* what we wish....

Our lot to be sure has been caste in evil times, but this should only make us stronger. If
God has appointed for us a greater work than for others, we should be thankful that we are
permitted to accomplish it.... The future of our country, although it may be dark to some, is
to me bright. I am just now beginning to feel that this republic will fulfill its destiny. Slavery
has well nigh destroyed it, & for a time I feared it was gone, but my hopes are brightening
every day. Still I am confident that two or three more disasters like that at Bull Run would
do us more good than a hundred victories. The public sentiment of the country is so corrupt, that it is incapable of distinguishing between honesty & dishonesty, between heroism
& cowardice. Witness the orations given to the men, who run like sheep from Bull Run, &
disgraced themselves & the whole nation. They should at least have been permitted to slip

quietly to their homes, without any demonstration which only served to bring into public notice their cowardice. To say the least possible our men acted cowardly at that battle & the less we say about it the better.

Another thing which has disgusted me lately is the triumphal march & speeches of the windy Gen [Benjamin F.] Butler.[6] His expedition, although it succeeded through the folly of our enemies, the part he acted was a complete failure. And yet he goes about the country receiving dinners & congratulations on account of the great victory he achieved. And the country looks on & praises. Alas, what are we coming to. I am truly ashamed of things like these. Have the American people no more discrimination? It seems to me that they ought to have, & until they do have[,] need we expect them to do any thing great & noble as a people.

Well, Harriet, you will observe that we are back again to Camp Tenally. We had a long and tiresome stay at the Falls. We were out on guard every other night while there & during the whole time had not more than half enough to eat. At last we are beginning to hope that our commissariat will be properly managed. Dr King the Brigade Surgeon, was here this morning & on learning how we were treated while stationed at the Falls was not a little indignant & declared that he would put a stop to the matter....

Yesterday ... our tents were struck & together with our baggage put into the wagons. Supposing the wagons were to accompany us we put every thing into them, our knapsacks, blankets & some even their haversacks. About half past five o'clock we got under way. The wagons took the country road & we took the river road which the wagons could not travel, though it was the shortest. Just here we were informed that the wagons would lay up during the night, & would not reach Tenally before to-day (they have just arrived 4 o'clock P.M.). He[re] were we in a good condition to march, but in a very bad condition to pass the night.... Of course there was nothing to eat here. There was a little fire burning in the "kit," but that was all. It was a cold, comfortless, cheerless home.

Besides our clothing was wet with perspiration & we had nothing to cover us. Some dropped down nearly exhausted as soon as we got into camp, others crowded around the little fire, some ran here & others there to find a comfortable place to pass the night. [William] Allen & I succeeded in getting enough hay to protect us from the damp ground, but had nothing to cover us. But before lying down, I took off my shirt & dried by the fire, & this being done I was able to keep warm all night....

Sept. 24th, 1861

Night before last I was taken very ill. Yesterday forenoon I was so prostrate that I could scarcely walk. In the afternoon I began to get better.... During the night I was very cold, it was this that brought on my illness....

The Pittsburg rifles have not all got the ague, though I believe that nearly one half of the company is ill. There are one or two cases of ague — two cases of typhoid fever, & the rest are ailing about like me with cold & headache.... Our company turned out but forty out of one hundred & one. So you can imagine what is the condition of the company. Our company has the reputation of doing more work than any other company in the brigade & so far as my observation goes I believe the reputation to be well deserved.

...I am sorry — yes more than sorry that the President cannot comprehend the troubles of the nation. It is a fight with slavery & with nothing else. As soon as the spirit of slavery which has taken hold of our people both north & south is thoroughly rooted out our difficulties will end, not sooner.... The President is trying to save Kentucky. How much of it will he save; let us wait & see. He saved Virginia & Missouri & behold what a salvation he has given them. Gen. [George B.] McClellan catches slaves & under the direction of the President, I suppose returns them. Besides being very impolitic is not such a course very silly....

... Remember that I *love* you.

Sept. 25th, 1861

I feel much better to-day, in fact almost restored to my former health....

I am sorry this morning & a little indignant on being compelled to believe that we have suffered another great defeat in the fall of Lexington, although it was nobly defended for four days by a few brave men against great odds. We have hundreds of thousands of men in the field, can we never have a sufficient number in the right place. We have been thus far unfortunate in our generalship at headquarters.... While in Missouri our army was generaled by as good men as ever took the field. They were never allowed a sufficient number of men to cope with the enemy, notwithstanding men were offering their services to the government every day. One of our best generals fell a victim to this weak policy, & now nearly a whole state has fallen by it.[7] In vain may we attempt to end this rebellion if such a policy is pursued. It is wanting in vigor & never will succeed. It seems the President does not wish to send an army into a border state, lest he may cause a few slaves to run away & thereby incur the wrath of a few slave holders. I hope that he is not too old to learn. If he is not I think another months experience will teach him the fallacy of his present course. Under our laws through the influence which slave-holders have exercised on our congress, slavery has for the last half century been a sacred institution. Shall it be sacred still when it imperils the very existence of our government.... Every slave state which has not openly rebelled is now so rent with internal faction that they never can be restored to peace unless slavery be abolished.... This reverence [of Northern men for slavery] it seems cannot be educated out of them. It is to be sincerely hoped that it will be whipped out of them, & the sooner this is done, the better it will be for us. Whenever the causes which produced this rebellion are thoroughly understood by the men in power & they have courage enough to act according to their convictions we may expect it to be crushed, not sooner.

...I hope further that [General John C. Frémont] will not be hampered any more by the administration.[8] I have more faith in him than I have in any general now in the army but if he is continually checkmated by orders from headquarters, what can be expect[ed] of him. Since Lincoln's last order to him I am ready for almost any thing to eminate from the White House....

John C. Breckenridge has fled.[9] One more stumbling block removed. Wont a few more fly that the president may be free to act his convictions. As long as these villains stand up & look him in the face & bagguard him, he is unable to do any thing effective. At the next meeting of Congress these men will be so few that they need not be noticed except to arrest them. But have we any officer who has courage enough to arrest them; I believe not.

...Our army is already suffering from the effects of cold nights, & the rebels must be suffering much more; and when you add to this bad food in insufficient quantities their suffering must be great.... I believe that McClellan is a careful general & that he will not move until he is "master of the situation["]. The only thing we lack now is means of transportation for the enormous army which is collected here ....

[Regarding the rumor that our company might be added to McClellan's bodyguard,] I am not at all anxious for the position. It is not a position of great honor because it is not a position of great danger. But for this same reason a great many prefer it. They like the reputation of having soldiered, but they do not like soldiering itself....

Sept. 26th, 1861

I am still better today....

Day before yesterday on the line of pickets opposite the chain bridge a skirmish took place between our pickets & those of the rebels in which four of the latter were killed & some of ours wounded. Yesterday the contest was renewed resulting in the death of two more rebels. At this juncture they sent in a flag of truce, under cover of which it was agreed that there should be no more picket firing on that line. The business had got a little too hot for the rebels & they thought it prudent I suppose to cease for a short time....

Last evening a sad thing happened in our regiment while on picket. Two men of Co. I Capt. [William] Lynch & formerly the "McKeesport Union Guards" quarreled & one deliberately shot the other with his rifle, killing him instantly....

This is the National Fast day appointed by the President. It is observed here the same as the Sabbath.... We have no drilling, thanks to Gen. McClellan's proclamation prohibiting drilling on the Sabbath. The Rev. [James B.] Piatt [usually spelled Pyatt] chaplain of our regiment, is now preaching at Headquarters; but as I have very little faith in either the honesty or religion of the man, I never go to him & shall not to-day. The chaplain is generally regarded by the regiment as a "wag." He has at least no influence on the men & the government had better retain his salary & send him home.

...I shall return to you saddened it may be, but purified I hope by the trials of a soldiers life. Those who have never been so circumstanced can have but a faint idea of what we have to endure. But with a firm reliance on a High Power I hope to endure successfully to the end. My love to all. Remember Your <u>Bird</u>

Sept. 27th, 1861

This is a wet & gloomy day — such a day as gives one the horrors in camp. We have nothing to do, cannot go out, are crowded into small tents & are compelled to live a miserable day.

...In the afternoon the body of William Coyne who was killed the day before, was sent to the city accompanied by a small escort. Nothing remains now to remind us of the sad transaction, but the prisoner who is still held under a strong guard....

We live very fast here. An excitement, no matter on what subject dies away in an hour. The old saying that "every day brings something new," is changed here, so as to read "every hour brings something new." The transactions of this morning although they may be important, are forgotten by evening. Those of the evening by the morning, & thus we live from day to day, time flying so fast that we sometimes find it difficulty to count the days as the[y] pass. We are "living in history." "In a history" whis [sic] is destined to be read by generations yet to come & to be looked up to as a period of great success or of awful disaster.

I feel proud of my position humble though it be. I would rather be a soldier in the great American army than be a king. I am as proud of my country as the old Roman was of his. The day of calamity is upon her; I rejoice that I am permitted to aid in her defense. Those who wish may stay at home. I cannot, while the danger continues, & when it is averted I can go home & enjoy the peace I have helped to conquer. I could not enjoy it without the satisfaction of having borne my part in the struggle to obtain it.

Yes, Harriet, I have often envied the men of '76. And I have sometimes thought that in my day there would be nothing to <u>do</u>. Little did I think that so soon so great a responsibility was to fall upon the shoulders of the young men of this country. This present struggle though not in its present shape, perhaps will continue during my lifetime & likely during two or three more. I have taken my stand, years ago, upon the unchangeable principle of justice to all & I shall try to persevere in this cause until the end. How long I shall be allowed to work, what I shall do, where & when I shall fall, God only knows & in His hands I leave it.

I am in a sanguine mood today. I feel that I was born to do some thing great, & I likewise feel that the talents have been given wherewith to do it....

Sept. 28th, 1861

To-day it is quite cool — the wind is high & chilly & good warm clothes are in demand. Fortunately I provided myself with good warm underclothes before leaving home & I have nothing to want in this respect. A few days ago too we were furnished with long heavy over-coats, so that in the way of clothing we have all that could be asked.

...I am myself again, though by way of precaution I shall not do any duty until Monday.

...I cannot imagine how or by whom the rumor [that my arm was shattered] was started but presume that some fool in the company has written it home. Several members of the company have already written home things equally as foolish & fully as censurable & it would not surprise me to learn that the rumor relating to me had been set afloat in the same way....

...It is a relief to know that [Lexington] was bravely defended.... A few more such victories will destroy the rebel army.... Every day we expect to hear of Frémont doing something, that will clean that state [Missouri] of rebels.... I have faith enough in Frémont to believe that whatever is done will be well done.

...In one of your letters you asked me if my messmates are agreeable. I have to reply that they are tolerable & as no more. One of them is a very fine fellow, another one is good enough to be a companion for any one, for the other two I have nothing to say. None of them are companions for me, for the simple reason that I cannot have a companion. It [is] something that I never had in my life, & I suppose never will have. My thoughts & feelings are known to no one but myself. I am constrained to say that you know as little about me as the rest of the world. I promise you that you shall know more by & by....

Sept. 30th, 1861

Orders have been received this morning for a general movement over the river....

I do not apprehend there will be any fighting for some days unless there should be some thing in the condition of the rebels to warrant an easy victory. Every thing is life here. The soldiers are ready for the advance, & will go forward toward Manassas without ever thinking of returning until they have finished the good fight....

Oct. 4th, 1861

The order which was received was however misinterpreted. It was not an order to go over the river but to go to Great Falls where the rebels had made their appearance in force. Our brigade Col. [John S.] McCalmont was formed on the road ready to go forward, but an order came countermanding the order to march & we returned to camp to hold ourselves in readiness. We have remained in camp ever since.... The rebels will not attack our line here, & Gen. McClellan will [be] very cautious about attacking them at Manassas. I do not think he should be, for I believe he has force enough here if properly handled to sweep them away. It seems now to be the policy of the administration to remain on the defensive here & do the fighting in other parts.

[There is little likelihood that the Pennsylvania Reserve Corps will be sent to Missouri, as we are part of the line here].... Besides Gen. McClellan is not going to send troops to the support of Gen. Frémont. He will either be superceded, or be left to perish as was Gen. [Nathaniel] Lyon. This war is not going forward fast. A villainous pack of intriguers have command of our army & navy & so handle it as to defeat it every where. The worst of our calamity has not yet been felt. Missouri will continue for some time to be a place for ruining or killing good generals. It is to be hoped that we may be whipped into an appreciation of our cause.

Camp — — — —
(Near) Lewinsville
Fairfax Co. Va
Oct. 11th, 1861

On Wednesday while we were eating dinner in Camp Tennally we received an order to prepare to march with two days rations in our haversacks. This was the same order that we had been receiving for two months & we paid but little attention to it, not expecting to leave camp at all. We however made preparation according to order. Scarcely were we prepared, when the order was given to fall into ranks. The regiment was formed, & marched off towards the chain bridge.... [It] crossed the chain bridge into Virginia & proceeded ... to a small village called Langley ... then emerged into a freshly plowed field where we halted to remain for the night. It was not dark & we began to think about making our beds for the night. There was a large stack of sheaf-oats in the field, which was quickly confiscated for this purpose, which spread upon the ground made a bed soft enough for any one to lie on ....

When I awoke in the morning regiments were scattered around so thickly that I could not count them.... It now appeared that our wing of the Grand Army was on the move which pleased us all for we were beginning to be impatient & to grumble at the tardiness of our general. Our tents left Camp Tennally yesterday morning & reached us yesterday in the afternoon....

Camp Pierpoint,[10]
Fairfax Co. Va.
Oct. 15th, 1861

Since my last letter we have been lying in camp not quiet but inactive. Our officers are anticipating an attack by the rebels & keep the army merely on the defensive ready at all times for any thing. We are in a very strong position here & in case of an attack we could fight to great advantage. Hence McClellan prefers to wait a while on the rebels & if they do not make an attack he will make another advance.

...There is no probability of an attack by the rebels on our position here.... To suppose that as cautious a general as [Confederate General Pierre G. T.] Beauregard will attack a strong position when it is wholly unnecessary to do so, is to suppose an absurdity. A good general will always fight to advantage if he can, the rebels have entrenchments at Manassas behind which they can fight with safety can we expect them to fight any where else unless compelled by the force of circumstances to do so.

It is all folly to say that they will be forced to lead their army against us in order to keep it together. I dare say their army is as well organized fed & clothed as ours.... A week ago they occupied the farms which we now occupy. When we came here we found every thing untouched.... There was wheat in abundance & it was not taken therefore they could not have been without provisions; there was hay, & oats in like abundance & these too were left. Some belonged to Union men, some rebels, both were left....

The army has not the faith in McClellan that it had a month ago. He is too slow. They begin to believe that he is carrying on the campaign so slowly that bad weather will overtake him before any thing can be done. He is simply absorbing the resources of the country & doing nothing. If it is the policy to only defend Washington why keep so large a force here to do it, while one half the force could do it.... Our men have showed a lack of vigor from the beginning. It is time for them to wake up, [if] they wish to establish the authority of our government on this continent.

Throughout the summer General McClellan continued to exercise caution, asserting that his forces were greatly outnumbered by those of the Confederates — scarcely the case. McClellan implied that the delays were primarily due to General Scott. The latter was allowed to retire and in November McClellan gained the post of commander-in-chief in addition to command of what he now named the Army of the Potomac.

Among his various dispositions of that army McClellan assigned to General Charles P. Stone's division responsibility for observing crossing points on the Potomac River north of Washington and east of Leesburg, Virginia. On October 20 a small observation force thought it spied an unguarded Confederate camp near Ball's Bluff, halfway between Conrad's and Edwards' Ferry. Stone ordered an attack on this target of opportunity. The next day this camp was found to be only a row of trees. But with few Confederate forces evident, more Union troops were sent across the Potomac. The process was slow, and Southern reinforcements arrived before Union strength was well assembled on the Virginia side of the river. The Confederates were all the more able to move because Brigadier General George A. McCall's division after advancing to Dranesville, south of Leesburg, had withdrawn in compliance with McClellan's original plan, though Stone was not informed of the withdrawal. At Ball's Bluff Confederate and Union forces matched at about 1700 men; the Confederates chose better positions, however. The battle turned into a rout after Colonel Edward D. Baker, commanding the Union right, was killed. The Confederates lost 150 men, the Union 900 killed, wounded, drowned, or missing.

This defeat, following on that at Bull Run, led Congress to establish the Joint Committee on the Conduct of the War to investigate these battles. McClellan and Stone publicly placed the blame on the dead Baker, an Oregon senator and close friend of the Lincolns. Radical Republicans who alleged Stone held sympathies for the South saw to it that he was arrested and imprisoned for six months without charges ever being filed. Later investigations suggest there were many miscommunications and errors of judgment committed by multiple Union officers; the blame should not be placed on any one individual.

In the West, Frémont proclaimed free all slaves owned by Secession sympathizers in Missouri. Lincoln, bridling at a military officer setting government policy and fearing that such actions might turn border states against the Union, asked Frémont to alter his order. The general ignored the request, and Lincoln rescinded Frémont's order. A few weeks later the president replaced the ostentatious general as commander in the West and transferred him to a lesser post in the East.

Camp Pierpoint
Fairfax County, Va.
Oct. 21st, 1861

I have just time to write you a line to inform you that I am living & well. We have just returned from a two days march up the Leesburg road, & have received orders to march again immediately....

Allegheny City
Oct 25th

My Bird;

I recall with loving pride, that the highest motives alone prompted you to do as you have done. I cherish the thought that this must give you strength and comfort. I know I am comforted, when most distressed by thinking, that only love for Justice and Right has taken you away.... There is no need for haste one man's life is worth millions of dollars. Gen. McClellan is no laggard....

Harriet

Camp Pierpoint
Fairfax County, Va.
Oct. 26ᵗʰ, 1862

Day by day we lose ground & our army loses prestige, yet day by day our commanding generals continue to make blunders, & the President is either to blind to see them or too weak to remove those who make them.

The great campaign is about closing without any thing being accomplished.... I thought when Lincoln was inaugurated that we had put the right man in the right place, but I do not believe so now. This war should now be closing & if we had had a President during the last three months it would be closing. But our men have pursued the do nothing policy while our enemies have acted vigorously, the result is before you: a nation with a half million of soldiers in the field & plenty of material for soldiers at home rich in every thing that can add to the strength or glory of a nation yet this nation is *dead*....

...Yesterday we were arranging our company's affairs, that is filling the vacancy occasioned by the death of Lieut. [E. R.] Darlington. This was done by promoting [James P.] Beatty to be 1ˢᵗ Lieut, & [Hartley] Howard orderly sergeant to be 2ⁿᵈ Lieut.

...I must forbear to speak of our last blunder namely that of Balls Bluff. Who is responsible for it is now the question. I believe that Gen. McClellan, himself was the author of it....

Nov. 1ˢᵗ, 1861

I promised to give you my version of the Edwards Ferry affair. So far as I can learn there was a plan formed to capture Gen. Evans [Confederate Col. Nathan G. Evans] .... by a simultaneous movement by Gen. McCall & Stone. The plan failed in the execution either because Gen. McCall retreated when he should have advanced, or because Gen. Stone did not attempt to cross the river soon enough.... It looks to me very much as if Gen. McClellan was moving both armies—that either through some fault of his or his couriers, he failed to have them move at the same time. This it was that caused the disaster. It will be years probably before we know the truth, & in the mean time the name of Baker will bear the odium.

I received your box.... The socks are very nice & are not too large.

In compliance with your request I send you an autumn leaf.

Nov. 6ᵗʰ, 1861

It is cold & chilly today, but notwithstanding I shall try to write you a short letter. It is impossible to be comfortable here in camp in the sense in which comfort is understood at home, yet *as soldiers* I suppose that we are as comfortable as we can expect.... I hear very little complaint among the men on account of being left here in tents during the cold weather, they only complain that they are allowed to do nothing towards the accomplishment of the object for which they left their homes. Every day it is asked: Why do we not move on? I hope that Gen. McClellan & the President will be able to answer it....

Another sorrow has fallen upon us this morning, one which I fondly hoped would not come, the removal of Frémont from the command of the Western Department. I could almost wish that with this act the government might perish. I have but little faith in the government which uses its best citizens only to disgrace them.... I expect now to see Missouri lost beyond possibility of recovery before next spring. Others may think differently but I must say that a people who will silently permit the removal of a good general in obedience to the cry of those who are jealous of his success deserve to be trampled beneath the feet of thieves & traitors. Frémont has not yet fulfilled his destiny. He may live to shame those who have so long attempted to disgrace him.

...McClellan has assumed command of the U. S. Army. He has yet to show that he is worthy of this high position. The retirement of Gen. Scott, will not in any material respect change the administration of affairs at present.

...Everything here denotes the approach of winter. The storm of Saturday last stripped the forest trees of their leaves, & their bare branches remind us that there are days of discomfort in store for us. However, I think I can live through them, but many I am sure can not....

2

Promotion

The fiasco at Ball's Bluff enhanced General McClellan's caution. Union troops settled into quarters for the winter as did the Confederates about twenty-five miles to their west at Centreville, Virginia. A few naval gunboat expeditions were assayed, but mostly the soldiers drilled and concentrated on making their lives as comfortable as possible. The presence of thousands of horses and mules in the camps of both armies called for frequent foraging efforts. By coincidence, forces of both General E. O. C. Ord and Confederate Brigadier General J. E. B. Stuart converged on the farmland near Dranesville on December 20. An attack by Stuart was stymied by the Federals, and he withdrew. The short firefight resulted in 194 Confederate casualties and 68 in the Union forces.

In the days before Christmas attention turned to the controversy caused by the stopping of the British ship Trent *off Cuba by an American warship. Two Confederate envoys on their way to England, James Murray Mason and John Slidell, were seized by the Americans before the* Trent *was allowed to continue on its way. British Prime Minister Lord Palmerston promptly demanded the men's release and threatened to dispatch troops to Canada. Despite opposition within his cabinet, President Lincoln decided on Christmas Day to let the two envoys go, saying, "One war at a time."*

Camp Pierpoint
Fairfax Co. Va.
Nov. 13th, 1861

The Washington Republican hints this morning that this portion of the army may be called up to do something. I sincerely hope so, but I fear it is not well enough organized and officered to make a successful campaign from here to Richmond. A poorly organized army may suffice to operate against another in the field equally as poorly organized, but it would generally fail when batteries are to be taken & forts stormed. I am sorry to say it but I have very little faith in our success should we to-day make an advance on Manassas. A month ago we might have done some thing because the army was under some sort of discipline. To-day the army in addition to being discouraged by recent events is a good deal demoralized by the lax discipline which has prevailed since we crossed the river. We might do something yet if we advanced under the belief that the Great Expedition has withdrawn a large part of the Manassas army, or per force of some other advantageous circumstances; but if we advance relying on our courage & discipline to overcome all obstacles in my judgment we will meet with a terrible disaster. To give you some idea of the discipline prevailing here I need only mention the fact, that out of about eighty men fit for duty in our company only about forty can be found [to] go on regimental drill or Dress Parade, & the other companies in the regiment are ditto. To say the truth, our officers (with the exception of 2nd Lieut. Howard who has not yet learned to get drunk) are drunk half the time. Some times we do not see them for several days & when they are present they never look after the interest or the comfort of the men. These company matters are <u>inter nos</u> of course.

It is this condition of affairs around me which cause me to have little faith in McClellan. It is urged in his behalf that he can not see all these things. I have only to reply that they stare him in the face every day, & unless he is blindfolded he must see them....

...You inquire of Taggart.[1] He is not dead as reported. He was left in the Hospital at Tennally when the regiment marched into Virginia. Before our regimental Hospital was brought over the river he was taken to one of the Georgetown Hospitals, where he began to improve but very slowly.... All the patients in the Hospital near Washington are sent to Baltimore as soon as they are able to take care of themselves....

Nov. 26th, 1861

Though the night was cold & my covering was only a thin canvass, I slept warmly & soundly after reading your letter. You came to me, watched over me during the night & sat with me in the morning & are with me still....

Will you not quit using that harsh term "Mr. Duff"? Do you not know that I dislike it & think that you should not be guilty of using it in our talks with each other.... It chills me when one so near me as you make use of it. Why should you doubt that you are writing to Levi?

...On Tuesday evening, just after I had got myself snuggly arranged for the night, the call was sounded to fall in with guns & with over-coats on. I arose dressed myself & put on my equipment, little dreaming of what was immediately before me. Five companies of the regiment turned out, the Major [John McKinney Snodgrass] took command & marched us towards Lewinsville.... We halted about 2 o'clock, we had started at 9 o'clock marching sometimes slowly & sometimes fast & in the meantime gained a distance of ten miles from our lines.... We were within a half mile of Hunter's Mill, where the rebel pickets are stationed. We were sent out to ascertain their locality & having accomplished the object of our scout about-faced & marched towards camp. Ten miles lay before us to be traveled before day light. The ground was hard-frozen, we were tired out almost by our previous march (forward march) & the prospect for a return march was not inviting. The men nerved themselves up & stepped off briskly & we reach[ed] camp just before the break of day, tired foot-sore & hungry ... [and I] slept nearly all day having been excused from all duty.... I saw no indication that the country was occupied by an army or even by scouts. It occurred to me that the people pursued their daily avocations without any disturbances.... Abundant crops were either stacked in the fields or about the barns. No foraging parties had carried them off, & no one looking on the country before him would ever have supposed that Virginia was at war.

On Thursday evening I went on guard, continuing until Friday evening. On that evening we got orders to be prepared to start on picket at 4 o'clock on Saturday morning. I was somewhat fatigued....

...If you have any fears of my fidelity dismiss them. Let me assure you that I take no thought of the future without your presence....

Dec. 10th, 1861

You will no doubt soon conclude that I am neglecting you. Two weeks have passed since I wrote to you. During that time I have received two letters from you & in answer thereto I will now try to write one. Week before last I might have written any number of letters, but last week I was quite busy & had but little time to spare from guard & marching.

On monday evening I went on cattle guard & remained on guard until Tuesday evening.

Monday night was so cold that I was not able to sleep much, Tuesday night was about ditto. On Wednesday I went out & helped to cut poles to build us a "shanty" or rather a base for our tent. We make our tents quite comfortable by building a square pen about four feet high and putting our tents over them. Having no boards we are obliged to build them of poles, which we cut about two miles from camp & then hire some villainous Quartermaster to haul them. We got the poles for our pen cut & hauled on Wednesday, & began early on Thursday morning to put it up. We got through with the building with the exception of a little fixing to be done to a recess which we made in one side to put a stove in. On Friday we marched up the Leesburg turnpike on a reconnoitering & foraging expedition of which I suppose you have seen accounts in the newspapers. However, as you have not seen account of the part I took I venture [to relate it], although to a stranger it might appear very insignificant. We left camp about seven o'clock in the morning. It had been cold the night previous, the ground was hard frozen & the air bracing & the men moved off briskly. A mile from camp we halted, stacked arms & rested full an hour & a half, waiting for the wagons of the expedition to come up & pass. These being passed we started forward & soon reached our picket line where we halted again. Our Brigadier, Gen. Ord came up and ordered skirmishers to be thrown out on both sides of the road. Our company was ordered to take the right & company B the Garibaldi Guard the left. Here was an opportunity for our company to exhibit their knowledge of tactics & especially skirmishing, & to do something to support the high reputation we have always had as soldiers. But alas! We did not do it. After a good deal of "fussing around" we got started. But before we were able to start Captain Smith who was in command of the company showed that he knew nothing about skirmishing & that the company knew about as little as he did. But after all his efforts Gen. Ord could only give us a sort of a start. Our company officers have frequently tried to learn us the skirmish drill but not knowing it themselves they were of course incompetent to teach it. Every time they attempted to teach us they were openly laughed at & finally the[y] relinquished the task. Thus we were left without the knowledge of that which it was most important for us to know. By whose fault you have learned from this narrative.

Well, we started out skirmishing scouting or whatever you please to call [it]. We march in Indian [style] each man following the next one in front not very closely but about five paces behind him. First we marched through corn-stubbles, then through a narrow woods & then we came upon some fallen timber & here was the "tug of war." Our captain who was in front soon began to lag behind; he is too old to jump over logs & crawl though tree-tops, which here became necessary. After going some distance he got down into a ravine & the men had to help him out. Out of this he swore he would go to the road & not attempt to get over the tree-tops any more. Nearly all of the company considered themselves privileged to follow him & did so. A few in front kept straight on as directed & the rest of us soon joined them. We had gone but a short distance farther when we were called in by Gen. Ord to cross a very deep ravine. After the ravine was crossed we struck out again, but this time we got along better. The woods was open & we were able to march through them as fast as the regiment marched along the road. At Difficult Creek the skirmishers were called in & were not sent out again. Difficult Creek is five miles from our camp & we halted here to get some water. No sooner had we halted than the men began to open their haversacks preparatory to eating. Gen. Ord turning to his aid indignantly remarked, "That's the <u>hell</u> with them volunteers they never halt but they eat." He told them to put up their haversacks & shoulder their arms & march forward, which was done. We went about three miles farther & halted & were ordered to eat our dinner. This was on the very spot where Col. [George D.] Bayard had a skirmish with the rebels about two weeks ago. It is eight miles from here & four miles from Drainsville.

You will recollect that Col Bayard with his regiment the 1st Penn Cavalry was returning from Drainsville & was fired upon by the rebels while riding at the head of the regt. The rebels were concealed in the pines along side the road but were hunted out of their ambush by Col Bayard & his men. One rebel was killed five or six taken. Two of our men were killed, one of whom was assistant surgeon [Samuel] Alexander. Col. Bayard's horse was killed his carcass was lying by the roadside & was the only thing remaining to bear testimony of the fight. Nearly opposite the pine woods where the rebels were concealed stands a house, which is occupied by a Union-seccesionist as we call them. I walked around the house several time[s] looking for a flower to send you as a memento of the spot, but could see none. The only thing that I was able to find I send you enclose — a bunch of rose leaves. Neither the house nor the spot looks inviting, but it will do no harm to keep in mind the fact that a fight occured there.

After eating our dinner we remained an hour or so, when the wagons having secured their forage we turned towards camp. The return march was devoid of any incidents worth relating. We reached camp at dark, tired enough of the days march. The day was very pleasant almost too warm, to march comfortably. All of us were pleased with the trip & would be glad to repeat it two or three times a week.

On Saturday we put a floor in our shanty & made some little conveniences about. We will be able to live quite easily when we get our stove, which we expect in a day or two. On Sunday we did nothing but lay around as usual, in the evening I went on guard again & was relieved at nine o'clock yesterday morning. Yesterday remains to be accounted for. On that day I did my washing, simply because I could hire no one to do it for me. This washing is hard work for me, but I sometimes am compelled to do it; & when I do it I generally do it better than I get it done hereabouts. You would no doubt laugh to see me do it; indeed I almost laugh at myself, but it is one of the horrors of war to which I must submit. There is no ironing to be done of starched clothes I wear none & my handkerchiefs I fold up in small squares and press the wrinkles out of them with my hands or any thing else that I find convenient. This may seem novel to you, but it is not uncommon here. These things all looked queer to me once; now they are as much a part of every day that they go unnoticed. A soldier's life is somewhat different from a citizens: its hardships one soon gets used to & its inconveniences are forgotten. It will [not] do a man any harm to be a soldier if he is half prudent, on the other hand it will do him a great deal of good. The temptations are not so numerous as generally represented; they are not to be compared in number with those of the city, yet we hear men say daily that they are afraid to go to war or are afraid to send their sons, lest they become demoralized. After some experience I am prepared to pronounce this excuse the meanest exhibition of cowardice, or better express an exhibition of the meanest cowardice. You hear this excuse, I suppose every day, & you will have occasion to observe that those who make use of it, have some other excuse and use the former only as a pretense. At least whenever you hear any one make use of it, just give them the road & let them pass, they are not good for much.

You mention something in one of your letters about expecting a big battle near here. On this point I believe I can set your mind at rest. Judging from what is transpiring about me & from what I hear, I have concluded that the grand army of the Potomac will remain in its present position for some time, perhaps all winter. The only thing in my judgment that would cause a forward movement of our army would be some change in the rebel tactics either by diminishing their force at Centreville or by withdrawing from there altogether. The whole war may be ended successfully on our part too, without another battle on the Potomac. I was once the advocate of a forward movement, but lately I have begun to think that it would be folly to take our raw troops to storm the Manassas batteries. If they would exhibit a little more energy in organizing the army I would be satisfied. I think that our generals in command are not doing their duty when they will permit a drunken incompetent officer to exercise authority for a single day. But there are thousands of them, several in our regiment & no apparent effort is made to get them out of the way. It is wise I believe to keep our army until it is well disciplined, but it is folly to waste time in pretending to discipline. The administration has an excuse for not advancing against Manassas in the fact that our troops should first be well disciplined, but it has no excuse for the lack of vigor that has been shown in weeding out incompetent officers. More vigor will have to be shown by us in this respect before we are able to compete in equal numbers with the rebels. I have thought that we have had disasters enough to teach us the necessity of bestowing particular attention on this subject, but it seems not. Other humiliation will have to be endured by us before this war is ended; my prayer is that they may be forthcoming soon, then we will soon see the end.

Well what do I think of the President's message? You say that "it will do no harm." This is severe enough. I would make about the same criticism in different language & say that it is wanting in character. President Lincoln is trying to play the politician, or in other words is playing the politician. He is trying to straddle the slavery question, it will prove his ruin just as sure as it has proved the ruin of any man that has attempted it. We have a history, slavery is a part of that, & President Lincoln should read it & learn that there are only two sides to the slavery question. If he can make a third, he will do what I think is not within his or any other man's power. But wait & see what Congress will bring forth. Harriet, let me make a prediction, this rebellion & the trouble growing out of it is hardly begun. We may live to see it ended & we may not. At all events I thank God that I have been permitted to live in these times. We are living in period that will be looked upon either as the brightest or the darkest in human annals. Be patient, be calm await God's good time & all will re right.

I have just room, Harriet, for a parting word. I am with you as often as you are with me although we are miles apart.... And now let me bid you good night....

Dec. 16th 1861

I received your letter of the 9th on Saturday morning on my return from picket. We had been out twenty four hours at the usual place. In fact, although we have been doing picket duty for nearly five months we have been only in two places and neither of them were places of danger. In the summer time in Maryland picket day was a holiday. We hailed it with joy & were always sorry when it ended. But now it is some what unpleasant. It is too cold to sleep at night, & it is generally uncomfortable the greater part of the day. If, however, we have to perform no harder duty than picket this winter, we may consider ourselves fortunate.

You will be pleased to learn I am sure that I am comfortably housed or rather tented at present. I told you in my last letter, I believe that we had built a square pen of logs & put our tent over it, & were waiting for a stove to warm it. Last week becoming impatient and not seeing any immediate prospect of receiving the stove, we determined to build a chimney. On Saturday morning we got to work, the brick were brought & I began the chimney as master mason. There were a good many critics about & some suggested this & others that but I had determined from the beginning to carry out my own ideas as near as I could. Nearly every chimney in the company had been built & nearly every one smoked, & it was generally conceded that a chimney could not be built with our limited amount of material that would not smoke. I believed that it could be done & I was now compelled to express my belief in a manner that would settle the question at least with me. I had great faith in my own ideas so I went on the chimney. Towards evening I finished it & immediately put a fire in it to test it & was surprised to find it drew better than I expected. It satisfied all in the mess & that was all I

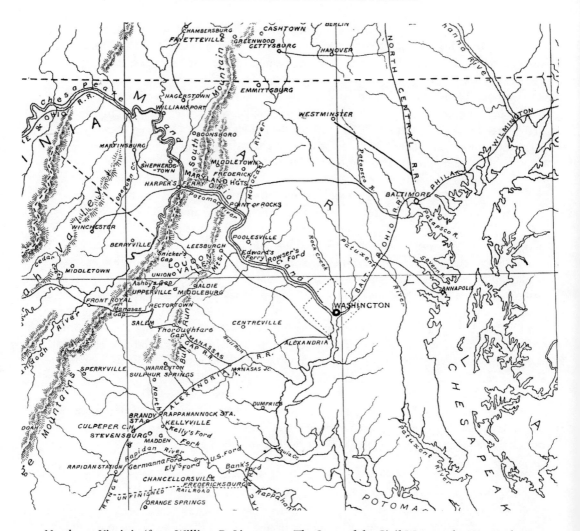

Northeast Virginia (from William R. Livermore, *The Story of the Civil War*. 3 vols. New York: Putnam, 1913. III).

care for. Several of them were very much opposed to the chimney & in favor of the stove & [I] wish[ed] to make a chimney good enough at least to silence them & believe I succeeded. Just now Torrence[2] came in & was praising the chimney & [Sgt. Isaac M.] Sowers who was most violently opposed to it remarked that he thought he liked it better than he would have liked the stove. It looks very cheerful, & I can sit down & read & write in comfort, something that I have not done for at least a month before.

    ...After I had finished the chimney I observed that it did not correspond with the ideas with which I started out.... Thus it is with every thing. We look at a piece of our own workmanship & although it may be beautiful & even exquisite we are dissatisfied with it throw it aside & turn to something else. Thus we toil & toil always unsatisfied, yet it is a blessing to us that we are compelled to toil.

    Well here comes the mail & a letter from you.... Everything is quiet here. You may never expect to hear of a fight here until our army advances. There have been supposition[s] that the rebels were going to advance, but they have not yet advanced & probably will not. I just now recollect that last Wednesday we received marching orders with two days rations in our haversacks. We were unable to explain the order when it was first received, but supposed it to be a reconnaissance towards the enemy's lines to keep up appearances. We afterwards learned that an alarm was caused by a reconnoitering party from [Gen. Samuel P.] Heinzelman's Division approaching B——'s. They were at first taken for rebels, but were soon discovered to be our own men; but the alarm was sounded throughout the whole army before the discovery was made. The newspaper reporters I presume laid hold of this alarm & spread it over the country & created a general alarm. Such reporting is a great nuisance yet it must be born with until men become more honest & more prudent.

I cannot think who it was that made the remark concerning me, nor do I care. I give very little attention to them. The words which you give in your letter look very much like Capt. Smith's: if they are you need not believe implicitly in them, for he has a habit of saying not what he believes to be true, but what he thinks will please. However, I have tried to do my duty in everything, & I suppose have done as well as any of them. I was off duty one week at camp Tenally when I was sick & lost one tour of guard out & with this exception my record is clear. I have not slept out of camp except on duty one night since our arrival at Washington. The last night that I was absent from the company was spent with you. How I wish I could have a night with you now.

...The army is not so large here at present as it was some time ago. A good many regiments have been taken away to join the various naval expeditions. The policy I am at last compelled to believe is to do nothing here this winter but to occupy the attention of the rebels as much as possible, so that they may neither impede the naval expeditions nor our operations in Kentucky. I am not prepared to pronounce this bad policy. Next spring our army will be sufficiently disciplined to cope with the rebels on any field. I will then have more confidence in a forward movement....

Dec. 21st, 1861

A letter from me at the present time will no doubt be welcome, although it must be brief. I have a story to tell you, but have not time to tell it now. You have heard of the battle of Drainsville yesterday & will read the particulars of it before this reaches you. I was in the hottest of the fight & escaped uninjured. One man in our Company was severely wounded & will probably die. His name is Alex. B. Smith. He is a young man about twenty-two, was formerly in the coal business. I believe his relatives live somewhere on the Monongahela. He was shot through the neck & was brought to the regimental hospital last night. He rested easy last night but was worse this afternoon. The surgeon thinks he cannot live many days.

In the Regiment there were two killed & about 20 wounded, several of whom will die. But I need go no further into details. You will have heard all before this reaches you. When I began I only meant to tell you that I am safe and well....

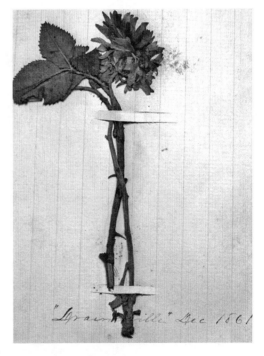

Flower from "Drainsville," December 1861. Levi early established the practice of sending to Harriet flowers, leaves, and twigs as mementoes of his thoughts and affection for her (courtesy Allegheny College).

Allegheny City
Dec. 24th/61

My Dear Levi:

If I could kneel beside you in thankful prayer my heart would seem to be satisfied. The news of the battle [Dranesville] reached me Saturday night, but not the fact that your Regmt was engaged — on Sabbath I was unable to leave my room with headache; occasionally the thought that you had been in the fight came into my mind, but I dismissed it at once — how wisely our thoughts are controlled for had I fancied you in danger without knowing any certainty the suspense would have been terrible. When I did learn the truth it was sad indeed but I knew that I could thank God for your spared life — with my dear friends, whose loved one, is I fear, mortally wounded, I feel most deeply....

Harriet

Camp Pierpoint
Fairfax Co. Va.
Dec. 27th 1861

...You are anxious to hear all about the [action at Dranesville] I know, & I will give you a full account of it when I find time. It will pacify, if not satisfy you to learn that I am safe: the rest you shall know but not now.

Alex. Smith is still no better & no worse. There is a possibility that he may recover but the chances are against him.[3] It is a great wonder that many of us are not in a worse condition than he, but more of this hereafter. Since our return from Drainsville I have been on guard once, & during the rest of the time have been busy at other things.

Christmas was rather dry. I might have had & expected to have a jolly time; but circumstances prevented. Firman sent me a box containing many good things for Christmas, but it did not reach me in time & has not reached me ... yet, & I fear will not until every thing in it is spoiled....

...On Christmas I went to the house of a negro woman, near here to get some washing done. I ask[ed] her some questions about the winter in Virginia.... We can not expect to do much now before the spring opens. We may have a bigger war on our hands by that time than we have now, but I hope not. Yet rather than sacrifice one jot or tittle of national honor, I am willing to fight England & if necessary the whole word besides. If we cannot preserve our government & our country we can preserve our honor, which is worth more than all.

You said that you would like to hear my opinion of the English question. Well I do not know that it is of very great consequence, yet I am free to express it to any one that desires it. I have not yet learned on what grounds England rests her demand for the restitution of Mason & Slidell, or for an apology, or for whatever her ultimatum may be; but it is plain to my mind that she is acting the "bully," that which nothing is more dishonorable to a nation. I was never an admirer of English governmental policy, never a warm friend of the English, but when most people expressed admiration of the one & love for the other I was willing to be silent. I have always felt, however, that England is our natural enemy. There has no doubt descended to me some of the enmity which the revolutionary struggle engendered in our people, & this has been increased ten fold by the course she has taken since the commencement of our difficulties. She is jealous of our prosperity & power & desires to see us humbled. Many months before the Trent affair, I had several discussions with Mr. Allen one of my mess mates, about the conduct of England during the present war. He is a warm friend of England & could see no injustice in her conduct towards us; not so I, I point out to him the fact that she had all along openly sympathized with the rebels. I at the same time took occasion to observe that Mr. [William H.] Seward [Secretary of State], in his dispatches to the English Government, did not speak boldly or rather manly enough. He ignored the fact that while they pretended friendship for us, by their acts they gave aid & comfort to our enemies. He replied that in all probability if the course of policy marked out by me were pursued, it would lead us into a war with England. I answered him by saying: Let it come, if we cannot be men with honor let us be slaves. England with all her boasted power cannot conquer us, nor even humble us. I feel, Harriet that right is all powerful, & that whether this contest be long or short it will in the end prevail. We are a powerful nation, if we had men in power who could call forth our strength.

Whether the <u>Trent</u> affair, does or does not bring on a war with England I feel certain of one thing & that is that we will be involved in a war with her before many years. I believe in peace, yet I believe that we must fight England & humble her, teach her that her unjust interference in our affairs was wrong — was a crime. This once acknowledged by her we can afterwards live in peace.

In one respect I have thought that a war with England just now would be a great blessing to us. It would compel our rulers to have regard for the principles of justice & equity in the conduct of this war, which I am sorry to say they have not now. It would then be a life struggle in reality, through which we could not carry ourselves safely, unless we humbly atoned for our national sins past & sinned no more in the future.

Jan'ry 22, 1862

Dear Bro:

I have your letter of the 19th inst tonight. I had received intelligence of the flood at Pittsburgh by the days papers, & supposed it would prevent you from leaving home. Although the rain may damage you, it can not annoy you more than it does us. For a whole week we have been confined to our tents on account of rain. It has not rained for two days past but the mud is so deep that we are afraid to venture out into it. We expect to be "holed" as we call it, until the 1st of May.

I am well as usual, but confounded and disgusted at everything.

Jan'y 29th 1862

Our love, Harriet, is too strong to be disturbed even by a passing storm.... <u>I</u> am yours, you are <u>mine</u>....

I told you in my letter that on Sunday morning we would have to go on picket. At the time of writing it was raining & desperately muddy, & I feared though I did not say it, that we would have a very disagreeable tour of duty. During Saturday night, however, a strong North-wester sprung up; it got very cold, & the mud was suddenly frozen up. On Sunday morning when we came to start, although the

Firman K. Duff. Levi's older brother, with whom he felt closeness. Although Levi was critical of those who did not enlist, this criticism did not apparently extend to Firman, who was needed at home to assist his father in his business (courtesy Allegheny College).

wind was bitter cold, we thought ourselves fortunate in escaping the mud. The wind continued all day Sunday, but at night ceased & for the rest of tour the air was quite pleasant. But every thing was so damp that most of us were compelled to pass the night without sleep, & on returning to camp the next day we felt a good deal fatigued. One night of sound sleep on a soft pine board entirely restored me....

Our picket line, or line of Pickets, is about two miles in front of our camp & extends from the river Southwardly to near Lewinsville....

Saturday Febr'y 1st, 1862

I had written this far when in stopped Firman.... I did not make any particular inquiry after you, fearing to arouse his suspicion...

Col. Jackson as well as our company officers, had informed us that Gen. Ord, would sign but <u>five</u> passes a day for a regt., which is one to a company every other day.

[While seeking Gen. Ord in order to gain a pass] ... being well acquainted with Mr. [James] Chadwick, the clerk at the Gen's Quarters, I sat down to talk with him & to wait for the Gen. I staid with him nearly all afternoon.[4] He gave me some information concerning the 105th Regt from which I have not heard directly for nearly a month. Col. [Amor A.] McKnight had requested him to visit the regt. with a view to a commission but when the Col. asked him to undergo an examination he declined fearing that he might fail to come up to the Col.'s standard. I learned from him that the Col. was well pleased with me, & was anxious to receive my commission which still lingers in Harrisburg.... [Regarding the pass] I felt however that I had been badly treated, & it will be a good while before I forget it. Lieut. Beatty cheated me, the Col. lied to me.... I shall probably soon get out of the co. & the regt. & I shall not be grieved when the day arrives.... The officer's pets can get passes when they want them; but I am not one of them & I am very thankful that I am not.

...[Along the turnpike to Lewinsville] are several fine farm houses located with an eye to the surrounding scenery, & complete & convenient in all their arrangements. These ... have a quiet & cozy appearance about them which is seldom seen any where in our country except in the vicinity of the cities.

...The Head Quarters of the first company on the left of the Turnpike is at one of these houses built I should suppose about eighty years ago by a man named Ball, & lately occupied by some of his descendants.... The owners of it are rebels & left the house very hurriedly the day we crossed the river. They left behind them some of their furniture. Some of their slaves the[y] took with them, others ran off & the house was entirely deserted.

When we first visited it, we found it but little wrecked. The barn the slave huts, the icehouse & in fact all the out-houses of which there was quite a number were standing undisturbed. The soldiers were occupying every room in the house, & feasting on the cabbage & potatoes which they found in the garden, & amusing themselves at reading over his old letters, thousands of which were found up stairs in one of the small rooms. These letters deserve a passing notice. There were several thousand of them — all the letters of the family for about eighty years extending almost through three generations.... Among all of them there was not found an illiterate or unseemly letter.... These were the best evidences to me of the high character of the family. Call them rebels if you will — & they deserve to be called such to be treated as such — but the fact cannot be denied that they were a highly cultivated people. All the houses ... [show] that the country was inhabited only by such ... essentially an aristocratic people.... They were descendants of the aristocratic families of the old world, & having lived always under the influence of the institution of slavery never knew nor practiced democracy as understood by us at the North. It is not surprising to me that they rebelled. They were jealous of the encroachments of the federal power and of the advancement of the lower classes, hence they had a double motive to rebel. Never till I crossed the river did I comprehend the true character of this war. I never before knew how the war affected the people of the South. I have now learned that the people of the South differ in many respects from the people of the North. They are controlled by different ideas, they were descended from a different ancestry & have always lived among different institutions, & one cannot expect them to agree with us in governmental establishment concerning which men are sure to disagree if they disagree about any thing. Standing in one of the deserted houses of the Virginia aristocracy looking at the rude characters & illiterate sentences scratched upon its finely polished walls by northern invaders, I said to myself: ["]Here are the powerful vandals of the North again overrunning the country of the effeminate aristocracy of the South." And so it is; & this war will never end until the whole Southern country is overrun. This is a war now, not for the political union of the people both North & South, but for the territorial unity of that portion of the country lying between the great lakes & the gulf. Whenever our rulers comprehend this & make war for the accomplishment of this object we will have begun to work to some purpose. You may think that we are near the end of it, but do not be too sanguine. So large a country as the South cannot be conquered in a day, nor in a year. We every day despise the power of the rebels & every day we are reaping the fruits of such folly.

The last time that we were on picket we were stationed at Balls house. But how changed in four months occupation by soldiers. As the cold weather began to come on the soldiers began to knock down the barn & carry off the boards to make floors for their tents. Commencing with the barn every other building on the farm has been carried off for a like purpose, till nothing remains but the frame of the house, with a part of the roof over it. The furniture, the letters & all other relics left by the owner in his rapid retreat have been carried off or destroyed....

[One slave cabin remains, inhabited by an old couple with their two great-grandchildren.].... They tell us that Ball had only about a dozen slaves, seven of whom he sold & the others he took with him [These people were too feeble to travel.].... Ask them about freedom, & they know not the word. They have heard of Massa Lincoln, but do not know what he is doing.... They are ignorant, but it almost seems a blessing to them. Yet in looking at them I am reminded of a sentiment contained in a poem by John G. Whittier....

> The laws of changeless justice bind
> Oppressor with Oppressed;
> And, close as sin & suffering joined
> We march to Fate abreast.[5]

Feb'y 5th, 1862

I told the boys in the mess to-day that I felt a little homesick. Sowers was shrewd enough to suggest that the girl I left behind me, was the cause of my home-sickness. I am not sorry to confess that he was exactly correct. Did circumstances permit no one would go home more gladly than I.

...[Firman]speaks highly of the [105th] Regt, thinks it a much better one than the 9th & suggests that if I get a captaincy in the Regt I will get a pretty snug thing—which by the way is pretty true. He further says that Col. McKnight is more anxious for the commission than I am; that the company is without a captain & has been for a long time. He leads me to infer that I am quite popular down there....[6]

Well, Harriet, we still remain here idle & without the expectation of having any thing to do, for some time. We have little faith in Gen. McClellan's "Anaconda," as Curley called it. We have discussed the war pretty freely to-day — the Gens who are conducting & every thing connected with it, & it was the unanimous conclusion that Gen. McClellan is "played." I feel sorry to say it but I fear that McClellan has failed. What Gen. is left to conduct the war? The man who is to lead us triumphantly Southward is not yet at our head. The country is almost ruined, it will require a bold determined man to restore it. The night is not yet passed, the morning may never come.

> Camp Jameson near Fort Lyon
> Fairfax Co. Va.
> Feb'y 13th, 1862

Since my promotion it behooves me to write to you promptly, lest you may think that a change in circumstances has caused a change in me. An advance in life frequently puts bad notions into a man's head but I hope it will no[t] so affect me. On thing bear in mind, that you are with me in all fortunes, whether good or ill....

In order to tell you how I got here, I will begin my narrative at least a month back, a little more. On the 29th day of Dec. last, I received a letter addressed simply "Mr. Duff" in a bold firm hand. I opened it, & after the caption, which was the same as of this one, it read thus:

"Mr. Duff

    Sir,

There are several commissioned offices vacant in this regiment, and hearing that you are a gentleman of considerable natural ability & of some practical military experience, if you will visit me at an early day, the result may be mutually advantageous," and was signed Yours etc.

> A. McKnight
> Col. 105th Regt Pa Vols.
> Alexandria Va.

After looking at it for some moments in astonishment & in silence I handed it to my friend Mr. Sowers.... I did not know A. A. McKnight, had never heard of him, but after considering the letter for a short time I concluded that it would be no harm to make the acquaintance of a Col. Having come to this conclusion on the 30th of Dec. I started for the Regt which is encamped about a mile and a half beyond Alexandria.... I was wondering all the while who had given Col McKnight my name, & what would be the result of my visit. I supposed it to be some monied way of getting a commission which some of my mistaken friends have frequently advised me to adopt. But I had my mind made up before I started to do nothing to compromise my dignity or honor, no matter how glittering the prize might be. For many reasons I desired to leave Capt. Smiths Co, but I determined that I would submit to almost any thing rather than yield up one jot or tittle of my self respect.

After some wandering I reached the camp just at noon, was pointed out the Head Quarters, entered & found the Col. & Lieut Col. [W. W. Corbet] both present. I was so much abashed or bewildered I do not know which that although the two men were seated near each other, & had on their distinctive badges by which at least a soldier should be able to designate the one that was Col. & the one that was Lieut. Col. — I addressed the Lieut Col. instead of the Col. Taking off my cap looking at him & bowing I said "Col. McKnight." "no Sir" said he "there is the Col" pointing to him. Here I discovered my mistake & blushed deeply. I soon rallied, however, & looking at the Col. stammered out "Mr. Duff." He looked at me very coolly & asked "Is that your name"? "Yes Sir" I replied, "I had the honor to receive a letter from you & called in answer to it." "Very well Sir" said he "take a seat." I sat down, but he immediately said "our dinner is just ready have you been to dinner"? "No Sir," said I. Well he replied "Come in & take some dinner with us." He got up & I followed him into an adjoining tent, where we sat down to dinner. As soon as we were seated, he began: Mr Duff, have you ever studied tactics? "No Sir" was the reply. "What is your military experience?" "Eight months in the service and a months militia training." Other questions passed of no great importance & which I will not repeat. After dinner we went back to Head Quarters. I took a seat as directed by him, he said he would attend to my case by and by. The officers began to drop in one by one until quite a number had collected to all of whom I was introduced. I felt a good deal embarrassed, & conducted my self very poorly I am afraid. By & by a man came in, dressed in a Chaplain's uniform. His countenance looked a little familiar to me, but I did not quite recognize him. He peeped at me through the crowd & said "Mr. Duff I believe." "Yes Sir" said I. "Mr. Steadman," for when he spoke I recognized him.

Mr. [Darius S.] Steadman is a Methodist Minister & at the breaking out of the war was stationed at Brookville. Last August when Col. McKnight raised this regiment he appointed him chaplain.... I was on "familiar terms" with him [in the summer of 1858 as I] ... would converse with him freely about our experiences at Allegheny College, where he too had got his education, although he did not graduate.[7] I ... had long ago forgotten him.... He, having heard from some one that I was in the service & where I was gave my name to Col. McKnight....

...I went with him telling the Col. that I would see him again.... In a very short time Col. McKnight came in, & said to "Pete" mr. Steadman['s] boy: "Pete go over to company B's Quarters get a gun & bring it to me." I now began to see what was on the board. I will not tell you how I felt, that would be impossible. In came the musket, however, & the Col. says hand it to Mr. Duff. I took it. He told me to go through the manual. I started, the first shift was wrong, the second ditto & my spirit sunk so rapidly that I was almost afraid to open my mouth. But on he went into the School of the Company. In this I was better posted than in the manual of arms & I began to get a little confidence. He asked me the position of the rear rank in the oblique firings. I described it for I knew it perfectly. He sort of intimated that I was wrong but he did not say so. I appealed to the book, & after some hesitation he opened it. I was right, & this little victory straightened me right up. I now began to bear down upon him a little. He went on into the battalion drill. In this I was still better. After an hours examination, he rose from his seat, & said "Mr. Duff we will give you a position here, your examination is very satisfactory." This was a great surprise to me for I thought it a miserable failure. With his remark about the examination he left. As it was drawing near night I concluded to remain all night with the chaplain & had so informed the Col. After supper, the Col. called at the chaplains tent, & asked me out. I went out, & he asked me if I drank. I told him that I some times took a drink of whisky, but never got intoxicated, & further said that if I came there (here) & he found any thing objectionable in my character to let me know & I would leave. He turned away again without giving me an intimation of what he wanted me for. In a very little while a summons came for me to appear at Head Quarters. I went up & on entering found present only the Col. the Lieut. Col. & their confidential clerk [Jesse J.] Templeton.[8] The Col. harangued a while, beginning with the statement that there was several vacancies in the regiment one captaincy & several lieutenancies. He then told me how & why he had created these vacancies, & the kind of men he wished to fill the vacancies with, & wound up by telling me that he would appoint me captain of Co. "G" & immediately directed the clerk to write out an application for my discharge from the 9th Regt Penn. R. C. With this I left him. I staid all night with the chaplain called on the col. next morning when he again harranged me for a short time after which I left for Camp Pierpoint.

I went back home with queer thoughts in my head. Is he sincere, said I to myself? He is so different from any Col. I ever met, that his singularity caused me to doubt his sincerity. I pondered the case for several days & finally concluded that he meant what he said. Having come to this conclusion I wrote to Pittsburg for a uniform, & went to work to learn all about tactics. I was convinced that Col McKnight had made application for my discharge & felt certain, that he would have sufficient influence to carry the day. In this faith I rested & went to work. In a day or two I received a note from the Col. stating that he had forwarded the application for my discharge to Gen. Heinzelman's Head Quarters, & it was sent back with the statement that it required more evidence than his word to prove that I had been appointed a captain in his regiment, in other words it required the commission. He further stated that he had written to Harrisburg for my commission, & he hope[d] to have it in a few days. I wrote in reply that I would await the order for my discharge, & when discharged would report immediately.

Thus the matter rested until the 6th day of Feb'y about noon. I was in my tent at Camp Pierpoint, when Capt. Smith sent word to me that he wished to see me at his quarters. I went up & he showed me an order for my discharge. I told him that it was right, to make out the discharge. He became inquisitive of course; ask[ed] me if I was getting a commission etc. I told him I was. Lieut Beatty who was making out the discharge asked me if it was a first or second Lieutenancy; I replied that it was a Captaincy, at which the Captain blushing rose & congratulated Capt. Duff & Lieut Beatty blushed too but went on with his writing. He did not seem pleased with the prospect of me outranking him.

The discharge was made out, I took it to the Col. had it signed, packed up & started without any ceremony to Washington. I reached Washington about an hour before dark, & took lodgings at the Avenue House. Next morning I started for Georgetown, got my uniform which was lying there in the express office tried it on & found that it fit me very well. I had now every thing but a sword & fixings, & to get these I had not the money. I had written to Firman the evening I reached the city to send me some money, but it would not arrive before Tuesday, so I thought I would be compelled to wait until Tuesday before joining the regt.; but on Friday Col. McKnight as well as Lieut. Col Corbett of the regt. came to the city, remaining there over night. On Saturday morning Col. McKnight asked me to come over as soon as possible for he had two companies almost without officers. I told Lieut. Col. what I was waiting on, & he just handed me the money & went with me to a store where I could get my outfit. This was bought in a short time & I went to the Provost Marshal, got a pass & was then ready to join the regt.

I left Washington & after a very muddy tramp reached the regt. about seven o'clock. I took supper with the Lieut. Col. but stopped all night with the chaplain. Next morning Sunday I was called to Head Quarters. I went up, the Col said to me "mr. Duff, I guess we will send you over to Co. D" & told Templeton to call Mr. [Charles H.] Powers. Mr. Powers came in, the Col. introduced him, & I went with him to the company; we went through the tents he introducing me to the men as their "new Captain or as the man who was to run the machine." This done I was shown into the officers tent, & immediately took up my abode there. Mr. Powers was formerly the orderly sergeant of the Co., but is now one of the Lieuts., the other lieut is not yet appointed. The company was formerly commanded by a man named [John] Rose, a very ignorant & tyrannical man, if I may believe all that is told me. The company is from Jefferson & Clearfield Counties about half from each. I find them very deficient in some parts of the drill, but I think it a good average company. The men so far seem pleased with me, & judging from present indications I will be successful in my new undertaking; at least I have not yet seen any disposition on the part of the company to be displeased with me.

On Sunday evening I took the company out on "Dress Parade," the first time that I had ever made my appearance as an officer at drill or parade. Of course I was somewhat timorous, but I got through it very well. On Monday I went out with the company to brigade drill, & got along much better than I expected. I now began to find out the fact that I knew about as much as any captain in the Regt. & I believe that in a short time I can leave them all behind. I am gradually gaining confidence, & every time I go out I get along better. This week has passed off smoothly. All of the officers seem friendly & are generally men of good character....

Allegheny City
Feb. 18th 1862

Dearest,

Need I <u>say</u> how gladly I read the <u>literal</u> evidence of your promotion — the story you tell, was interesting to me. I <u>felt</u> every bit of your embarrassment. I know not what Col. McKnight thought. I have <u>seen</u> your embarrassment <u>very</u> becoming. I do indeed wish that I could "salute" the Captain. My heart kisses you, and is so thankful and happy — beside the honor, which I <u>know</u> you have <u>earned</u>, you will be comfortable and able to feel yourself among respectable people.... You have been in the ranks and know how a Captain looks, you can try then, to be to others as you would <u>have had</u>, others be to you. My own little secret in this matter has always been to become really interested in people — they will soon find it out. I know a leader must be <u>firm</u> but he need not be <u>unkind</u>. An unchangeable answer, may be brightened with a smile. Your position will often require decisions and caution.... The gladness in my heart tonight is a very solemn joy.... I hopefully pray that the blessed Jesus may keep you ever, and eventually lead you to Himself....

Harriet

Camp Jameson Va.
Feb'y 25, 1862

Your letter of the 18th found me about eight miles from here on the direct road to Richmond, in a place called Pleasant Valley doing picket duty. I was very sorry to learn that you were ill....

I am busy here from morning until night. We have two officers drills & company & Brigade drills the rest of the day. To-day we drilled from day-light till dark. Col. McKnight is determined to have a well drilled regiment, if work will make it so. He told the officers the other day that they must think about nothing but military science; that they must forget their families at home & only think about their religion occasionally. He asked me when I first saw him if I was a single man. I told him I was, & I doubt not that this had some bearing on my appointment. I did not tell him, however, that I was as deeply "involved" as most married men.

Every thing is quiet here at present. The People of Washington are in daily expectation that this army will move forward, but I do not expect it to move for some time. The roads are still very deep & if they were good I do not believe that transportation enough could be found about the city to move it. In other words I believe that a forward movement at present is an impossibility. When we do move, however, I think we will find no difficulty in dislodging the rebels from their strongholds.

Mar. 5th 1862

Dear Father:

My out-fit & expenses up to the present time have amounted to $150. leaving me at present about $50 in debt. I have however enough coming from the Government to square me up & a little more. I have pretty hard shoving at present, we are not likely to be paid for a month yet, & we are all pretty well strapped. If we go on a march soon as we expect to, we intend to steal our living if we can get it in no other way....

Mar. 5th, 1862

To-morrow morning early we go on Picket, & the night is already well advanced so I must be brief.

Before receiving this letter you will have received the intelligence of the death of Capt. [Charles W.] Chapman Quartermaster Lyle [James M. Lysle] & a private of the 63rd Regt. [Alexander] Hay's [Hays'].[9] Of course when you hear of this & learn that I have gone on Picket you will be anxious to hear of my safe return. I will return on Sunday (at least I hope so) & if in the meantime you do not see any notice of us in the papers you may consider us safe. The men above named it is well understood here lost their lives through carelessness on their part & Lieut. Col. [A. S. M.] Morgan who was commanding the Scouting Party. I think that such carelessness will not be found in our Regt. Gen. [Charles Davis] Jameson told Col. McKnight this evening that he wanted just to catch the men (Texas Rangers) who are annoying our Picket Line & outpost. We shall probably make the attempt what may be our success I cannot say. I have no personal fears but perhaps I am too-confident.

...I hope that I may return to you after our country is at peace, but if it should fall to my lot to make a sacrifice of my life in this cause, it is a great satisfaction to know that you will not regret that I did my duty. To serve my country & then to return to "take care of you" is my only ambition now....

[P.S.] Pay no attention to the absurd rumors that are now flying about Pittsburg that this that & the other regt. [were] torn & cut to pieces. Whenever the story runs that such a regiment was "cut to pieces," set down a lie, & don't let it bother you.

March, 11th 1862

On last Thursday we went on Picket to Pohic Creek about fifteen miles from here. We started at 8 o'clock in the morning & reached our post about 1 o'clock P.M.... We remained on Picket until Sunday noon when we returned to camp. But I am anticipating a little. On Friday night I received an order from Major [Mungo M.] Dick, commanding our wing to have all my men except two at each post, ready at four o'clock next morning to scout through Mason's Neck, the country lying between Pohic Creek & the Occoquan River. I had about thirty men ready at the time, with which I started towards Major Dicks Head Quarters. Arriving there my forces were joined to a detachment from Co. A also one from Co. F making in all about one hundred men, under command of Major Dick. We started in the direction of Colchester, a small town on this (North) side of the Occoquan River, & three miles distant from our Pickets. We marched strait on to Colchester seeing nothing on the way & arriving there a little while after day-light. A small party which was in advance saw the Rebels on the opposite side of the River, & Major Dick I believe concluded to fire on them & retire. He told Capt. [Robert] Kirk to take thirty men & go forward in the road until we could see the rebels & to fire on them, & told me to take an equal number & go round a field to the right of road to fire at them from there. I immediately started off with my men, but had not gone far, when Capt. [John] Hastings of Co. A who was to direct me where to go, called out to me to double quick my squad up to an old house where he was standing. I did so, he told me to fire on them, said I where are they? Why over the river there, he replied. Looking over the river about a half mile I saw some rebels running down the hill toward the river. Why said I there is no use to fire at them at that distance. Yes you can hit them said he. Well said I perhaps, & called out to the men to fire & they did, doing I think very little harm to the rebels. They continued to fire for five or six times, when I got disgusted with the thing, & told the men to stop it. I marched them back to Major Dick & told him it was no use to fire on the rebels from that point. He said, he guessed not & that we would retire. We did so, & marched strait back to our Picket Line.

The other officers in the affair thought it a great thing & have been talking about it ever since. I think it rather small, however. There was no one hurt on our side & it is rumored that two were hurt on the rebel side but this is doubtful. You will probably see some exaggerated account of it in the News Papers.

Well I have only to add that we expect to leave here in a few days. It seems to be confirmed that the rebels have left Centreville & Manassas, & there is no longer any use of our staying here. My love to all. In haste

March 14th, 1862

All is stir & confusion here this morning. We received an order last night to draw six days rations & to be ready to march at a moments notice. We have been busy since and we are now fully prepared to go, & expect to leave every moment.

March 16th, 1862

We all believed that we would move on Friday & so I stated to you in my hurried note. Friday night however found us in camp, then Saturday, & still to-day we are here, expecting to leave on Tuesday next.... A large fleet will sail from here in a short time for some point on the Southern Coast. We go with (or in) it....

...Something (perhaps it was natural) had taught me to disbelieve in the sincerity of woman. She seemed to me to be a "pest" at least an annoyance to be shunned at all times. Of course this belief did not entirely smother my nature. I would still instinctively look at the women as they passed me, & a pleasing face would sometimes suggest to me happiness. But ambition, selfishness, said to me that time should not be wasted on any such useless objects. Many a time in day-dreams my life was <u>finished</u> gloriously without the smile or blessings of a woman. I would go to my room & would lock the door then sit down to study, to labor to build up a name—for what—for naught. I could not study unless I was alone, & was annoyed at any disturbance—it seemed to me when any one appeared that they were trying to rob me of my time, & thus of my ardently wished for greatness. Thus I was living, hardly living for such can hardly be called life, when one night I looked into your face.... It went with me to my secluded room.... In a very short time she went with me in all my day-dreams.... During all this time what was I doing, why trying to shut my eyes & to forget the ministering angel, because said I, if I recognize her my race in life will be encumbered with "useless baggage."

But after a year's endeavor, I found it impossible [to] displace my companion & I was compelled to recognize her. Yet she knew nothing of it did not even suspect it. It was necessary, therefore to notify her of it. This was a very difficult thing, you know how gallantly (rather how awkwardly) it was done....

I more than half regret that you are not — —. You seem so near & dear to me that I cannot think of you in any other light. I would rather meet you as Mrs.—than to meet you as Miss—as I shall be compelled to. What did your "if" mean? You would not say, but I believe from the connection that you were thinking as I have thought for a long time that your name should be — —. Now tell me is not my surmise correct. Nothing would induce me to go home but to effect this....

Ever your's, Harriet, do not forget this.

3

The Peninsula

Persuaded in large part by faulty information gathered by celebrated detective Allan Pinkerton, who served the Union as chief of intelligence, General McClellan consistently over-estimated Confederate strength. In consequence, he was convinced throughout the winter that the Southerners' troop deployments between Washington and Richmond were too numerous and their fortifications, especially at Manassas (Bull Run), too substantial for the Army of the Potomac successfully to assail them. Frustrated by McClellan's delays, at the end of January President Lincoln directed movement on the Confederate capital by Washington's birthday, including assault on Manassas Junction. McClellan countered with another plan: shipment of Union troops down the Potomac through Chesapeake Bay and up the Rappahannock River, where they would disembark and march northwest to Richmond having circumvented the main body of Southern troops. This plan the Southerners undid by shifting south toward Culpeper. McClellan stuck with his flanking approach, however, modifying it to involve advancement up the York and Pamunkey rivers or up the James River. The Union movement was not well concealed and executed so slowly that the Confederates had time to reposition.

Camp Hamilton (near) Fortress Monroe
March 23rd /62

I wrote you a note on the 20th, informing you of our safe arrival at this point [on the east-ern tip of the peninsula between the mouths of the York and James rivers]. We embarked as I told you, on Monday but did not leave Alexandria until Tuesday at noon. There were thirteen steamboats in our fleet, which in the Potomac looked quite formidable but when we got out into the bay it could scarcely be seen. The day that we were on the Potomac was very pleasant & I stood on Deck nearly all the time. The country along the Potomac from Washington to its mouth is very poor with the exception of a few spots. The only respectable looking house that I saw was the house at Mount Vernon & it is in a dilapidated condition. The whole country looks impov-erished, deserted & I had well nigh said detestable. As we neared the Bay, the bottom land on each side of the river spread out into wide marshes covered thickly with stunted cedars & pines.

On Tuesday evening at 5 o'clock we passed the famous Aquia Creek Batteries. A dense smoke was seen rising from the creek some time before we approached it. When we neared it, nothing could be distinguished by the naked eye, but with the aid of a good glass we could see the smoking ruins of the Railroad Depot at the terminus of the Fredricksburg & Rich-mond Railroad. It had been fired the night before by the rebels & was consumed but the ruins were still smoking. We could also see sixteen guns mounted on an embankment along the creek shore. They looked like Columbiads, but may have been painted logs, such as the rebels used to deceive us, at Manassas. The Gun Boat Yankee which accompanied us, fired a shot when we were just opposite the Battery to let them know, I presume that we were there.

Soon after passing Aquia Creek it got dark & I retired to the cabin. About 8 o'clock the fleet stopped & anchored in the river for what purpose I have never been able to learn. At eleven we got under way again but stopped again at one, but I was asleep when we stopped the second time. When I awoke on Wednesday morning we were floating on salt water near the mouth of the Potomac. I washed myself for the first time in salt water on that morning. Nothing occurred worthy of remark during the remainder of our passage. We could just distinguish the shore of the bay, but could not form any opinion of the country. At 5 o'clock on that evening we landed at Fortress Monroe. We disembark just at dark, marched from the Fortress almost due North. Where or how far we were going I knew not. We had only gone about a half mile when it began to rain & storm terribly. The Col. was leading the regt. & after we had marched about two miles from the Fort, the regt was halted & the Col gave orders to the officers to do they best they could for their companies. In disembarking my company had got in the rear & I ... did not hear the Col.'s instructions. I stood for a short time in the rain awaiting orders when all of a sudden the companies in front of me scattered every where some went to neighboring camps some to the cavalry stables, & others to fires which had been built by regiments which had come in before us & were without shelter, but had good fires. When I saw these companies scatter, I went forward to where they had stood to see the Col. but he had scampered off to some shelter supposing that all the officers & men would do the same. After searching in vain for some time I had my company stack arms & told them to go to the fires until I could find some quarters for them. I still continued my search for the Col. or some field officer but found none. I returned to the company intending to march them to the Cavalry stables, but I met in the mean time a Captain of a Massachusetts Regt who said he thought he could find quarters & also get us some coffee. He told me to wait until he would return. I waited on him for an hour, when I began to lose faith in him & sent my first Lieut. out to hunt quarters. He soon returned & said the men could find good shelter on the "lofts" of the cavalry stables. I directed him to march the company off while I remained. He did so & I stood by the fire in the "pelting storm" expecting every moment to see some one of our field officers, but none came. In a short time a man came along near me wanting to know if there was any commissioned officer there who had no quarters for the night. I spoke up & told him that I had none. He told me to come along with him & he would find me quarters & also asked me if there were any more officers about there. I looked around at the fires & saw a sword hanging by a man's side & pointed him out, he called him & we went off together. The man whom I pointed out was found to be a 2nd Lieut. of the New York 87th Regt. Our guide took me to the Quartermaster's of the 11th Penn cavalry. On entering his quarters I found [my] 1st Lieut. seated by a warm stove drying himself. I took off my over-coat, when the man who brought me in looked at me & exclaimed. "I got a captain any how." Why, said Lieut. [J. P. R.] Cummiskey, that is the man I sent you after. Well said the man "I had the name on my tongue but I fell into a mudhole & I forgot where I was going & whom I was going after. But he continued, I went ahead & I came upon a lot of soldiers & I cried out for a commissioned officer & he was the first man that answered me." ... I staid with the Quartermaster all night, had a good bed & a breakfast the next morning. I was so sick that I could not eat anything. During Wednesday on the Bay we had quite a breeze, & a great many of the men got sick, but it did not affect me then. On Thursday morning, however, twelve hours after we had disembarked I was just as sea-sick as a man could be. It continued all day Thursday but towards evening I got better & the next morning, Friday I felt quite well. On that day we went into camp where we are at present....

Troops are continually arriving here. We expect to move farther up the James River tomorrow. I took a walk through the ruins of Hampton to-day. I enclose you a few flowers plucked therefrom among them a peach blossom.... All I can give is yours.

March 25th 1862

Dear Father:

There are here now two Division's, [Charles S.] Hamilton's (formerly Heinzelman's) & Fitz-John Porter's. These two division together with [Joseph] Hooker's constitute Heinzelman's corps. This last mentioned division will be here in a few days....

The rebels it is said are in considerable force at Great Bethel only five miles from here, consequently, if they make a stand our first days advance will bring us upon them. We may have a fight here any day. The two armies are so close together that it will be difficult to prevent it.

The weather here is very fine, peach trees in blossom, flowers blooming, many things about as far advanced as May in Clarion....

March 27th, 1862

I received yours of the 24th today. It was as unexpected to me as mine was to you. I had felt during the morning a little homesick, but your good words drove the feeling away.

Your answer to my question I read with a good deal of pride. I am proud of you; you seem to me to be endowed with capabilities superior to other women, fitted willing & eager to make me happy. Whatever of life there may be to me (if you will accept the poor bone) shall be yours. I am willing to acknowledge that I love you, truly & sincerely.

...It is now almost April & nothing done here; and what is worse every thing looking as if nothing will be done for some time. To me there has always been a perceptible lack of energy & promptness in the Potomac army. It still continues & how long it will continue I do not know. One thing at least is certain, that is, if Gen. McClellan does not ruin this government it will be because he is deprived of the opportunity very soon. He is either grossly incompetent to command an army or a traitor. It don't matter much which. He should be removed from his command forthwith.

You ask why were we brought here for. I am sure I cannot tell you; but I believe this to be a more favorable point than Washington from which to approach Richmond.

...The soil is very deep & rich, by far the best that I have yet seen in this State. Just north of the Fortress there are several fine farms, now deserted & lying waste.... On the North side of this [Hampton Creek] was situated the town of Hampton, burned by the rebels last fall. It was a clever little town.... From one of these gardens I plucked the flowers which I sent you....

...[Captain James Hamilton of Co. I] says that they [a reconnoitering force] discovered a force of five thousand posted just beyond Bethel & learned that there are fifteen thousand at Yorktown. I asked him how they got their information, but he could not tell me. You can set it down that they did not exactly find out all this.

Both of my Lieutenants are now sick....

Remember & love

March 29th 1862

Dear Father:

...My pay here is $106 per month & a servant. My out-fit cost me a good deal but aside from this, there is no great expense attending the office. I think I shall be able to save a good deal in a year....

April 2nd, 1862

In many respects, Harriet, I am just as I was when I left you. I am a little wiser in the world's ways; but I believe I can say with truth that I have passed unscathed through many

Oil-cloth toilet kit. Made for Levi by Harriet, he used it to store the precious letters received from her (courtesy Allegheny College).

temptations & trials. You can never know (for I cannot tell you) how much the remembrance of you contributed to my safety....

We are still lying in camp near Hampton. There is no stir here. It is not at all different from our idleness on the Potomac. Our career here is beginning just as it began at Washington last summer — that is with reviews.... When we are to advance to drive the enemy from Virginia is not known & is not supposable. The winter time, during which we should have made our campaign in the Southern States is gone, the Spring is almost gone too & nothing is done. The days are already getting hot here & in a month I dare say we will begin to suffer some from heat....

Camp (near) Yorktown, Va.
April 7th, 1862.

On Friday morning at 7 o'clock we left Hampton for this place. Fitz-John Porter's Division was in advance, ours next, what was in the rear of us I am unable to tell. The morning was warm, the sun bright & we moved off at very brisk pace. The soldiers had very full knapsacks & had only marched two miles when they began to throw away extra clothing, & in a very short time the road was strewn with overcoats blankets & all description of clothing. As we passed along the slaves from the neighboring plantations were busily gathering them up. These slaves allow me to remark were all old & decrepit. I did not see a young negro (& I saw a good many) during our journey. The young & serviceable men have either all run away or been sent south. These slaves too were all clothed in rags: the usual clothing of all the slaves I have seen within the slave states. They may be well fed, but I assure you they are not well clad.

Towards noon it became more pleasant, a firm sea breeze relieving the warmth of the sun. Our march too became slower on account of the advance of our column encountering the barricades placed in the roads by the rebels. In fact towards night it became tedious. Just at noon we reach Big Bethel the scene of gen. [E. W.] Pierce's Defeat. The rebels had occupied it that morning, but evacuated it without any demonstration on the approach of our column. They had thrown up some slight embankments more for "scare-crows," than sub-stantial defense. Their works irregular incomplete & apparently built without a plan. It was sufficient to frighten our generals until they got a hundred thousand men & a hundred pieces of artillery with which to advance upon it.

We only marched about two miles beyond Bethel to a place called Russel's where we stayed all night. The advanced Division reached the North Branch of the Buck River about four miles farther on & about nine miles from here. At this latter place the rebels had thrown up earthworks, more formidable than at Bethel, yet not of any strength. The position is nat-urally very strong, & I am a little surprised that the rebels did not make better use of it. Just in rear of their works is a dense forest in which a few of them were concealed & when our troops gained the hill on which their works were built, they fired on them & fled. I have not learned whether they killed any or not. We reached that place about noon on Saturday: we did not halt & I had no opportunity to examine the position. There had during the winter been a considerable force there for their barracks or quarters were still standing.

Here the face of the country changes.... As soon, however, as we crossed the Buck River the soil became heavy & the land low & swampy. It had rained heavily during the forenoon & so large a body of troops passing over them had made them [the roads] very deep & muddy. The remainder of our march was difficult & tiresome. We reached the vicinity of the York River about five o'clock & were first told to pitch our tents about a mile in rear of our pres-ent location. But before we had made much preparation were ordered to fall in & were moved to our present location....

On Saturday evening two of our guns were put in position & threw a few shells into the nearest Fort. The rebels immediately replied, killing two & wounding three of our artillerists. It is not known what damage we did to them. While the firing was going on a heavy ball came over our camp passing directly over my company, struck & buried itself in the ground about two rods from us. It waked the men up, caused a good deal of dodging & some little sport. The firing ceased just at sun-down & every thing assumed its quiet & peaceful aspect.... I was notified in the evening that I would have to go on Picket in the morning at six o'clock. In order to prepare we rose at 5 o'clock, & at six we started. I knew not where we were going but followed the guide, knowing well that I was going into a dangerous position. We went about a mile in advance of our camp to a road, just in front of which beyond an open field is one of the Rebel Forts. The Pickets are strung along the road to keep a lookout toward the rebels.

The day was bright & pleasant, & during most of the time quiet. I enjoyed myself look-ing at the rebels until I got tired then sat down & whiled away the day as best I could. We were in range of the rebel guns, but they did not molest us. We could see them moving around some on foot & others on horseback. Some dozen of them at one time climbed up on top of the embankment, sat down & watched us for a long time. Directly in front of us over the cen-ter of their works floated their flag bright & beautiful. To the unaided eye it looked red, but a glass revealed to us the white stripe in the centre. Their flag from its bright colors, red being predominant can be distinguished at a great distance. In this respect it is very good; neither is it devoid of beauty, but it expresses no idea or sentiment except slavery, & this is enough to render it detestable, in all places & to all men.

The day soon wore away & night came on. It was still clear & pleasant & we congratu-lated ourselves that we were having a fine time on Picket. We gathered piles of leaves & made beds so that those who were not on watch might sleep, & having made these arrangements settled down for the night. The rebels had not disturbed us during the day & I felt assured that they would not during the night. Being of this mind I lay down & went to sleep, leaving orders to be wakened at four o'clock. But I was not permitted to remain undisturbed so long. At two o'clock I was aroused by the rattle of musketry just to the right of my position. I listened to it a little while & then believing that it did not concern me lay down again. I was wakened as ordered, but no disturbance appeared. At eight o'clock we were relieved & returned to camp. In all we had a very pleasant & safe time considering our proximity to the enemy.

I have since learned that the firing that disturbed me during the night was our men firing on some rebels who were felling timber to give range to their guns. They were heard chopping & a force was sent out to stop it. They did so by firing on those engaged at it.

During yesterday nothing was done by either party so far as I can learn.... About noon it got very cold & began to rain & has continued to rain incessantly ever since. It is the most constant & disagreeable rain that I have encountered since I entered the service. It impede[s] our operations here very much. The roads are so deep, I understand, that our heavy artillery can not be brought up. It is not probable that any thing important will be done here for a few days. Gen. McClellan is here commanding & has a balloon with him. He has been reconnoitering with it, but has not seen fit to send to me the result of his observations. I only hope that he may be able to take the town, for I am afraid that a defeat here would settle the contest against us.

Though Union troops outnumbered those of the Confederacy on the Peninsula, McClellan remained convinced that the latter's line defending Yorktown was stronger than it was in actuality. Rather then venture an assault, he settled for a siege which only allowed the Southerners more time to shift forces to the region.

April 11th, 1862

It began to rain on Monday & did not cease until Thursday morning.... Tuesday we did nothing; Wednesday there began to be whisperings that the rebels were about to shell us; & it was talked that we would have to move back. We were in range of their guns & in an exposed place & every moment I expected the rebels to open on us. Thus passed the day. At night [we] were ordered to be ready to march at a moments notice. We packed every thing except our blankets, put on our overcoats & lay down to sleep. At twelve o'clock there came an order to us to get the men out under arms immediately. It was reported that the rebels were coming out of their entrenchments to attack us. The men were got out & stood shivering in the rain for an hour when they were permitted to return to their quarters. The men commenced to build fires to warm themselves, but the Gen. ordered them to be put out because they afforded too good a target to the enemy. The fires were put out & you can imagine how we felt standing in the cold rain. By & by they satisfied themselves that the alarm was false, & the men were allowed to break ranks & go into their tents. But they were so chilled that, not being permitted to have fires to warm themselves, they were uncomfortable the balance of the night. They got up Thursday morning feeling "<u>miserably</u>" & somewhat despondent. I am free to confess that I felt a little despondent myself. We had been on short rations since we left Fortress Monroe, the roads being so bad that it was impossible to transport them. Half-starved, half-frozen men are not accustomed to have the same elated feelings with well fed & well housed men, & we felt sensibly (at least I did) the effects of bad weather on our spirits. However, we whistled & kept our courage up & today feel as well as if we had not undergone such trials.

It was cold enough to snow, in fact did "spit snow".... At nine o'clock we received an order to be ready to march immediately with every thing. It did not take us long to get ready for the men have become so well accustomed to taking down & putting up their little tents that they can do it in an instant. After the regiment was formed we marched to the rear about a mile into the woods & were told to put up our tents. As soon as we entered the woods we felt that in a storm trees would be a great shelter to us; we were rather pleased with the prospect of living in the woods. Just at this time the sun began to penetrate the woods & the sight of it made us still more glad....

This morning is again bright & pleasant & the men are again in good spirits. This morning too, for the first time since we left Hampton we got a full ration....

It is also rumored that [Confederate] Gen. [Joseph E.] Johnston is falling back from Gordonsville to Yorktown & that Gen. [Irvin] McDowell is in pursuit, that Richmond has been abandoned & that the rebels intend to make a last effort at this place to prevent Virginia from falling into the hands of Northern vandals. I only hope the rumor is true, but it is too good to be true.

April 11th, 1862

Dear Father:

Since last I wrote you we have done comparatively nothing here. On yesterday morning we moved our camp out of range of the rebel guns. On Wednesday we were aroused by a threatened attack, but did not move out of camp. This afternoon the alarm was sounded again. The pickets were attacked but not by any great force. The rebels were easily driven back. We lost two men killed & five or six wounded. Our regt. was not under fire.

On Wednesday last while the 63rd was reconnoitering near the enemy's works, they were fired upon by the rebels, & your [David] Irwin of Reedsburg in Capt. Reeds [Benjamin J. Reid's] Co. was killed. He was shot in the neck, or rather his throat was cut by a ball....

April 11th evening

At three o'clock this afternoon an alarm was sounded, & the men were put under arms, it being supposed that the rebels were coming to attack us.... We marched out into the open field in front of the camp where we halted. The 63rd Regt. Col. Hays was on Picket & some portion of the line had been attacked, & it was supposed that the rebels were coming in force. In a few moments Adjutant Cortes [George P. Cortz] of the 63rd Regt. came riding along very much excited, & told the Gen. that Col. Hays was not able to hold his left flank & that he wanted a couple of regiments to sustain him. The whole of the Brigade that is three regiments were put in motion immediately towards the left of the Picket line. We are on the left of the Brigade & this movement threw us on the extreme left. When we arrived in rear of the Picket line at the point designated we found no disturbance, & learned that attack had been made on the <u>right</u> instead of the left <u>flank</u>. Adjutant Cortes in the excitement of the moment had forgotten, I guess, which was <u>right</u> and which <u>left</u>; he should have told the Gen. that the <u>right</u>, and not the <u>left</u> flank needed support. This mistake (as I think it was a mistake) threw us where there was no firing. We lay in the woods however, until dark, when we returned to camp. The 57th Regt., however, which was on the right of the brigade & behind the right of the Picket line got into a slight skirmish with the rebels, & had two men wounded. The 63rd had two killed & I believe one or two wounded. A number of the rebels ventured beyond their works & when our men approached them, the force that was out retreated precipitately.

Morning April 12th, 1862

Another night has passed without disturbance....

How the siege of Yorktown is progressing I cannot tell.... So far it seems McClellan has only been getting his forces into position. I believe all of our artillery is not here yet, & I suppose not all the force that it is the intention of the Gen. to bring to bear against this place.... There is no doubt of our ability to take the place unless the attack is very badly conducted which is not likely to be the case. How long the siege will continue is altogether a matter of conjecture. "Eddie," thinks that he will be home on the 4th of July. I will be satisfied if by that time we have driven the rebels out of Virginia. Three months is too short a time within which to subdue a half a continent with such a formidable enemy to contend against. It will require next winter yet to finish the war, although, if we are successful here, some [of] the troops may be dismissed before that time. I am content to think that I will be permitted to go home when my term of three years expires.

According to the Tribune Correspondent we had a terrible fight here on Saturday last. It caused a broad grin on every soldiers face when he read the exaggerated accounts of <u>nothing</u>. A very small sprinkling of truth is enough to fill a page of the Tribune. The best advice I can give you is to pay no attention to these highly colored statements....

April 15th, 1861

We were on Picket during Saturday night & Sunday. We were in sight of the rebel forts & within range of their guns but they did not disturb us. The generals were quite indignant at Col. Hayes & his men for raising the alarm of which I wrote you in my last. They think that it was caused by the rashness of our own men, provoking the rebels to make an assault. We had strict instructions not to fire unless we saw a body of the enemy approaching. They were content for the present to look at us & we were content to look at them.

...Gen. Jos. E. Johnston, has fallen back from the Rappahannock to this place, with his whole army, so it is generally believed. This makes them so strong here, that an assault on their works is a little hazardous unless a part of their force can be diverted by an attack on Richmond at the same time. McDowell when re-enforced by [Gen. Nathaniel P.] Banks, will [be] strong enough to take Richmond, or at least be able to divert a part of the force from here & thereby secure the place.

We will soon have 100,000 men here (that is not the aggregate of the regiments) but the force that we can bring on the field in case of a fight. This is a formidable army & if properly handled would be invincible....

What glorious fighting they are doing in the West. A little of the energy which they have there if sent to the East, would be of great service to the country. The battle at Corinth or Pittsburg Landing, shows what has been shown in more than one battle during this war; the superiority of the <u>rebel</u> <u>generals</u>, & the superiority of <u>our</u> <u>troops</u>. Yet our generals on the Potomac, have the presumption to assert that they are ready any moment to battle with the enemy, & that <u>their</u> <u>forces</u> need disciplining before they are fit to cope with the enemy. This dogma in which every one seems to acquiesce is costing us millions of dollars of every day & may yet cost us defeat....

April 16th evening

Yesterday was rather quiet but to-day there has been considerable cannonading, the result of which I have not learned. It is hazardous to be a spectator at these artillery fights, & I do not go near them unless duty calls me there. To-day while the firing was going on, a sergeant of a Maine Regt., who was standing in rear of our guns watching the firing was struck by a ball from a rebel gun & cut to pieces. He was out of his place, & there was very little sympathy expressed for him.

I have not heard from the Reserve Corps for a long while. Did Wallace say anything particular about Co. A & the 9th. In a paper a few days ago I saw a statement that "the troops left at Manassas were in a mutinous condition, & that the officers & men of the 3rd Reserve were seen mingling in the most disgusting exhibitions of drunkenness." I inferred two things from this, that the Reserves were left at Manassas & that they were fast becoming demoralized. It is a sad thing to think that the flower of Penn. youth, are about to prove a great disgrace to the state. There was never mustered a finer body of men than the Reserve Corps of Penna. Yet it is far behind many other Division[s] in what constitutes soldiers.... McCall is a poor man to lead it, & many of the lower officers are a good deal worse....

...Remember & love me & I will see you some day. My love to all.

April 19th, 1862

I received yours of the 14th inst. yesterday.... Your letters are received many times when I need to be cheered, when I feel fatigued & despondent but your kind words give me comfort & strength....

The siege here goes forward slowly.... On Thursday two officers of the Engineer corps were near the rebel battery just in front of us, making a sketch of their works. They were observed by the rebels, who threw a shell which exploded near them wounding both of them & killing a picket who was on post not far off....

During Thursday night heavy firing of musketry was heard just on our left. We were called out to be ready for any emergency, but the firing cease[d] after one or two volleys & we went back to quarters again. In about two hours we were aroused by firing in the same place, but it was of short duration and we did not go out. I have since learned that the rebels made a <u>sortie</u> in that direction to take a gun of ours which was playing on their batteries & annoying them I suppose. They were unsuccessful in their attempt....

Yesterday our regiment was working on a road which Gen. McClellan is opening ... in order to approach their most formidable battery.... The road is pretty well underway, but a great deal of work is yet required to complete it. It will be some days yet before we are prepared to attack the enemy's works.

This evening we go on picket again. They manage their roster so as to put us on picket every Sunday. To-morrow will be our third Sunday at Yorktown, & we have picketed two of them & will picket again to-morrow. The weather here is delightful.... The warm sun, however don't seem to affect the swamps much. They look as if they might be summer residents; if so, this is certainly a very unhealthy place during that time. But I hope that before the sickly season, we will have gained higher ground, purer air, & purer water.

Are you proud of me? It is something to know that a woman as intelligent & good as you are feels proud of whatever I do & say. I shall endeavor to so conduct myself that you will always feel proud of me & then I know that I will have no difficulty in retaining your love & esteem.

...Be loving, be truthful, be <u>frank</u> & kind, (I know you will) & you will be able to guide my life in uprightness....

April 23rd, 1862

We are encamped in the woods & picket in the woods but between the woods in which we are encamped & the woods in which we picket is a cleared spot about a quarter of a mile wide, over which we pass on our way to the picket line. While passing over this open ground we can be seen by the rebels from one of their batteries, & frequently they throw shells at us. They threw two on Saturday the first falling short, the second bursting above & in front of us scattering the pieces in all directions over our heads. Nearly all the men when they heard it coming fell down flat on the ground but this precaution was unnecessary, the shell bursting so far away & so high, that it was [more] likely to injure one lying on the ground than standing up.

...About seven o'clock there came up a heavy rain-storm ... so heavy as to wet us a great deal. In a short time we began to hear straggling shots, on our right, left & in front, but were unable to judge whether they were our own men or the rebels.... But it still continued & continued all night but not one of our men fired a shot.

About ten o'clock the rattle of musketry was heard away off on our left quick & loud. In a few minutes the reserve came up & this swelled it still more. I woke all of my men that were sleeping fearing that the attack if such it was might be extended along the whole line. But the firing ceased in about ten minutes & again all was still as death save the occasional crack nearby us. The rain, however, continued. The hours hung heavily upon us & I thought the night would never pass away.... Thus passed the night, slowly drearily.... All was still. Two hostile armies lay face to face, each preparing to meet the other but neither inclined to break the peace of the Sabbath. This silence is not infrequent; yet one who has never witnessed it could scarcely believe it could be. I would that they could remain silent forever did not justice demand that an insolent enemy be destroyed.

...The straggling shots again commenced. I now ascertained that they came from the rebels & learned that the shots during the night had been from them. They had come up close to & in front of our line, we could not see them nor could they see us & I presume they fired in order to get our men to fire, & having discovered a post by the flash of the gun to shoot the men that were on it. But our men were too cool, not one of them fired, consequently rebels did not have an opportunity to shoot any of them. In the day time our sharp shooters got out in front of the line & their fire was directed at them & we were out of danger.

At eleven o'clock Gen. [Charles Smith] Hamilton our Division commander, & Gen. [John Gross] Barnard of Gen. McClellan's staff came along with their glasses to examine the enemy's works. Gen. Hamilton is a very plain man, nothing striking in his features or bearing except his eye, which is dark & unfathomable. This was the first time I had met him face to face & I liked his gentle modest bearing. He reviewed us at Hampton, (the first place I saw him) & I was not well pleased with his appearance. He had on himself & his ... horse all the gold & tinsel of his office, & being one of those men who do not at all look becoming in this "rig," he appeared like a man that was trying to make a "show" but was failing. I saw him afterwards in plain clothes & he looked better; & when I saw him face to face on Sunday I felt that he was a man competent to fill the place which he occupies. I have as much if not more confidence in him than in our higher Generals.

Gen. Barnard is a fussy looking, seedy old gentleman reminds me a good deal of an old school teacher, whom the boys have harassed all his life-time. He may be a great military man but I failed to observe it....

Monday it rained nearly all day. We did nothing; the ground on which we are encamped is low, & our time was principally occupied in keeping the water out of our tents, in doing which we did not succeed very well. The night following was rather unpleasant. The floor of our tent was damp, our clothes were wet & our blankets damp. However, we got along & are still enjoying as good health as usual.... I was detailed to take charge of two hundred men to work on the roads.... We worked rather lazily all day but finished all the work that was assigned to us.

During the forenoon I strolled out to a house on the York river.... There were several officers with me & while standing on the bank of the river one of them observed a rebel slipping along under the bank towards us. We were outside of the picket & he was slipping up to shoot us. When he saw that he was discovered he put back, probably fearing that he might get shot instead of shooting one of us.

The house near which we were ... is the same in which Lord Cornwallis, signed articles of capitulation to Washington.... I enclose to you a couple of flowers plucked from the garden in rear of the house....

While returning to my working party I saw Gen. McClellan out strolling about with three or four of his staff. I had never seen him before afoot; & I am compelled to agree with

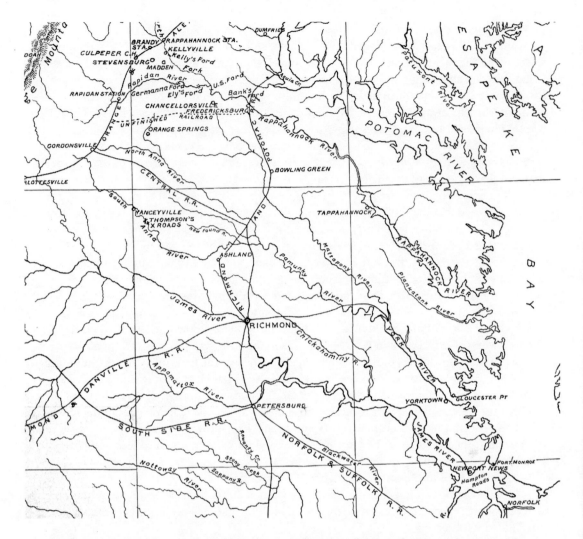

Southeast Virginia (from William R. Livermore, *The Story of the Civil War*. 3 vols. New York: Putnam, 1913. III).

others who say he makes a finer appearance on horseback than on foot. He is a man of about my height, but heavier bodied. His legs are slightly "bandy" to use a low term & this gives him a very squatty appearance. He was unshaven, his face was flushed, whether with liquor or victory I am not prepared to say & he had in his mouth the everlasting segar. Altogether he looks like a German of ample means who makes free use of Lager & the pipe. I failed to discovery any of the signs of greatness which others have seen in his personal appearance. He may be a good general nevertheless.

Your heart is not "<u>just as near</u>" mine as it was last July, but a good deal <u>nearer</u>. Every days separation brings us nearer each other....

The siege progresses slowly. About the time we are ready to bombard, they will evacuate & fall back to Williamsburg & there put us to the same delay that we have met with here. I am afraid the summer will be consumed in preparing to attack the enemy just as the winter was.

Camp Winfield Scott
(near) Yorktown, Va.
April 28, 1862

During all day Saturday it rained, creating a good deal of despondency. We are encamped in a swamp (in fact the whole country is a swamp) & when it rains the water lies on top of the ground & a little tramping makes terrible mud. This, you know, makes the men uncomfortable, uneasy & discontented; consequently there is a deal of grumbling at every body. But it all passes away with a day of bright sunshine & they all become as happy as ever.

...We have hard work here [on the roads] which together with bad weather & a coarse unvaried diet is causing some sickness.

...My boy who has been on the hunt of something for me to eat has just returned with crackers purchased at 20 cents per lb. butter 50 cts eggs 50 cts per dozen. These are what might be called <u>war-prices</u>. Give my love to all. Remember that I am yours as ever

Extract from Kate M. Scott, History of the One Hundred and Fifth Regiment of Pennsylvania Volunteers *(Philadelphia: New World Publishing Company, 1877), 39.*

"Nothing unusual occurred until Saturday, May 3d, when, while the regiment was occupying the front line of works, about noon, General [Edwin] Sumner passed the redoubt where Captain Duff was stationed, and the Captain called his attention to the fact that the rebels were moving along their lines toward our right, and that he believed they were retreating. The General, however, paid no attention to his statement. During the night, when the officer of the day passed, Captain Duff told him that all was quiet in his front, and that he believed the rebels were gone, but the officer gave no heed to him. At daylight Captain Duff was relieved. Before the relief reached Captain [J. W.] Greeenawalt, who was on Captain Duff's right, he sent forward some scouts, and ascertained that the rebels were actually gone, but no attention was paid even to his report, and it was high noon before it was known at army headquarters that the rebels had evacuated Yorktown. The consequence was that the army did not begin its forward movement until in the afternoon."

At daybreak on May 6th Duff's Company D and Company I of the Wild Cat Regiment P.V. were sent forth to reconnoiter. They discovered Confederate Fort Magruder near Williamsburg abandoned and quickly took its possession. As a souvenir the captain claimed a packet of letters on blue stationery. Written in French, these few notes constituted correspondence between a Creole soldier and his wife. Most interesting of these papers is a poem, Chans des Confédéres, that may be found in Appendix A.

Williamsburg, Va.
May 8th, 1862

You are no doubt very anxious to hear from me, & I shall relieve your anxiety as soon as possible. Yorktown was evacuated on Saturday night last, & we started on the march on Sunday....

...I shall give you full particulars as soon as I can find time.... We did not reach the battle ground on Monday until just before dark when the enemy retired. The loss on each side is about two thousand including killed wounded & missing.

We were thrown forward early in the morning & took possession of the town. It is quite a fine place....

Evening.

...Since then [this morning] our baggage has come up....

We are under marching orders again & will no doubt leave early in the morning going towards Richmond. I have not time to give you the particulars of the battle of Williamsburg.

It would require more time than I have at present. Suffice it to say that it was a fierce & bloody struggle, in which bad generalship was shown on our side & the most determined bravery on the part of our troops. I shall never forget that eventful day & the day following. You say that the sight of those wounded at Shiloh has given an idea of war; but allow me to say that you have seen nothing ... approaching the horrors of war. I should be afraid to tell you what I have seen. It is best to leave it unwritten at least.

I am now looking for a speedy termination of the war. Our troops fight so nobly & so bravely that I do not think that any serious disaster can overtake us. There may or may not be another great battle in Virginia. At all events Richmond will soon be in our possession.

Within the last few days I have begun to have some longing to return to civil life. I can now see the end of this dark & bloody struggle & I am becoming impatient to have it achieved....

> On the Road to Richmond Va.
> 16 miles South West of Williamsburg
> May 11th, 1862

We halt here for a short time to-day to get a supply of provisions. We have been on the road two days & have marched only 16 miles....

If the rebels make a stand on the Chickahominy, as it is said they will, it may be a couple of weeks before we reach Richmond. I believe it is confirmed that Norfolk is taken & that our Gun boats are up the James River. If this be so, Richmond must soon fall....

> May 11th. 1862

Dear Father:

We left Williamsburg on Friday [May 9] & reached this point yesterday evening. We are halted here a short time to get a supply of provisions.

The rebels are still retreating....

The weather is very warm here. It will require two months for us to reach the southern line of Virginia, by which time we will be obliged to halt on account of the heat. Notwithstanding our late success the war I believe will continue through next winter. I think however, that I may have an opportunity to get home this summer.

I am well. The health of the army has been good since we left Yorktown. The country here is elevated & healthy. Give my love to all.

> Cumberland Landing on Pamunkey River
> New Kent County Va.
> May 16, 1862

I wrote you on Sunday last from near Burnhamsville. We remained there until Tuesday, then started forward but the road being filled with troops in front of us we were able to move only three miles. We started the next morning at four o'clock & marched six miles & halted near New Kent Court House.... We did not start [again], however, until Thursday morning (yesterday) when we marched to our present location. It rained on us all day yesterday & a part of last night making the march & the encamping very disagreeable....

Cumberland Landing ... is a beautiful place.... Notwithstanding the many natural advantages & attractions of the place it looks like all Virginia farms decayed & wasting. You can never know the injurious effect of slavery upon a country until you have looked over this peninsula, now wild & desolate but only wanting the impulse of honest industry to make it one of the finest countries on the globe. North of the Pamunkey River the land is low and swampy, I presume, and heavily timbered. The stream is narrow, deep and sluggish, navigable for heavy schooners as high as White House, at least.... It will be some time I think before we reach Richmond, unless the Rebels evacuate, which seems probable to me....

...I desire you to bear in mind that I still love you & hope to meet you soon. But do not interpret that latter clause wrongly. This is the month & this about the time when I expect[ed] to receive from [you] a gift of yourself but fate cruel enough in this instance has declared otherwise....

Allegheny City

May 16th /62

Dear Bird:

Yours of the 11th has just come, and with eager eyes I have read it. My precious one is still safe, still thoughtful of me — surely there is no cause for tears; and yet they come; weary, hopeful, sad, joyous tears, all at once; and the woman's heart would not be content until the rain cloud had emptied itself. Now I am strong and glad again.... You always write to me of the bright side but I can clearly picture to myself the dismal, cheerless days and nights.... What would the happiness be if this night I could talk to you....

Harriet

Cumberland Landing, Va.

May 18th, 1862

Lying in my tent to-day sweltering with heat & thinking of my far distant yet nearest friend ... when in stepped the Post Master, with a letter of the 12th inst. Never was a letter more welcome....

I have been an eye-witness to almost every thing that has transpired on the Penninsula. I know all about the evacuation of Yorktown, was on Picket the night they evacuated. There has never been a correct account of it published. When I get home you will know all about it. The same is true of the battle of Williamsburg. It is a matter of surprise to us that newspaper correspondents cannot give a more correct account of the movements of the army. In generals they are some times correct; in particulars universally wrong. All you can read in the papers gives you no idea of what has taken place.

...You will have to wait a few days for the occupation of Richmond by our troops. I believe it will fall into our hands without a struggle, if it is true as alleged that the Monitor can go to the city. Gen. McClellan I am satisfied is waiting on the movements of the Gun Boats on the James River, Gens. [Ambrose E.] Burnside & Frémont. There is one thing evident to me: if the rebels do not evacuate Richmond they will be captured. I shall be well satisfied if they do not evacuate, & I think Gen. McClellan is trying to prevent them from evacuating....

While McClellan slowly approached Richmond, another Union commander, General David Hunter, proclaimed free all slaves in what was called the Department of the South, encompassing Florida, South Carolina, and Georgia. Union forces actually controlled only a few islands and enclaves along the Atlantic Coast, however. The president, who was still striving to maintain a coalition of strongly differing groups, could no more allow Hunter to determine political policy than he could Frémont in the fall of 1861. He therefore revoked the order. To anti-slavery Republicans, the president's action was disappointing, as was Confederate General Thomas J. "Stonewall" Jackson's defeat of Banks at Winchester in the Shenandoah Valley. On the other hand, the apparent impending fall of Richmond was a source of encouragement.

At the close of May, Confederate General Joseph Johnston saw opportunity to save Richmond. The Chickahominy River separated McClellan's forward forces from the York River, which was their supply base. It also divided the Union army. Heavy rains on May 30 turned the stream into a torrent that threatened to destroy the bridges linking the halves of the Army of the Potomac. The next day Johnston sent his forces against the two Union corps south of the river. Confusion delayed the Confederate advance and additional Union forces crossed the flooded bridges. The attackers were forced back to the road between Fair Oaks and Seven Pines. The battle could be counted a victory for the Union, but the Federals' 5,000 casualties were only a thousand less than those of the Confederacy.[1] The affair heightened McClellan's caution, and it brought a new commander to the Southern army. General Johnston was wounded, and his replacement was Robert E. Lee.

Camp (near) New Kent Va
May 19th, 1862

This morning we were ordered to be ready to march at 7 o'clock. We were ready at the hour appointed & started, not towards White House, as we had supposed, but towards New Kent, which gave rise to a number of conjectures as to what our destination was. When near to New Kent we halted, to rest for an hour the Gen. said, but instead of resting an hour we rested till 2 o'clock. We got under way again, but instead of going to New Kent, we turned to the right & took what they called the Richmond road.... We are in the rear of the whole army. I really do not know whether our merits or our demerits have placed us here. It is a fact nevertheless: it would take some considerable disaster, it seems to me, to get us into a fight.

Well let us talk politics a little while. The Democrats still incline to the belief that we cannot keep the South in submission to the laws. How do they propose to remedy it. These men do not care any thing about the country, they only regret that they are not in office.

What do you think of Hunter's Proclamation. This I think strikes at the root of the evil & if sustained by the President will do a great deal towards ending the war. But I fear the President will recall Gen. Hunter & countermand his Proclamation. Then comes the long talked of rupture in the Cabinet; then what? Will Congress support the President or will it support Gen. Hunter: this is the question I am debating now, & I believe it will sustain the Gen. I am sure it ought to do so. The transactions of this week will be looked for with anxiety. What if Richmond should be taken, the Confederacy be recognized by the Great Powers of Europe, on condition that it emancipates all the slaves within its boundaries; & that Lincoln should recall Gen. Hunter. How would we stand then. How near the end of the war would we be: The end would be afar off it seems to me.

Allegheny City
May 26th /62

Dearest:

How, or what, shall I write to you this gloomy night? This has been the saddest day of all the sad new year. Bank's army defeated, and retreated to Hagerstown. What can it mean? I tried hard not to believe, yet it is true. Knapp's [Joseph M. Knap's] battery <u>totally destroyed</u>— most of these men from here—some dozen my own pupils, who held a warm place in my heart.... Your letter of the 19th received tonight, was so ... doubly welcome.... When troubled my thoughts are <u>to you</u> always, and here you come, with bright words to cheer me—for a while at least, the woman forgot her country, and thought only of you.... Do you feel the touch of my lips on your forehead? ... God alone knows, where this fair evening finds you—you are doing your duty in this hour of need, and whether your reward be life or death it will come from a Father's hand.... I sometimes feel that when you come home we shall not be the same people at all that we were.... You cannot know what it is to feel that you are in danger of loving something better than you love yourself, and at the same time know that <u>all</u> the future depends upon it.... The end of the war does not appear — it will come when we as a nation have repented of our sins and have manifested it to the world — the events of this week may change the whole face of affairs, but the cause of the <u>slave</u> will triumph.... Be strong, be brave, love God, serve Him and you will be ready for life or death....

Harriet

Camp (near) Summit, Va.
Saturday, May 24th, 1862

Since my last letter to you ... we have been quite busy marching & picketing. On Tuesday morning we left New Kent & marched to within 5 miles of the Long Bridges on the Chickahominy, & then encamped expecting to remain several days. My company & another which during the march had been the advance guard, were sent on picket as soon as we reached our camping grounds, & were not relieved until the next day at noon. We were about three miles from camp & by the time we got to camp I felt like taking a little rest. The next morning, Thursday, I had scarcely got my breakfast, when we were called out to drill. After we had drilled for a couple of hours, the whole regiment was ordered to prepare again for picket. We did so, this time going to the Long Bridges. My company was held during the day & part of the night as a reserve. At 2 o'clock in the morning I was ordered to cross the Bridges with my company & post them so as to be able to catch a party of rebels whom it was supposed would visit the bridges during the morning. I stationed my men so as to entrap any party coming to the bridges & then awaited the coming of the party. But no party came, & after remaining until after day light I returned with my company to this side of the creek, or River as it is called. At eleven o'clock we were relieved & had a fatiguing march back to camp through the hot sun, & over a sandy road. Soon after our return to camp we were order[ed] to prepare to march immediately. This done we started "on-ward to Richmond" again. We marched until ten o'clock last night making about six miles. We stacked our arms on the road side & lay ... down to rest for the night. We lay down very quickly & were soon asleep. This morning we were ready early & started on our way, but after marching about a mile halted & were ordered to camp....

Our advance is at New Bridge, scarcely eight miles from Richmond.... Whether we will succeed in getting Richmond during the [next] week I am not able to say. I am not yet convinced that the rebels will make a stand for the city....

The repulse of our Gun Boats [at Drewry's Bluff May 15] was not [a] very serious affair; although I have no doubt it gives some hope to the rebels. Our Boats will be able, I think, to silence the battery & remove obstructions in the river & go up to Richmond....

A Baptist minister who lives near Long Bridges told us that Jeff. Davis has changed his entire war policy; that he intended to withdraw all of his army from every point where they could be reached by our gun boats & expects to protract the war for years by the adoption of this policy. This minister who is a bitter rebel, thinks that if they break up their army into guerilla parties they will be able to destroy our armies by constantly harassing....

Camp on Chickahominy Creek
Near Railroad Bridge, Henrico Co. Va.
May 31st, 1862

Yes, Harriet, you deserve more than I can ever give you. Your constancy during my long uninterrupted absence is worthy the love of any man.... If you knew with what pleasure I read your letters, how often I think of you, how often I sit down by your side, kiss you, tell you how I love you & receive in answer your pleasant smile & look of <u>perfect</u> confidence; <u>you</u> would <u>feel</u> "that the love which is to be your life portion is unbounded"....

...I could tell you all my hopes, my ambitions, my fears, and I could listen patiently to the gentle reproofs of one whose nature is purer, lovelier, holier....

But I trust that by my own determination, aided by the strength derived from your love will enable me to withstand all, endure all, conquer all, that I may return to you with a pure & single heart with as sacred lips as those you kissed so often on the July morn when I left you....

We are the extreme left of the army & are left here to guard the Railroad over which all of our support pass from the Depot at the White House.... It is not likely that we will be moved from here during the operation before Richmond.... The rebels I think will be compelled to evacuate Richmond with a battle....

The repulse on the upper Potomac is of no consequence, if the disgrace of a panic be excepted. The troops made no show of fight at Winchester. The cowardly scamps deserved to be whipped. As for us here you need have no fears. That raid has not the slightest influence on us, more than to make the soldiers mad & make them more impatient to wipe out the rebellion.

My health is still very good. My first Lieutenant [J. P. R. Cummiskey] has returned from Fortress Monroe. Yesterday my company was detailed to worked on the roads. Only one commissioned officer was required: the Lieut. took the co. & I was allowed a holliday, the first one since I took command of the company....

> Hospital, near Battle Field,
> June 2nd, 1862

Mr. Samuel Duff,[2]
Clarion, Pa.
Dear Friend;

Levi has requested me to write you a few lines to let you know how he is. He was severely wounded in the battle of Saturday. His wound, as I say, is severe, but it may not be extremely dangerous. He rested quite well through the night, and this morning is quite comfortable. He distinguished himself as a brave man in the battle, and his patient endurance and cheerful disposition distinguish him here. Whilst with us his conduct has been such as to endear him to all. I have made arrangements for forwarding our wounded to Pennsylvania. They will probably leave this afternoon. Levi's wound is in the Right breast, the ball coming out of the back below the shoulder blade. He is very hopeful, yet he would not fear to die. Please excuse my haste, as I have to write many letters. Our loss is not less than 200 — loss in our army not less than 5,000. I am

> Yours Truly,
> D. A. Steadman, Chaplain,
> 105th. Regt. Penna. Vols.

Levi B. Duff official report of battle May 31st, 1862, Fair Oaks, or Seven Pines:[3]
On Saturday May 31st. about Ten o'clock the firing began on our front. It rapidly grew heavier and came nearer, and about Four o'clock in the afternoon we received an order to go to the front. There were but eight companies in the regiment, Companies C and I being detailed on fatigue duty. We left everything behind and marched down the railroad past Savage Station at double quick, then took the Richmond Road, and after going about half a mile halted for a few minutes in the woods. By this time the shells were flying over our heads pretty briskly. To our Right was an open field, across which was a rifle-pit filled with our men, apparently awaiting the onset of the enemy. Just in front of them was a narrow slashing, in front of which was the field in which was Casey's Camp, then in possession of the enemy. We

turned to the Right out of the woods, marched by the flank in front of the rifle-pits, and between it and the slashing, until our Left cleared the woods, were then brought to the front, and in line ordered to go forward through the slashing and attack the Rebels. They were more than ready for us, for they had already started to attack us, and we met almost on the edge of Casey's Camp. The Right of my Company, as we advanced, was on the Richmond Road, and we had scarcely started forward when my men began to fall. Just as we reached the further edge of the slashing, beyond which was Casey's Camp, and the enemy had approached to within about twenty yards of us, I was struck and fell.

4

Recovery

Harriet first learned of Levi's wound from the Pittsburgh newspapers of June 1. She received no further news until Firman Duff told her on June 4 of his father's receipt of Chaplain Steadman's note. Samuel Duff promptly dispatched Firman to New Haven with instructions to bring Levi home as soon as possible. Worry for Levi placed additional stress on Harriet's fragile nervous system. Worn out at the end of the school term, she took to bed with her chronic throat infection. About June 18 Levi reached his brother's home, barely able to walk and speaking only in a whisper. Yet he managed to visit Harriet on June 20, told her that he planned to be well enough to return to the army in six weeks, and urged her to marry him immediately.

Joyful at Levi's return, Harriet agreed to the marriage but delayed setting a date, hoping that the assumed imminent capture of Richmond by Union troops would mean the end of the war. Levi pressed his case, and Harriet agreed to wed on July 21. On the eighth of July Levi traveled to his parents' home and told them of the wedding plans. They did not object to the match, but all his family — as well as the family and friends of Harriet — urged postponement, partly as a way of keeping Levi from returning to military duty before the war ended. Harriet succumbed to this pressure and wrote to Levi suggesting a postponement of the ceremony. Levi reacted against these suggestions strongly and the large wedding was held as scheduled.

Allegheny City
June 8th

Dear Bird

I cannot come to you and words, written words will be of small moment to you in your sufferings — and yet I cannot let your brother start without a few lines. We hope that he may soon find you — you will need his love and sympathy. How long the past week has been — our hopes were just rising when the word came alas! "seriously wounded through the breast" I dare not think what or how much the words mean. Oh! May a merciful God heal the wound and make you ready for much good to come — My anxious heart forebodes that you may be very dangerous I feel that I must be ready to bear the worst — until better news reaches us. I try to think over the long hours you must have spent since your kind good letter was written (I could not count the times I have read it) I hope that you were able to trust in God, and be comforted.

Levi I cannot write more my heart is too full — it may weary you to read this much — you know I will pray continually for you. Hoping that you will soon be home and that your pain is thus relieved. I remain your anxious

Harriet.

State Hospital
New Haven, Conn.
June 10th, 1862

My long silence will give you warning that you are to receive bad-news. I telegraphed to Firman on Saturday giving him my condition at that time; & I hope that you have ere this heard from there that I am not dead, but in a fair way to recover.

My last letter to you was written in the forenoon of Saturday May 31st. I little thought when I wrote it, that the afternoon would find me in the battle. But such was the case. I can not, however, write details now. Suffice it to say that I was wounded about six o'clock in the evening & by great exertion & a piece of good fortune succeeded in reaching Heinzleman's Head Qtrs. where I had my wound temporarily dressed.

The wound is severe, by a large sized round musket ball through the chest. The ball entered above the right nipple & lodged against the back-bone just under the skin. It was at first pronounced fatal by all the surgeons; & not until I reached White House did I receive any assurance that I would recover. I suffered terribly for three days but since have been tolerably easy. I am able to be up nearly all day & can walk out a little. I think I will be able to get home in two or three weeks. I am very comfortably fixed & kindly waited on here.

I cannot write further at present. Remember & love

Clarion Pa
July 10th, 1862

I left Pittsburg on Tuesday evening at 4 o'clock & arrived at Kittanning just at dark. The cars were very full when I entered them & I was obliged to take a poor seat & was very much fatigued by the ride.

I had a good night's sleep before attempt[ing] to go farther; & I felt so well on Wednesday morning that I thought I would be able to get home without much discomfort. But in this I was disappointed. The road was so rough that I dare not lean my back against the buggy seat & I did not go far before my back gave way & the ride from there home was very annoying & when I reached home I was well nigh exhausted.

This morning I was very sore all over, caused by the jolting in the buggy & I felt quite languid. I got weaker during the day & this evening I do not feel well. I think, however, that it is only the fatigue of travel & that I will be better in a few days. I was at the store a few moments this morning but remained in the house the rest of the day.

The folks are all very well at home & Winnie [younger sister Winifred], & her "baby" are well. They look upon me as broken down & are trying to persuade me not to go back. They expected me to stay at home a month & feel not a little disappointed that I am only going to stay a week. I have not told them why I am to return to the city so soon.

You will have to excuse me this evening, Harriet. I cannot write. Give my love to all & accept a <u>kiss</u>

P.S. Please write me a short letter, if you can find time.

The bullet that wounded Duff at Seven Pines (Fair Oaks). It came close to ending his life, traveling through his chest and stopping near his spine beneath his right shoulder blade (courtesy Allegheny College).

Clarion, Pa
July 15th, 1862

A letter from you this morning made me feel happy all day. Time flies <u>too</u> swiftly when you are present, but when you are absent the hours, the days, are long and wearisome. The hope that a few days will bring me to your side is all that reconciles me in my present situation.

I feel stronger today than I have felt since I was wounded. I think that I am now able to return to my regiment & every day that I remain here idle only makes me the more impatient to get away. You think that our arrangements could be readily postponed. I am rather of the contrary opinion. The 1st of August at farthest will find me on the way to Virginia. The longer I stay here the shorter will be my stay with my —. If I stay here a week longer I will only have three days to remain with you, surely you do not wish this. There seems to be a tacit conspiracy among some <u>women</u> to prevent me from going back to the army or at least to detain me at home as long as possible. All hands must understand that their schemes will not succeed. However much I desire to stay, I feel that my duty calls me elsewhere — there I shall go. As I tell mother "There is no use to talk about the matter." Perhaps this may seem a little decisive, but it dont mean any thing except that you will find me rather decisive in many things. I have been thinking since I came home that you do not fully understand my character in this respect. You will find me to be a very unruly self-willed man. Have a care before it is <u>too late</u>, is the advice of <u>one</u> who wishes well for you.

I will leave here on Friday morning next, will be in the city the same evening, & expect to see you also. It may be as late as 9 o'clock when I reach your house but I shall be there without fail. Winnie is coming with me, and perhaps Sardis [younger brother born in 1840]. I can not afford to allow a postponement. Had I known 2 weeks ago that today would find me well, you would have been requested to fix an earlier day. How glad I shall be when this week is ended. I am getting <u>desperate</u>.

I have told the folks here all about it. They seem surprised at nothing, except that I am going to leave you so soon. They wonder how you can permit it.

This is probably the last letter I shall write to my "<u>sweetheart</u>." The first one was written from here. Do you not recollect it? A naughty fit placed it in my hand, and a naughtier hand put it into the fire. But for this misfortune the series would be complete.

This is a bright pleasant evening, Harriet. How are you this evening? I hope your cold has left you. I believe I am the <u>better man</u> now. How delightful would it be to sit alongside of you & hear you talk — to see your smile & to feel your lips press gently my forehead. Hope says by and by. Give my love to all. Accept a kiss

Contrary to Northern expectations, Richmond did not fall to the Union forces. In a series of contests known as the Seven Days Battles at the end of June, Robert E. Lee undermined McClellan's military confidence even though the Union won all but one contest and sustained significantly fewer troop losses than did the Confederates. Despite the advice of some subordinates to counterattack, McClellan retreated and finally ordered his army to retire all the way back to Harrison's Landing on the James River. That is where Captain Duff rejoined Company D of the 105th Regiment of the Pennsylvania Volunteers following his departure from Pittsburgh on August 6.

The Army of the Potomac needed more men, and in July these were recruited via the militias of the separate states. Lincoln brought in a new leader, General John Pope, from the West to take charge of the armies formerly led by Nathaniel Banks, John Frémont, and Irvin McDowell. The president also appointed another general from the West, Henry W. Halleck, as commander of all the Union armies — an appointment far from pleasing to McClellan. The latter was also less than happy about the latter two men's decision to send the Army of the Potomac north to reinforce Pope's Army of Virginia, given the approach of the "sickly season" in the swamps of the Peninsula.

Springfield Farm
August 7th, 1862

My Dear Husband;

Time's wings are leaden today, though yesterday the hours were swift-winged.... I have tried to be brave and strong, and have succeeded thus far — but your presence is still so vividly here that my heart cannot ache so much as it will.... This want [for my husband], how great it will be, and yet, strange paradox, because the want is great I am a happy woman.... I hope that other days to come will be so full of happiness, we shall forget when the thought of parting saddened the brightest moments. I think of you today with pride as you have turned your back on all you love to do what you can in this strange contest. May strength of body and happiness of mind be yours.... I dare not follow you today on your far journey lest I should know what a distance separates us....

Flower from graveyard of Quaker meeting near York, Pennsylvania. Plucked on July 16, 1862, it seems a memento of Levi and Harriet's honeymoon (courtesy Allegheny College).

Harriet

Baltimore Md
Aug. 7, 1862

News from my journey has been rather pleasant. I arrived here today at noon; & will leave on the Mail Boat this evening at 5 o'clock. I reached Harrisburg this morning & remained there one hour & a half. During my stay I had a talk with Col. Hays (Alex.) who says that all of our field officers have resigned; that McKnight has not been heard of since the battle of Fair Oaks; & that the regiment is in command of a Captain [Calvin A.] Craig. This is a queer story & rather improbable, the author of it being regardless generally of what or where he speaks.

I also met Orlando Gray our Adjt who has been sick for some time & is now on his way to Annapolis. He remained with the regt. a month after I was wounded & knows a good deal about the late troubles, but he evinced a disinclination to talk about the regt. From this I am led to infer that there is something wrong, what I am unable to conjecture. I shall know in a few days.

Please excuse this hurriedly written note. I shall write again tomorrow from Fortress Monroe, if I have an opportunity....

Camp (near) Harrison's Landing Va
Aug. 10, 1862

I arrived here safe on Saturday morning early, found our regiment in a good place & in good spirits. In the afternoon I visited Charles & Edward & also Co. A. of the 9th. Charles & Edward are both well & looking well.[1] Todd Wallace & Torrence are also well. They are all in good spirits.

I found the army in much better situation & condition that I expected to find it. The location here is healthy although it is very warm. Good water is got by digging deep wells & fresh bread & vegetables (Potatoes & onions) & furnished to the men <u>twice</u> a week. This is so great an improvement on previous rations as to provide a marked difference in the most of them are really growing fat.

I found my 2nd Lieut. In charge of my company with 28 men fit for duty. Our regiment can now turn out about 350 effective men. Col. McKnight has resigned & very probably the Lieut. Col. & Major will resign.[2] I have not time to give you particulars at present. Capt. Craig is in command of the regt. & will likely be the Col. It is not yet ascertained who will be the other field officers. I have lost all of my friends by the resignation of the Col. Every man who was his friend has now to keep quiet, so that you need not flatter yourself with any expectations for me.

Aug. 12th, 1862

I had first seated myself this morning early to write you a letter when yours of the 7th was laid before me. The perusal of it made me so happy that I had to drop my pen "& sit & muse" instead of writing. The morning wears away & I again take up my pen to write.

The caption of your letter is new to be sure; but as you say it is not strange. The conviction that I am a "dear husband" is sincere & it does not seem inappropriate that it should be expressed. It is not impolitic to let me know that much I am sure. I am quite as content with my portion I am certain as you are with yours.... But this separation is hard; I can scarcely muster courage & strength to endure it. Did I not feel that you can bear it with faith & hope, I fear I should give away. There are happy days for us in the future.

[Duff continues with a detailed description of his trip. He writes of his breakfast in Harrisburg.] I went to the United States Hotel for breakfast because it was convenient; I was not disappointed in getting a poor one. There met Col Hays & several more Pittsburgers all more or less drunk. I did not meddle more than to talk a short time with the Col, who told me all sorts of stories some true & some untrue.... I reached [the mail boat] about 5 o'clock. We did not start however until ½ past six & I am certain I was never nearer burnt up than I was during the time the boat lay at the wharf crowded as the boat was with passengers. The boat was heated by the boilers & sun conjointly until it was almost as hot as a bakeoven. [Once the boat moved, he was somewhat cooled by the breeze as he watched a lovely sunset. But he could not help but think that] the boat was bearing me away from all that was near & <u>dear</u> to me to a gloomy dark uncertainty & I could not help feeling somewhat despondent; yet the strong faith within me that I would again return to enjoy your society buoyed me up & I resigned myself, not without a struggle however, to my present situation.

[Duff did not sleep well that night because of the heat and the next day the air was stifling.] I floated (if I may be allowed the expression) in perspiration all afternoon. [The boat docked late in the evening. The next morning Duff sought out his unit.] I met the company on the drill ground some distance in rear of the camp & as I approached them they gave me three rousing cheers. They were all very glad to see me & I to see so many of them present for duty.

When the regt came to Harrison's Landing but four men of my company could stand on their feet, although there were about thirty of them left, that is that number had actually escaped in battle. All of the men here with one or two exceptions are now fit for duty & in good condition so much has a months rest done for them. The regt that is what is left of it is now in as good condition as it ever was, & the men are in good spirits. To be sure we are without field officers, but the Col. is the only one who[se] absence is felt & his place is filled by a man in whom the men have a good deal of confidence.

[Duff tells of his visit with Charles, Edward, and others.] I had a long quiet talk with Charles on Saturday evening & enjoyed it very much. He said that he had never yet regretted that he came to the army. He did not seem to feel very despondent over the situation although he was disappointed that our work was not nearer done than it is. I had a talk with his captain [John R. Brooke]. I think very little of him. He is not the man for the times I am sure.

I have done nothing since my return. Since the regt came off picket on Sunday we have been lying idle in camp. Yesterday morning at day light we recd an order to get ready to march by two o'clock. We struck our tents & in a short time were ready to leave, but before noon we were told that we would not move that day. We have remained in readiness to go ever since. The probability is that we will go to-morrow.

No one will venture to make a conjecture as to our destination. We do not know, but there is one thing that we feel certain of, & that is that when we move we stand a very good chance of getting into a fight, since the enemy are around us & we cannot move in any direction without encountering them. We might move down the James River in transports without meeting with them, but there is no indication we are going that way. Our knapsacks & extra baggage have been put ... aboard boats to remain there "until a permanent depot is established" as the order reads but it did not state <u>where</u> the depot was to be established. Our wagons loaded with ammunition & provisions are to go by land, & from this it is evident that we are to march.

It seems to me to be too hot to make any aggressive movement at present, but I am ready for any thing. I think I can endure as much as the rest; & I would not be the least displeased if we should gain a victory, for I believe a victory would scarcely impress us at present.

The weather here is extremely warm, too warm for men to labor hard in. It is I believe fully ten degrees warmer here than it was when I left Pennsylvania. The heat too is all pervading. In Penn, get into the shade in the warmest day & lie down quietly & you will feel rather comfortable, yet here you cannot escape the heat go where you will.

We are encamped in the woods in a very pretty location; our camp is kept clean & looks neat & the men all say they are sorry to leave it. The flies are very numerous & give us some trouble, but strange to say the mosquitos do not annoy us.

...My health has been very good since I came here & I feel that I am almost as strong as I was before I was wounded.

Catlett's Station
Prince William Co. Va
Aug. 23rd 1862

After a long forced silence I am permitted to write you again. You cannot image what pleasure it gives me to be able to write. I know how anxious you will be to hear from me & how often you have looked for a letter & been disappointed & I desire that the disappointment shall continue no longer than I am forced to be silent.

For nine days past we have been constantly on the move, & if I had an opportunity of writing I had no opportunity of sending a letter. I wrote a note in pencil from Williamsburg on Monday last directed it to New Alexandria & put it into the mail of the 4th Cavalry but I do not expect it to reach you.

We left Harrison's Landing Friday morning Aug. 14th [Friday was Aug. 15] marched to Yorktown by Tuesday evening embarked on the Steamboat Long Island Wednesday, reached Alexandria yesterday at noon & here by cars this morning at nine. Our regt. is guarding the railroad between this Station and Manassas Junction a distance of ten miles. We do not know how long we will be permitted to remain here. Our army (that is Pope's army) is on the South side of the Rappahannock about fourteen miles South of here. The two armies, (the rebel & ours) have been cannonading each other for three days past. The rebels it is alleged trying to cross the river & our men preventing. The attack has been on the right, where Siegels [Franz Sigel's] Corps is stationed, & up till yesterday evening Siegel held them in check. The cannonading ceased about ten o'clock this morning what is the result I have not yet learned. Troops are arriving rapidly from the Penninsula. All of [Philip] Kearney's [Kearny's] Division is already here & I look for [Joseph] Hookers this afternoon.

Last night some rebel cavalry (what number I have been unable to ascertain) made an attack upon our trains, which are nearly all near this station & succeeded in burning some twelve wagons, but doing no serious damage. A fight of course ensued between the guard here & the rebel cavalry in which four of our men were killed several wounded & quite a number taken prisoners. The rebels lost two killed & three or four prisoners, & lost also eight horses. The attack caused a great fright among [the] teamsters, & there is no end to the wild stories they tell.

I am well as usual, remarkably well considering what I have undergone since I left home. I will give you particulars of our journey to this place at another time.

I cannot add more. Excuse this hastily written letter. What should I say in conclusion? Shall I say to my wife that I love her? No, this is unnecessary, she knows that I think of her constantly. My love to all & a kiss to <u>my Harriet</u>

The action Duff described in the above letter was a result of Lee's effort to defeat Pope before his army could be reinforced by troops arriving from the Peninsula. Jackson was sent to swing around Pope's troops and attack the Federal supply depot at Manassas, which he did August 27. On the 29th as the Confederates retreated they encountered Union troops on the Warrenton turnpike, inaugurating the Second Battle of Manassas. Fierce fighting took place in a railroad cut. The first day's contest was inconclusive. On the second day substantial reinforcements led by General James Longstreet and undetected by Union leaders until too late fueled an overwhelming Confederate counterattack resulting in yet another Confederate victory. Union forces did hold firm on September 1, stopping the Confederate advance at Chantilly.

The 105th Pennsylvania Volunteers were much involved in these battles, especially the fighting along the railroad from which it was the last Union regiment to be driven by the graycoats. That retreat was organized by Duff and Lieutenant William J. Clyde, as all other officers were either killed, wounded, missing, or detailed elsewhere. After leaving the battlefield of Chantilly, the regiment reached Camp Jameson on September 3rd, "few in numbers, half naked, and almost worn out," according to Kate Scott's history.[3]

Cedar Creek
Prince William Co. Va
Aug. 26th, 1862

[Envelope marked: This letter was taken prisoner and released]

I wrote you a letter the day of our arrival here, & gave it to a man to mail at Alexandria, but doubt if ever reaches you. Our regimental post master has not yet come up & we have no way of sending off letters except by chance. To it I trusted my last & to it must I trust this one.

Since my last we have moved to Cedar creek, about a half mile beyond (South) of Catlett's station. We are very pleasantly situated, & have very light duty to perform & will probably remain here some time. Our baggage has not come down from Alexandria & we all feel the want of it very much. I have not had an opportunity to change my clothes since I left Harrison's Landing, & am beginning to be very uncomfortable on this account. They will not allow any thing to be transported on the railroad except troops. When the troops are all up we will get our baggage.

But what annoys me most is the stoppage of the mail. The change of operations from the Peninsula to this place has so disarranged our postal facilities that we have not had a mail since Aug. 14th. I have recd but one letter from you, Aug. 7th, the day after I left. You can perhaps imagine how I feel by this time. If ever I was home-sick it is now. I do not know how I will endure the privation much longer. There is a prospect of a mail today, but nothing is certain & I shall not feel disappointed if it does not come.

I do not know anything about the situation in front. It is about fourteen miles from here. This place is thirty eight miles from Alexandria on the Orange & Alexandria Railroad. The country has been very fine, but is devastated by two armies & at present is not attractive. My health still sometimes good, & the health of the regiment is good.

I must close this letter as there is a man waiting to take it to Alexandria.

I must not forget to tell you that I saw Edward at Yorktown. He was well & had stood the march remarkably well. Charles was sick & had taken a boat at Harrison's Landing.

Centreville, Va
Aug. 31st, 1862

After passing through many dangers during the last four days I am able to send you a note to inform you that I am safe & well. I dare not think how anxious you are: I can only hope that you have born the trials of the last month with spirit.

Our army fell back about six miles last night, having been badly whipped. We lost about 40 pieces of artillery & I do not know how much more <u>materiel</u>. I think that we will be obliged to fall back on Washington, but I hope not. We have plenty of men, but our Gen's seem to be made of blunders.

P.S. We have not yet recd our mail nor our baggage.

Camp (near) Alexandria, Va
Sept. 5th, 1862

I am truly thankful that I am again permitted to write to you. I am safe still, but am not well. The toils of the last month have worn me out & a severe attack of diarrhea has added considerable to my infirmity. I feel better this evening however, & if allowed to rest a few days will be well.

I had intended to recount to you the events of the last month, to tell you what toils what dangers I have passed through, but I can not. Besides not being able to write a long letter I have not the time we are again ordered to be ready for a three days march. We may go any moment, whither we know not.

My letter to you from Cedar Creek date 26th ult[imo] has a little history which I suppose you will be interested in. After writing it I gave it to a man named W Dillon to carry to Alexandria. He took it, but being at Manassas Junction Tuesday night Aug. 27th was taken by the rebels. He, however took care of the letter & after he was released mailed it. I saw him on Friday the 30th just after his release & he told me that he had the letter & would mail it as soon as he had an opportunity. I never saw a man more delighted than he was when he got within our lines.

I wrote you a short letter from Centreville Sept 1st which I presume you have read. Many things have transpired since which will no doubt renew your anxiety, but this letter will I hope relieve you.

We left Cedar Creek on the 28th [27th] under command of Hooker & were in the fight at Bristow on that day.[4] I had a very narrow escape from a shell, which passed over my head so near to me that the wind of it raised my hat. On the 29th [28th] we marched to Centreville, & on the 30th [29th] to Bull Run & were in the fight all of that day losing about 43 of our men. You have no doubt seen accounts of it in the papers & it is unnecessary for me to give particulars. On Saturday the 31st [30th] we were under the fire of cannon, but suffered very little. After the left & centre of our army ... broke, we covered the retreat remaining on the field until 11 o'clock. Sunday we remained inactive at Centreville. Monday afternoon we marched to-wards Fairfax & had the fight at Chantilly in which Gen Kearney was killed. We remained on the field until 3 o'clock in the morning then fell back to Fairfax. The next day we marched towards Alexandria by way of Pohic Church, halting near the church that evening. Wednesday at two o'clock we reached our present camp. As I said before we recd orders this evening to be again ready to march so we are at sea again although we expected to have a little rest here.

...What can I say further. The future looks dark. I can not bear to look forward, I can only trust that it may be well with us. I never cease to think of you & of home. My absence I know is felt. I hope it may not be long. Now my dear good wife I must bid you adieu. Let me kiss you before I go. My love to all, & let me hope that I may again meet you all.

Camp (near) Fort Worth, Va
Sept. 9th, 1862

Since I last wrote I have your letters of Aug. 15th & Sept. 5th.... Last night I was just about to seat myself to write you a letter when we recd an order to be ready to move in half an hour. This of course caused letter writing to be laid aside for the time. We started about nine o'clock & arrived here at eleven. We marched about five miles halted & were to encamp for the night. This morning we were assigned a place & told to pitch our tents, which we did after clearing of the grounds. We are three miles from Alexandria, on the Fairfax road, near Fort Worth as my caption indicates. The 123rd P.V. lies near us & the 141st has been temporarily placed in our brigade. It was announced to us in an order today that in the absence of Gen. McClellan in the field Gen. Banks would command that portion of the army left for the defense of the capitol. From this we are to infer that Gen. McClellan has taken the field with a large portion of the army & left the remainder for the defense of Washington, we being in the latter. This is cheering to me for it will give me a little rest which I very much need. I do not expect to hear of very much being done in the field at present notwithstanding it is announced in the papers that Gen. McClellen is after Jackson. Gen McClellan is not a man of enough dash to catch Jackson & I shall be very much surprised if he does it. I do not much fear the presence of the rebels in Maryland. They have not yet crossed the Potomac in any great numbers & are not likely to. Unless we are betrayed by some traitor, or sacrificed by the blunders of some incompetent Maryland & Washington are safe. Touching the end of the rebellion I will not speak. I will say this much, however, that until we changed [change] our policy from one of cruelty & injustice to one of justice & righteousness we shall never succeed. We may marshall more men than ever were marshalled before, but without a <u>cause</u> to fight for they can do nothing. Men cannot fight without something to inspire them. War can not be carried on successfully without a cause. History is full of examples on this point. We will have to wait with patience until God turns hearts & heads of our leaders before we shall see any successful termination to this war.

Sept 12th, 1862

I recd your kind letter of the 9th yesterday evening. How glad I was to learn that you are still well & hopeful. I hope you may not lose courage while I am absent. I know how difficult it is to look on constantly repeated disaster ... & be faithful & courageous. Yet I am sure that if any one can do so my wife can. I hope with you, Harriet, that these sad times will be over some day & we be permitted to enjoy the happiness of peace.

I know your solicitude for me to well not to believe that you are anxious concerning my health. I thank for your good advice & also for the powders you sent me. I shall try to make good use of both. I [am] happy to be able to say that I have been somewhat better for two or three days. My diarrhea has left me but only for a short time I presume, as I am not yet well. We have not had hard work for a week past and are not likely to have for some time & I think I will get well now before we have hard campaigning....

Since my last letter we have moved a short distance about a half mile, from the left to the right of Fort Worth. This occurred day before yesterday in the afternoon. The 155th Col [Edward J.] Allen lies near us now. I visited them yesterday. They are in good health & spirits as all new soldiers are. It is a good regiment & if properly officered will do good service.

This morning we are ordered to be ready to move immediately, tents packed & wagons loaded. How far we will go, I do not know, but not far I think. I have not had a paper this morning & do not yet know what transpired yesterday, nothing I presume. A higher power than our President or our Gens. must help us out of our difficulty or we will never get out of it.

I have a letter from father yesterday; he is very despondent thinks that if we can do no better that we had better quit sacrificing lives & money, which is the conclusion I have no doubt of all sensible people; but it is to be hoped that something better may be done....

Lee also thought something better might be done: an invasion of Maryland could win it to the Confederacy. A few more victories, even seizure of the strategic Union rail connections at Harrisburg, Pennsylvania, might persuade Great Britain and France to recognize the insurgent states and lead the North to sue for a negotiated peace. He divided his army as he moved forward. By chance Union forces came upon a lost copy of Lee's special order No. 191, which detailed his plans, and McClellan gained information that might have enabled him to pick off separately each portion of the Southern troops. Again he acted slowly. Lee had time to cluster some of his forces, and with news that Jackson had captured Harpers Ferry, the Southerner decided to fight at Antietam Creek near Sharpsburg, Maryland. September 17 was the single bloodiest day of the war, a battle from which Duff was spared. Both sides took legion casualties. Confederate losses were such that they had to withdraw to Virginia. McClellan failed to pursue with any vigor, but Antietam could be listed as a Union victory (not by much). This gave Lincoln the occasion for which he had been waiting to announce his "Preliminary Emancipation Proclamation" that all slaves in states that remained in rebellion on January 1, 1863, would be emancipated.

Camp (near) Long Bridge, Va
Sept. 13th, 1862

Let me greet you with a husband's love on this our mutual birthday. With a husband's grateful heart, let me thank you for your forbearance, your kindness, your love. With a husband's pride let me call you my <u>dear good wife.</u>

During the past year we have loved, we have wedded. We have been made happy in the knowledge that we are all in all to each other. [Duff continues in similar vein, then turns to their different views of religion.] Is it not strange too, that a man whose only religion is indifference to the future should love a woman ... [who looks] afar off to something he knows not what, but something toward which she can look steadily and not get bewildered. She calls on him to look, he tries to look, but is soon lost in the vagueness of his own mind. [Duff refers to an incident during their courtship.] I did not then believe that you could love a man of my character.... When I returned you threw yourself into my arms, without any questioning, willing to be my wife, asking nothing more.... [He urges her to feel free to speak about religious matters] I wish to have nothing standing between us. Let this day leave all misgivings behind.

I am still improving in health. The rest is doing this for me. All is quiet here....

Allegheny, Pa
September 16. 1862

My Dear Husband:

I begin my letter with regrets that I have not written sooner. I meant to write you a long letter on your birthday, but could not, everybody seemed to drop in that day.... Just as I had penned the last word your letter of the 13th was handed me ... sincerely do I thank God for every word.... I know that you will see Him [Jesus] also. I was silent, and have been so, on this subject, not because for one moment I forgot the peril of your soul. When I learned from your own lips (that which I had always hoped) that you did not <u>disbelieve</u> the truth of our Holy Religion, the hope sprang up in my heart, with certainty of fulfillment that God was leading you to Himself.... Levi, it is because you will look with a doubting intellect that you cannot see.... The only way is Christ Jesus.... Come with me, I can show you the way, if you are but once willing to walk in it — united in this, there cannot come unhappiness. I must tell you something you will be surprised to hear. I have spoken to you of numbness that occasionally troubled me. During the past month I have been worse than usually, annoyed so much that for days I could not guide my pen. Mother became alarmed, and, at her request, I had medical advice. The mistakes of physicians are numerous, or I should be anxious indeed. Dr. Hamilton tells me that I am in imminent danger of paralysis in the Right side, the pressure, or cause, being in my brain. I think him mistaken, believing the cause to be in my stomach, but will nevertheless submit to his treatment, it will do no harm. He cauterized my back with hot irons all the way down my spine. I was at once relieved, and have continued so. The operation is repeated once a week. I am quite well in every other respect, and have no fears, that whatever the cause of the trouble, I shall soon be well.... The State troops are mustering with enthusiasm — if they were only permitted to do something....

May God keep you, and cause
His face to shine upon you.
Harriet

Camp Fairfax, Va
Sept. 16th, 1862

I have been busy all day performing the duties of Brigade Officer of the Day, in a Brigade scattered over several miles of territory. This evening finds me a little tired but ever ready to write to you which I have the time.

I recd yours of the 11th day before yesterday. I thank you for all the love it contained & the confidence expressed. I hope to fulfill your expectations to requite your love and to obtain worthily all the honor which you think is awaiting me. So long as my Harriet continues so good so live — and I know she will always continue so — I shall not fail to so conduct myself that she may feel proud.

Yesterday I got a pass & visited Washington. I found it very quiet & dull. In afternoon, when the good news came in from Maryland there was a little stir but hardly noticeable to a stranger. Congress is the life of that place; and I do not know how the people live there when it is not in session. There are few troops in or about the city; they have all moved up into

Maryland except the few on this side of the river. Our Division alone I believe remains near the city. Since the death of Gen. Kearney it has been commanded by Brig. Gen.[David B.] Birney; but the papers state that Brig. Gen. [George] Stoneman, formerly Chief of Cavalry on General McClellan's staff is to command it. I know nothing of his ability except that, although he had many opportunities, he did nothing brilliant on the Peninsula. Birney is a fancy man from Philadelphia—called by Gen. Kearney "slow-coached Birney" & I hope he may be superseded before we go into the field again.

I have not heard the news from Maryland to-day. Yesterday the news brought indicated success of considerable importance to us. Our generals, however, have such a habit of exaggerating their successes, that we have to hear from other sources, before we can form a true judgment of what has taken place. If the rebels have been badly whipped I shall be satisfied. I am willing to forego bagging them if they are only whipped & demoralized. I feel sure that, if we have had this much success, their army can never get back to Richmond in a proper condition or in numbers sufficient to defend it.

Since I last wrote we have again moved a mile & a half to the front. We are now about three miles from the Long Bridge on the famous Arlington Heights. We have orders to keep two days cooked rations in the haversacks & three in the wagons & be ready to march at a moments notice. Of course we are always ready to march when we have our rations & it was unnecessary to add the latter clause. I do not think it is the intention to move us away from here, except in case of a great emergency — in case of a disaster to some portion of the army now in the field. It may be however, that we are to join in the pursuit of the rebel army; if so we may leave here any hour.

While in Washington yesterday I got a portion of my pay $500. [Duff expressed most of this to Pittsburgh and asked Harriet to pay off various debts he had contracted at an interest rate of one dollar per month; he urged her to feel free to use the rest.]

Sept. 18th, 1862

I expected a letter from you this evening but it did not come. I have recd none since that of the 11th. I know you have written since then if you are well — the fact that I have not received a letter makes me think that you have not written — therefore that you are not able to write.

We are lying where we were when I wrote you last. All is quiet here. I believe it is the impression at Division HQtrs. that we are to move soon — where it is not known. I do not know what foundation they have for their belief, no more than I presume than I have for the belief that we will not move for some time — not until the movements on the upper Potomac have developed some course of policy or some plan of campaign. The news we got from that region this morning is cheering. It is now generally believed that the rebels will be badly whipped & disorganized. This being the result, I suppose a campaign against Richmond will be immediately determined upon. What will be the plan of that campaign is a matter of conjecture with us. Some think that Richmond will never be approached from Washington — others that it will not be approached by way of the Peninsula. What will be done in the future you well know, depends on the issue of the present contest near Harpers Ferry.

Two officers of Co "H" of our regt who were taken prisoner at Bristow Station Aug. 26th, have been paroled & visited us to-day. They say that they were very badly treated. They were at first confined in prison with Pope's Officers, but were subsequently released & then paroled The whole rebel army they say has come North from Richmond and that the citizens are following the army expecting — or professing to expect — to reach New York in a short time. Judging from recent reports they will be disappointed.

The Reserve Corps has again been engaged in these recent battles. This time they were under a leader in whom they had confidence & who was worthy of their confidence. They have at last had an opportunity to prove that they are the best troops that our State has sent to the war. They never before fulfilled expectations— never behaved more than creditably— hardly that — yet I believe it was because they were badly officered.

I observe that [Ed. D.] Dithridge & [Willam] McClurg of Co. A are wounded. I presume there are others, but their names have not yet been published. This company has escaped with remarkably few casualties— perhaps it was not so fortunate this time. We were much pained to hear, this morning of Hooker's wound. We presume, however, that it is not serious. The taking of [Confederate General James] Longstreet which seems to be confirmed will partly off-set our late heavy losses in Gen's.[5] He was one of the rebel's stand-by & his loss is a heavy blow to their cause.

Sept. 19th— This morning the news is not so cheering. The battle of Wednesday seems to have been a draw one. The great contest is not yet decided; it is to be hoped that it may be decided & in our favor in a short time. The loss of Harpers Ferry with ten thousand men, fifty pieces of artillery & large quantities of ammunition & stores is a severe blow to us— while its gain is of great moment to the rebels. I still believe that this rebellion will be determined almost finally within a short time — still I have fears when I think of what has so often happened. If God is with us we are safe, if not we will receive further punishment. I can not feel that we have been sufficiently humbled, to asked [sic] for success yet I can not but hope that this disastrous war may be terminated soon.

For three days past I have not been so well as usual. On Monday being in Washington I walked a good deal. On Tuesday being Brigade Officer of the day I was obliged to keep moving all day & part of the night. This constant stirring about started the diarrhea, which has continued for three days. Yesterday it was quite annoying this morning however I feel somewhat better. I think I will get well again until I am compelled to march or move about, when it comes back.

Camp Prescott, Va
Sept. 21, 1862

I have been thinking of you all day long....

This evening finds me in the same camp, from whence I wrote my last — named yesterday by order of our Brigadier "Camp Prescott"— in health as well, but not any better: my spirits are lively however & my hopes as high as ever....

I have read & re-read yours of the 16th inst. I will try to remember your words of wisdom & study to profit by them. You know — yes I am sure you do— the difficulties in my way — you can too & will help me to remove them....

I cannot but feel anxious concerning your numbness— not that I think it at all serious at present, but because I fear it may become so. Physicians are frequently mistaken, but their opinions are not to be despised. In respect to your being in imminent Danger of paralysis I should think Dr. Hamilton mistaken — as to the cause of your numbness, however, I incline to think his opinion right. Your brain I think is a little too strong for your body & your present labors don't do much towards restoring the equilibrium. On the other hand your brain work exhausts your physical powers & this it is that causes your numbness. More physical exertion and less brain work will cure you.... Allow me to ask you to consider the matter of quitting your school....

We have no news since yesterday morning. Matters are still in doubt in Md.

Sept. 22, 1862

I am glad you are well — sincerely hope you may continue so— know you will, if you do not overwork yourself & are not over-anxious about your — "Levi".... Your good letters are cheering. I love to read them whether long or short....

Like you we are, in a measure, in the dark in regard to the movements of our army. McClellan's army has failed it seems to catch the rebel army or even to rout it. They have retired leisurely across the Potomac so say latest advices. If he pushes them hard he may yet rout them, but I do not expect to hear of such a result. Gen. McClellan is too slow to catch a man of rapid movements like Jackson. As the result of the battle on Wednesday last [Sept. 17] our army has gained some confidence in itself & in its leaders, beyond this we gained nothing. We were too slow as I supposed we would be. If Gen. McClellan had attacked a day sooner Harper's Ferry might have been saved, notwithstanding the blunders of those who commanded there. If this point had been held McClellans army could have routed, perhaps captured a great portion of the rebel army; but in losing this we lost all.

We have not moved yet. We had another warning from Gen. Heinzelman this evening to be ready to march at a moments notice. I do no know what plan of campaign may be or may have been decided upon, but I am confident that wherever it may be we will take part in it. I think, however that we will not set out, before something further transpires in the Shenandoah Valley. The troops here are awaiting the issue of that contest, and will be moved either to complete a victory or retrieve disaster just as circumstances may require.

I enclose you a fine photograph of Major Gen Kearney....[6]

Sept. 26th 1862

What shall a man do with a woman who has fallen in love with him beyond recovery? Shall he neglect her, despise her love, & leave her to brood over the misfortune of having loved one who is either too foolish or too fickle to return it: or shall [he] accept the love as a divine gift return it with a grateful heart & receive her who proffers it to guide & counsel him, to smile on him in prosperity & her him in adversity.

By me the question has already been answered. I have made my choice — such as few have had the opportunity and fewer still have had the good fortune to make. I have taken to myself one whose only pride is to be my wife, whose only ambition is to "win my praise" by a gentle & modest bearing in my presence & by wifely conduct in my absence.

I almost laughed out when I read in your letter of the 20th the acknowledgement that you are in love. Did you know that you were talking to a man? How then could you think of speaking thus? I have it — I told you (you will remember) that I would compel you to love me. I have compelled you to acknowledge it — I am content. Henceforth let it be known — just to you and me — I love you — you love me. Now kiss me and let me kiss you & look into those beautiful eyes where I first met my doom & where I see reflected all the virtues that a husband's pride can name. — my harp to-day would sing only of love. I must turn it to something else.

We still remain where my last left me. We have not hard work but this is our play-day soon to end I suppose. The weather is unpleasant — the days are too warm & the nights too cold for comfort. Our soldiers who have only the shelter tents are beginning to suffer some. I presume that if we lie here long we will be furnished with better shelter. The troops under McClellan on the Potomac must suffer considerably, while the rebels who in addition to being without tents are without the necessary clothing must suffer terribly. It is coming the time of year now where our superiority in equipping our soldiers is of some advantage, while our enemies will feel the sad disadvantage of their thin wardrobes.

There is nothing new in army matters; all is quiet here as well as on the Potomac. But during this dearth of war news we have abundant food for conversation in the President's

Emancipation Proclamation. It struck us like a thunder-clap at least it did me, for I thought that Lincoln was firmly chained to the fatal jugernaut of Border state influence. His long submission to the dictates of pro-slavery union men, who are not heartily loyal & whose respect for and adherence to the constitution is subservient to their love for slavery, his rejection of the advice of all the best men in the country, who long urged him to adopt the policy which he has finally proclaimed, led me to believe that little was to be hoped for from him. I had already begun to fear that another revolution would be necessary to rid this country of the incubus of slavery. But to my surprise & gratification there is now a better prospect before.

But a few days ago I would see the end of the rebellion only in the triumph of Southern arms & in the success of their confederacy. I could see beyond only continuous strife between two nations, contiguous & without natural boundaries dividing them — embitter[ed] in their feelings towards each other by a long & bloody war. And still slavery existed to degrade and brutalize the black man, & to curse with its blighting influence the white man. But one thing was needed to throw sunshine on this dark picture, but one thing was necessary to be done, to give us permanent & prosperous peace — to do justice to the black man, whose wrongs stand in our light. Has it been done, so far I think as we can do them justice. The President's proclamation is not a recompense for their long withheld rights. It is no atonement for our long continued brutality & wrong — we can make no atonement for this — we can offer no recompense for that, we can only say to our enslaved brethren rise up & be free & ask God to forgive us for having held them in slavery from generation to generation.

Many times during the last few months I thought I was almost committing a crime in exposing my life for a government which knew no law of action but wrong to a weak and despised race. More than once did I think of throwing down my sword & returning home. But I was encouraged to continue by the reflection that this war — whether intended to be so or not — must prove more or less disastrous to slavery — & I trusted that God was working out some grand result which it was not proper for us to know then. I am glad now that I did not turn back. I am encouraged to go forward by this last just & righteous act of the President. I now know for what I am fighting — for what I am periling my life and all I hold dear. And I know too that whether I live or die the great result will be attained — the rebellion will be conquered, slavery will be abolished, & we will have a government of which we may be proud — one which — freed from the foul blot of slavery — will give us dignity among the nations of the world.

I have room to say but little further than close. In regard to my health I have no improvement to note. I took some of the powders you sent me, but they did me no good, rather they made me feel worse. My diarrhea is not an ordinary diarrhea, — nor is it very severe as yet only troublesome. It arises from derangement in my system caused by my wound & not removable by diarrhea medicine. The derangement is probably in the liver as I have a soreness in my right side so severe some times as to make it difficult to rise off my back. I shall consult our Surgeons about & have it removed — I believe it is nothing serious, but may result seriously if not attended to. Mahlon B. Loux of my co. — just returned — a prisoner since the battle of Fair Oaks says I look different from my looks then. He poor fellow, has had a hard time of it too. He was very rugged when he was taken, but looks badly now. Four months of hard usage has done its work.

I need only add that my constant thought is of you....

Oct. 1st, 1862

Since Sunday I have done no duty except attend to business matters of the company, which have kept me quite busy. I have concluded not to do duty until I get better. On Monday I went to the Surgeon & stated my case & ask[ed] him what he could do for me. He said that he could give me some pills but could not assure me that they would cure me. He said that the army diarrhea was a very hard thing to control in many cases they could do nothing with it. As mine was not a violent case, he thought I could be cured. I have taken the pills according to his directions, & discarded several articles of food which he thought injurious, & I am beginning to think to be better. I think, however that my improvement is more owing to my dieting than to the effect of the surgeon's pills.

Every thing about the army here remains quiet. Other troops hereabouts, except our corps Heinzelman's, have moved & are moving: but there is no indication of our going. On Sunday our Brigade, [General John C.] Robinson's, was reviewed by him: & to-day our division was reviewed by Gen. Heinzelman. This is all the stir we have in our camps.

Col. McKnight has been reappointed & has again taken command of his old regiment. We have now McKnight for Col. Craig for Lieut. Col. & [J. W.] Greenawalt for Major. A good many officers are chagrined at the return of Col. McKnight, & it is probable that our difficulties are not yet ended. What has transpired concerning our field officers is too-long a story to write, consequently I will not attempt it. Suffice it to say that I am treated with more consideration by Col. McKnight than by any other that has yet been at the head of the regiment.

I made inquiry of Capt. [Hugh B.] Fulton concerning John Johnston. He told me that he had had two John Johnstons in his company. One belonged to the company when it first came into service, was wounded at Charles City Cross Roads June 20th 1862, & is now in the Hospital. The other joined him as a recruit on the 26th of Aug. last, was killed at the battle of Bull Run Aug. 29, 1862. This is probably the one of whom you imagined.

The last few days have been very warm. We have had no rain for a long while — two weeks at least.

I have heard nothing from Charles and Edward Smith since the battle at Antietam; are they still safe?

What qualifications to command a gun-boat does Mr. Chamberlain possess, or does he expect to get the command of one, by influence without reference to fitness. With regard to quitting your school, use your own judgment....

Oct. 4th, 1862

Capt. Duff is glad to be able to say to Mrs. Duff that his health is much improved during the last few days & that with care he is in a fair way to be well again. — I asked the surgeon as I wrote in my last & gave you his opinion. He left the impression upon my mind that medicine would not help me, but that careful dieting would. So I have left off eating almost every thing except boiled bread & milk mush & milk & quit coffee & taken to tea. I have quit doing duty also, as I would not able to do much duty on such diet. This course has been continued for a week & I have improved much. I shall continue it until I am entirely well. I will have an opportunity to rest here for a month yet I think for there are no signs of moving our division. We at present seem to be left as a reserve to protect Washington.

Our cause I think is brightening every day. I believe with the National Republican that our cause touched bottom when the rebels invaded Maryland. We shall never again see as dark days as those were. Besides the hope of recovering Maryland is forever gone to the rebels. They now know that that state is not in active sympathy with their cause.

And then the dignity added to our struggle by the proclamation of the President. The Richmond papers now talk of hoisting the black flag. Let them do so. The civilized world will then look upon them, as they deserve to be looked upon, as pirates & highway robbers. Our sympathy with slavery has always relieved them of the odium attached to the institution; now that we have cut lose from it, the world will judge them by the true standard.

...I hope you are well & happy. Do not fret about me. I am getting well.

Give my love to all. Kiss me then I can bid you, adieu.

Oct. 5th, 1862

When in camp this day [Sunday] is with us usually a day of idleness. In a military point of view we do nothing. Sometimes a very <u>regular</u> officer has us out on a review, but this seldom happens. We are, however, obliged to remain in camp, & may read, sit around & talk think, or do what we have a mind to.

This morning is bright & cool — a pleasant bracing October day. Every one around me is apparently happy — possession of the happiness only which arises from the submission to an unpleasant duty. I too am well & as contented as morning usually finds me. But my mind wanders. I do not love although obliged & willing to endure my present surroundings. To a man of my education & habits, there is nothing loveable in them. Others may find satisfaction here. I can not: my home, brightened by the presence of a wife too good to be forgotten for an instant absorbs my thoughts.

When I think of you on this day I am always reminded of our different habits — how widely different from me you spend the day. On every other day we walk together — in thought & action one. But today I go over the usual routine of daily life: you turn aside to another way which to me is unknown....

When I first thought of religion, that is gave it any serious attention & began to apply it to my own case, I questioned whether there was such a thing outside of education or family predilection, whether a man was not more or less what he was brought up. My early impressions— not very decided to be sure — told me that there was while my present belief taught the contrary. After considering the subject for some three months it became a settled conviction with me that there was not. I was content to believe that if one lived uprightly so far as he knew how, or as was the Roman maxim lived honorably & gave to every one his due ... he would have done all that in reason would be required of him. I knew that it was difficult & sometimes impossible to do this on account of the perversity of our nature, but disbelieving in the renewal of our nature I accepted this as an evil I could not avoid. The perversity of nature was not acquired by but descended to me & therefore I could not believe that I was responsible or would be called on to answer for it.... I believe then and still believe in a future state that there is another world where our conduct in this is judged & rewarded according to its deserts.

Previous to this time I had regularly attended church & frequently a bible class. It now occurred to me that if religion was nothing but the superstition I supposed it to be there was no use to attend church nor study the bible except as I would study any other book....

...When you first wrote me a note on the subject.... I now thought that I could talk to you and explain to you my views, & if you could entertain such a man well: if not my duty was plain however hard it might be. It is unnecessary to recite what followed. I thought but little on the subject from that time until after our marriage. I was then first brought into close sympathy with a person of deep religious feelings & character.... Could it be possible said I, that one so intelligent so wise in the ways of the world could be deluded into believing and countenancing a weak superstition. I readily answer, no; and this opened the subject again to my thoughts. You looked beyond yourself for the guidance of your conduct & for strength to endure the trials of life. You seemed morally stronger than I.... You pointed out to me the only true way: that if I would come with you I must make an effort to do so myself — that God would hear and answer earnest prayer.

I have tried often, Harriet, to think about it, but my mind wanders from the subject. I shall try to think of it more, & hope by your aid to receive the true light....

One word more & I close. I love my wife with all the ardor of a man's first love.... I feel assured then that she will not overlook the errors of my life, but forgive where I have been unwillingly led astray. Give my love to all.

Oct. 6th, 1862

I can only write "All is quiet on the Potomac." We have not moved & there are still no indications of our moving. It is stated in some of the papers that most of the new troops are sent to Gen. McClellan on the Upper Potomac. If this be so we may be counted out of the next campaign. There is still some doubt as to the plan of a fall campaign adopted, or whether any plan has been adopted.

The news from the west looks bright, but telegrams seldom tell the truth. I hope the campaign is begun in earnest in Kentucky. Gen. [Don Carlos] Buell, I think, should be removed & someone who[se] heart is more in the cause be substituted.[7] It is time now to remove all lukewarm generals. Let us have no half way work. Congress has passed laws the president has issued [a] Proclamation, let the latter now appoint generals who will recognize the Proclamation & enforce the laws. Gen. Hunter & Gen. Heinzelman have been mentioned as fit men to take command of the army in the Mississippi valley. Let either one be appointed. I would be satisfied.

I have no doubt you have a good many invalids in the city at present. Is not Kennedy Marshall a nice young man. I should be ashamed to walk the streets with a certificate of disability, possessing the constitution which he has. It is a pity that such men escape the draft. These are fit for nothing but food for gun-powder. Their loss would not be felt in the community.

I enclose you an autograph of Gen. Kearney, which I chanced to pick up to-day. Capt. Caine, our brigade Commissary asked me to assist him at a Court Martial to-day. This paper fell into my hands, & being of no use to him, at my request he gave it to me. The autograph is genuine.

...I am feeling better than I have felt at any time since I was wounded. When the weather gets cool, I shall get strong & hearty again.

Oct. 7th, 1862

Another day has passed in quiet and comparative idleness....

So far as we can see from here, our army is doing nothing: but our observation is limited, being confined to our division. Gen. McClellan may be doing great things of which we know not, but will be permitted to read about one of these days. We wait patiently for the result.

From the far West we have cheering news. [William S.] Rosecrans has beaten [Confederate General Sterling] Price badly, as say the papers & official reports. Gen. Ord, formerly of the Reserves has risen again into pubic notice, and our former Division Gen., Chas. Hamilton, who was removed from the command of our division while at Yorktown has distinguished himself. I do not know what bearing this victory may have on the struggle in Kentucky between Buell & [Confederate General Braxton] Bragg, but I presume it is of great importance to us. If we can whip them severely in Kentucky & also in the Shenanadoah Valley, their course will soon become hopeless.

We hear from home that Col Hays of the 63rd has been made a Brigadier Gen. I am inclined to believe the rumor, for he is a man better fitted for the position than hundreds that have been appointed. Our present Brigadier, John G. Robinson, is about as good as a wooden man. He has no brain at all.

Is Gen. [Stonewall] Jackson dead. I have heard his death contradicted. You wrote to me that he had died of an old disease. We don't hear much of him in the papers.

I am beginning to be exercised about our State elections. I have no anxiety but I would like to know how it is going. The democrats are making desperate efforts, as usual, to carry the Congress. It is to be hoped they wont succeed. Sardis writes me from Clarion that the democrats boldly preach treason there, & he sends me a Clarion Democrat, the contents of which prove his aspertion to be true.

Oct. 8th, 1862

I feel lonely without you this evening. Sometimes the desire to be with you almost overcomes me. It is so now: I can think of nothing else but my home — no one but my good Harriet.

Today has passed as usual with the exception that the order to be ready to march with two days rations was repeated to us. If we move I presume it will be to support Siegel: some think that we will move, others that we will not. For my part I think but little about, & care less. I have always had that feeling of "don't care where we go["] since I have been in the army, & talk about moving never disturbs me.

I have felt kind of queer to-day. The idleness of camp life does not agree with. I long to be doing something, especially do I long to be home at my old business.

I have some notions of resigning. Our regiment now has about 150 men for duty nine companies being represented. In my company there are 20 for duty. I have still an aggregate on my roll of 63, — 37 present with the regiment. Of the absent 26, at least 20 will never return, being disabled by wounds & disease. This reduces my company to near 40 men, just half the minimum standard allowed by the Government for a company organization. Ten of these are required for regimental duty outside of the company, musicians etc. Leaving me 33 men, a good many of them spirit-broken by hard service.

There are several companies in the regt about like mine, others are a little better; but it is evident that our nine companies must be consolidated into half that number, & the regiment filled if it is to be filled at all, by the admission

Pennsylvania Governor Andrew G. Curtin. Elected one month before Lincoln was elected president, Curtin was a member of the "People's Party," a coalition that favored Republican policies on tariffs and public land, but out of distaste for war took a more conservative stance on slavery. He soon joined the Republicans, threw his support to Lincoln, and was re-elected in 1863. Curtin was called "The Soldier's Friend," but Levi held distaste for him because he allowed political concerns to influence the appointment of regimental colonels (**Under the Maltese Cross: Antietam to Appomattox**, 1910).

of new companies. This will dispense with quite a number of officers who will have to be mustered out. I know that they will not muster me out, but I believe they would accept my resignation if I should offer it at present. I feel indignant that Gov. Curtin has not filled up our regiment and all of the old regiments. Instead of filling them up & giving positions to officers & non-commissioned officers who have served faithfully for more than a year, he has made new organizations in order to make offices for many who remained at home until forced to come out. The government that refuses to recognize & reward the services of a faithful soldier, has no right to the services of any one.

If I knew of any thing to do at home, I should surely resign. I shall wait this month yet, & if matters dont change for the better I shall make the attempt.

I am still improving in health I believe....

[P.S.] <u>Send me a letter</u>

Excerpt from journal of Harriet N. Duff:

Oct. 8th 1862 — My journal has been long neglected almost a year. How many things I might have written. — Many changes have been to my self and dear ones.... God's mercies have been without number. Mother and Aggie were both very ill but soon recovered health and strength. Perhaps to myself the greatest event came July 21st my old name was no more and I became the wife of Levi Bird Duff. Aug. 6th I bade my husband farewell since which time he has been in dangers oft and imminent, but God still spares him.

5

Fredericksburg

Don Carlos Buell was not the only general Lincoln let go. On November 7, 1862, the exasperated president cashiered George B. McClelland as commander of the Army of the Potomac. The cautious general was popular with the troops, and many observers feared a mutiny. Ambrose E. Burnside, his unconfident successor, chose to move on Richmond from the north, rather than up the Peninsula. He maneuvered his troops quickly to the Falmouth shore of the Rappahannock across from Fredericksburg, but his advance stalled as the pontoons necessary for crossing the river failed to arrive until the end of the month. By that time Robert E. Lee and Stonewall Jackson were ready. Though the Union forces on the left, after crossing the river on December 11, briefly pushed the Confederates back, reinforcement did not arrive; the Federals had to withdraw. On the right, the blue were slaughtered on the slopes of Marye's Heights. Union casualties, numbering 12,600 in the December 13 rout, were two and a half times those of the Confederacy.

Camp Prescott Smith, Va.
Oct. 9th, 1862

Another warm but pleasant day: nothing done nothing to do. Thus we pass the time. I am feeling to day just as I felt yesterday as though I was wasting my time. I told the Col. to-day that unless the regiment is soon filled I would resign: he said that my resignation would not be accepted. I told him I thought it would. He said, however, that he had made arrangements to have the regiment filled, if so I may hold on. Tell me what [you] think of my desire to leave the service, under the circumstances....

Does every thing in the city go on as usual, since so many have gone to the war. I imagine the city looks lonely. I wish I could come back to it. I really feel home-sick to-day. Don't you pity me....

Oct.10th, 1862

My mind today has been chiefly occupied with thoughts of you. I sometimes fear that by getting married, I destroyed my usefulness ... when I am done thinking of you I have no time left for other pursuits....

To-day it is cloudy. Our bright weather I believe will leave us. For six weeks past we have had but little rain, the heat has been very unpleasant & the dust almost intolerable. I now look for fall rains, which will in all probability convert the dust into mud, something equally as disagreeable. We hear no further word of moving. Tomorrow I am informed we lost one of our regiments, the 114th Penn. [Charles H. T.] Collis' Zouaves. It was put into our brigade a month since. It goes to join a Zouave brigade, in Gen Porter's Corps I suppose. We will still have five regiments in the brigade, or rather two regiments & three remnants. Gen. Birney's Head Quarters which have been at Fairfax Seminary were to-day moved to Fort Lyon. This would indicate that, although we may move from here, we will not leave Washington. I hear of no movement of any portion of our Virginia army. Gen. Siegel [Sigel] remains quiet on our front, & the papers tell us nothing of McClellan. It is to be presumed that he is quiet too. It is about time for him to move against the rebels. If he don't move against them soon, he may lose the opportunity of doing so this fall.

I have a letter from Sardis a few days since. The political fever is running high in Clarion this fall, as I presume it does in Allegheny. There is no danger, however, of Allegheny voting against the policy of the President, but Clarion is almost sure to do so. It seems to be the general opinion, among those who profess to know, that the democrats will carry the State. For the sake of our good name I hope not. It would give so much encouragement to the rebels; whereas if the state should vote Republican, every hope of aid from Southern sympathy would vanish. I regret that the President is not using all his power to compel a result favorable to his policy. He could help himself and the cause greatly, if he were not so careful of the constitution.

Oct. 10th, 1862

I wrote you a letter this afternoon when all was quiet.; I did not then expect that we would move soon. Now every thing is bustle. We have received orders to be ready to march immediately. We have packed every thing and are waiting for the teams. We will start I presume about 12 o'clock, it is now 8 P.M.

Rumor says our destination is Poolesville Md. forty five miles from here. This rumor is probably correct but whether we will stop at Poolesville or go on to reinforce Gen. McClellan is more than I am able to say. It is three days march from here to Poolesville.

I felt blue all day but since we received the order to march & I have stirred around some I am feeling better....

A month's rest has done me a great deal of good....

Camp in Fair Grounds at Rockville Md
Oct. 11 1862

We left camp Prescott Smith this morning at half past 5 o'clock A.M., our regiment acting as rear-guard marching behind the train. As I surmised our course was toward Maryland. We crossed the Potomac on the Georgetown Aqueduct (now for a year past used for a bridge) & turned out of Georgetown on what is known as the Rockville Turnpike. About a mile from Georgetown we made the first halt in front of the residence of an old citizen of southern style and habits & of secession sympathies. He and his family, of course, come to the door to look at us. On seeing him Capt Hamilton & myself recognize it as the place where the 9th Regt P.V. halted on the 6th of Aug. 1861, when on the march from 3rd Street Washington to Tennallytown. We went up to the old man & asked him if he recollected the 9th Regt & the hot day on which it halted at his home: he said he did, he recollected the day & that it was one of the hottest of the season (it was I assure the thermometer standing at 110° in the shade & 132° in the sun).

As their breakfast was just ending, he kindly invited us to take a cup of coffee. This invitation I gladly accepted, for I had but an indifferent breakfast & and that too early, & have not drunk a cup of coffee for a month. We went in & had a cup of coffee and some corncakes <u>from the hands</u> of a <u>slave</u>. We had some conversation with the old man but said nothing touching secession. We knew his feelings & did not wish to make ourselves disagreeable under the circumstances. He has two sons in the rebel army & a son-in-law in the Union army. When I passed there a year ago, he frankly acknowledged that his sympathies were with the South.

On leaving the house I could not help referring to myself, now in a capacity widely different from the one in which I was then. From a private I have risen to a captain. I congratulated myself that in a worldly point of view, my life during the last year had been a success. Shall I pass that house next year, & if so in what capacity?

We reached here (about eighteen miles from where we started) at five o-clock P.M. I am quite tired but feeling well. I had a good supper of bread & butter (nice fresh butter bought of a farmer to day) & tea. As soon as this letter is taken to the town Post office I shall go to bed. Excuse mistakes for it is too dark to proof-read my letter. Give my love to all. A kiss to you my own

Camp (near) Poolesville, Md
Oct. 13th, 1862

We left our camp at Rockville (from where I wrote you last) at 2 o'clock yesterday morning. As we had been the rear-guard on Saturday, we were made the advance-guard yesterday, three companies of our regiment (A. F. D.) with a section of Randolph's Sixth Rhode Island Battery, marching about half a mile in advance of the column. I felt well enough at starting, but soon got very tired. We marched right along however without halting until we reached this place, about a mile North of Poolesville. We halted here about one o'clock, having marched the distance of twenty miles. Our regiment stood the fatigue very well, but men from the new regiments lay down by scores. Fortunately it was cool enough to march even at a rapid pace without becoming heated, else many more would have been left. I was so weak when I reached here that I could not stoop to pick anything off the ground without falling. Lieut. [Charles H.] Powers said that I was older than his great-grandfather. A cup of tea & a little rest made me feel better.

On arriving here we learned that [Jeb] Stuarts Cavalry, which had lately been on a visit to Pennsylvania, was returning to Virginia, & would probably cross the river near this place: It was further stated that all the fords were guarded & that the celebrated cavalry would surely be captured this time.—At four o'clock we received orders to march immediately with only haversacks & shelter tents. Tired and worn out as they were, the men fell in promptly & we were off again, towards Conrad's Ferry on the Potomac five miles from here. We arrived at the Ferry at 7 o'clock P.M. & were told to lie down & sleep. It was then raining quite hard & the ground was very wet, notwithstanding I laid down on the rotten weeds, because I could not stand up. I had on a good army overcoat which kept me dry, but my knees ached so much & I was so chilled, that I could not sleep. At half-past ten we were aroused again & told to fall in; we did so, although not very promptly, because many of the men were so tired that they preferred to lie down in the rain rather than march. We were brought to an about-face & marched back to camp, arriving here at 1 A.M. this morning. Here I had a tent to go into & plenty of blankets to keep me warm & I laid down & slept soundly until long after daylight. I got up feeling strong enough, but having a slight head-ache, which will leave me after I have stirred around a little.

This morning Stuarts Cavalry is safe in Virginia, having plundered a portion of Penn. & Maryland & befooled our generals. "Just too late," is again the melancholy story. Stuart with his cavalry crossed the Potomac at Cooley's Ford six miles above here yesterday at 2 P.M. just before our troops (two regiments of infantry) reach[ed] the Ferry to prevent their crossing. After they had crossed our forces approached the river on this side when, the indefatigable Stuart turned his artillery on them & shelled them off. This is the end of the story. Again we can say somebody is a block-head, or a traitor.

I do not know where we will go next. We will lay here to-day at least. Give my love to all.

Oct. 15th, 1862

We were aroused yesterday morning at three o'clock, put on our haversacks & canteens & marched to Conrads Ferry. Here we halted & our general took divers observations as though about to cross the river. At twelve o'clock, however, we started up the river & marched six miles to the mouth of the Monocacy. A few minutes after we arrived there we got an order to return to camp. As soon as we had got ourselves a little supper (for it was near night) we started back & reached camp here at nine o'clock, making a march of 22 miles during the day. I was very much fatigued & would have reached camp with difficulty had I not succeeded in getting into an ambulance at Conrads Ferry & riding from there to camp....

In regards to my resignation, I am just now waiting on the Colonel. He is making some effort to fill up the regiment and wishes me to remain. I will remain during this month, at least.

Oct. 17th, 1862

I might write to you often from here if I could send my letters away. As yet proper postal arrangements have not been made, & our mail is irregular both in its arrival & departure....

Yesterday passed almost in quiet. At eleven o'clock we received an order to be ready to march at half past twelve. We began to prepare but before we had finished the order was countermanded. So we remain where we are for the present.

Last night we had a very heavy rain which overflowed our whole camp & drove us out of our tent....

The portion of the army about here remains quiet. We heard yesterday the cannonading of Gen. McClellan's reconnoitering force sent to Charleston & supposed that a fight of some moment was taking place. This morning's paper states that nothing of moment was done or suffered by either party. This seems to indicate an advance of his army, which I did not expect to take place so soon. We possess many advantages over the rebels now, but will have more in a month; hence I do not expect our forces to move for at least a month unless the enemy should retreat.

...[I have heard enough regarding the elections] to warrant the assertion that the administration has been triumphant. I am glad of this for if the democrats had been successful our course would have been endangered. The allies of the rebels in the North made desperate efforts but have been defeated; now let Lincoln go forward with his army & clear the South of all armed traitors & we will be done with this "gigantic rebellion."

It is rumored here that our division is to winter on the line of the Potomac between Washington & Harper's Ferry, in order I presume to guard the Chesapeake and Ohio Canal, & keep down guerrillas on the border....

I must ask you not to entertain any hopes of seeing me soon. For several reasons I have postponed my resignation until next month. The situation may [be] so changed by that time as to cause me to continue....

Oct. 19th, 1862

These are sad, sad times full of sorrow and privation every day breaks at least one heart & makes one home desolate yet out of this sorrowing will come joy — out of these sacrifices will come great results. We too have our dangers & privations, but while we have faith to bear them cheerfully they can little harm us. I am glad that you can bear your part so hopefully. I can bear mine while such good cheer comes to me from home.

You ask about the disposition of our division. Before we left Washington, one brigade Birneys was stationed here; the other two Robinson's (ours) & [Hiram G.] Berry's brigade were at Washington. Birney's brigade is now at Conrads Ferry, ours at Poolesville & Berry at

Edward's Ferry. Gen. Stoneman's Head Quarters are at Poolesville. Our division is detached from the main army defending Washington to act as a "corps of observation." At the same time that we do this we guard the Chesapeake and Ohio Canal from the mouth of the Monocacy down to Great Falls. This canal is now open & is of great moment to the government, & it is necessary to preserve it against malicious citizens were the enemy not near.

Oct. 20th, 1862

Last night and to-day have been quite cold — so cold that one cannot sit in a tent with any comfort. We will soon have to begin to build chimneys. The men are still obliged to live in the Shelter tents. It is to be hoped that those that are not to take the field will be furnished with better quarters.

I have nothing to write concerning the army. All is quiet on the Potomac. For the past four days we have not heard the sound of a gun, something very unusual at this point. From Washington we hear nothing....

Having nothing to write about I might as well close my letter. I am well as usual, we can live pretty well here, being in a good farming country, although eatables are very high.

We expect to be paid shortly after the 1st of Nov when I will send you some money. I hope you may be able to get along until then without any inconvenience. My love to all.

Oct.22nd, 1862.

We go on picket to-morrow morning to remain three days. The Picket-line is on the Potomac & along the Canal about five miles from here. There is no great danger from the enemy, it is merely to guard the Canal against malicious citizens. Stewarts [Stuart's] Cavalry might make a raid on us, but this is not probable.

[Duff comments on the elections, noting the loss of Republican seats.] If Lincoln, however, has courage to arrest the traitors he can reduce the opposition sufficient to give him a majority.

Oct. 26th, 1862

The picketing was light work & pleasant until to-day. This morning early it began to rain hard & has continued all day & still continues (6. P.M.) Of course we got quite wet as we have only been home some two hours.

I have not time at present to reply to your sweet scolding. It is partly merited, but I am not quite ready to resign. I think my health is improving rapidly since I came here. I know I am gaining flesh & think I am gaining strength....

It seems that we are not to lie here idle this winter as I supposed we would. Just when I expect a little comfort they come along & disturb us. We received an order to-day to be ready to move to-morrow morning....

Monday morning Oct. 27

It is now half past four & they have just routed us & ordered us to be ready to march by day-light. It is raining & blowing from the South West a bitter gale, but notwithstanding this we must go....

And first in the way of news, we are now under a new commander. I have informed you I believe that we are in Stoneman's Division, formerly Kearney's & formerly in Heinzelman's Corps. We have been transferred, it seems, to [Orlando B.] Wilcox's Corps, which is under the command of Burnside. Who Wilcox is, I do not know, never heard of him but presume he is some dashing Brigadier whose merits have not become known to the public. Burnside is well known & has I suppose some independent command, but where and what to do I have not the slightest idea.

I have been thinking that he intends to cross the river here & march towards Richmond in order to cut the line of communication of the rebel army with their capital. If he attempts this we may expect hard knocks. Each man is ordered to carry with him 100 rounds of ammunition, which is extraordinary, & leads me to the belief that some important blow is to be struck by him. In the direction of Richmond appears to be the only direction to give it. I am ready for any thing, as I have always been, but our poor little regiment will make a bad show after it undergoes a hard march. There is one consolation, however, that a hard march & a fight will finish it. It will then be about time to muster out the remnant.

Camp near White's Ford. Va.

Oct. 29th, 1862

To-day finds me again in Virginia. We left our camp near Poolesville yesterday morning at 5 o'clock marched to the hill overlooking the Potomac at White's Ford, halted there until 1 o'clock then crossed the river & marched about two & a half miles beyond where we encamped for the night, making a march of about five miles....

The only hardship about yesterdays march was crossing the river. We were obliged to wade it. The water was about three feet deep & very cold. You can imagine how disagreeable it was to wade it & how we felt afterwards. Many took off their trousers & the crossing was the most ludicrous picture I ever beheld.

After we halted we built large fires & dried out clothes, & although the night was cold we were all quite comfortable & do not now feel the effects of our bath.

The whole army is now advancing on the rebels. What part we are to play in the advance I have not been able to determine, but suppose I will know in a few days. Burnside I am informed commands three army corps, the 2nd, 9th & 12th We are in the 9th, the Corps formerly commanded by Burnside himself, afterwards by [Jesse] Reno and now by Wilcox. We are the 4th Division in that Corps & I think the extreme left, unless Siegel be included....

Leesburg Va.

Oct. 31, 1862

We lay near White's Ford until to-day at noon, when we broke up camp, started on the march and arrived here at half past 4 o'clock. We are again quietly encamped just South of the town. Leesburg is an old town of, I suppose, some two thousand inhabitants. It is a very aristocratic place and of course all of the people are "secesh." I saw more men as we passed through the town than I have seen in any place in Virginia. It is surrounded by a fine country, which has been but little devastated by the war.

Soon after our arrival we heard some cannonading in the South West quite a distance off. I presume it was a skirmish by our advance. It lasted but a few moments & could be of but little importance either way. Our whole army is now over the Potomac and advance, & I suppose it will not be long until we have more fighting....

I laughed when I read your remarks concerning Bella Lawson. Women can't keep a secret: that is a well known axiom; but I am surprised at the funny way they have of telling them....

I saw a paper of to-day. It gives a very cheering account of our prospects. I hope they are not too highly colored. With one thing I am highly pleased; namely, the removal of Gen. Buell. He should have been removed at least six months ago. But that curse of our country and our cause — "pro-slavery unionism" — kept him in his position. Is it not a fine thing that such unionism is now outlawed. The democrats may conspire to prolong the war but I think that Lincoln's proclamation abolishing slavery will render of no avail all of their conspiracies.

...I hope McClellan will not prolong his movement until the weather is unsuitable.

I have no "night-cap" & one would be very acceptable. If you have an opportunity you may send me one....

Camp (near) Rappahannock River
Fauquier County, Va.
Nov 8th, 1862

Before going farther I might as well tell you where we are, then I can tell you how we came here. We are on the North Fork of the Rappahannock River, sometimes called the Hedgemon [Hedgeman] River, at the mouth of Custers Run, & about eight miles South West of Warrenton.[1] The rebels burned the bridge across the River at this point, & it not being fordable we are stopped until it is rebuilt, & until our supplies come up. We arrived here yesterday morning at 10 o'clock.

My last was written Oct. 31st just after our arrival at Leesburg. The next morning (Saturday Nov. 1st) we went on picket some two miles from Leesburg, remained on picket until the next day (Sunday) noon. We were then called in & ordered to prepare to march immediately. We did so, but did not start until 4 o'clock. We took the Winchester Turnpike, crossed the Kattactan Mountain, then turned South, & marched in that direction until 11 o'clock when we halted at a small town called Mount Gilead. The next morning we started again & marched to Millville, a town containing one house & a mill, situate[d] on Goose Creek, near where that stream enters to Kattactan Mts. We remained at that place during Tuesday, & on Wednesday morning started forward again. We marched through Middlebury, thence to White Plains & to within a mile or two of Salem & encamped. Thursday morning we started again marched through Salem then took a by-road & crossed Carters Mountain & halted just at the foot of the mountain and encamped. On Friday we marched about two miles to our present location. The country though which we passed is generally well improved. It was never before traversed by an army & of course it does no[t] present the desolate appearance of other portions of Virginia. On Thursday we passed the residence of Col. John A. Washington. It is on Carter's mountain, about five miles from Warrenton, & is I presume one of the finest & most comfortable places in the state. The house is supplied with water from a spring in the mountains, high enough to throw it to all parts of the house. Everything is arranged with an eye to comfort, & it is hard to conceive why a man would abandon such a place to engage in rebellion against his government. May his be the fate of all his associates.—The weather during our march was very fine until yesterday, that is fine for this time of year, days pleasant but nights cold. Yesterday morning it began to snow & snowed all day, during the forenoon very hard. At one time the snow on the ground was full two inches deep but it soon melted away. To-day is again pleasant & I hope we may not be again visited by a snow storm. I am very well and in good spirits as usual. I am not a little provoked at one thing. Our baggage including blankets is back at Leesburg. During the last week I have had nothing for covering at night except my overcoat. You can imagine that it would be a little uncomfortable with this light covering when in the morning the frost is half an inch deep on the ground. But we can accustom ourselves to almost any thing, & I have no doubt if this war continues we will learn to run like wild-beasts. The men are better off than the officers for they carry their blankets in their knapsacks. Were it necessary for us to endure this privation I would be silent. But our luggage was left through a blunder of our Quartermaster & I feel like scolding about it.

Our advance is South of the Rappahannock & I presume a large portion of the army will cross to-morrow. Our Pioneers are building a bridge here to-day. Our rations will come up this evening & I look for a forward movement to-morrow. I do not know the whereabouts of the main body of the rebel army, have not yet learned of their leaving Winchester, but presume they have from the position occupied by our army. There is said to be a large force of rebels at Culpepper C. H. about 20 miles from here.

Yesterday I saw a paper of the 5th inst. It contained no news save the announcement that New York has gone Democratic. Ever the traitor blood is elected to Congress. I should despair over this result, had not the President issued his proclamation. The edict has gone forth which will destroy slavery, & this mite of justice will save us a government.

...In your next, send me $10, if you have it & can spare it conveniently. I am now out of money & I do not expect the Paymaster to visit us while we remain in the front although there is 4 mos. pay due us.— Also if you have an opportunity to send the cap of which you spoke and with it a good pair of wool gloves.

I almost forgot to tell you that our regiment is to be filled up with drafted men. The Col. has asked for 600, & has sent Capt. [Cassius C.] Markle to Harrisburg for them. They will be here soon I suppose. This deprives me of all excuse for resigning & you must resign yourself to my continued absence. I do not expect to get home before next summer.—

P.S. Nov. 9th. We go on Picket this morning. We have no indication of a march to-day. Our forces are said to be in Culpepper....

Camp (near) Rappahannock River
Nov. 14th 1862

Sunday morning the 9th we went on picket on the Rappahannock & were relieved on Monday. In the afternoon of the same day the rebels drove in our advance pickets at Amissville & in Culpepper Co. which caused a general alarm, & all the troops were put under arms. Our division was ordered across the Rappahannock & took a position about a mile & a half South of the River. Here we remained until Wednesday evening (the alarm of Monday proving false) when we returned to this side (North) of the river & encamped about a mile East of our former encampment where this morning finds us. Our army is on the North side of Rappahannock and at a stand still; Head Quarters at Warrenton. The rebels are not supposed to be in force south of Culpepper C. H. Such is the position this morning & "all is quiet on the Rappahannock."

The removal of McClellan was rumored in camp the first of the week, but was disbelieved & was not confirmed until Wednesday. When it was announced officially every one was astonished—some were indignant & talked loud—some were pleased—quite a large majority regretted it; why they could not tell. The few who were indignant saw impending ruin to the country cursed the abolishionists, & some of them went so far as to proclaim themselves traitors in ambiguous language of course. This was the state of feeling two days ago. To-day McClellan seems to have been forgotten. Very little is said concerning him & I dare say that in a month his name will hardly be known in the army. Although he was popular with his army, that popularity never rose to any thing like enthusiasm. His control over the minds [of] the men under his command was lost the moment he lost his command. The country need not fear a mutiny in the army on account of his removal.

I need not tell you how I received the news of his removal. I believe I lost confidence in him fully a year ago, & confidence was never restored by any thing he has since done. Day after day have I proclaimed him a failure—I really believed it & I was delighted when I heard of his removal. When you asked his friends what he has done, they point to his Maryland Campaign. This I consider the greatest failure of his military career—history will write it down such.

...In Burnside his successor I have full confidence but I am sorry that he takes the army under such unfavorable circumstances. The advanced season of the year will I fear prevent him from doing any thing decisive before spring. However if the weather in December is as good as it was last year, I think he will be able to take Richmond. Our army is in good condition, good health & good spirits & if properly led will triumph over any opposition.

The Democrats are becoming very bold in the North. The only hope of the country is now in the army, if it fails, all is lost. How careful then should be the president in whose hands he places it.

Camp 10 miles NorthWest of
Fredricksburg, Va
Nov. 20th, 1862

We remained at the camp from which I last wrote until Sunday morning, when we broke up camp & marched to Warrenton. On Monday we marched again taking the road leading from Warrenton to Fredricksburg, & halted late at Bealton, a station on the Orange & Alexandria Railroad about four miles North of the Rappahannock River. The next day we continued our march toward Fredricksburg & halted two miles South of Morrisville. The next day (yesterday) we marched to this place, which is about 10 miles distant from Fredricksburg. Our destination is Fredricksburg, but we will not likely march today. Nearly the whole army is now in and about Fredricksburg. I do not know where the advance is, but it is said to be 10 miles South of Fredricksburg.... It is presumed or rather it is certain that Fredricksburg is to be made the base of future operations. So fighting is likely to occur soon. I think the rebels will fall back to Richmond before they will give general battle. The roads are now getting bad & it will require some time for us to reach that point. It has been raining for the last three days (to-day very hard) with no prospect yet of ceasing. It looks like the beginning of bad weather and bad roads. There is every indication that a winter campaign against Richmond is determined upon; and it is not well for us to look for any thing like pleasant soldiering at present. If we are only successful, I can willingly endure my share of the discomfort.

Since the appointment of Gen. Burnside in the command of the Army of the Potomac numerous other changes have taken place.... Gen. Stoneman now commands our Corps & Gen. Birney our Division. This arrangement is satisfactory enough to me, with the exception of our division general. He was formerly a lawyer in Philadelphia, of very common renown, got to be the colonel of a regiment then by political pressure a brigadier general. Since the death of Gen. Jameson, he has been senior brigadier in our division, & on the promotion of our Division General succeeded to the command of the division.

...Be as cheerful as possible. I still think of you, & love you as dearly as ever....

Camp (near) Fredricksburg, Va
Nov. 25th, 1862

I hope our mail communication will be better. The route from here to Washington by way of Aquia Creek is now pretty well established and I do not look for any more changes of base for some time. It is now generally believed that we are to advance on Richmond from this point and in this belief I share. There will be a delay, it is said, of some ten days at this point — then the army is to move rapidly. This is the old promise, so oft repeated & so oft broken that one is inclined to doubt its fulfillment.

Our Division marched from where I wrote last to this place on Saturday. The roads were a little muddy but not so muddy and impassable as we expected to find them. We had very hard and constant rain on Wednesday and Thursday last. On Friday the storm ceased & the air got quite chilly; on Saturday the clouds disappeared, the sun came out & the weather has been bright ever since. Every thing is still favorable for military operations. The men are in good spirits and healthier than usual. There is not half the sickness in our regiment that there was during the Peninsular campaign. I do not know how we may be affected by the swamp near Richmond, but I am of opinion that fewer will die there of sickness at this season, than died in May and June. The winter, I am coming to believe, is the proper time to approach Richmond: one thing alone will impede our operations, that is mud, and this will impede the enemy as much as it does us. Nothing but the blunders of our leaders can now prevent us from taking the rebel capital.

The situation here at present is this: our main army is concentrated at this point occupying a front of about three miles in length on the North side of the Rappahannock river, extending two miles above and one mile below Fredricksburg. Our pickets are on this shore of the river the rebels on the other, about 150 yds. apart, but no firing takes place between them. There is no agreement between them not to fire at each other, but there is a mutual forbearance under the conviction that such firing would be productive of no good to either. I do not know what force of rebels lies opposite us, but it is reported that there are 20,000. No one believes that their main army is there: hence it is not thought that we will have any trouble in crossing the river. Their demonstrations are merely for the purpose of delay. Since Gen. Sumner notified the authorities of Fredricksburg that if the rebels did not leave the town within sixteen hours he would burn it, most of the inhabitants have left. There are a few rebel soldiers in the town. The main rebel force lies back (South) of the town, the smoke of their camps can be seen from this side. Gens Longstreet and D. H. Hill are reported to be in command.

As our army is very much concentrated we have an opportunity of visiting most of the division. On Sunday I paid a visit.... The [120th] regiment is in very fine condition, in better condition than any new regiment I have seen. The reverse is true of the 135th. It looks "salty" to use a vulgar but expressive term. It has either been badly cared for or much abused, the former the more probable. Col Allen is under arrest and has been for the past six weeks.[2] If restored to duty I hardly think him competent to have charge of a regiment. You need not make public any of my remarks disparaging to the regt. or the Col.... Richardson's old division, in which is the 53rd I have not been able to find. If I knew who commanded it I would be more successful. Divisions are known only by the name of the commander, hence it is necessary to know his name in order to find his division.

I have been somewhat unwell for the past week, very much troubled last night with my old complaint diarrhea. It has been brought on by the hard food I have been compelled to eat constantly since we started on this march. Hard bread, mess pork & coffee & sugar have been our rations with the exception of twice I believe we had rice & beans. The coffee was only an aggravation in my case & I have to quit it. I have lately been able to get a kind of tea which makes a passable drink. As soon as they get the railroad completed from here to Aquia Creek (it is now nearly completed) we expect to be better provided for. I think if I can get something better to eat I will get well again. The box which you & Firman would like to send — with the exception of fruits, which I dare not eat — would be very acceptable. But it cannot be sent at present. The railroad is so occupied in transporting subsistence to the army that nothing else is allowed to pass over it. We can not even have the baggage which we left at Leesburg brought to us.... I have just heard a salute to a Major Gen. fired. Hooker or Burnside must be reviewing. By the way Burnside passed by our camp on Sunday morning. I did not know that he was about until he was almost out of sight. I had a glimpse at his face. At a distance he looks a little <u>tame</u>. He may appear more fierce on a closer view. I am inclined to place confidence in him no[t] so much on account of what he has done but because by all of his actions he has shown a desire to terminate the war. If Gen. McClellan was not the willing, he was at least the unwilling tool of those Northern politicians who desire to prolong the war, until the nation is exhausted. There never was a more diabolical scheme devised and attempted to be executed, than has been devised by the Northern democracy & is attempted to be put into execution. They would destroy this army if they could, and if the administration is not careful they will so paralyze its efforts that it will fail of its object. The[y] have raised a great cry about the removal of McClellan because they knew he never would take Richmond, & disparage the merits of Burnside because they fear he will take it. I have not lately seen many Northern papers, but I have seen & read enough to convince me that democracy is only another name for treason. What they secretly wished for before the elections they now openly advocate in all of their organs. The president should suppress every one of them. Men who say aught against the government or president at the present time have <u>no right to live</u>. Such is at least human law and it is the duty of the president to enforce it....

Dec. 4th, 1862

It is already more than a week since I wrote my last, and I fear you may begin to be anxious....

Yesterday I was quite busy all day long, putting up a tent building a chimney & making a bunk. Evening found me with all this done, & ready to write you a letter had not my wood been too scarce to keep up a fire while I wrote. This morning I got a supply and having my tent warmed I am now ready to begin.

Since we left Leesburg (Nov. 2nd) we have been without tents or blankets, I may say without every thing except overcoat & haversack. Our baggage, all of which was left at Leesburg has never been forwarded to us, and probably never will be, but yesterday we managed to get a small "A" tent for the officers of each company and a supply of new blankets. With these we can make ourselves tolerably comfortable. To make me still more cheerful our mail (the first one we have received for twenty days) arrived yesterday....

On the line of the Rappahannock all is quiet. Our forces hold the same positions they held when we arrived here. Some three hundred of our pickets (infantry) and two squadrons of cavalry have been captured by the rebels. On this subject I need not particularize, as you will find more information in the papers than I can give. It is rumored this morning that the rebels have evacuated the line of the Rappahannock. I have not yet been able to learn whether the rumor is true, or not. It is not unlikely.

Last Friday I visited Charles and Edward.... Charles got me some bread.... Although it was not very good it was quite a treat.

Day before yesterday I visited the Reserves. They are lying about five miles from here in the direction of Aquia Creek. In company "A." I found all of my friends well. There is only a small number of the original members left, but they are fine looking soldiers, and seem to be in fine spirits.... I found stronger feeling for McClellan among the Reserves than I have observed any where in the army. In the 3rd Brigade [Conrad F.] Jackson's, they are so foolish in their attachment to him from Gen. to private that they would wish disaster to fall upon Burnside. I feel certain that they will be disappointed in their wishes. I took supper with Gen. Jackson and his staff. I always pity my country when I meet with a Brigadier & such a staff. If there are no better brigadiers than he let us have none. Lincoln has at least made some mistakes in appointing brigadiers and this is one of the most patent. I heard language at the table which in the mouth of an officer of the army is surely treason....

...The money you sent was right. There is no scarcity of change here for Treasury notes. A letter from our paymaster yesterday informed us that we would not be paid for some time yet, not until the middle of January I presume. In consequence I will need $20 more....

Dec. 8th, 1862

If I could only kiss the troubled brow or look into those <u>sweet eyes</u> to quiet the apprehension which I know cannot be concealed....

Day before yesterday I received the package of tea.... Good tea is a luxury that is not easy to find hereabouts. In fact we can get nothing but bread and meat — hard bread & the coarsest meat. This is not a very healthy diet, and any thing in addition is very acceptable. Sutlers have even been prohibited to bring stores here, till within a day or two when the prohibition was taken off. In a short time I presume they will bring us some luxuries, but they will furnish them at a high price. It is with us a choice between two evils, starvation and <u>robbery</u>, I prefer the latter, and hope the sutlers may come along immediately.

In army matters I have nothing new to write. I have not been at the front, that is at Fredricksburg since I last wrote. I believe the situation is unchanged. Our soldiers are generally building huts, to make themselves comfortable expecting to remain here all winter. If the weather continues as it has been for the past four days (and I have no hope that it will not) we will be obliged to remain here for some time. Early in the forenoon of friday last it began to rain, in the afternoon the rain turned to snow and it continued to snow until midnight. Since then we have had every night a succession of hard freezing. The nights have been very cold, as cold nights as I ever experienced in Virginia. I presume you have real winter in Pennsylvania. There is no sign in any department of a forward movement here. There are some slight indications to the contrary. The condition of the roads the weather and the fact that the Gen. has to know how many tents we need seem to us to indicate that we are to remain here during winter. I do not know what the papers will do if we should remain. They have made so many predictions that we were about to advance that they will be stultified if we do not. It is laughable to us to read the excuses the papers offer for the halt on the Rappahannock. They assume to begin their story that Gen. Burnside should not have halted here. Here is their great mistake. I think that this army is halted here by orders from Washington. I do not believe from what I have seen and heard that it has been intended to take Fredricksburg. If it was the intention to do so I have only to say that our generals one and all have acted very foolishly, and if this be the case we would have heard some notes of displeasure from Washington ere this. Winter has set in a month earlier than it did last year. It may be that our generals divined this and halted here for the purpose of wintering the army. It is much better than in front of Washington, besides the advantage we have of being nearer the enemy and nearer our field of operations when the spring opens. We are yet in doubt as to what is to be done with us this winter, but it seems most plausible to us all that we are to remain here.

Nothing has yet been done towards consolidating our regiment, and it is not supposed that any thing will be done. Gen. Halleck in his official report says that he hopes some legislation may be had whereby the old regiments may be filled. This is an indication that the government desires rather to fill than to consolidate these regiments, and I should not be surprised if Congress should authorize a special draft or there will be a neces-

A sutler's coupon. Because coinage was scarce during the war, these purveyors of non-military goods (sugar, tobacco, coffee, etc.) often made use of coupons or tokens that could be initially purchased in quantity (courtesy Allegheny College).

sity in about five months hence for a new call for troops. In that time, the period of enlistment for most of the five months volunteers and militia will have expired and if the war continues (and we cannot hope that it will end sooner) their places must be filled. Filling up the old regiments would partially and I presume sufficiently accomplish this. The papers concerning the consolidation of our regiment have gone to the Adjutant General's office, and their return is daily expected, but I do not expect that they will return approved.

Gen. Bank's Expedition sailed on Thursday last, so say the papers. Here there are great many conjectures as to its destination....

I see that the poor Pennsylvania Militia have left for Washington. What next will Gov. Curtin attempt in order to surround himself with office seekers. In this military business he has disgraced himself and the state. First yielding to them the organization into companies, which prevented the old regiments from being filled, then appointing field officers from among the politicians that congregated at the capital, instead of taking them from the field, thereby making the regiments inefficient, and finally by permitting one of them to run away, he showed that he had but little patriotism and less sense. Suppose it were necessary to make another draft from Pennsylvania? Will any man think himself under obligations to obey the call when drafted. I fear not, and Gov. Curtin will find himself powerless to compel them. Persons who have been in Pennsylvania lately say that the people (that is the democrats) would not permit another draft. How is this? If it be true, then verily we are exposing our lives for a state that is worth nothing to us. There has been a little too much dish water business in this war, is it never to end.

The President's message has been received here and read, but has been very little commented upon. It does not make the stir that his previous messages made. Concerning the war he says nothing except that he puts forth an impracticable scheme for the abolition of slavery, as an excuse I suppose in case of its rejection which is undoubted for abolition by proclamation. It may be necessary for him in order to hold his seat to pander to the proslavery prejudices of the North, but I think not and I was sorry to see this feature in his message. I thought that when [James] Buchanan's term [of] office expired we had done with political demagoguism but it seems not. President Lincoln is following in the wake of his predecessors, building for his re-election. Who can doubt that his success will equal theirs. [Secretary of War Edwin M.] Stanton is more frank in his report. He points out how the rebellion may be crushed and is not afraid to advise the adoption of his plan. Gen Hallecks report is more commented upon in the army than any other. It has stirred McClellan's friends to wrath. They now say that it was Gen. Halleck that removed Gen. McClellan, yet they say that it was done for political reasons. How inconsistent? Gen. McClellan's friends are very angry that he has been removed, and catch at every strain to prove that it was wrong. I have no high opinion of Hallecks abilities, so I tell McClellan's friends that as far as it concerns me it is "dog eat dog," that I would have been better pleased had Halleck been removed at the same time that McClellan was. Halleck proved himself unfitted in the field as well as did McClellan. Why should one be considered better than the other.

Concerning the delay imputed to McClellan in evacuating Harrison Landing and joining Pope on the Rappahannock I can testify, and my testimony is in Hallecks favor. Our corps, Heinzelman's, covered the march of the army from Harrison's Landing to Newport News and Yorktown, marching twice as far as any other corps, yet it was the first one to reach Pope and the only one that was of any service to him in his battles. There was great and criminal delay in moving the other army corps, to whom it is to be imputed I can not say, McClellan or his generals I do not know nor do I care. His favorite generals were equally incompetent with himself & I do not care to make distinctions when speaking of them. Gen. McClellan's letter to Porter requesting Porter to do all in his power to aid Pope as though it were not his duty unless McClellan requested it goes far to convince me that he heartily wished for Pope's failure. I do not like the language of the letters emenating from McClellan recently published. He protests too often that he is actuated by the purest motives, talks too much like a self convicted criminal for one to believe what he says. His friends think these letters at least show his patriotism and exclaim how unjustly he has been dealt with. Touching the removal of McClellan, the views of the English press (always hostile to us) convince me that great good will grow out of it: They call him a "conservative martyr," say that he was opposed to the violent acts of the executive (President Lincoln) & was therefore removed. The latter I have always believed and have therefore continually argued his removal. His heart was not in the cause and our enemies express their sorrow at the loss of a friend. I hope they may lose many more.

...It may be, Harriet, that I now think less on the subject of religion than I did a short time ago, but I think not. It was brought prominently before my mind by constantly thinking of you. I cannot think seriously of you without noticing it. You are the first and the only person that impressed me with the belief that there is such a thing as religion....

I wish to ask you about your numbness. I felt sorry when I read your letter written in pencil. It seemed like an ill omen. Can nothing be done to cure you.... My last attack of diarrhea lasted only about ten days, but it was very severe occasioned [by] a severe cold I presume. My ability to throw off my disease is not so good as it used to be, but I feel that I am gaining in strength every day.

Dec. 9th, 1862

I have just received Carrie's letter informing me of your serious illness.... Quinsy, I believe, is not reckoned a dangerous ailment and although your attack seems to have been severe, I do not anticipate any fatal result. I still fear more than any thing else, the numbness in your arm and side....

I am quite well again. A little rest has restored me....

...Unless you get quite well again I shall expect you not to continue teaching. You must not forget how dear you are to me, and how much my happiness depends upon your life....

Dec. 10th, 1862

Our marching orders received this morning mean something and we will move without doubt some time to-night. We are ordered to carry in our haversacks rations sufficient to last us until the morning of the 14th, and are to have sixty rounds of cartridges to a man. It is generally presumed that we are to cross the river and occupy Fredricksburg — it being supposed that the enemy has left with the exception of a small rear guard.... We have not yet got used to Burnside['s] manner of moving & consequently I will not presume even to guess where we are going....

In the Woods (near) Fredericksburg, Va
Dec. 12th, 1862

Yesterday morning at 8 o'clock according to the orders mentioned in my last letter we left our camp & advanced a short distance toward Fredricksburg. Here we lay in line until dark when we marched into the woods in the rear (East) of Falmouth. We remain here still & will probably remain here during the night.

...During the night of the 10th a pontoon bridge was thrown across the Rappahannock by our men just at the upper end of town. At 5 o'clock in the morning of the 11th (yesterday) the rebels opened their batteries on the bridge & at least partially destroyed it. Our batteries immediately opened on the rebel batteries & we had terrific cannonading during the whole day. In the meantime our men were busy at work building bridges under cover of our guns. Although annoyed a good deal by rebel sharpshooters who fired from the houses in Fredricksburg they succeeded in placing down 2 bridges by 4 o'clock. Our troops immediately began to cross and I am informed th[at] the whole of [Oliver O.] Howards Division (formerly) Sedwicks [John Sedgwick's], crossed before dark. None crossed during the night, but early this morning our troops began to cross again and are still crossing. Nearly all of Sumner's Grand Division is now across. The rebels have a battery in position North of the town, & this morning fired a few shots at our troops in the town. It was quickly silenced by a battery of our's posted on this side of the river midway between Fredricksburg & Falmouth. This occurred at 10 o'clock this morning. From that time until present writing our troops have been permitted to cross in silence. Just as I began to write, however, the rebels opened on our men (as they were crossing one of the bridges) with seven guns & since a brisk fire has been kept up from both sides....

Although the rebels seem to be very tenacious, I do not anticipate a general battle here because I think it is the policy of the rebels to avoid a general engagement at present.... We bivouacked in the woods last night and although it was very cold we did not suffer much....

Battle Field (near) Fredricksburg, Va.
Dec.15th, 1862

We crossed the river below Fredricksburg about noon on Saturday & immediately went to the front to check the rebels who had repulsed the Reserve Corps & the 2nd Brigade of our Division. They were driven back to their entrenchments & we rested on the field. We remained on the front line during Saturday night, Sunday & Sunday night this morning we were relieved & came back to the 3rd line. We have had one man killed & 11 wounded in our regt. One man of my company wounded. I have escaped injury thus far & feel quite well this morning. The Reserve Corps lost heavily on Saturday.... Capt. Fulton of the 63rd Regt. was killed or mortally wounded.

...Everything looks favorable.

Camp (near) Fredericksburg, Va.
Dec. 18th, 1862

After a week of toil and hardship I find myself again comfortably seated in my "wee" muslin house....

At 5 o'cock A.M. of Thursday the 11th inst. I heard the first gun fire into the city of Fredricksburg.... From that time until 6 o'clock guns were fired at intervals, and then the firing began in earnest. I presume our men opened with fifty guns. The cannonading was the most terrific I ever heard.... We could neither see the town nor what was transpiring so dense was the smoke of our cannon....

Friday ... we were moved near to the lower bridge in order that we might cross when needed....

Saturday morning early skirmishing began along the whole line, but the fog was so thick that great operations were not attempted. At 2 o'clock we were moved to the bank of the river near the lower bridges. About noon the fog cleared away and the struggle began. Our troops formed line and advanced to attack the rebels in their works. The Penn. Reserve corps charged on the works in front of them and say that they carried them, but not being properly supported and they censure Gen. Birney of our Division for not coming promptly to their support. This charge was made about one o'clock and at the same time we were ordered to cross the river. After crossing the river we went to the front on a double quick. It was fully a mile from the bridge to the place where the Reserve Corps were engaged to whose support we were going. After going half [that distance?] we met some wounded and many stragglers, and although they did not tell a doleful tale (as they usually do under such circumstances) it was evident to me that our troops were breaking and giving ground. Notwithstanding this our brigade went forward confidently and formed in rear of Randolph's and Livingston's batteries which were busily engaged firing on the enemy. Our line of infantry had been entirely broken and the rebels were just preparing to take advantage of our misfortune. They were advancing rapidly to take the batteries, and were already within fifty yards of them. However, when they saw our brigade formed in line in rear of the batteries they despaired of success & began to retreat towards their entrenchments. Seeing this our general ordered our brigade forward with the exception of our regt. and the 141st P.V. and fired a few volleys at them before they got beyond reach. Our forces did not pursue farther than to get a secure position in front of the batteries. When this was gained the firing of musketry ceased at this point, but the fire of artillery still continued.

Soon after we had formed line a shell struck a man of my company on the shoulder and side burning the shoulder and breaking one or two ribs but not injuring him seriously In a short time another shell struck in company "F" just on my right killing one man and wounding another. At about 4 o'clock the fire of artillery and musketry on both sides ceased and we had a calm. At 5 however the rebels opened on us again with seven guns and used them rapidly for half an hour and then the firing again partially ceased. Just at this time, about sunset, as Lieut. Col. Craig, Major Greenawalt, Capt. Hamilton and Lieut [Isaac N.] Tuller of Co. "I" and myself were standing in a group engaged in conversation in rear of the left of Co. "I" a shell struck the ground some six feet from us and exploded, killing a private of Co. "I" wounding four others and Capt. Hamilton blowing Maj. Greenawalt's hat off and throwing the dirt and burnt or refuse powder over us all. It is wonderful that any of us escaped with our lives. We were so busy talking that we did not hear the shell coming and it surprised us so much that it seemed as though some one had quietly laid it down in our midst. Capt. Hamilton's wound is quite severe. A piece of shell knock[ed] a strip of flesh an inch wide off the top of his right arm midway between the elbow and the shoulder. He has gone to Washington, I believe. The last time I heard from him he was doing well. The artillery continued to fire until after dark, but ceased entirely at 7 o'clock. Our regiment was now moved on the front to fill a space between the 63rd & 68th Regts. We went forward and lay down on our arms. The ground was very cold (although the day had been warm the frost was not yet all out of the ground) and our beds you can readily imagine were uncomfortable and cheerless. Thus we lay all night. All firing had ceased and night was as quiet as usual with the exception of the cry of the wounded for help. A large number lay between our pickets and those of the rebels and no aid could be sent to them. Their cries were most piteous and continued all night long. Morning came and with it we expected a renewal of the battle. But the morning wears away and no fighting takes place save some skirmishing on our right. We wonder what causes the delay, not feeling ourselves whipped and not knowing that the army was. But night comes and nothing has yet been done: then we say to-morrow will come the battle. During Sunday we were obliged to lie close to the ground in order to avoid being shot by rebel sharp-shooters. Several of us had narrow escapes. There was one sharp-shooter who very seldom missed. He shot the Maj. (Hawkworth) [Thomas Hawksworth] of the 68th he shot at Col. McKnight and the ball passed the Col. but was uncomfortably close. I was on my feet several times during the day and was shot-at once and very nearly struck in the head. Gen. Meade and his staff came on to the field in the afternoon, and the sharp-shooter knowing him to be big game leveled his gun and fired. The ball struck the Gen.'s horse but did not injure the Gen.

Sunday night was much like Saturday with the exception that it was not quite as cold and the men slept some. Monday morning came and we were informed that we would be relieved, & permitted to fall back to the third line. This information was welcome for we were well nigh worn out; we had been lying on the damp ground for two days and nights and during all of the time had no warm drink nor any kind of stimulant. Just at dawn [John Henry Hobart] Ward's brigade relieved us and we fell back. I was much exhausted. I have slept not more than 10 hours during the last five days and nights: add to this the nervous exhaustion caused by being under the fire of the enemy for 60 hours and you will conclude that I was somewhat reduced. A cup of coffee and a cracker made me feel much better, then the day was so pleasant as to make any one rejoice. But we could not imagine why the fighting had ceased. Some thought that we were waiting for this, others for that, but no one suggested that we were going to recross the river. The day wore rapidly away. In the afternoon a flag of truce was sent to the rebels commander and permission was given us to take off the wounded that lay between the lines and bury the dead. This we knew would prevent fighting that day and again we postponed the decisive shock until Tuesday. We spread our blankets immediately after dark and lay down to sleep. In a few minutes and [sic] order came to pack up and get ready to move. We did so, but were hardly ready when we were informed that the order was wrong & we lay down our blankets again and got under them. At nine o'clock we were again order[ed] to pack up. Having done so, we built fires and sat around them until 12 o'clock, when we were hurried into ranks and started off at a double-quick. This was continued until we crossed to this side of the river when we took a more leisurely gait. About a mile this side of the river we encamped at 3 o'clock A.M. The next morning at nine we packed up again and moved back to our old camp where we still remain undisturbed, and probably will remain some time. We now learned our attempt to drive the rebels from the hills in rear of Fredricksburg had proved a failure. However our army was withdrawn in safety. Our loss I cannot estimate, but I presume it will reach ten thousand. Most of our wounded were got off a few were taken prisoners....

On the day after our arrival here I heard that Charles had been wounded. I immediately went to see him. I found him in a house (good quarters) in Falmouth. His wound is not serious. A musket ball struck him on the back of the head, cutting the head slightly and passing down into the right side of the neck (to the depth of a couple of inches he says). His neck is not the least stiff, & I think he is very slightly injured. He is looking well and in good spirits. Edward I did not see; he had gone over the river to help bury the dead. Capt. Coulter had his right arm shattered by a minie ball and it was amputated near the shoulder. His company lost a great many, most of them slightly wounded.—On Monday while yet on the other side of the river I saw Co. "A" of the 9th. Todd Wallace is uninjured; the company lost seventeen. 1st Lieut. [Reuben M.] Long was killed Capt. [Charles] Owston mortally wounded and left on the field.[3] Lieut. Sowers escaped uninjured. Gen. Jackson was killed as also Capt. [F. B.] Swearingen his Adjutant.

...I feel sorry that the box was stopped. An order was issued some time since that all boxes for officers and soldiers would be sent to the Provost Marshals of Grand Division, and that they would be delivered over to soldiers and officers on their signing a statement that they were for their individual use. I presumed that this order would bring us any box that was sent, but it has been since suggested to me that this order was issued in order to prevent boxes from coming to the army....

I am pleased to hear that you are again well....

Allegheny City
Dec 18ᵗʰ 1862

My precious husband;

It is "thank God" oh! what grateful hearts we have to night. The terrible disaster has shrouded every thing in gloom — we did hope for victory, but alas! to learn of the costly defeat, seemed worse than we could bear. The papers give full descriptions of all the terrible scenes. Who is to bear the blame of all this? "They say" that the directors at Washington must answer for the blunder — it will matter little whose fault it is to those whose hearts are broken. My own joy is so great to night that I cannot see all the fearfulness of the disaster — the effect will be "winter quarters" and then the clamor for compromise will begin in earnest — and indeed if the present administration can do no better than murder our brave brave men — we cannot be worse off. But my dear husband I forget every thing in the happiness of knowing that you are safe — from Saturday noon until to night the suspense has been terrible — knowing that so many were killed and yet so few names given — room for hope was but scant. I sat up every night until one o'clock to hear the telegrams whilst you were over the river — on Sabbath night I dreamed that you had fallen during Saturday afternoon. I did not believe, though, that you were dead. I thought you were among the wounded. I have firm belief that I am to see you once again. Levi what are we? that God should visit us with such tender mercy.... Tomorrow morning we have our yearly examination — how different my energy will be. I shall be the gladdest woman there — today I felt that I <u>could</u> <u>not</u> go back in the morning unless I heard from you....

Harriet

Camp Pitcher, Va.
Dec. 20ᵗʰ, 1862

I had better say first that "Camp" Pitcher is near Fredricksburg or the same camp in which we have been for the past month. Gen. Birney has ordered that it be called Camp Pitcher in honor of some officer who was killed on Saturday last.

To-night it is bitter cold it requires a good fire in our rude chimney to keep us warm. However we have no reason to complain since we are more comfortable than many others. The soldiers are daily adding to their comfort by building low huts of pine logs and covering them with their shelter tents. Some of them are quite comfortable others are not, but all are some protection from cold & storm.

Nothing new has transpired here since my last. The papers still cry out for onward movements and hint at another change of base. Thirteen Senators it is stated have waited upon the President to urge a more vigorous prosecution of the war. What does this mean. Do they wish that fourteen thousand more may be killed on the banks of the Rappahannock. The also cry "onward to Richmond." I wish this cry were once hushed. I ... feel very sure that it will require a great deal of time and a greater sacrifice than it is worth to take Richmond. How end the rebellion then? You may ask. Throw our army South of Richmond & they will be obliged to leave Richmond and fight us. Richmond is too well fortified now to take it in a short time, and we cannot afford to waste time besieging a place that is of not great importance to us. What we wish to get at is the rebel army, not their fortified cities. If we can by some "strategy" allure them or compel them to come out of their fortifications we can whip them in a short time; if we attack them in their fortifications we will get whipped as the result here proves. What we want is a general. Already many intelligent officers in the army believe that we are whipped that foreign nations will interfere and oblige us to acknowledge their [the rebels'] independence. Something must be done and done quickly in order to save us if we are not already lost.

The next thing to be expected is the President's Proclamation freeing the slaves. But what effect will such a proclamation have now. At the beginning of the war when the black man thought we were strong enough to give him freedom and protect him in it, it might have done some good; but I fear that he will now take counsel of our defeats & disasters and turn away from us. Should he do so, we are doomed. An alliance with him is now our only salvation. There is a dark cloud ahead of us through which I cannot see.

Dec. 22nd. 1862

I was pleased to read the letter to "my precious husband["]: It is a great privilege to be precious.

The prospect of conquering the South is now very dark. What ever is done, must be done between now and the first of May and the time is so short that I cannot see that much can be done. About that time the term of the nine months volunteers will expire and our army will be so reduced that aggressive operations will be impossible. Men who come from the North state that the people will not acquiesce in a further draft, so here it ends. But will the end be the acknowledgement of the independence of the South, or a democratic compromise. I will wager that it will be the latter.

...There is nothing new in army matters. Everything is not only quiet but stagnant....

Dec. 26th, 1862

Yesterday, Christmas, was spent in quiet. The day was very pleasant but I was out of sorts with myself, and I enjoyed it but little....

I have ceased to talk and ceased to think of our country. My patriotism is about extinct and I am beginning to think of personal safety and comfort. No man entered upon this war with purer feelings than did I, and no man I presume has more completely lost faith in the government and people. In this country a patriot is a fool, and he needs only serve in the army a short time to be cured of his folly. I am much gratified with one sentence in your letter; "she (Rachel) may love her country next to her God, I cannot and do not." This is really more good sense than one can expect of a woman.

Like Rachel I am still hopeful, but when I look for something on which to base my hopes I find nothing.... By no human calculation can I now see a successful termination of the war. It seems we are given over to the devil.

Dec. 29th, 1862

I have been out of humor for several days in consequence of having nothing to do & I need a letter to restore my spirits....

6

Winter Quarters

The demoralized Army of the Potomac licked its wounds in camp while Burnside's assisting generals complained of his incompetence. January was mild, and the commander attempted to retrieve Union fortunes by crossing the Rappahannock north of Fredericksburg. But rains came, and the Federal troops, artillery, and wagons bogged down in what came to be called the "Mud March." Burnside had to order his troops back to camp and then threatened to resign unless President Abraham Lincoln dismissed several criticizing subordinates. Lincoln did transfer some of these, but he also accepted Burnside's resignation perceiving that the general had lost the confidence of his army. His replacement was Joseph Hooker.

Lincoln was experiencing other difficulties as well, for the defeat at Fredericksburg stirred a Republican senatorial caucus to demand a reorganization of the cabinet. It hoped to oust Secretary of State William H. Seward, who the senators considered insufficiently hardened against the Confederacy and slavery. They hoped to promote the status of Secretary of the Treasury Salmon P. Chase, a radical Republican. Lincoln maneuvered until he achieved resignation letters from both men, pocketed them, quieted the uprising in his own party, and kept his cabinet intact.

Camp Pitcher, Va.
Jan'y 1ˢᵗ, 1862 [3]

A happy "New Year" to my dear good wife....

...In army matters every thing is quiet. We had orders two or three days since to be ready to march at 12 hours notice with nine days rations.... But we have received no further orders yet.... We have had several intimations that the government intends taking some of the <u>three years</u> troops to Washington & sending nine months troops to the front, in order to save as many as possible of the <u>three years</u> troops.... It is certainly sound policy to throw the nine months troops to the front. If they fight the battles to be fought between now and the first of May (when most of them will be discharged) there will be fewer of them to be discharged & our army will be less weakened.

I look now for an entire change in our war policy. The campaign to Richmond will be abandoned, an emancipation proclamation will be issued and our army thrown into the Slave States so that they can liberate the slaves. This will make it a life and death struggle to the South. In this way we can conquer in no other way can we conquer.... Is our President firm enough, here is my only fear.... I am sorry that the cabinet embroglio ended as it did. I had hoped that Seward would be removed and that some staunch man like [Senator Ben] Wade or [Senator William P.] Fessenden be put in his place. Such a change would give confidence to those who really desire the success of the government, & would break down all hope of the traitors to use President Lincoln to subserve their purposes.

...To be sure my life is risked here—this risk is common to us; but you feel it more keenly than I do. At this moment I make a narrow escape from death, the next moment I forget that my life was in danger; but not so with you, you cannot forget it.... We see men killed here by hundreds and thousands, we soon forget however that death has been among us; but the slain are remembered at home and years will not remove the sorrow and anguish of their death. I have to make out to-day a list of the casualties in my company since it entered the service and when I came to write May 31 1862 I said to myself, that was a day of calamity to us. When I looked at the long list of men who went down in the fearful struggle of that day I could scarcely refrain from weeping. When I presented the report to the Col. he looked at it & remarked that it always vexed him when he was reminded of the death of Cummiskey. Of all the officers that have left us, his name alone is mentioned with reverence. When after the battle of Fair Oaks Col McKnight was informed that Capt. [John C.] Dowling Capt. Duff Lieut Cummiskey were killed & that one half of his regiment was lost he exclaimed that he was ruined. Then & there his spirit was broken; he has never since shown himself to be the man he was before.

...I have well nigh come to the conclusion that honesty is not the best policy in this country. I have been cured of many of my absolute ideas since my entry into the army; in other words I have been a good deal demoralized....

The latest from Jeb. Stuart is that part of his force was near Alexandria.... It is a little singular that our cavalry can never perform such marches & scouts as the rebel cavalry are famous for. They lack in the first place a leader & then they lack training. Enough attention has not been given to this branch of the service. In the infantry a man needs only to be trained to fight, in the cavalry he must be trained to manage a horse & fight at the same time. Our cavalry man, when he gets into action finds it requires all his skill to take care of his horse, & having none wherewith to oppose the enemy turns and rides away.... But what will the people at home think of these [rebel] "raids"? They look upon them as disasters, which they are not. They are great annoyances, however, which by a little foresight might be rendered less frequent. There is one thing which aids the rebels very much in these undertakings, they are acquainted with the country & can get exact information of the position & strength of our army from the citizens. Our commanders are not vigilant enough of the citizens....

Jan'y 2, 1863. This morning early I went to the Depot ... & there found the small black trunk. It looked as though it had once been broken open.... There is a Division Review ordered at 11 o'clock today & I suppose by Gen. Joseph Hooker. This is in order that he may know the condition of his troops at the beginning of a year. What a strange contrast between them now and the same men one year ago. The year of 62 was one of disaster to us.... [I] can see as clearly as you can the absolute necessity of coming home, but I cannot see the way. Should I start some Provost Guard would arrest me and send me back to my regiment....

...I love my dear good wife.

Jan'y 8th, 1862[3]
[Letters have not come.] I hope that my dear good wife is not ill....

...Burnside reviewed our Corps the other day. Of course to the soldiers the affair was fatiguing and unpleasant but I presume it was brilliant to the Generals.

...The news that reaches us from the West is cheering.... People I presume are not now so despondent as they were....

Jan'y 11th, 1863
It is quite as difficult for you to keep up your spirits as it is for me. I keep mine up by the hope that some day I will be permitted to return to you. Sometimes, however, the day of

my return seems so far distant that with all my buoyancy of spirits I fail to see it. But that does not happen often.

...Every time my feet get damp I feel a slight soreness in my throat ... I have been very well since the first of December.... I am much better than when I left you. When I think [of] the time I left home I am [a] good deal surprised that I did it. I now know that I was not well but I thought I was....

Jan'y 12, 1863

What will you have first? News from the army. I must answer there is none. We are resting quietly in our small but comfortable huts....

...We must have a home.... Even if love fails which I do not fear, your strong & firm convictions of duty will make you a loving wife.... I sometimes think that serving as an officer in the army will unfit me for being a good husband, not because it exhausts my patience or makes me ill tempered, but because my word is accustomed to be law. Having become habituated to command, & to receiving implicit obedience, I might give commands, and expect obedience, after I have left my present sphere and entered one where my relation to others is entirely different. I trust though that your love will smooth down this rough feature of my character and make me as kind and gentle as though I had never been to war.

Jan'y 17th, 1863

We received an order to be ready to march at <u>reveillé</u> this morning with three days cooked rations....

This movement prevents me obtaining a leave of absence for which I intended to apply the day we received the order.... I hardly believe that they would put this army into battle under present circumstances....

...There are many temptations here that are not known at home and it requires all my strength to resist them....

...Hooker has the advance this time. I expect a hard time. It is very cold to-day.... To lie out & sleep would be impossible on a night like last night was. The consequence would be that the men would soon wear out....

...I shall need a little more money. Our paymaster has not found us yet.... In your next send me $10....

Jan'y 24th, 1863

We left camp on Tuesday last for the purpose of crossing the river at Bank's Ford about three miles above Falmouth. Our Division was to have protected the laying of Pontoons & to have crossed first. We arrived at the place of crossing about four o'clock in the evening, where the pontoons were ordered to meet us at that hour. The pontoons however failed to be there & we encamped in the woods near the river. The pontoons did not begin to arrive until late in the night after a terrific rainstorm had set in & broken up the roads. A half dozen of them arrived during the night, & in the morning the rest of them were found sticking in the mud so deep in the mud that the horses were not able to move them. During Wednesday details were made from the brigades ropes were attached to them & the men dragged them to the plain just on the bank of the river where men horses pontoons & all sunk in the mud. Here they were abandoned & of course the forward movement countermanded as it was impossible to go forward.

The order to go back to camp was not received, however, until Wednesday morning. The mud was now so deep that ... it was impossible to get the artillery back without corduroying the road for the distance of a mile or more. This was done on Thursday & on Friday we began to move back. We reached our camp just at dark.

Jan'y 26th, 1863

Since the army of the Potomac "stuck in the mud," there has been no talk of movements. We are lying quietly in our old camps. There is to be a review of our Division to-morrow in order I suppose to keep the army in a healthful motion.

Yesterday (Sunday) the Paymaster paid us four months pay—from July to November—There is almost three months more due us, but the paymaster said he did not have the money. He says he expects to return in a short time but his word is not better than a tailors or shoe-makers & I do not put much confidence in what he says. However we can get along now. I send you a check for $503 $^{13}/_{100}$. It should be worth a small premium in Pittsburg. I have put it in that shape in order that I might transmit it more conveniently.

...I have about concluded to resign. I had thought of coming home first, but I now think that one bother is sufficient. My reasons for this course I can not give you at present. I have not time—but you shall see me some time soon if it be possible for me to resign. I desire you to keep this matter secret until I come. Very few here suspect that I have any intention of leaving.

...I do not trouble myself about you. I would like to feel that you are happy—but can-not, knowing that you cannot be happy unless I be with you. I hope it will not be long....

Jan'y 27th, 1863

You are very unfortunate in starting boxes. The first one you tried to send, was taken to the Express office just before the battle of Fredricksburg, & when the Express Co. knew that the army was moving, hence they would not take it. The same misfortune befell the last one.... Dont trouble yourself with sending or attempting to send any more—because if the box does reach me it will probably be robbed of half the contents—& it is extremely improb-able that any of it may reach me.

Col. McKnight is now at Gen. Berry's H Qrs. As soon as he returns I expect to send in my resignation. I do not know that I shall succeed in getting it.... I will tell you why I resign when I come home....

I am of opinion with you that the war will not end in a dishonorable peace nor will it end soon. I expect, however, that in a military point of view nothing will be gained in '63. We need & will have another political revolution in the North before we will have any mili-tary success. The army of the Potomac is not likely to throw down their arms soon, but it cannot be denied that a great many are deserting. The truth is, the army of the Potomac never was an army and never will be one until we get a general who understands the necessity of discipline, & has the firmness to exact it.

...I do not know what Hooker may do, but I believe he is the best man that has yet taken command of the army.

...The mud here is wonderful in depth & still it rains....

Jan'y 28th, 1863

We are not accustomed to chose our rulers in the army consequently don't feel much interest in a change. I may say as I have said before that our Division is well pleased with Hooker. He will do something whenever any thing can be done. The appearance of the weather this morning [snow] indicates a long delay here. I do not expect that we will be able to move before the 1st of April. This is too late a start to take Richmond before the expiration of the term of enlistment of one half this army. In consequence I expect that nothing will be done in Virginia towards crushing the rebellion during the coming summer.

...The sending in of my resignation has been unavoidably postponed for a short time. I hope however, to get it through soon....

Camp Pitcher Va.
Feb'y 1ˢᵗ, 1863

I am very much obliged to you for postponing your dress-mending to write to me. Yet I believe in dress-mending. It is a great virtue in a woman to keep her dress in good trim ... I wish I was at home that you might take care of my shirts, for although I can sew a button on a shirt it is a "pesky business," & I am loath to undertake it. Consequently my shirts sometimes have a run without buttons.

...They circulate many foolish rumors at the North, which we never hear in the army.... The exposure and fatigue of that march did not injure me any. On the third day I felt slight pains in my right side & arm reminding me that I had once received an injury there. The pain was caused by the cold & it passed away entirely when I returned to my tent. But I was made sensible that my power to withstand exposure was somewhat diminished by wounds, although I had well nigh forgotten that I had ever been wounded.

I was not surprised at the change of commanders, but I was surprised when Sumner left, for I have never heard him charged with incompetency, although I have many doubts after the battle of Williamsburg of his ability to command a large force. He is gone. [William B.] Franklin too this was to be expected when Hooker took command, for Franklin is a warm friend of McClellan & Hooker is McClellan's enemy. I could tell you many things in regard to the changes of general officers, if space would permit.

When McClellan's army began operation on the Peninsula, Fitz-John Porter was his idol, but unfortunately Lincoln had not chosen him a corps commander; on the contrary he put him & his division in Heinzelman's Corps along with Hooker & Hamilton (afterwards Kearney) As these generals were all desirous to distinguish themselves, each was anxious to have the advance. Hooker happened to be the senior officer & the first position in the Corps could not be denied him. This was another block in the way of Porters advancement. But McClellan was not to be balked in his efforts, so he made two new army corps, by detaching Porter from Heinzelman & giving him [George] Sykes Division of Regulars, thereby constituting a corps of two divisions & giving the command to Porter. He also detached [William F. "Baldy"] Smith from Keys [Erasmus D. Keyes] & Franklin from Sumner forming another corps of two divisions & gave the command to Franklin. Thus he had his friends fixed. But alas in all the battles of the Peninsula they achieved nothing while the names of Heinzelman, Kearny and Hooker became famous, notwithstanding McClellan always attempted to keep them back. Consequently there grew up an ill feeling between McClellan & his generals & the three latter generals.

Just as he was about to receive a reward for his industry & ability Kearney was killed. Next Heinzelman was put into the defenses of Washington & Hooker alone remained in the Army of the Potomac. Then began the removal of McClellan & his friends. First the chief himself was removed then the right hand man Porter, then last comes Franklin, & Hooker is left in command of army of the Potomac. The wheel of vengeance has revolved full circle. Hooker who was at first "snubbed" as an insignificant brigadier now fills the place of him who first despised him.

...[A friend of a friend in Washington reports] that the feeling in Washington was that the army of the Potomac had fallen into bad hands, that Hooker was reckless & would go to Richmond or destroy the army. She further stated that Stanton was removing all of McClellan's friends & promoting all abolition generals, & that they looked for the return to the army of Gen. Fremont and others.—The term "reckless" applied to Hooker means that he is in favor of handling the rebels with ungloved hands in other words he believes in fighting the rebels not in playing with them; in no other sense is he reckless....

I received the cap this morning. It is pretty: will my wife accept a kiss for it?...

Feb'y 3rd, 1863

I have been often reminded during the last few days of my wife['s] thoughtful care concerning me. The cap has been admired by everyone....

I shall send up my resignation to-morrow. I could resign if for nothing more than to have a talk with you. There is no longer any interest for me to stay here, I am really no use to the government. I shall go home, if I am permitted, & help father settle up his business & then if it be so determined by us, return to the service again. I have no fear of losing any thing in rank by so doing. My friends can certainly do something for me on the data of twenty one months experience.

Feb'y 5th, 1863

I sent my resignation up day-before yesterday.... I hardly expect it to go through on the first application....

...There seems to be an impression in the North that nobody has got any brains but McClellan. But let me ask these people where McClellan ever showed any brains. If he has I have failed to see it. Every day's experience convinces me that McClellan is the villain I always supposed him to be....

Feb'y 6th, 1863

And you really hope to begin life. Ah! Harriet I fear you will be disappointed again. This dreadful struggle is not yet closed, and I cannot think of remaining at home until it is closed. And yet there are many reason[s] why I should stay at home. I must have a talk with you before I can determine any course. My life has not been since my marriage, what I fancied it would be when I learned to love you. My good wife my quiet home are ready to receive me but I come not....

Feb'y 9th, 1963

My resignation ... was disapproved at Division Headquarters.... If the second one fails I shall try to get a leave of absence for ten days, which is allowable by Gen. Hookers late order....

We have no army news. Every thing is quiet. The mud is so very deep that a movement cannot even be thought of....

Feb'y 10th, 1863

I had the pleasure just now of reading yours of the 4th & 5th. I read it twice, then re-read it, then closed my eyes to dream of my "dear good wife." The letter so lifted my heart....

You no doubt know my feelings, know how I am troubled betimes with despondency, yet if I could sit down beside you & talk to you, I would feel better....

Feb'y 12th, 1863

Although I did not get a letter this morning I still feel better off than some of my neighbors. Lieut. [Charles H.] Powers (my second Lieut.) has a lass at home with whom he generally keeps up a regular correspondence, but from whom he has not received a letter for an unusual length of time. Of course like all doubting lovers he thinks his lady offended, and is in great distress of mind — because he does not know what she took offense at and cannot make the proper amend. He finally concluded to write her a letter, the contents of which I have not the least knowledge of; but when he sealed it, he exclaimed: "There my destiny is sealed let it be good or bad."

Feb'y 14th, 1863

...It is whispered hereabouts that the President's Proclamation of emancipation is to be sent to the army for the signature of approval of all of the officers. Some of the officers say that they will not sign, although this is very quietly said....

Feb'y 17th, 1863

...I went to Div. Hd Qrs. last evening and ascertained that he [Gen. Birney] had written on it [Duff's second application for resignation]: "Respectfully forwarded <u>disapproved</u>." A second paper of this kind is not likely to <u>provoke</u> an acceptance: it is more likely to <u>provoke</u> a hint that the officer sending it is a little impertinent, and that hereafter it would be well for him to avoid such impertinence.... They dare not accept a resignation for any other reason than physical disability. It would be too dangerous a precedent to be established.

Feb'y 18, 1863

Yesterday I took it upon myself to inquire about a leave of absence, & received for an answer that one could not be obtained before the middle of March after the return of Lieut. [Robert I.] Boyington who is promised a leave after the return of Capt. Kirk who is now absent but will return in a day or two. I was promised a leave by Lieut. Col. Craig (who was commanding the regiment) after the return of Kirk, ... but Col. McKnight has seen fit to over rule Col Craig's promise & my leave is postponed....

...Ere long a loud voice will be raised in the North against Northern traitors. The revolution which is to settle forever and finally the condition of the people of this continent is now impending.

It is announced that Gov. Curtin will be a candidate for re-election to the office of governor. I hope he may be defeated let who will be his opponent. It is said that he is popular with the army. Granted, yet I don't believe it; but the organization and discipline of Penna Reg'ts full proves how he obtained his popularity in the army. The Government of the United States must bear a portion of the odium of our past ill success; but a much greater portion must rest on the state Governments, for inefficiently organizing & improperly officering the bulk of the army. Gov. Curtin has been one of the most prominent offenders in this respect. Though his successor be a traitor he cannot do us much more harm than he did.

Feb'y 21st, 1863

Our mail misses about every other day.

...The storm has had the effect to raise the streams, and last night for the first time since our arrival here I heard the roaring of the Rappahannock.

I am quite well to-day and feeling some what more cheerful.... I have had the good fortune to pick up a pleasant book or two lately.... I am longing for the army to be again put in motion to relieve us from the disagreeable monotony of camp life. I know you will be more anxious when we start again.... For my part I would rather risk the field than the camp ... my surroundings are singular at least. Going into the field will not alter them, but it will lessen their evil influence. I do not fear any great injury but I hate to be compelled to associate with men in whom I cannot see even a spark of manhood....

...My second resignation came back yesterday morning "Disapproved"....

Feb'y 22nd, 1863

My hand trembles with joy to write "Harriet." Could I have a wish to-day it would be that I might be transported to your side to receive your kiss, to hear your words and to be made strong....

...The snow is at least a foot deep in the thinnest spot, and in places it is "<u>drifted</u>" into piles several feet high. Our tent is "<u>bunkered up</u>" all round with snow to the depth of three feet. <u>We can scarcely get out and in</u>.... If this snow goes off with rain as most snow does in this country it will make very high water. The mud that it will make will be unspeakable. To talk of army movements now is folly. Were this day not a prognostic of what we are to have through all of March we could accept it with better grace. But if the "Conscript Bill" becomes a law, all will yet be safe.

March 2, 1863

Were the disappointment all I could bear it, but to be trifled with and made a fool of, is more than I can brook. To be promised a leave of absence, then have a "tody" substituted in your stead, to be promised again and to have another "tody" substituted, this is my complaint.... To be twice lied out of a leave provokes me almost to madness....

If I were not compelled to serve under men who are entirely devoid of character, & who lie to me every time I ask them a question, & for whom I cannot feel a spark of respect, I would not feel that I am wronged so frequently.

March 3rd, 1863

When I was informed yesterday morning that I would again be denied a leave of absence, I foolishly got angry — the first time for five years that I have allowed that passion to get the better of me. Happily no one but you know that I was guilty of such a weakness, for I kept myself calm while speaking to others. The triumph of the fit, however was but momentary, for the instant that I was conscious of my condition I determined it should not rule me....

Camp (near) Potomac Creek, Va.
March 5th, 1863

Camp Pitcher has been evacuated. On Tuesday evening we received order to march to our new encampment on Wednesday morning at nine o'clock. I was detailed to take charge of a squad of men to work on the roads and was obliged to start a[t] seven o'clock & was not present at the breaking up of the camp. I was on the road all day, and did not get to the new camp until about five o'clock when I found all of the men busy building huts. They slept last night in their half built huts, and this morning early they began to hew & hack, and no other sound can now be heard. The day is bright and pleasant, and ere the storm comes again the men will be comfortably housed.

Our new camp is in the woods, where of course wood is plenty which was our great want at Camp Pitcher....

March 7th, 1863

The roads are still so deep that it is almost impossible to get a wagon through them....

We have better quarters now than we have had any time during the winter. Knowing that we would remain here at least a month, we took more care in arranging our quarters. We determined to be comfortable....

I had a letter from Sardis this morning.... He also says that Rev. D. N. Steadman and wife were with them a short time since, and that Steadman left there that precious relic of mine the ball that went through me at Fair Oaks. When you go home you must get it.

The long anticipated ten-day leave was suddenly granted, effective March 10. Levi hastened to Allegheny City, where he spent six days with Harriet.

Allegheny City
March 18th, 1863

My dear husband;

The first day of your absence is past — how it has gone I will not tell.... The memory of your dear presence is so like the reality, that I am silent as when the thoughts in my heart were <u>breathed</u> to you.... No matter how short the time may be until your return, I shall find it long—but our duty is to make our trials light as possible.... How shall I talk to you, Levi, of the happiness of the past week—it is too great for words.... I pray God keep him [my husband] from temptation and sin—from sickness pain and death. The memory of the past, will give strength for the harsh present....Your banishment from peaceful pursuits <u>will</u> <u>end</u>, and you can be happy and diligent once more.

...I kiss you a good night....

Harriet

Camp near Potomac Creek, Va.
March 22nd, 1863

My visit home, though productive of much happiness to us both, is now troubling me some. You have been made aware that the train on which I started was delayed at Birmingham Pa [by a broken bridge] for several hours and failed to reach Harrisburg in time to connect with the Baltimore train. The loss of this connection caused me to be a day over my leave in getting to my regiment. When I arrived at the regiment I sent a note [to] the Col. stating the facts, supposing that he would answer it by putting me on duty or arresting me. I received no reply to the note until yesterday in the forenoon when it was sent back to me with the statement that it was not properly endorsed. I immediately sent it back insisting that it needed no endorsement. He returned it again with a message to the effect that if I wished to report for duty I might report in person. I then went to the Adjutant and reported in person; the Adjutant said "it was all right." I thought nothing about the matter until evening when I got an intimation from a friend that it was not all right. I then went in person to the Col. determined to come to some issue in the case. I told him the circumstances of my delay and ask[ed] him what he would do with me. He replied that he had no discretion in the matter, that he was obliged to arrest me and send me before a court martial. I then requested him not to make any delay in the matter but to have it disposed of immediately. I returned to my quarters & had been there but a short time when the Adjutant came in and stated to me that "by order of the Col. I would not exercise any command until further orders." Charges against me for overstaying my leave were written out and forwarded last evening, but were returned from Brigade HdQrts. For what reason I have [not] yet been informed. I think when the charges reach Gen. Birney he will order my release. If I am compelled to stand a trial I do not fear any disgrace. I think I can show that I started to my regiment in time.

I[t] was merely personal spite that caused the colonel to arrest me, and although he would like to give me trouble he has no case with which to do it. I shall be at liberty again in a few days....

March 23rd, 1863

It will require at least two weeks of good fair weather to put the roads in even a passable condition....

...[There are rumors of a move.] If we are obliged to leave our baggage I shall send home every thing that I cannot put on my back.... If I leave them in rear of our army, they will be taken either by a federal or confederate thief.

March 24th, 1863.

This morning the Adjutant called at my tent and told me that I might consider myself on duty. So I suppose my accounts are again square and I am not to undergo a trial by Court Martial for losing a day. I do no know who restored me to duty but I shall find out by & by. I troubled myself so little about the matter, that I think the Col. has not congratulated himself very much on my arrest. At any rate he has not made any thing off me.

Watch chain woven from Harriet's hair. Attached to it is a Kearny red diamond medallion. About the time of the Fair Oaks (May 31-June 1, 1862) battle, Gen. Philip Kearny directed that all men of his division wear a red patch so that they could identify each other. The patch evolved into the red diamond and into the practice of divisional patches throughout a modern army (courtesy Allegheny College).

To-day at 11 o'clock we have Brigade inspection and to-morrow Division Review....

...The roads dry very slowly. Sickness is beginning to appear among the troops. Yesterday our Surgeon said he had several very sick men, sicker than any he had for several months. This is a bad indication.

...On my return to the regiment I found here a letter from father devoted exclusively to the Provost Marshallship. I answered him in this way: That no recommendation from him would be of any avail that political influence alone would secure the appointment; that although I did not desire the position I would accept it if offered to me and he desired me to accept it. I then stated that if he could secure the recommendation [of] Amos Myers Congressman from the District, he might either have me appointed or detailed.—Just after writing the above I received a letter from Capt. Hamilton of our regiment now at Washington disabled by a wound received at Fredricksburg, requesting to procure for him a recommendation from the field officers of the regiment to be appointed to the same position! What can I do now? Can I be true to myself & friend too?

March 25th, 1863

I have met with a slight advancement in my fortunes—in point of dignity only. I have been detailed as Acting Assistant Inspector General, for our Brigade. This though no great promotion, sounds big and will do to talk about. So "wag your tongue."

My duties are to inspect the Brigade to see that the troops are kept in good condition and properly instructed that the camps are properly arranged and kept clean, and that all the regulations of the service are complied with. My Headquarters will be at Brigade Head Quarters. I will have a horse and will constitute a part of the General's staff. The pay and emoluments will be the same.

In one or two respects this position is much to be preferred to the one I now hold. There is less labor required and less responsibility and I will be relieved from hard marching, having a horse to ride. The latter is to me the most important, for although I look strong and am healthy, I am sensible that my right side is weak and that I could not undergo the fatigue and exposure I underwent a year ago. In this respect my advancement has just come in time.

March 26th, 1863

I think I forgot to tell you in my letter yesterday that I have been released from arrest. The Col. sent up charges against me. When they reached Birney I had a friend there ready to explain the case. The explanation being made Gen. Birney ordered my immediate release. When the Col. received the order he threw [it] down on the floor and directed the Adjutant to release me. He felt disappointed.

This morning I went to Col Hayden at Corps HdQrs. to receive instructions as to my duties in my new office. Having received the instructions I almost feel that I am taking upon myself too great a burden by assuming the office. I will do the best I can....

March 28th, 1863

This day I permanently establish myself at Brigade HQuarters. I have a week of hard work before me, once through that I can work more leisurely. I had intended to commence the inspection of the Brigade to day, but a rain storm interfered.... I sincerely hope the mud may not interfere with us [in any troop movement]. Mud in this climate is so filthy sickening that it is an abomination. Besides being an impediment to any movements, it breeds sickness and death.

...I love you, dear "Hattie," now don't blush.... My heart aches for your presence this morning. My love to all, and to my own dear wife a kiss....

Hd. Qrs. 1st Brigade
March 29th, 1863

The rain storm yesterday was terrible and continued for full 12 hours. I don't know that I ever saw it rain harder for so long a time....

...I am glad that my visit home did you so much good. I know, Harriet, that when I come home to stay with and this evil war is over, you will get well, your arm will no longer trouble you because your heart will be happy.... I have been made happier in my wife than ever I dreamed I could be....

April 1st, 1863

Last night about midnight an alarm was raised on the picket line and our Corps was roused and put under arms. It was reported that the rebels were advancing in force, but as nothing has been heard of them to-day I presume the report was false....

...We are all prepared for a move and the army is I believe in better condition that it ever was....

Apr. 3rd 1863

My associates here are a brigadier general — Chas K. Graham formerly of Brooklyn N. Y. his two A.D.C.s the Asst. Adjt Gen., the Ast Qrs. & the Asst Cam. Some good some bad I have not time to go into particulars. My situation in respect to associates is much better than it was in the regiment. I expect to learn a great many things and improve in manners.

Lieut. Powers of my co. has just been here showing me a letter from his unknown correspondent. What a silly woman she is, or a very great deceiver. From the tone of her letter I judge she is becoming interested in the Lieut. He is entirely unworthy of her confidence....

April 5th, 1863

The Brigade went on picket this morning in the storm. I did not have to go, thanks to my new office. My new position adds greatly to my comfort.

...I had a letter from father yesterday. He still thinks I should use my endeavors to secure the Provost Marshalship. I care nothing about it now; the reason that I might have had for accepting now ceases to exist & I have no desire to take it. I[t] would bring me home to be sure, but if I am to be in the army I had much rather be here.

April 7, 1863

Yesterday I was present at the greatest review I ever witnessed: the review of [Major General George] Stoneman's Cavalry Corps, by the President. I left Hd Qrs. here about 11 o'clock with Gen. Birney. He dashed off at full speed and about fifty mounted officers of his division followed him. Arrived at Gen. Sickles Hd. Qrs. We received an accession consisting of himself & staff & then proceeded to the review ground. We arrived there before the president, but did not wait long before the firing of the salute announced his approach. Gen. Hooker and his immense staff were with him. He looks like old "Abe" yet, but he is quite thin and haggard, not so well as I have seen him look.

The great thing of the day was riding in review. The President started accompanied by Gen. Stoneman and all the mounted officers on the ground at least two hundred in number dashed after them, myself in the crowd. The whole crowd went at full speed and as the ground was rough and intersected by many gulleys and mud holes there was some dangerous jumping and some amusing falls. A horse's foot would stick in the mud, he would fall and through [sic] his rider sprawling a rod from him. I heard of no one getting hurt. — And then the mud: there was so much splashing that it fell all round and all over one. I was bespattered with mud from the crown of my hat to the tow of my boot. To make me look still worse, coming home my horse went into a mud hole, stuck fast & went down. Of course I went off, but I alighted on my feet, and held on to my horse. I was on him again in a second & into the crowd at full speed. I feel a little sore to-day but not so badly as I expected to feel. — the President was to review the Infantry to-day but I believe on account of the mud the review was postponed. —

April 10th, 1863

Our army is in good condition but will be in better condition by the 1st May, as it is improving every day....

The President is to visit our Hd. Qrs. This morning at ½ past nine, when I presume we will all be permitted to take him by the hand. He is looking closely into the condition of the army, visits almost every camp in order to see what the army looks like.

Have you read in the report of the committee on the conduct of the war the reason of Burnside's resignation. If you have not read it. It is a page of imbecility so weak, that one wonders on reading it whether we have a government. Gens. John Cochrane and John Newton, should be hanged. I cannot say what should be done with Lincoln.

Hd.Qrs. 1st Brig. 1st Div.
Camp Sickles
April 11th, 1863

You need not presume on reading the caption that we have moved. Our camp has only been christened. It bears the name of our Corps General....

I will have to ask you to send me $50.... Dont send a draft of any kind, but the money. I have had to get some new equipments for my new position & besides it costs me more to live here than it did in the regiment.

April 15th 1863

Yesterday morning we received orders to prepare to march. The order specified that each man would be required to carry 8 days rations of bread (5 in the Knapsack) and three days rations of meat. It also stated that he should take ... in his knapsack 1 shirt 1 Pr. Drawers & 1 Pr. Socks & his overcoat strapped outside. The men were busy all day yesterday sending their extras, expecting to start this morning....

Last night at 12 o'clock a cold severe rain storm set in.... It really seems as though Providence is against us. Every movement we have attempted here during the present year has been prevented by bad weather.... We will not get off for three or four days at least.

...I am very well. I was never better prepared for a campaign....

April 16th, 1863

This morning when I awoke my good wife was by my side, her head nestling in my bosom. I kissed her and had a long talk with her....

I have got into difficulty with Gen. Birney commanding Div. How serious it may prove I do not know. He alleged that in my reports of my inspections of the Brigade I have been too severe in my <u>strictness</u> especially on officers. He has sent one report back twice refusing to transmit it to Corps Hd Qrs. I do not know how I will get through with the affair. I have not yet altered my report & I think I shall not. The difficulty may set me back to my company again, but I can survive the disgrace. I hope you will not go to school until your throat gets well again. It were better to quit entirely. I must insist that this term shall be your last. Were I not convinced that you injure yourself physically every day you remain in school I should not ask you to leave....

April 17th, 1863

My difficulty with Gen. Birney is about closed. He has however to answer to his superiors for having treated my reports with disrespect. I have the whole matter explain[ed] exculpating me for being tardy with my reports & inculpating him for detaining them. There is a feeling getting up in the matter which may breed a difficulty. I have kept my own counsel & held on to all written evidence coming into my hands, and I am prepared to defend myself.

We have recd no further orders to move, & do not expect to receive any until Monday. The blankets taken from the men have been returned to them....

April 19th, 1863

This is the Sabbath. We are to be visited by the Swiss General Fogliardi. The troops are to be formed in their camps. Of course he will be very complimentary, & the papers in the North will say there is another evidence of the efficiency of our army. But don't trust to the judgment of these foreign Generals. They [know] no more of our army and the enemy it has to contend with, than my grandmother would.

Our move has not yet taken place.... We will not move far before having a fight. The rebels are determined to dispute every inch of ground. The rise in the river caused by the rain of last week is now delaying us.

April 20th, 1863

The [Swiss] Gen. however, did not come, having gone to Aquia Creek with Gen. Hooker to see President Lincoln. Gen. Sickles came and rode through the camps accompanied by Gen. Birney. He was not received very enthusiastically. If he was proud of his reception he can afford to be proud of rather cold horrors.

At these Hd. Qrs. especially by the Gen. & his personal staff Sickles is held in great esteem. I cannot however, do him so much homage. He is just the kind of general that I dislike. He has gained his position of Major Gen. not by services in the field, but by political intrigue. In every sense of the word he is an untried general and I do not know why or how he has been given so large a command. I am willing to admit that he is a smart man in some respects, but I am mistaken in my judgment, if he makes any great mark as a military man.

...Our Cavalry which had started out ... was stopped at the Rappahannock by the swollen stream.... As soon as it is able to move we will move also....

April 25th, 1863

The roads are as muddy now as they have been any time this spring. Men here are beginning to ask if it will rain always....

I have forgotten heretofore to say that my difficulty with Gen. Birney has been settled. I rather had the inside track & kept it.... I do not anticipate any further trouble with him.

April 28th, 1863

In one hour we march, so says the order & part of that hour I must take to write you a note. I cannot say where we are going but I think we will cross the river a short distance below Fredricksburg.

You may expect to hear of a battle soon. Perhaps you may hear of one ere this reaches you. There has been no fighting yet, although all of the army except our Corps has moved. I hope for success but my faith is not very strong. My faith is weak because I do not think that our army will enter the contest with the same determination that the Rebel army will: A few days will tell the story.

I am quite well and as well prepared as I could be for a march. I am getting stronger every day. I do not think that the exposure will hurt me any now.

...Kiss me my good good wife....

7

Chancellorsville to Gettysburg

General "Fighting Joe" Hooker reorganized the Army of the Potomac and did much to rehabilitate its morale. The question remained "How well will it fight?" At the end of April, Hooker set out to test the matter. His plan was to leave a small force facing the Confederates in their trenches along the Rappahannock at Fredericksburg, while sending the majority of his men to cross the stream some miles to the northwest. He aimed to outflank the Southerners at a rural crossroads called Chancellorsville. Rather than press his opponents, Hooker positioned his army south of Chancellorsville and waited for Lee to attack. The outnumbered Lee did, in the course of which he outflanked the unsuspecting Union soldiers. The apparently unnerved Hooker failed to throw all his available troops into the fight and erred in abandoning key positions. He also allowed Lee time to dispatch sufficient of his troops to defeat the attacking Federal force at Fredericksburg and have them return to help push Hooker back across the Rappahannock. Federal losses were greater in number than those of the Confederacy. But the latter lost important leadership with the death of Stonewall Jackson from pneumonia May 10, after his arm had been amputated consequent to wounding by friendly fire.

Camp (near) the Rappahannock
April 29th, 1863

We left camp yesterday at 5 P.M. & reached this point about 4 miles distant from camp at 8 o'clock. We are now near the Rappahannock on the North side about 6 or 7 miles below Fredricksburg. The[re] are two Army Corps here the 3rd & 6th. The 2nd & 5th 11th & 12th preceeded by the Cavalry have gone to the right. The whereabouts of the 1st Corps I have not learned. The Cavalry had crossed the river yesterday in the neighborhood of the Orange & Alexandria Railroad, & were skirmishing with the enemy. It was thought that a general battle would begin this morning but there are no indications yet. The main contest I think will be on the right the largest body of troops is there & I presume they were sent where the work is to be done. We may and no doubt will have a fight here but it may not be a large one.

The weather is damp & foggy, favorable I think to our operations. The pontoons were to be laid at 3 o'clock this morning, so the [order] ran last evening, but it is now nearly seven and no sign of a move yet. As we had quite a shower yesterday & the roads were slippery it may be possible that the pontoons have failed to come up at the appointed time.

A very few days will determine whether we will be able to cross the River. But of six regiments we have only 2000 effective men in our Brigade. This is about half what six regiments should turn out.

[P.S.] I have just heard a few musketry shots near the river. It is possible that they are attempting to lay the pontoons.

Near the Rappahannock Va.

April 30th, 1863

Yesterday we moved only a half mile, going towards the river. I have not heard the situation this morning, but as yet every thing is quiet on the Rappahannock. Yesterday I went to this river near here, and I saw distinctly all the progress we have yet made. At the point where Franklin crossed before[,] Gen. Sedgewick laid three Bridges & put over about a Division of his corps. He had not advanced further than to take sufficient ground to protect himself. The Bridges at that point were laid without much difficulty. Our men went across in boats & drove the rebels away, having only fifteen men wounded, & taking a hundred prisoners About a mile below Gen. Sedgewick's crossing, Gen. [John F.] Reynolds laid two or three Bridges & had succeeded in taking over about a Brigade. About 5 o'clock from both points they were advancing skirmishers along the river so as to connect the points of crossing. As the enemy were not close to the river this was done without any fighting. And this I believe to be the situation at present.— We have heard nothing from the right except that all was going well. We did expected [sic] that the fight would open early this morning but as yet we have heard no firing. It is now 7 o'clock. So far as I can see there is no prospect of a fight here to-day. We anxiously waiting [to] hear of the beginning of the contest on the right for that is where the larger force is, & where Hooker is. Sedgewick commands here. I forgot to say that they made some resistance to Gen. Reynold's crossing. He lost in killed & wounded about 200. He also took a few prisoners but what number I have not heard. Looking at the whole field it may be said that nothing has been lost nothing won. Last night about 10 o'clock it began to rain quite briskly....

Near Chancellorsville, Va.

May 2nd, 1863

I could not find time nor opportunity to write you a letter yesterday, we were so consistently on the move. I have a leisure moment now & can write but I do not know that I can find a messenger by which to send my letter. You will observe that we have moved quite a distance from where my last was written.

In the forenoon the 30th we recd Hooker's Genl Order No. 47 announcing that he had succeeded in gaining a position in the enemy's rear with the 5th 11th & 12th Corps & that the enemy would either be compelled to fly ingloriously or fight on ground of our choosing. Soon after receiving this order we had orders to move. We got under way at one o'clock. We took the road leading to Warrenton. We marched on rapidly until 12 o'clock at night when we halted on the Warrenton Road North of U. S. Ford. Before getting to sleep we received another order to move at 5 o'clock in the morning. We started at the appointed hour going towards U. S. Ford a crossing on the Rappahannock three or four miles below the junction of the Hedgemon & Rapid Ann Rivers. We crossed the River reached Chancellorsville at noon. Our Brigade had orders immediately to go up the Orange C. H. road on Picket. After marching a mile or more we were stopped by Gen. Howard who commands the 11th (Siegels [Sigel's]) Corps, who informed us that we we[re] not needed. We then halted & sent back Staff officers to explain our situation. They returned by & by & we got orders to returned [sic] at 6 o'clock. We returned to Chancellorsville & halted our Brig in close Column of Regiments in a field South of the Orange Road. The rebels opened a battery on us, & we had a pretty warm time until we got a battery in position & silenced them. We had one man killed (114th Reg.) & 5 wounded. We lay there during the night & at day light this morning moved a ½ mile to the right & put 2 Regts. on the front, at which place we now rest. Every thing is quiet except some skirmishing on the left, towards the river.

The line of battle as formed yesterday consisted of the 5th 11th & 12th Corps. posted as follows: 11th Gen. Howard on the right, 12th Gen. [Henry W.] Slocum in the center, 5th Gen. Meade on the left. On the right & center there was no fighting worth mention, but on the left Gen. Sykes Div. Advanced to uncover Banks Ford & lost considerable. I have not learned certainly that he succeeded although I think he did. Our army seems to [be] waiting an attack to day at least it is not attempting to advance. The rebels got a battery in position a little while since & then threw some shells near Hookers Hd Qrs. I believe they did no injury, they are silent now.

The May days are very pleasant. I am quite well, & every one about me is in good spirits....

Our movement[s] thus far have been I think a grand success. We have completely turned their position & can now fight them advantageously. The men are in good spirits....

Hd Qrs. 1st Brig. 1st Div. 3rd Corps
May 4th 1863 (4 P.M.

We left our position below Fredricksburg from where I last wrote on Thursday afternoon. On Friday we crossed the river and marched to Chancellorsville. On Saturday afternoon we attacked the enemy & drove them some two miles from our front, but in the mean time the 11th Corps which was on our right gave way & the rebels got into our rear. On account of this we were not only obliged to retire, but were placed in such a position that we had to fight our way out. On Sunday morning the enemy attacked us in great force & we retired fighting for half a mile where we got him checked. The fighting was terrible and our loss is severe. In our Brigade we lost Col. McKnight killed, Major [Joseph S.] Chandler of the 114th P.V. killed & Lieut Col. [Guy H.] Watkins of the 141st mortally wounded.[1] In our regiment the 105th besides Col. McKnight, Capt. Kirk, & Lieut Powers of my company were killed. Lieut [Isaac L.] Platt also of my company wounded slightly. The loss of E. M. [enlisted men], was about seventy. The loss in our Brigade will be I suppose 800 — 500 killed & wounded & three hundred prisoners. All of our wounded are prisoners. The fight began at 6 o'clock & lasted until 12. I saw Charles on the field about 10 o'clock he was well & safe there, but as there was a very hard fight just afterward in which their brigade took a prominent part, I cannot say that he is safe now. I passed through it all uninjured. My sword scabbard hanging at my left side was stuck by a ball. I had a narrow escape from being taken once.

The enemy will not again attack us in our present position. It is too strong for them to carry.... Our success here is quite certain although it will not be as great as the people expect.

What Hattie will be most pleased to know is that I am safe & well. I did a hard days work yesterday I got the credit of having done my duty well....

[P.S.] We have had no fighting to day & are not likely to have any.

Camp Sickles, Va.
May 7th, 1863

Back again at Camp Sickles.... Such backward movements are common with us. I have not heard what transpired in Sedgewick's portion of the army but rumor says that he was badly whipped. We on the right were not badly whipped but were so much crippled that we could not attack and were too far off to render assistance to Gen. Sedgewick. This being the case we had nothing to do but retire. We reache[d] camp yesterday afternoon, after a very hard fatiguing march. Our men notwithstanding our defeat are still in good spirits. They have born themselves remarkably well through the terrible contest. There is a general impression here this morning that we will move again in a day or two: this move if it takes place means back towards Washington I presume.

I felt very much worn out yesterday but I am feeling quite well to-day. I thought that I was not very well, but I guess I was only fatigued. I do not know what may be the feeling at home about our defeat, but I can say for myself that it has not affected my spirits in the least. Although I hoped for success I was not one that believed it certain. I have not so much faith in our army as many have. The discipline is too lax for it to operate under adverse circumstances, and as we generally have to operate thus, we generally fail.

I have not time to write you more to-day for I have to inspect the whole Brigade to-day & report its condition....

May 8th, 1863

This morning finds me busy making reports but I must take time to write you a short letter. I am feeling quite well this morning and almost restored to my former strength. The air is very chilly with drizzling rain and every thing is dark and gloomy. We have received an order to be ready to go to the picket line at any moment from this I presume the line is threatened. I do not anticipate an attack on us here by the rebels but you will soon hear from their army in the Shenandoah valley. Some think that they will invade Pennsylvania, but I do not believe that they can sustain themselves so far North. They may and probably will attack Harpers Ferry, but whether they will be able to take it remains to be seen. At all events look out for squally times.

We are just now trying to get our Brigade in condition for the field, and a great labor it is. Our loss has been very heavy in both men and material. Gen. Graham is now commanding [Amiel W.] Whipples Division and Col. Eagan [Thomas W. Egan] of the 40th New York commands our Brigade. We have about 1200 men for duty in six regiments. We had twenty-two hundred when we started on the move.

Before leaving here I left with Mrs. Gen. Graham $690 to be sent to you in case any thing should happen [to] me or she should leave before my return.... I love you

Allegheny City
May 9th, 1863

My own precious one

I am too glad and thankful to write many words. This time the suspense has been worse than ever. We have not had anything <u>reliable</u> from the army this morning, when Stanton's dispatch to Curtin announces Hooker's return to Falmouth. The week to look back now seems to have been a horrid dream. Now that I hold the blessed assurance of your safety in my hands I <u>begin</u> to think of the movement and its effect — every one you talk with has a reason for Hooker's failure — it is a terrible disappointment. alas for the lost lives.... I see that Gen Graham had two horses shot from under him. How or why is it that the same men always have the fighting to do. Kearney's men have seen many a battlefield.... I cannot tell you how much more dear and precious you become every day....

Harriet

Camp Sickles, Va.
May 9th, 1863

The great battle was not fought on the 4th as Mr. Riddle told you, but on Sunday the 3rd, and the most terrible contest took place about 11 o'clock A.M. just when you were quietly listening to a sermon. I think I never was in greater danger than I was at that time. The battle began a little before six in the morning and lasted until 12 noon. During the whole six hours I was under a terrible fire but escaped without a scratch. Our loss was about 12000 in killed wounded & missing, perhaps two thousand were killed, two thousand taken by the enemy & the rest 8000 wounded, 2000 of whom were left on the field & fell into the hands of the enemy.

I have not been able to learn the particulars of Sedgewick contest at Fredricksburg further than that he was "badly used up" so says rumor. The whole contest may be thus summed up.—The plan adopted by Gen. Hooker, of dividing his army into two portions was a dangerous one & very seldom succeeds. With him however it was a success, but this success was lost by subsequent blunders.—He succeeded in placing the Chancellorsville army in a position threatening the enemies rear, & they were obliged as he said to fight him on his own ground. But he permitted the enemy to hoodwink him & turn his right flank, which drove him back into a position where he threatened nothing & could do nothing. Thus ended the operations of the right wing.—On the left Sedgewick likewise succeeded but pushed too far was surrounded & was obliged to cut his way through the enemy & recross the river. Had he fortified the heights of Fredricksburg & held them, we might have joined him & Fredricksburg at least would have been ours. But this was thrown away & we lost all.—It is said that our cavalry expedition was a complete success and that the enemy are retiring from here but I do not believe it. I do not know what will be done next. The 9 mo. troops are beginning to go home. 123rd P.V. went home yesterday.

May 10th, 1863

Our Division passed through a terrible ordeal and our brigade was the most exposed of the Division. It is almost wonderful that I escaped but such was my good fortune. Every thing is again quiet on the Rappahannock. I was down at the Lacey House yesterday. Looking over the river no indication of war could be seen: only on this side could be seen a few of our camps, and our railroad depot. They were bringing some of our wounded over yesterday & will begin at 12 o'clock to-day to bring all over. There must be quite a number over there yet.... The New York Herald & World are again to work trying to embarrass the government.[2] I wish the government would silence those sheets. It would be a great service to humanity to do so.

...My good good wife how I would like to sit down beside you this pleasant morning & talk to you.... This morning when I first awoke I beheld your bright face and received your warm kiss. Take one in return....

May 11th, 1863

The Herald (although I have not seen it) exhausts itself abusing Hooker. I understand the Provost Marshall at Aquia Creek confiscate[s] that paper when it comes there & will not permit it to be distributed in the army. This is just. Hooker is only exercising the right of self defense. If President Lincoln would do the same he would stop the printing of it.... We hear good news from the West.... We are almost ready here for another forward movement. Our men are not the least dispirited. Although obliged to recross the Rappahannock we succeeded in inflicting as severe a loss on them as they did on us. At least I believe they are so much ... crippled that they cannot take advantage of our present idleness. Notwithstanding Hooker committed two blunders as I think, he did very well in his first advance. Had the 11th Corps, stood all might have been well in spite of the blunders, but it giving was destroyed all hope of success. I do not think the North has any good grounds to be dissatisfied with the results. I know the army has lost no prestige.

Our Corps was reviewed to-day by Gen. Sickles. It looks full as well but much smaller than two weeks ago. Our Corps will have to be filled up with troops from some where & I do not know where they are to come from—The loss of Col. McKnight leaves a vacant field-commission in our regiment, & by the death of Capt. Kirk I become senior Captain in the regiment & am properly entitled to the position of Major but am afraid the Governor will refuse to commission on account of the smallness of the regiment.

At the review to day I was thrown from my horse by foolishly attempting to read a newspaper, the rattling of which frightened him. I had the left side of my face skinned slightly & my knee bruised. I will be well again in a day or two.

May 12th, 1863

I feel cross this morning.... I hurt my face yesterday as I wrote you, I had the toothe ache all night ... I have the head ache this morning. Besides I feel generally mean.

The weather here is oppressively warm. The summer has fairly set in. Soon we will have an ocean of flies then the disagreeable time we had at Harrisons Landing. There are no signs of a move. Every thing is quiet along the Rappahannock, not exactly either, for Lieut [Harvey] McAnnich [McAninch] of the 105th Regt was shot while on Picket this morning. He was on the river, & the rebel shot across the stream, the first instance I have heard of picket shooting for some time.—Ambulances started early this morning to bring our wounded from the other side of the river. Poor fellows how they must suffer. I am very very glad that they are to be brought within our lines where they can be taken care of.

I have been detailed as Asst. Inspector for the 3rd Division of this corps. This Division was Whipples. He was killed in the late battles & it is now commanded by Gen. Graham who commanded this Brigade. This is a promotion. The Division is small, but still it is a Division. It will give me less work & better opportunities to become known.

May 13th, 1863

I feel quite happy this morning.... My toothe-ache has left me. It got so bad yesterday evening that I was obliged to ask the surgeon for something to stop it. He gave me some mustard which had the desired effect & I slept soundly....

I came home yesterday evening feeling very low spirited. On entering my tent I saw on the table an envelope with a familiar hand writing on it.... Now that I know that you are assured of my safety I can be happy again.

...It is not thought here that the army will move for some time not I presume until the conscripts begin to arrive at Washington when we may receive reinforcements from there. We can wipe out the rebels this coming fall. We could do it now, but for the evil of a portion of our army going away just when we need it most.

...My new position is a very agreeable one, but I do not like it very well because there is no out-come in it. I do not like a staff position because promotion is so slow. I would like to get home this fall or summer & get a regiment. As all these matters will be determined by politics this summer & that being out of my line I suppose I must stand back. I could get the very best recommendations from here.

Hd. Qrs. 3rd Div. 3rd Corps
May 14, 1863

I came to this place yesterday & will get to work to day. I do not know how long I will stay here only three or four days I guess. Gen. Birney objected strongly to my leaving the Division and its probable that I will be ordered back. Birney must have a high appreciation of my services or he would [not] take so much trouble to have me retained in the Division. If he calls me back he will have to give me something handsome. The truth of the matter is I would willingly go back for I find this Division in such utter confusion that it will be an Herculean task to set it right. Besides it is so very small consisting of only eight small regiments that I presume it will be broken up or consolidated into a Brigade. In this case I would be no better off than if I had remained with the Brigade not as well, for the staff of the 1st Brigade is likely the best in the army. Gen. Graham has been trying to transfer it to this Division but has failed with every one except myself, & it now appears that I am to be sent back. Gen. Birney is sharp enough to retain within his Division men who are competent to discharge their duties and this is the reason of my difficulties. As I have my reputation pretty well established I do not think that I will lose any thing by the refusal to transfer me to this command.

May 15th, 1863

...In the afternoon of yesterday I discovered that my face and neck was swelling on the right side. I was frightened for a moment for this was my first discovery of it. I thought for a moment that it might be your disease quinsy, but on examination I found ... that all the inflammation came from my toothe. It was the back toothe in the lower jaw, close to the throat and of course any ailing to it affected the throat. The ulcer was so large that I found a difficulty in eating my supper. Last night it broke and ran quite freely and this morning my throat feels better. The toothe has ceased to ache and as the disease has gone the full round it will get well now I hope.

...[Capt. Joseph B. Sackett of the 155th] told me that [Andrew A.] Humphreys Division now contained only four regiments and that two of them would soon leave, there would then remain only two regiments when there was a large Division. In the face of such facts the army cannot move and people need not expect that it will. It was a great mistake last fall to enlist troops for 9 months. They are just going out of service when we need them....

I hope you have received the money I sent you.... Going where I thought there was a likelihood of loosing it I ... handed [it] to Mrs Graham.... Send me $10. It will require this to reorganize.

May 18th, 1863

We have indications during the last two days that we are to spend the summer here. We will have to wait for the conscripts. The rebels at present are as helpless as we are. Two deserters came from them yesterday. The name of one was Duff, a tall robust fellow "<u>sandy</u>" too.... They did not talk despondingly of the rebels. They had just got tired of the business, saw a chance of escape and took it.

May 20th, 1863

No movement care taking place, the soldiers are cleaning and arranging their camps for summer residence I presume.... There is no need for hurry just now. Time is wearing out the Southern Confederacy and there is no probability of any foreign nation coming to their aid. Europe has now got a complication of its own....[3]

I like the aspect of affairs in the West and South-West.... I think, that notwithstanding our defeat, the war is progressing.

...I send you a flower which I picked up in the garden here. This is the old residence homestead of the Fitzhugh family ... about 2 miles from Fredricksburg....

May 21st, 1863

I have presumed that he [Gov. Curtin] will not fill up many of the old [regiments] and this will cause the formation of many new ones. It is when these new ones are formed that I wish to get a regiment. I don't want a volunteer regiment. I am after "ye conscripts." Volunteers I have always believed to [be] a humbug. Drafting is the only proper way to raise an army. Whenever it is time to move in the matter I will send you a recommendation which your political friends can lay before the Governor. A Major's Commission has been ask[ed] for me in our old regiment. I am still in doubt as to whether it will come....

Yesterday quite a large party went over to Gen. [Thomas Francis] Maegher Hd Qrs. to bid him good bye.... Unfortunately we found Maegher so drunk that he could not see, and the whole party turned away in disgust. Maegher has resigned....The service has lost nothing.... Every dog has his day & Meagher's is past.

May 22nd, 1863

I go to-day to attend a court Martial as a witness to testify in the case of Col. Collis of the 114th P.V. who is charged with cowardice at Chancellorsvillle. It is an important case. I do not know how it will result.

All is quiet along the line of the Rappahannock. The soldiers are making their camps comfortable & healthful for hot weather....

I have an item of <u>personal</u> news for you. <u>Captain</u> Duff the distinguished gentleman that you married, is no more. Major Duff takes his place. I hope you can bear with the Major's society.... I received the commission day before yesterday & was mustered in that is took the oath yesterday. Calvin A Craig of Greenville Clarion Co is Colonel. J. W. Greenawalt of Westmoreland Lieut.-Colonel.... It is not yet determined whether I will stay. One thing I have escaped by the promotion I cannot be a Brigade Inspector, my rank is too high for that. If they wish me in the Inspector General's Department they give me a Division. So much is settled. I rejoice that after two years toil in the army I have got above the hardest work.

Soon, however, Duff would be deeply involved in difficult duty. Defeat at Chancellorsville did not demoralize the Union forces as had the previous defeat at Fredericksburg. Confederate leaders recognized that despite their victory they were hard pressed on all sides. In the West Ulysses S. Grant strove to take Vicksburg and with it control of the Mississippi River. He launched frontal assaults on the city on May 19 and 22. These proved unsuccessful, and Grant commenced a siege.

Meanwhile, Lee convinced the Confederacy leadership that the best chance of saving Richmond, relieving pressure in the West, and perhaps bringing either European intervention or negotiated peace offers from the North was invasion of Pennsylvania. He began to shift his troops north and did so with sufficient stealth that the Union army was for some time confused as to his position. When it became apparent that Lee was indeed moving north, Hooker took precaution to keep his own troops between Lee's army and Washington. He, however, seemed more interested in taking Richmond than in confronting Lee's army. Like McClellan before him, he called for more troops. He quarreled with General Halleck over the garrisoning of Harper's Ferry and offered to resign. Perhaps to Hooker's surprise, Lincoln took up the offer and appointed General George G. Meade to command the Army of the Potomac. The date was June 28.

May 25th, 1863

The news from Vicksburg yesterday had a very happy effect here. Grant's achievements are considered as brilliant as any in history. The country in which he operated is very unfavorable for rapid movements, but it seems not to have impeded him....The loss of this river [the Mississippi] is a fatal blow to the Southern Confederacy.... Although this success is of great importance to the army here, yet it is at home, its influence will be most felt. We know & feel the weakness of the South better than you do at home. Notwithstanding all of our defeats we feel that the South is weak & that finally we will overcome them.

Insignia of major worn by Duff on his cap (courtesy Allegheny College).

What will now become of Copperhead Stock. It is surely flattened....

...I am now obliged to buy a horse & equipments. I will want $200.... If Firman should see any one coming to our regiment he might send me a good horse. Horses are very high and difficult to get here.—

May 26th, 1863

I have frequently in my letters alluded to my 2nd Lieut Powers.... He seems to have been a real "heart smasher" and, without wishing to be unjust to the dead, somewhat unprincipled in his dealings with the ladies.

This afternoon I received two letters, one ... inquiring on behalf of Miss Emma J. Alexander, what disposition had been made of Powers body.... I answered ... that his body was left in the hands of the enemy and could not now be recovered.. I enclosed for Miss Alexander her own likeness which [he] had in his pocket when he fell.

I received another letter from Miss Lettie E. Grey.... She said he was "her own loved one" that all the "aspiring expectations of her heart centered on him".... Poor child she will feel sadder still when she receives my letter for she cherished a hope that he was still living. However it is probably her first love and she will soon forget him. As for the other one Miss Alexander nothing need be said. She cares very little for him & will soon forget his name.—

May 29th, 1863

[The rebels] can not attack us here with any prospect of success, & the rebel generals here do not make mistakes. However much they blunder out West, I can safely assure you that their blunders are not repeated here....

...Nothing has given me so much courage as the death of Stonewall Jackson. If there was a Christian, a man that feared God in the South, he was one. And too he was one of their greatest leaders. His death is to them a calamity. To me it is full of significance. By taking him away God seems to say "Wicked people thy race is run."

June 1st, 1863

The light of a bright June morning brought with it happy thoughts of you — of you my dear good wife, whose love, given to me three years ago hath not faltered or failed me, but hath cheered many a lonely hour and kept alive within that hope of future happiness without which the life of a soldier would be dull indeed. Thankful I am this day that I am spared in health and strength and that you are spared to love me. God has been good to us, Harriet: the future is in his hands, let us be content to leave it there.

The first anniversary of our <u>love</u>-<u>union</u> (for that day we were united in love) was spent together just after the cloud of distrust that passed over us had parted. We were both happy. Naught could then come between us to mar our pleasure. Although my departure was foreshadowed in the uniform I wore our hearts were too light to search the future for anxiety and trouble. You were mine, you rested in my arms, so quietly that you seemed to partake of my life. Your loving eyes, your warm gentle kiss told me you were more than a friend, and my spirit said this woman has been given to me, to cheer and comfort me. I shall love and cherish her. Our hopes were one — of fears we had none, the evil angel could not intrude in that moment of happiness.— A few days and I left you. You will remember how you clung to me, never expecting to see me again. I went off with a better hope.... [later, your loved one] was brought from the dreadful field mangled bleeding, dying they said but God in his mercy spared him. His spirit was calm, but ever and anon in his half conscious state would come the thoughts "my Harriet, my mother" what to them if I am taken away! But something whispered to me you will yet be spared to see them. And I was spared.... The mishaps of life are many. No one knows the uncertainties of the future but nothwithstanding I am very confident that this rebellion will be crushed & that afterwards I will be permitted to come home & live happily with you. Yet I know many with hopes as bright as mine, have perished when the[y] thought themselves secure. How many of the gifted of the land this cruel war has already carried away, and how many more will be carried away. When I think of the many brave & good men that have fallen I feel that let what will come this contest cannot be given up. It has cost us too much. The blood of the slain will cry unto us from the ground if we give it up. Whether I live through it or not I have determined that I shall not abandon it while there remains any thing to be done. My wife I know shares this feeling with me....

June 3.... I think a large portion of the Virginia army has gone west probably to reinforce Bragg who has no doubt sent a portion of his forces to Johnston. This game of transfer will answer for two or three months yet, but when our conscripts come, the game will be stopped. The only news that I have to give you is that we are doing nothing. Yes we are doing something, we are spreeing. Some ladies are here on a visit from Penn. They are stopping with Capt. Buchanan of Gen. Graham's staff, & the staff (this is the unmarried portion of it which is all except Lieut. Bullard and myself) are "handing them around." Unfortunately there is only one young lady in the party. You may be sure she gets enough attention....[Miss Cameron] is I judge about 26 is well educated & quite sharp. She is not possessed of much beauty, but her intelligence & good manners make up for this deficiency. Lieut Benson of Gen. Graham's staff went to Gen. [Winfield Scott] Hancocks Hd. Qrs. to see them before they came here. On his return he said Miss Cameron was rather good looking & a very interesting woman. This was after a night view of her. The next day they came over to our Hd. Qrs. & Benson remarked that Miss Cameron was not so good looking in daylight as she was afternight. He was a little dazzled it seems when he first saw her. This detracts nothing from the lady, it only argues weakness on the part of the boy.

Night before last we had an entertainment for them here. Gen. Hooker was present. Miss Cameron played the agreeable to old Joseph right well. He got a little weak in the knees before he left, the result of too much "grog." A number were laid out just at the close of the entertainment. Our Adjutant General rolled off the stool & had to be carried to his room. Two paymasters clerks who were here from Washington were "laid out" to use an expression & low term, & the Quartermaster who made the last bucket of Punch strong to lay the crowd out got laid out himself. Don't smile when I talk about buckets full of punch, for the crowd which was not a large one drunk three <u>horse</u> <u>buckets</u> full, or to express it in dry measure a bushel & a half. Drinking is a science in this army. It is hard for an officer to keep from it for every officer he meets offers him a drink. Sometimes I think that our plenty is our ruin. I feel confident that if we were farther from the great cities, we would have a better army. Men may talk as much as the[y] please about the effects of liquor, but no matter how little a man may take, when he once gets to drinking for sport, he is greatly injured if not ruined. The practice is so undignified, that if there were no other considerations I could not adopt it. I never can believe that smoking chewing & drinking are essential to gentillity.

Yesterday they went to Gen. Hookers Hd. Qrs. to dine. We expected them back here early in the evening & had a band & other things arranged to have a lively evening. They did not return, however, until it was very late & our part of the entertainment yesterday was short. The band remained & kept playing until very late. I went to bed before the party returned.... I do not care to see women in the army because men make fools of themselves while they are here.

June 4th, 1863

Last night our army or a large portion of it was put in motion towards U. S. Ford to check the threatened crossing of the rebels. There was cannonading all day yesterday at U. S. Ford so I am told. The rebels are no doubt making a demonstration there, but I have not the least idea that they will attempt to cross there. If they are advancing toward Md. they will cross above, or go up the Shenandoah Valley. If they advance on Md. we will have more fighting and that soon. The general presumption here is that they will advance and that we will have a battle with them at or near the old Bull run ground. It will [be] some days yet before a battle on an extensive scale can take place.

...I cannot believe they ... can go up through Virginia into Md. but if our troops are properly handled I scarcely think that they can get back. Our army is probably weaker now than ever it will be again — this is the enemy's great opportunity and if he can take advantage of it he will. They must strike now or be ruined forever.

I intended to write for a suit to-day, but as there is a probability of a move on hand I will defer it for the present. The Major must have a coat & [or] it will not be known that he is major....

I am still quite well. I am not much afraid of sickness overtaking me. The army as a general thing is healthy. The weather is very pleasant. We have had no rain for 30 days.

June 6, 1863

The 5th Corps ... is up the river observing the movements of the enemy. It being very evident for the last few days that the rebels were leaving Fredricksburg a pontoon bridge was yesterday laid by the 6th Corps & a portion of it crossed, to reconnoiter I suppose.... A shot or two has been heard up the river but nothing of any moment. While the 6th Corps was crossing we received orders to be ready to march on short notice. We afterwards ... received orders to be ready to march in the morning (this morning) at day light. The last order was countermanded, the first is still in force....

[Enclosed with letter of June 7, 1863]   June 8th 1863

The situation has not changed since yesterday.... [Some think our movements] purely defensive for the reason that we have not troops enough to make an offensive movement. It is stated by many persons here that Hooker has been assigned to the command of all the troops in Virginia but I cannot believe the story. If it be true good bye troops in Virginia, they will come to naught. Gen. Hooker is not capable of handling so many troops so scattered as they are in this state. Officers here imagine that if Hooker handles the army of the Potomac successfully, he will have done all that ought to [be] required of a man of his ability. I think that we are only amusing the enemy here to prevent him from sending away his troops. If we can do so we may help Grant. There is no immediate prospect of a fight. This is suspended I think until fall.—

I return to the regiment this morning. Gen. Graham told me yesterday that Gen. Birney wanted me to report to-day.

Camp (near) Bealton Station
Fauquier Co. Va
June 13th, 1863

We left our camp on Potomac Creek on Thursday at 2 P.M., took the Warrenton Turnpike, marched that day about 15 miles halting at 10 o'clock at night. The men were almost worn out when we halted. The day was hot, & the dust thick; after dark the heat was very oppressive. Our regiment kept up well, but all of the other regiments straggled wonderfully. Yesterday morning at 7 o'clock we started again, & marched till 4 o'clock & halted in our present position. This day like the preceding one was very hot. The men fell out of the ranks by scores & before we reached here the Brigade was reduced to half its size. Our regiment kept up as it did the day before but the others were scattered & strewn along the road. This morning, however most of the stragglers are up.

Last evening I was appointed Brigade Officer of the day & had to post a picket, but only some 500 yds in front of the Brigade. Posted my pickets then went to a house near the picket line & took lodging. I slept in the house on a lounge. This morning I had breakfast in the house, a rather poor one, but it was a change from Camp fare. I had some hot biscuit & sweet milk. The people of the house are very poor I judge. The family consists of a woman ... & five small children & [an] old negress whom they call "Aunt Page." They have very few articles of furniture & these of the oldest & most rickety kind. There is no carpet on the floor. This house is old & filled with <u>pests</u> (as usual); & the whole concern is broken down & forlorn. The husband so the wife says was taken to Washington some five weeks since, for what I have not thought proper to inquire.

I am quite well. I have stood the marching remarkably well, because I could ride till I got tired then walk until I was rested.... There are no indications of fighting.

Manassas Junction Va
June 16th, 1863

We left our camp near Bealton on Saturday at noon going down the railroad to Rappahannock Station where we halted; we were put on Picket & remained out until noon Sunday when we were drawn in. Soon after we were ordered to march & returned to Bealton. Here we were detached & remained behind the Brigade to cover the withdrawal of our troops from that point. We did not leave Bealton until 2 o'clock Monday morning when we marched to Catletts, 12 miles. At Catletts we halted only long enough to get breakfast, when we again moved forward & reached this place at 5 o'clock. The marching yesterday was terrible. I never I believe felt so hot a sun. A number of men were sun-struck a few died, most of them will get well again. We are under orders to March to Blackburn's Ford on Bull Run & will move soon. There the bugle blows & we must be off. I shall close my letter when I get there.

Blackburns Ford 3 P.M.

We have arrived here and will remain I believe until to-morrow morning. This is historic ground. The first fighting of the war in this locality to[ok] place here. It is much more pleasant to lie here in the shade than to march.... Some think we left there [Aquia Creek] to follow the enemy who went up the Shenandoah valley, but I cannot believe this. I hear a great many rumors here of their movements in the Valley....

Centreville Va
June 18th 1863

Yesterday we moved only two miles, from Blackburns Ford to this place. Our whole army now lies here. We are the extreme left where the right is I cannot say.... The papers yesterday gave us more favorable news than I had anticipated. I feared that the whole rebel army had slipped by us & was in Penn some 75 miles ahead of ours & I began to tremble not for Harrisburg but for Pittsburg. If they are 75 miles ahead of our army & take the National road there is nothing in the way to prevent them from taking Pittsburg. The place may be easily enough defended, but it would require more troops than can be brought there on a sudden emergency to defend against Lee's Army.

June 19th, 1863

We have heard nothing & know but little of the whereabouts of the main rebel army. The cavalry raid into Pennsylvania is supported by [Stonewall] Jackson's old corps....

The great heat of yesterday culminated in a fine rain storm about six o'clock.... This is the first rain we have had since the battle of Chancellorsvillle and most welcome it was to every thing.

Gum Spring Loudon Co. Va
June 20th, 1863

Yesterday we received orders to march at two o'clock to this place. We did not get underway, however, until five, in consequence of the rain encumbering our way. After we started however we marched rapidly, the roads were good & the air cool. At dark there came up a furious rain storm, which continued until 12 o'clock an hour after we arrived & encamped. I never saw darkness more dense than that of last night. I could not see my hand before. The rain filled the road with water & the mud soon became deep. I did not suffer any from it, for fortunately I was on horseback. I had an overcoat and an India rubber coat which kept me dry and warm.

...I know nothing of military movements.... [From the movements of our army] I judge [the rebels] are in the Shenandoah valley....

June 21st, 1863

This is the 21st, one more month and we will have been married one year. Yet how little of each others society we have had. I can hardly think that I have endured such a privation, so hard does it seem. If the prospect for the next year were any better one might bear it more patiently, but there is not, and I feel a little dissatisfied.

I will make an effort to get home in July to celebrate the first anniversary of our marriage. Would it not be pleasant?...

June 22nd, 1863

It is the generally accepted belief that the rebel army is massed near us ready for a dash at Washington if by some alarming raid they can entice the army of the Potomac to the Shenandoah Valley. I do not believe that Lee has [a] large enough army to take Washington under any circumstances.... As usual every one imagines a great rebel horde in Virginia when I doubt if there is a rebel army of the usual size....

...Governor Curtin and his militia are a ludicrous set of fellows. That state will soon be in such a condition of anarchy that it will secede.... Our Government both State & National is growing so weak that the most contemptible citizens despise it. Instead of growing stronger as we should do we are growing weaker every day.

June 23rd, 1863

Nothing new transpired yesterday. It was very quiet here. Not a shot was heard in any direction. And it is just as quiet this morning....

I almost forgot to say that yesterday in the afternoon a wagon train was attacked about a half mile east of here on the Centreville road and before our men came to the rescue 4 wagons were burned. A party of scouts were sent after the guerillas & 8 of them were caught. The attack on the train was a very bold one. It was made about 200 yds from our picket line. All of the inhabitants in this country belong to this guerrilla band. Whenever our army comes to a place in force they remain at home in order to relieve them of the suspicion of belonging to it.

Point of Rocks Md
June 27th, 1863

We left Gum Spring Va. on Thursday morning last at 5 ½ A.M. & on the same day reached the mouth of the Monocacy going by way of Edwards Ferry. The distance marched that day was twenty three miles. Yesterday we marched from the Monocacy to this place seven miles.

This morning we move forward. We are ordered to go to Jefferson a small town on the road from Fredrick [to] Harpers Ferry. I do not know our destination, but I presume it will be governed by the movements of the rebels. We are moving towards them & will certainly over-take them in a few days. Harrisburg is certainly safe now if it has not already been taken by the rebels. Pittsburg is considered in greater danger than any other important place in Penn-sylvania, but I hope the militia are sufficiently rallied to delay them for a day or two if they make any demonstration in that direction.

By the way I am again a staff officer. I was yesterday detailed as Asst. Inspector General of the 1st Division. The Div. [brigade] is commanded by Gen.Ward Gen. Birney being in com-mand of the Corps [division]....

Taneytown Md.

June 29th 1863

9 o'clock P.M.

I wrote last from Point of Rocks. We marched from there to Middletown. On Sunday we marched from Middletown to Walkerville 6 miles North of Frederick, & to day we marched to this place which is about 25 miles North of Frederick & 5 miles south of the Penn line. We will be into Penn to-morrow. About day after to-morrow we will have a fight with the rebel army which is now I believe in York Co. I think that we will be able to drive them out of Penn, but I do not anticipate that we are going to annihilate their army.

You have no doubt heard of the change in commanders. It may surprise you but it did not surprise me. I have expected it for a month. Of Meade I know but very little. I have seen him frequently. He looks like an earnest patient man. I do not expect that we will meet with any great disaster under his command nor do I expect any great victories. We will be able to hold our own as we have done heretofore. Mead is not liked in this Corps and is especially disliked by Gen. Birney.

Our men are in very good spirits. The citizens here are very glad to see [us]. We have been cheered & feasted ever since we entered Maryland. Since our march through the state I am convinced that there are fewer disloyal people than in many parts of Penn. The coming week will be eventful....

You must excuse this poorly written letter. I will write to you as often as I can. I have confidence that I shall pass through the struggle safely....

General Birney's division was ordered to report to Gettysburg on July 1, marching up the muddy Emmettsburg Road. On the morning of July 2 the left of the division was at the foot of Round Top and the right, including the 105th Regiment of Pennsylvania Volunteers, was near Sherfy's house. In midafternoon the line moved to the top of the hill along the Emmetts-burg Road. The see-saw battle was fierce; eventually the regiment was forced back to a new line connecting Round Top with Cemetery Ridge. This line was held during July 3 and until the fifth of July, when an advance demonstrated that the enemy was retreating.

Battle Field (near) Gettysburg Pa

July 3rd, 1863. 9A.M.

I feel very happy this morning that I have an opportunity to send you a letter this morn-ing. Ere this reaches you, you will have heard of our fight & your anxiety I know will be very great. We had a terrible fight on our left yesterday. The rebels attacked us at 4 o'clock. Our Corps was first engaged & suffered terribly. The fight was closed at dark by portions of the 2 & 3 Corps. We held our ground except about a ¼ of a mile in the centre which was very much exposed. In every other respect we have been successful. Our army is well massed & I have strong hopes of a victory.

I escaped unhurt yesterday. I had my horse killed by a cannon ball. I regret to learn that Charles was severely wounded. I saw a member of Col. Brooke staff this morning & he told me that Charles had been shot through [the] face with a musket ball. I understood him to say that the ball entered the right cheek & came out under the left jaw. He said it was a very ugley wound. I have not an opportunity to hunt him up but think I can find him some time to day.

I am well and in good spirits. Harriet is present with me. You are my good wife & I love you. Hattie will remember & love me. Love to all. Send word to Clarion.

P.S. There is fighting on the right this morning with no result at present. We are about a mile south of Gettysburg.

Battlefield (near) Gettysburg Pa
July 4th, 1863. 9 A.M.

Since my letter of yesterday we have a good deal of fighting but have been successful at every point. In the morning of yesterday they attacked on the right & were repulsed. At 2 o'clock they attacked our centre and were repulsed with terrible slaughter. Our line is now in advance of the line of the 1st from which we were driven on the second. We took about 4000 prisoners yesterday. It was said this morning that they are in full retreat, but an examination of our front found them still in line of battle. Eventually I think we will whip them badly. Gen. [William] Barksdale of Miss. was wounded & captured day before yesterday. He died yesterday morning. Gen. Armstead or Olmstead [Lewis A. Armistead] was wounded & captured yesterday.

I am still quite well but much exhausted. I have not yet succeeded in finding Charles. On our side we have had Gens [John F.] Reynolds & [Gabriel R.] Paul of 1st Corps killed. Gens. Sickles & Graham 3rd Corps wounded. Gen. [Winfield Scott] Hancock of 2nd Corps wounded. We have lost in our Div. killed & wounded 114 officers & 500 men.

Our men are in good spirits & feeling confident of success.

[P.S.] I send you a kiss on a rose bud I pluck[ed] on the field yesterday while the battle was raging. It grew among the carnage.

Allegheny City
July 4th, 1863

My own dear husband;

My faith in God's mercy tells me that you live and that your eyes will read the thoughts I may write. Our hearts swell with joy to know that the rebel horde have been repulsed. The battle will doubtless be renewed, but we trust the power of God will be with you still. This day has been a great contrast to last "fourth." I cannot forget how happily it was spent. I have been lonely and sad today — so lonely that all the pleasant memories thronging upon [me] have failed to make me forget. The sound of the artillery for home defense speaks to me

Flower from Gettysburg battle, July 3, 1863. Harriet saved the flora mementos that Levi forwarded, most in a 1008 page volume by Thomas H. Prescott, *The American Encyclopedia of History, Biography and Travel, comprising Ancient and Modern History: The Biography of Eminent Men of Europe and America, and the Lives of Distinguished Travelers*, Columbus: J. & H. Miller, 1857). Some she carefully mounted and labeled. Others were simply inserted between the pages without record of their origin (courtesy Allegheny College).

of horrible sights and sounds not very far from me — it seems to me a desecration that the roar of cannon should fall upon careless ears this day, when to those, to whom we owe our peace and quiet, it has such a solemn meaning. I mourn this day for all the dead braves— men who have loved their country and died for her. I sit with closed eyes and see the red lips of wounds that say "it is sweet to die for one's country." Sleep softly brothers, no foe will o'er your cold ashes upbraid you — your last resting place is in the true "sacred soil" — now and forever sacred to your memories. And what to me if my precious one lies among the slain. I dare not think of this. Could there be a life left to me when my life were hidden beneath the sod? I have striven to pray as I should, to plead with God in the name of Jesus that for His own glory, your life might be spared. I have tried to put self far away — to be the humble unworthy child — for what indeed am I that God should hear me. To His name be glory what-ever the issue.... Nothing but a firm reliance upon God a loving trust can calm my troubled soul....

Harriet

Camp near Gettysburg, Penna.
July 5th, 1863

We still remain here, but the Rebel Army has left us. At daylight this morning they with-drew their pickets from our immediate front, & it was soon ascertained that they were in full retreat. We saw a line of battle beyond Marsh Creek supposed to be their rear guard, but it has likewise disappeared and their whereabouts just now is not known. Our forces are in pursuit but are not likely to come up with them today. We have encamped near the battlefield to rest for to day at least. The 6th Corps which has not yet been engaged, has the advance in the pursuit. We have gained a substantial victory & by a close pursuit may be able to effec-tually cripple their army. The fighting took place on the 1st, 2d, & 3d inst. The fight on the 1st between the 1st and 11th Corps & I believe [Richard] Ewells rebel Corps was a drawn fight. The fight of the 2d in which the 2nd 3rd & 5th Corps were engaged, when the Rebels attempted to turn our Left, resulted in our favor, but was not decisive. The fight of the 3d resulted glo-riously. It was very evident yesterday that they were retreating, but General Meade did not attack their rear-guard why I do not know. I suppose he has a sufficient excuse for not attacking. I think we will compel them to give us battle again before they get to Virginia. Their army is much demoralized and many are deserting. If General Lee succeeds in reaching Va. with half the army he left it with he will do more than we anticipate at pres-ent. One thing at least is settled by this fight and that is that Lee & his army are not invinci-ble.

Our loss has been about 18,000, that of the Rebels at least 30,000. The fighting on both sides was terrible. The dead of the two armies lay intermingled on the field, & have been buried where they fell. No one can realize what war is until they look on a battle-field like this. Cen-turies will scarcely efface the marks of the struggle.

In our division we lost 154 officers and 2157 men. This includes killed, wounded & pris-oners. There was very few of the latter. In the 105th Regt 1 officer was killed & 14 wounded & only three officers escaped without being struck. More than half the privates were killed & wounded 130 in all. The Lieut. Com[manding] my old Co. was wounded.

I cannot write further particulars today. We will likely be on the move to-morrow, but I will try to send you a letter. The homes of your Pittsburgh militia are now safe from inva-sion. Let them remember that the Army of the Potomac secured them.

What appears to be a page torn from a journal or a separate note, in the hand of Har-riet Duff:

July 6 1863

There has been a great battle the land sings with the shout of victory it seems that the glad day we have so long prayed and waited for is come — the giant rebellion is to sink down and our land is to be at peace But to me ... what has this battle brought — my husband my most precious self has I begin to fear fallen with the other braves that have purchased for us at a awful cost this hoped of peace Four days since the battle yet no message comes to tell me of his fortune in the fight Others have heard the glad tidings from their loved ones— wounded men from the dread field are home yet I have not a trace of him who is most dear My heart is dumb with agony for what can any one knowing my loss As days lengthen and pass away the hope which was so strong within me dies out I see that dear form still and cold — the careless hand hollows and the tearless eyes sees the damp earthy covering up, alas forever from <u>my sight</u> My brain reels can I do I think [abrupt halt]

Flower from the battlefield of Gettysburg where Harriet feared Levi had died. (Courtesy Allegheny College).

Emmettsburg Md
July 7 1863

We left Gettysburg this morning and have just arrived here. We are marching towards Harpers Ferry and will halt to-night I suppose at Lewistown 13 miles from here.

I have only time to send you a word. I am very well but feeling a little sleepy to-day.... No fight expected for a day or two. I do not know the whereabouts of the rebels.

Allegheny City
July 9th, 1863

My precious one:

The sad anxiety is past —forgotten in the joy of the present. Your letter of the 4th did not reach me until to day (I have had none since the 27th.) A mail from the army came yesterday & nothing for me — added to this I learned that Charles has reached home. What could I think in my inmost heart but that you were unable to write — unable to come home. How more than terrible the reality must be to those whose dear ones <u>are</u> the dead upon that battlefield? There was no strength left within me — and I had hope to buoy me above despair. You cannot measure the change which came to us in a moment's time, as Winnie, Mother and I sat waiting the postman. <u>Levi</u> was safe, <u>was safe</u>. The rose bud is a curiosity to all — not to me. To me it is magic itself — looking at the silent, faded thing I see pictures of the fray — the hot breath of the wide-mouthed cannon flushes my face — the sulphurous air stifles me. I hear the shouts. I see the unequaled valor of my countrymen. I am very near to you, my husband. I feel that God is with you — preserving your life that you may yet serve Him. To God belongs the glory of the victory. His mercy endureth forever.... Charles's wound ... a Minnie ball through his jaw — poor fellow I expect he will suffer greatly.... I dare not look back to the blank world I saw last night. Thanks be to God for <u>life</u>....

Harriet

8

Waiting

General George Meade, in command of the Army of the Potomac less than a week, felt relieved by the victory at Gettysburg. But he did not have the confidence, or yet sense of the spirit of his troops, to pursue the retreating Confederates. Despite Lincoln's urging that Meade attack the Southerners before they crossed the Potomac, Lee was able to get his men across the swollen river with minimal additional losses. Meade's delay may have prolonged the war, but Union supporters were cheered by news that Grant had taken Vicksburg. The Army of the Potomac followed Lee south, and the 105th regiment, Pennsylvania Volunteers, at the end of July made summer encampment at White Sulphur Springs. Since breaking camp in June to pursue Lee north the regiment had marched on 48 days and remained no more than two days at any one point.[1] It, and Levi Duff, were ready for a rest.

South Mountain
July 10th, 1863 10 A.M.

We are marching toward Sharpsburg to day, & have just halted on the West side of the mountain. Opinions differ very much as to the position of the rebels. It is generally thought that they are crossing at Williamsport. I think that we will fight another battle with them in a few days where I cannot at present say. We are all in good spirits. Gen. [William Henry] French commands our Corps.

Camp (near) Boonsboro, Md.
July 11th, 1863

I have written camp near Boonsboro because it is the nearest town I know of. I wrote you a note yesterday when we were on the western slope of South Mountain. We marched from there to Kedysville & after remaining at the latter place all day marched to this point. We are on the east shore of Antietam Creek 4 miles west of Boonsboro. Our Corps is held in reserve our front line is about 3 miles beyond here. This morning I heard that the enemy had disappeared from our front. I have yet heard where they have gone to. There will be no fight to day & may not be for several days & there may be one any day. I believe it is not Gen. Meade's intention to attack Lee, but to compel Lee to attack him. We are now between the rebel army & Richmond, & Lee will have to give us battle to open his line of retreat. If our generals are only vigilant we will finally destroy the rebel army. Although our army is somewhat larger than Lee's it is not yet strong enough to attack him, & there is no necessity to attack him when we can compel him to attack us.

...I felt content to know that you were calm & still looked for my deliverance. I thank God I have been again kept from harm, & I trust that God will keep me safe & return me to you. I realize, Harriet that I am in God's hands. I try to do my duty, trusting the result to Him. Of late I have derived consolation from your letters. Do not think that I overlook your religious letters. Although I cannot bring my mind to believe as you do, yet your faith expressed in living words is a great blessing to me....

...If we can again defeat Lee, I think there will be nothing to prevent [peace], but if we fail to do that, it may be postponed another half year. It must surely come within a year.... [P.S.] I send you some flowers from the Gettysburg field....

Camp (near) Antietam Md.
July 12th, 1863 9 A.M.

We are just on the eve of important movements. We received a circular this morning stating that the Maj. Gen. Commanding would attack this morning. We are in reserve but are ready to move forward immediately. The 5th Corps is in our front. I do not know where the attack is to be made, but I presume it will be made on one of the flanks. As yet every thing is quiet. Not a shot has been fired this morning. The rebel line of battle stretches from the Potomac near Williamsport to Frankstown. From the fact that the largest portion of our forces are on the right I presume the attack will be made there. That is the rebel left resting at Frankstown will be attacked. I will not be foolish enough to predict the result. The uncertainties of a battle are very great. Humanly speaking the chances are in our favor, that is we are stronger than the enemy. But God orders all things and will award the victory to whom it is due.

I have strong hopes of success. I almost believe that the rebellion is to end here and now. My own fate concerns me little. I know that, I cannot add to or take away a day from my life, therefore I can meet the great trial with calmness and without fear. If it be God's will that I fall let it be done. You will be taken care of. But I have bright hopes, yet I know of no reason why I should be spared when others perish.

Jones Cross Roads, Md.
July 14th, 1863

Very little has been done here since my last letter. I told you that an attack was to be made, but I did not know on what part of the line. It turned out that it was Gen. Meade's intention to occupy Hagerstown & Frankstown, & to do this he intended to attack the enemy's right. But the enemy relinquished these places & thus an attack was unnecessary. Our line now rests at this point (the left about a mile west of Jones Cross Roads & extends ... to Hagerstown (the right). Our Corps is in Reserve on the left.... Our army has been reinforced and I think is larger now than when we fought the battle of Gettysburg. I have no fear of the result, my only fear is that the enemy may escape before we can bring them to an engagement.... Lee's army defeated and scattered and the rebellion is ended.

Yesterday we had rain. Providence seems determined to keep the Potomac high, which is favorable to us....

Pleasant Valley (near)
Brownsville Md.
July 16th, 1863

You will have learned ere this reaches you that I am still safe, because the expected battle did not take place. Gen. Lee escaped with his army across the river. I can scarcely think that Gen Meade is excusable for permitting him to escape yet I trust all is for the best. It is doubtful if Meade could have whipped Lee, & since it is ascertained that a passage across the Potomac was effected by Lee, I think that Meade exercised a just prudence in not attacking him.

Many think that the last great battle of the war has been fought, & that further fighting would be merely a useless shedding of blood. Our victories in the west are complete. If Chattanooga has been abandoned by the rebels, then indeed is the war near its close.... I am now convinced the war will end in Virginia. It is the only place in which they have an effective army and it is now much reduced and dispirited.

But what of New York. It would be strange if the rebellion would <u>end</u> in <u>New</u> <u>York</u>. Some may regret the riot, but for one I am glad it occurred. Had it taken place two years ago we would now have been at peace....

Camp (near) Hillsboro Va
July 18th, 1863

Again we are treading the "Sacred Soil of Virginia." I hope our army shall never again go north until it disbands to go home, and I think it never will. I do not know any thing of present plans but our army is taking the same line of march it took last fall under McClellan. We got marching orders yesterday at 3 o'clock. We started for Harpers Ferry crossed the Potomac also the Shenandoah & passed to the East side of the Blue Ridge then took a direction almost due South along its Eastern slope. We halted at 10 o'clock but resumed the march at daylight this morning & reached here about noon and encamped for the day. We are now about midway between Harpers Ferry and Snickersville. To-morrow we will move forward again in the direction of the latter place.

...We have been marching mud ever since June 23rd when we left Gum Spring, Va.

I am just now waiting for this campaign to end. Perhaps it will not end until winter. Notwithstanding I still trust that I will be able to come home. I am better situated that I was when I last left for home, & I do not expect to find so much difficulty in getting a leave.

Woodgrove, Loudon Co. Va.
July 19th, 1863.

We marched five miles to-day and are in camp again for the night. Woodgrove is fifteen miles from Leesburg in the Piedmont valley. The town is located on a Cross Roads and consists of four or five houses. The inhabitants of the town are mostly rebels, in the country near are some Quaker non-combatants. We are stopping on a Quakers farm about a half mile from the town. This morning we stopped for a short time in the village at the residence of a man Headon two of whose sons were formerly in the rebel army. One, a captain, was discharged for drunkenness & the other is there still. We saw none of the family except some young girls, but they were bitter enough in sentiment. In order to provoke them we called a band and had the national airs. They listened to the Star Spangled Banner, for they said that it belonged as much to them as to us; but to Yankee Doodle they closed their ears. They were very brave, thought that Gen. Lee whipped us in Penn and would not believe in the fall of Vicksburg. Their boasted confederacy is almost extinct, but I presume they will deny its overthrow long after it has ceased to exist.

We expect an order from Corps Hd. Qrs. detailing officers to go to the states for Drafted men. I suppose within a month we will have a large army. Grant and Rosencranz will also have large armies then woe to the Southern Confederacy.

...Guerillas are very numerous here. They do not molest our column, but every straggler who ventures a half mile from the road never returns. A sergeant & a private of the Division Provost Guard were taken yesterday.

Upperville, Va
July 21^{st,} 1863

A glance at the date brings up thoughts of the past. A year ago to-day you stood beside me, & promised to be "loving & faithful." The beautiful remembrance is that you have nobly kept the promise....

July 22ⁿᵈ, 1863

I do not know what is the cause of our delay here, in fact no one seems to know.... I do not anticipate that [Gen. Lee] will soon attempt another invasion but I have no doubt that he will so manouvre as to reach the Rappahannock before we do, although we are much nearer than he is.

Our army must be reorganized before we can undertake a campaign against Richmond. Regiments are reduced to 200 & 100 men, & they must either be consolidated or filled up. Some I have no doubt will be filled up, but the number of conscripts called for now will not fill all of them. Penn. cannot I am sure fill half of her regiments.... The matter will end as it did last year, the details [sent to bring back conscripts] will return without men.

If the army is properly recruited and organized I have no doubt that the fighting will be ended this fall.

I lose my patience when I think of these things [the anti-draft riot in New York City] and I say to myself that a people who will elevate to a high public station a man like Gov. [Horatio] Seymour, & sustain a sheet like the New York Herald are fit subjects for the most debasing slavery. America has little to hope from the city of New York.

Camp (near) Warrenton,Va.
July 26ᵗʰ, 1863

On the 20ᵗʰ, the day on which I last wrote from Upperville, we moved to Piedmont & thence up the Manassas Gap to Linden Station 6 miles East of Front Royal. The next day we were ordered to move through the gap, but owing to our supports not coming up promptly we did not move until towards evening. We then advanced and had a slight skirmish driving the rebels a mile. Our Division and the Excelsior Brigade of the 2ⁿᵈ Div. were the only troops that took part in the affair. The rebels did not fight at all. They stood but a moment before our men then retreated. Our loss was about 120 killed and wounded. Lieut Preston of Pittsburg was killed. He was one of the Friend Rifles.

During the day the enemy's column could be seen moving rapidly down the Shenandoah valley. They were moving through Chester Gap in the morning, but about noon, when we threatened the road they were moving on, they turned their column towards Luray. Before this demonstration was made, the rebels had seemed disposed to remain in the Shenandoah valley, and even made feints towards turning to Maryland; but no sooner had they ascertained the whereabouts of Meades army than they turned towards Richmond. Ewells Corps which was in the rear barely escaped being cut off. I hope now that there will not be any more sensation stories in the Copperhead press, to the effect that Lee has been largely reinforced and is moving on Penn. again.

We are back again to the line of the Rappahannock. We left it on the 11ᵗʰ of June. What a history that army has made since then! As I predicted when we were here before and the rebels threatened an invasion of Penn., they have gained nothing but lost a great deal. Gen. Lee went forth from here a conqueror to conquer, he returns a fugitive flying for safety, his army scattered its spirit broken, its leader humbled. It will require several disastrous defeats to take from our army the prestige won at Gettysburg. I hope we can retain it.—

We lay in Manassas Gap during the night of the 23ʳᵈ, expecting to have a great battle with the rebels the next day. But in the morning, lo! The enemy as usual were gone. We then went as far as Front Royal, & having ascertained that their whole army had gone up the valley, we returned the same day to Piedmont. Yesterday, we moved to Cattail Run about 7 miles north of Warrenton & to-day (Sunday) we marched through Warrenton thence to this place, which is on the Warrenton & Sulphur Springs Road, about midway between Warrenton and the Springs. Our whole army is I think in the vicinity of this place. It is thought that we will halt here to receive our conscripts. If so we will be here a month. If we halt here a month, I shall make a desperate effort to get a leave....

I enclose you some flowers. These are from the garden of Chief Justice [John] Marshall, formerly of the Supreme Court of the U. S. He was one of the most celebrated American jurists. His residence was in Fauquier County near Piedmont. His grand son who owned the ... old homestead was a Colonel in the Confederate Army & was I believe killed at the battle of Gettysburg. The place is now occupied by a foreigner named Bartenstien. It has once been a beautiful place, but is now much neglected. It is known as "Oak Hill."—

July 28th, 1863

There has been no change in our position since I last wrote.... We are waiting here for supplies of clothing etc. Many of the men were near naked when we reached here. We received some clothing to day and will receive the rest to-morrow.... The main body of the rebel army has reached Culpepper, which places them nearer Fredricksburg than our army and consequently prevents us from gaining that place by marching. As we are not strong enough to take it by fighting I presume we will again have to halt on the Rappahannock to recruit.

...As the rebel army is past recruiting and ours is not I hope that before the 1st of January we will has [sic] subdued the Confederacy.

I have been thinking lately that I will soon be mustered out of service. There is not a sufficient number of men to be drafted in Penn to fill one half of the regiments now in the field, and as those regiments whose officers are influential politicians will be filled first and ours is not one, I conclude that it will have to be consolidated, in which event I will be mustered out. No particular effort is being made to keep up our regimental organization hence I think it will [be] broken up.

Leaves from the gardens of former Chief Justice John Marshall. His estate, "Oak Hill" was in Farquier County, Virginia (courtesy Allegheny College).

Warrenton Sulphur Springs Va.
July 31st, 1863

This evening finds us about 3 miles in advance of our former position at the place above mentioned. We moved to-day [at] 4 P.M. I believe it is the intention to halt us here for a while. We have a splendid place for Hd. Qrs. This was once a place of resort for a large crowd judging from the accomodation for visitors. The largest Hotel however has been burnt. It was burned last July when ... forces occupied this place whether by accident or design I have not learned.

There are two springs bath houses etc., every arrangement seems to have been complete. One of the Springs is clean, & untouched the other to-gether with the bath house & every accomodation almost have been destroyed.

Aug. 3rd, 1863

I do not know yet whether my wishes in regard to going home will be gratified....

The health of our army is very good. Our long marches instead of creating sickness have done the men good, and now that they are clothed, they look very well. Our regiments, however are terribly reduced, and we need the conscripts before we attempt further operations. Considering the sneers of the North I think the army of the Potomac has done very well this summer. This army has always been undervalued, and the disasters caused by its brainless leaders have been attributed to a want of courage in the men. We have outlived this slander, and have triumphed over the misfortunes sent to us by the imbecility of the President.

...I have no faith in the virtue of the North & its rulers, but the obstinacy of the South inspires hope. The subserviency of this people to the slave power is most thorough and most debasing. It would end in our own ruin were we not driven to extremes by this same power.

Aug. 6th, 1863

I am ... compelled to defer my visit home for the present, because I would not ask a leave while there is so much to do in the office. My work only begins when we halt, and I will have as much as I can do until the 25th of this month.... I fear that my visit home this summer can not take place.... [I] feel thankful that I was spared when so many others perished. But for what have I been spared — the future alone will tell.

Aug. 7th, 1863

[Sardis Duff] tells me that he is orderly Sergeant and that some of the men that did not vote for him curse him whenever he details them. So, so, such is the service, and Sardis will have to pluck up courage to bear it. The Position of Orderly Sergeant is a very difficult one to fill, and if Sardis fills it with any kind of satisfaction he will do very well. His regiment the 57th prevented [Confederate John Hunt] Morgan from crossing the river. Bravely done for the militia, they may congratulate themselves that they did not have any more to do.—

...[The renomination of Andrew Curtin for governor — which Duff strongly opposed] looks towards the support of the present administration, and the renomination of Lincoln. Look out for squalls.

The army is quiet every where even in Charleston. It is not to be wondered at that after such a succession of victories our armies remain quiet a little while.... Our regiment looks to Pittsburg to have its ranks filled. The officers we sent for conscripts are at their homes I understand enjoying themselves. I fear they will not exert themselves sufficiently to do any good....

August 8th, 1863

I only know that since [the war] began God has united us, and I trust it may end ere He separates us. The future is in His hands.... Although I do not feel as you do, yet I can trust God, and patiently endure every day's burdens and trials. The feeling of confidence in Him we have in common, and what ever other differences may exist, I know that it is good that we have loved....

Aug. 11th, 1863

Every thing is quiet in our army. Camps are all arranged for a stay of some weeks & the Inspector General's Department is busy over hauling every thing, which keeps me busy. Our army was running for 7 weeks without having time to stop for repairs consequently it is a good deal out of order. Things will be right I hope ... before this month closes.

The weather here is extremely warm. We can find no place to be comfortable....

...I [have] been several times just on the point of writing for a uniform & should do so now but it is stated that the uniform coat has been dispensed with by orders and a jacket, something like the Austrian Huzzar Jacket has been substituted. This will make our army look rather odd for a little while. The jacket will suit a man of my proportions very well, but on a tall man it will cut a sorry figure. This will be one good improvement, the uniform will not be so much like a civilians dress; neither will it be cumbersome, altogether I think it a wholesome improvement.

Aug. 12th, 1863

I could never belong to any [political] party, because I cannot always support the measure adopted by the party. I must exercise the right of private judgment more than is allowable under such a regime....

Every thing is very dull hereabouts. The scouts of the two armies occasionally have a "scrimmage" in Culpepper County. Beyond this nothing is doing here. A few conscripts, or rather substitutes, have arrived in the 5th Corps. They soon begin to come I presume in large numbers. I fear that the officers who went for ours are not active enough to succeed in filling our regiment. Of the two you met, [Alexander H.] Mitchel is quite intelligent, but he has not the experience to fit him for a recruiting officer. [William] <u>Kimple</u> (not Kelly) is too dumb to know any thing or too stupid to do any thing.

Aug. 14th, 1863

We have a good many visitors of all kinds here, but I have little time to enjoy them & less inclination. Most of them are Staff Officers of the rowdy style & I do not ... mix with them.

Aug. 15th, 1863

I glean from the Herald of yesterday that there is trouble brewing in New York and my impression is that if Lincoln stands firm he will have a collision with the Gov. of New York. If this takes place the secessionists of New York will get a taste of the loyalty of the Army of the Potomac.... I am gratified to think that we may yet get an opportunity to hang Gov. Seymour & a few other traitors....

August 17th, 1863

The Southern Confederacy is dead. The question of its existence is no longer debatable. The question which now arises is can we destroy slavery? If we can not then blood of this nation has been shed in vain. The President I think will stand firm & with Stanton to support him I do not fear the influence of the rest of the Cabinet....

Aug. 18th, 1863

Troops still continue to leave our army for Alexandria. They are shipping the Western troops from us as fast as they can transport them ... surely they are going to reinforce one of the Western armies. There are a good many Western troops in our army, and its numbers will be greatly reduced when they are removed. This looks as though the campaign from this point against Richmond has been abandoned. I do not think that any thing is lost by abandoning it.

Capt. Hamilton of our regiment who has just returned from Washington says that people now speak well of the Army of the

Flower from Hd Qrs/ 1st Div., 3rd Corps, Warrenton Sulphur Springs. August 1863 (courtesy Allegheny College).

Potomac. It is time as I have said before that justice be done to our army. Its day of disaster is past.

...Give love to all, and remember, Hattie, that your husband longs for the moment when he may receive you in his arms and kiss you. My dear good loving wife.

Aug. 22nd, 1863

We are to have a review of the Division to-day by Gen. Birney. Our Div. is very small now, numbering only 2800 men for line of battle. But we are getting stronger every day. We are receiving a great many convalescents and expect to receive a great many conscripts.

There is nothing new in army movements except that the celebrated Moseby [Confederate partisan leader John Singleton Mosby] has been reconnoitering our fortifications around Washington. Did you ever hear tell of a more impudent man than he? and did you ever know or read of a country where they permitted a gang like his to run at large so long. If our cavalry cannot catch him the President had better call on [James M.] Shackelford's militia.

...Remember your husband

August 24th, 1863

We had a little excitement here yesterday. A drunken officer threw a dog into the spring. As we have a guard over it of course he was reported. Two of our staff-officers who were with him were placed in arrest, as a warning not too keep such company. The matter was explained to be an accident (every thing is accidental you know)....

...I hope you will take better heart. I was never in better health never better situated, never had finer prospects. I can see no reason for your despondency. Your disappointment [that Duff did not take leave to return home] is very great but I hope you will take heart & not permit it to trouble you.

Aug. 26, 1863

Our conscripts come in slowly. We have received none in this Division, a few have been received in the 3rd Corps, & five are to be shot on Friday for desertion. There seems to be some vigor in the administration. I am glad to observe that it is no longer frightened at the disloyal party at the north, and that their policy is free from its influence.

Aug. 27th, 1863

The present war will be followed by a greater development of the west than took place in our years of peace and trade of all kinds will be increased.—

How does the draft come on in Copperhead Clarion. It comes on well in other parts of the country. New York submits but with a very bad grace. My wish with regard to her has not been gratified. I had hoped that Gov. Seymour would have attempted to resist the draft by force and given the President an opportunity to hang him; but he was either too wary or too cowardly & has avoided the difficulty. Henceforth we shall have no more riots in the North.—

We are to receive a small detachment of conscripts this evening for what regiment I have not learned. They are for a Maine regiment I believe. We will tame the fellows when we get them here. But few of them will get away when they once get into the army.—

Aug. 31st, 1863

The weather is still pleasant. The army is quiet. The 5 conscripts were shot as directed on Saturday. There was a large crowd of officers to witness the execution not many from our division.

I am still quite well....

Sept. 2nd, 1863

There are no indications of early advance here. Gen. Meade on receiving his sword a few days since hinted that it had come too late. Many here have the impression that the army of the Potomac will not undertake another campaign. But I can not look upon our affairs in that light. There is work to be done yet, and especially work to be done by the army of the Potomac. If the conscripts are not sent on more rapidly than they are sending them at present we will not get started this fall until it is too late to do much....

Sept. 3rd, 1863

This morning finds all things in statu quo, except some of our Staff, who are slightly excited. Last evening at dinner two Generals of the 2nd Div. were here to-gether with their respective Staffs. As usual the Staff took a little too much and became noisy, so much so that the General had to stop the noise. He has ordered the Officer of the Day to report in writing the cause of the disturbance and every one is on the qui vive to know what will be the report. It is thought probably that some one or two may be sent away. The matter does not interest me any further than as a spectator. I can generally manage to avoid these rows. Of late they have been quite frequent, and Birney's Staff will soon have an une[n]viable reputation.

Lt. Bullard, Gen. Graham's A.d.C. who was wounded at Gettysburg, returned yesterday. He reports that Gen. Graham was heard from as late at the 22nd ult. and that his wounds were healing but he was very thin and in poor spirits. He is a man of very little physical strength and a few months prison life may take his life. Great efforts are being made to exchange him but to no avail. If it be true that the Rebel chiefs have called or are about calling out 500,000 negroes, I presume ere long we will have a general exchange.

Gen. Sickles is expected back on the 8th or soon thereafter.[2] There is a good deal [of] feeling in the Corps against Gen. French and Sickles coming will be hailed with joy. I presume we shall then lose French and his Division, at least such is the rumor now. It wont be much of a loss to us. His Division is now smaller than ours and untried at that, and it is no great addition of strength to the Corps.

While the armies in Virginia lay quiet, political battles in the North heated prior to the fall election. The valiant effort of Black soldiers at Fort Wagner in July encouraged those who supported the Emancipation Proclamation and endorsed the notion of service in the army by former slaves. Copperheads and others argued that the war should not be over the fate of Negroes, and some even campaigned against the "danger" of Negro equality. Lincoln responded with a public letter written August 26 that extolled the heroic efforts of Black troops. Democrats hoped to make great inroads in the Republican majority in Congress and especially to take control of Pennsylvania and Ohio. They failed in reaching any of these goals, as soldiers furloughed by the administration to vote at home resoundingly supported the Republicans and the war. In September Union General Rosecrans forced the Rebels from Chattanooga but then suffered a tactical defeat at Chickamauga Creek. His army was trapped and under siege in the town until relieved two months later.

Sept. 5th, 1863

Last night was cold, so cold as to make my simple bed uncomfortable.... I have writing enough to do to keep me occupied all day, so I will remain at home.

In fact I am obliged to remain, for I lost my horse yesterday. My colored man let my horse loose yesterday to graze & he strayed off to-gether with four others belonging to the staff.[3] Mine was a very fine animal, I am sorry to have lost him, but as he is in the army I hope to find him again. Having but one I am dismounted. I shall get another before long.

Our army still remains quiet. The taking of the Gunboats [on the Potomac] did not give rise to any trouble on any other portion of the line than where they were found and consequently we have not been disturbed. The conscripts arrive very slowly and I fear we will be delayed here some time yet....

The Presidents Letter occasions very little talk here. It is nothing more than the army expected. Unlike the people, the army never doubted that the president would adhere to his present policy. We have settled down to war, and we do not hope much less desire that this struggle be ended in any other way. The New York Herald sees in the Presidents letter a desire to conciliate the South. What motives or what words cannot the Herald misconstrue. I am glad to note one thing. This paper is losing a portion of its circulation and consequently a portion of its influence since the issuing of Gen. Meade's late order requiring the News Boy to bring any paper that may be called for. Previous to the issuing of that order, if you ask[ed] for any other paper than the Herald, you were told that none came. This excuse will not answer now.

"Doctor" Melton. This contraband slave played a key role in Duff's life, first as a paid servant during the war and then as a household assistant in later years. Duff saw to it that he was always well dressed, even if the first suit Duff ordered for Melton was stolen (courtesy Allegheny College).

Sept. 6th, 1863

There is to be a review of the corps, and our Division will have to march 6 miles to the review ground. In consequence we will have to start early and will not get back until late in the day.

I have seen a list of men drafted in Clarion Co. Although it touched the Copperheads lightly in the Boro. in some of the townships it did them justice. It may happen that we will get these men in our regiment, for it will draw from that District. Send them along we can take care of them. We have recd. no conscripts in our Division. We have been expecting some from Maine for two weeks....

Sept. 11th, 1863

We have good news this evening. The evacuation of Morris Island and Chattanooga. This ends the rebellion in the West and it will not be long ere it ends in the East. Gen. Lee still confronts us here, but his army has neither strength nor spirit. If our army is judiciously handled when we next advance from here we may not be compelled to fight another battle on the Rappahannock. It crossed we can lay siege to Richmond and shell Lee out as [Quincy Adams] Gilmore is doing with Charleston. This war cannot last much longer. We may have our fears, but in my solemn thoughtful moments I think it impossible for the rebels to regain a tithe of what they have lost. In the course of a month or so English pirates may seriously damage our commerce but I hope that soon we will be able to chastise that perfidious nation. We will just be strong enough and mad enough too for a foreign war when we have finished the rebellion.

The rumors of Lee's advance are all very foolish. There is no danger of an advance from him now. Our army is stronger than his now and is gaining strength every day. The draft will produce quite a number of soldiers although the large majority of those drafted will be exempted.

I am quite well and in good spirits as usual. You asked me some time since to tell you if I thought I could come home this month. I am sorry that I can give you a definite answer. No leave of absence can be obtained now....

Sept. 12th, 1863

[P.S.] I send you a blue-bell & rose bud taken from the ruins, a kiss on the rose-bud....

Sept. 13th, 1863

Doubtless you recognize the date, if you do not permit me to say that it is the 13th day of September our common <u>birth</u> <u>day</u>. I have thought of my good wife to-day and wished her by my side but all in vain....

I have some news of army movements. Yesterday our Cavalry started on a reconnaissance towards Culpepper. They only got to Hazel River about seven miles South of this when they were stopped by the rebels. This morning they began skirmish with them and kept it up pretty much all day. For a short time about noon the cannonading was quite brisk. We have not yet heard the result of the affair, but I think that our cavalry did not gain any thing, as the cannonading did not seem to recede. As the firing ceased some time before night, it is probable that our forces withdrew. These are only conjectures based on the sound of the cannon. We will no doubt hear the result to-morrow....

Sept. 14th 1863

We have good news this morning. The Cavalry reconnaissance has been heard from. The rebels were driven out of Culpepper with the loss of 3 pieces of artillery. The firing was so distinctly heard here that I did not think it so far away as Culpepper. What information has been gained of the whereabouts and movements of the rebel army I have not learned. Many think that the rebel army has left our front....

Clarion
Sept 14th 1863

My dear husband.

How large a portion of life must be spent in learning what life is.... Not many lives, brief as yours have been so eventful — and I know you are better satisfied than if the passing days were spent in office work. Every dispensation of providence contains a blessing....

Hattie

Sulphur Springs, Va.
Sept. 14th, 1863

To day we received orders to be ready to move at a moments notice.... Precisely what the movement will be I cannot say, but it will be forward and may involve a battle. I suppose it has been ascertained to a certainty that a portion of Lee's army has gone to reinforce Johnson, and in consequence of this loss to Lee Gen. Meade thinks himself strong enough to attack him. I have not much fear of the result our army is in good trim and spirits and will make a good fight. They will fight too with more confidence than ever before because they now think themselves more than a match for the rebels.

...It is thought by many that we are not going to fight the rebels but that we are to confront them and keep them on the alert to prevent reinforcements being sent to other parts.

In Harpers Weekly for Sept. 19th 1863 you will find a sketch of our Hd. Qrs. Our tents are in one rank or row just in front of the ruins of the large hotel. The third tent from the right (as you look at the picture) or the one just on the right of the group of three [in front of] the ruins is Major Duff's. Unfortunately the artist omitted to sketch the tent. He only gives the fly which is in front, the tent was in rear of that. The picture of the spring is life like. I received a note from Boobyer yesterday stating that he had sent me a uniform suit by express the cost of which is $59....

Fox's Ford Va

Sept. 16th, 1863

We left the Springs at 5 o'clock and came to this place which is just 3 miles below on the river. This morning I believe we are to move to Freeman's Ford 5 miles below here & then await events.

A general forward movement at present is not yet determined. Our reconnaissances have been pushed to the Rapidan & the rebels have appeared to dispute our crossing. The 2nd Corps is in Culpepper or perhaps nearer the Rapidan. It is intended to attempt to cross with that Corps and the Cavalry to-day & the rest of the army is concentrated to aid them in case a battle should ensue.... Should it turn out that the rebel army is still intact on the South bank of the Rapidan, then most probably we will return to our camps again. But should it be discovered that their army has been diminished, then we will attack them & try to go forward — the bugle blows for the advance & I must close....

Camp 4 Miles South of Culpepper Va

Sept. 17th 1863

We left Fox's Ford yesterday morning just as I closed my letter about ½ past six o'clock. We marched to Freeman's Ford 4 miles south, forded the Hedgemon River, took a direction towards Culpepper, crossed the Southern River at Welfords mill, then taking a South westerly direction passed Culpepper on the West (leaving it about a mile to the left) & reached our present position at 7 o'clock. We had some supper lay down & slept & were awakened this morning just before daylight by the sound of bugles & drums etc. We were ready to march at six o'clock, but it is seven & we have not yet marched. To-days march will not be a long one.

I cannot tell the situation this morning. Our whole army is here: The sixth corps on the right, the third next, the 2nd next, the 5th next, & the rest of the line I do not know, the cavalry is in our front on the Rapidan I understand, which is 12 miles from here. It was whispered yesterday through officials that the rebel army was recrossing the Rapidan to attack us, but this is not probable. Their policy is to await our attack. There was some cannonading yesterday across the river on the left of Culpepper but I have not heard the result. Nothing of moment occurred. It is very quiet this morning, the fog is very thick, we will not move until it rises. From what I can learn it is not Meade's intention to attack the enemy at present but to take a strong position here and hold it....

We passed yesterday near Brandy Station the residence of Dr. Welford a noted & wealthy secessionist. He abandoned his property & went to Danville South Carolina some time since. His house is occupied by an overseer named Yancey. His wife gave us a doleful description of the condition of the chivalry. She dwelt especially on the fact that Dr. Welford had abandoned every thing except his "Tar pot niggers." These were the last things he would abandon & instead of being a profit to him now they are a burden. If Dr. Welfords condition is that of his class, then the South are poor indeed. Their only property now is human souls & bodies, and under present circumstances such property requires more to keep it alive than it can produce, so that in a short time slavery will fall of itself for the slave-holders will be obliged to turn their slaves loose to feed. I have observed several instances of this lately.

Jef. Davis may enlist or conscript into his army as many Negroes as he wants, but he can never enlist the sympathies of their race, or convince them that they are more friendly to them than the North. I am well satisfied that he will never venture in such an experiment.

I send you a rose from Dr. Welford's residence. It is the spot where what is called the Beverly Ford Fight occurred on the 9th of June last. I send you a kiss with them....

Stone-house Mountain, Va.
Sept. 20th, 1863

Seated before the fire this evening (for it is as cool as to make a fire very comfortable) along with Capt. Markle ... [I thought] how strange it is that I can enjoy nothing without you. You are a part of my existence and only with you can I be happy.

...I can afford to be patient for another eleven months. Even should it be necessary for me to return to the field again I will stay at home long enough to have a happy time with Harriet.

I enclose you a picture of Col. McKnight. Although latterly I did not much admire the man, his life is intimately connected with my history and for this reason I cherish his memory. Whatever may have been his faults as a man, no one questioned his ability as an officer. He went into battle with a foreboding of his fate, but died as bravely as ever man died on the field....

Sept. 21st, 1863

This evening we have an order to prepare to march immediately with 3 days rations in the haversack and 5 days in the knapsack. This is Hookers old order just before crossing the Rappahannock before the defeat of Chancellorsville. It is probable that we are about to undertake a like expedition. It is to be hoped that it may be more successful. What is likely to be [the] plan of operations I have not the least idea, but it is no doubt intended to attempt to turn the flank of the rebel army. Rosecranz is now fighting, we shall soon be fighting and our cause will either go back a year, or the rebellion will be entirely crushed.... [Rosecrans] is one of our greatest soldiers, and I have unbounded confidence in his success.

I have been working hard in the office all day and am quite tired.... We are about to enter another long & dangerous campaign. Many times you will be long without word from your absent loved one. The issue of all things is in his hands your country's success, your husband's life, your own happiness. Let us await this decision with faith and patience. Whatever may happen to me my Hattie will be taken care of.

Sept. 22nd, 1863

There is restless feeling and subdued excitement in our army but every thing is yet quiet....

The opinion is general here that another great battle will not be fought in Virginia. I cannot coincide with it. Our army to be sure is overwhelming in numbers, but then there are some fine defensive position[s] between here and Richmond where a small defensive army might hold a large offensive one at bay. A few weeks will determine the matter.

Sept. 23rd, 1863

Every thing has been quiet today.... We are now ready for a long march, the enemy (at least such is the general belief) is weak, the weather is good and the army is in good spirits then why not advance? Those who now know more concerning the enemy than I can answer the question.

The latest news from Gen. Rosecrans is bad.... I think that Gen. Rosecrans is our best soldier and I am reluctant to give up my idol. He has never yet met with a single disaster, and I shall be much disappointed if his brilliant strategy by which he gained Chattanooga is not followed by a decisive victory which will settle forever the fate of Tennessee and Kentucky. Long live the army of the Cumberland and its noble Commander.

Sept. 25th, 1863

But why does this army remain quiet. I can not understand why it is that Meade does not attack Lee. It may be as some suggest that the rebels are about evacuating Virginia but I do not believe it. We will have to fight them here yet and drive them out of this. The season for military operation is fast leaving us & by & by we shall be in the mud. Then we will have to delay until next June by which time a world of things may happen. I am not disposed to grumble but it seems to me that now is the time to strike an affective and decisive blow.

Sept. 26th, 1863

I do not feel unwell except the slight head-ache which I think is caused by the cold. I hope to be well to-morrow as I expect to have a little intellectual rest. For two days past I have been very busy making up reports & to-day I was engaged in a court martial defending an officer accused of dis-obedience of orders. This is the second case I have had since coming to the army. I have another on hand for Monday, if in the mean time we do not move.

...Everyone thinks the army should move immediately, but no one knows when it will move.

Sept. 29th, 1863

I was pleased to read your remarks on the late fashions.... What a fine thing this war has been in many respects. It has taught us self reliance & from being self reliant in the stern contests of life we have come to consider every thing of our own the best. We are about being Americanized. We have a country, people & government that have a history. Henceforth an American will be the representative of something besides a contemptible aristocracy.

Oct. 1st, 1863

...The 1st and 3 Corps are much stronger than the 11th & 12th, both in numbers and prestige.... Our corps is said to be the strongest in the army numbering 15000 effective men (Infantry). Our corps & I may say the whole army is getting many conscripts convalescents and deserters every day.

...I might as well answer Rachel's question. Gen. Meade is not what may be called an intemperate man. He however uses liquor constantly at the table & to entertain his friends etc. I have heard officer[s] say that they saw him drunk & others say that he never gets drunk, and I think the latter assertion the more truthful. He does not look like a man that drinks to excess.

October 2nd, 1863

To-day has been a dismal one. Some time before day light, it began to rain and has continued all day. Fortunately I have a good tent and it has not been incumbent on me to go out....

...I am glad to observe that the government is taking steps to punish the two generals who virtually lost us the battle of Chickamauga. [Alexander M.] McCook and [Thomas L.] Crittenden have been relieved from their command, & ordered to Indianapolis. I hope they may be punished as they deserve, for I think that our defeat is in a great measure due to their blundering. Rosecranz will fight a better battle the next time he fights. His army had been too long without a battle. It had undoubtedly become some what demoralized before the battle. This demoralization will be removed, by vigorous & strict discipline in camp & the army will go forth to better success than defeat.

Oct. 3rd, 1863

There is nothing new in army movements.... From an order received to-day I judge they are about to begin the reorganization of the army. They are endeavoring to get the 3 year troops to re-enlist for 3 years from this date making their term five years in all. The[y] are offering $400 bounty and an opportunity to go home. I have not yet heard how many will re-enlist but I think not many. The administration will have to conscript in order to get an army.

Oct. 8th, 1863

We have had a little stir here to-day. This morning early we received orders to be ready to march at a moments notice. From the tenor of the orders we judged that an attack was apprehended. During the day Gen. Birney received an intimation from an official source that the expected attack might be made on the right flank, the position he holds. A patrol was immediately sent out, which has just returned after having been to Hazel River (six miles). No enemy was seen or heard of. If Gen. Lee desires to attack the army of the Potomac I am very willing he should do so. I am satisfied that on a fair field we can whip him although we may not be strong enough to drive him from his entrenched line on the Rappahannock. Our army now has 80000 fighting men. I know it is generally underestimated at the North. You can rely upon the above figures.—

...I am sure my letters are very poor, for I never take the trouble to hunt up an[d] chronicle facts further than they affect myself. Had I begun earlier I might have written a very fair history of the army of the Potomac, but it is too late to begin now as I do not take the care I might to write interesting letters.

Camp 2 miles west of Culpepper
Oct. 11th 1863

Yesterday at 10 o'clock we received an order to put the troops under arms & form a line of battle facing west up the Sperryville Turnpike as if expecting an attack from that direction. We had not got into position before we received an order to form a ½ mile back near Culpepper & on the right hand side of the Turnpike. This done we were immediately ordered to the left of the Turnpike so as to connect our line with the 5th Corps and the 2nd came in on our right....

In the afternoon it was ascertained that there were very slight grounds of apprehension of an attack. In the morning our cavalry outposts on the Robertson river in the direction of Madison C. H. had been driven in, but the[y] returned to the fray & drove back the rebels & re-established their line. In the evening it is said that the rebels again drove in our out-posts and crossed the river with some force. It is said that A. P. Hills Corps is gradually working round our right.

Immediately after dark last evening our trains were ordered back to Bealeton, & this morning we are expecting to receive an order to go back also. Nothing has been heard of the enemy this morning.... From indications it is not presumed that Meade will fight here.... I think judging from the maneuvers that neither army desires to fight....

Freemans Ford, Hedgemon River, Va
3.20 P.M. Oct. 12th, 1863

You will observe that we have changed position. The movement began at 9 A.M. yesterday morning & ended by our arrival here at 2 A.M. this morning. The army retired from Culpepper without any difficulty except the Cavalry which retired along the rail-road & was attacked at Brandy Station & I believe badly used. The rebels at one time had our cavalry force cut in two parts, but it was reunited with some loss. Everything was quiet this morning. At noon we received an order to be ready [to] move immediately, stating as a cause for the order that an attempt was to be made to reoccupy Brandy Station, & the commanding General believes that the attempt may bring on a general engagement. Up to this hour there has been considerable firing in the direction of Brandy Station, but we have not yet received further orders. There has also been some firing on our right, in the direction of Waterloo, but what it is I do not know. So the situation is at present there is a good deal of noise and very little execution.— Here comes your letter of the 9th — I must stop to read it....

Centreville, Va.
10 P.M. Oct. 14th, 1863

I have been too busy to write, besides no mail has left our Corps for 2 days past.

You have heard that Meades army has been flanked and is falling back on Washington. It is now back at least to a point where the army is safe & Washington also.... On the afternoon of Monday the 12th our army was lying along the Rappahannock, the right at Freemans Ford, the left at Kelly's Ford, & the main body of Lee's army was south of the Rappahannock on the Warrenton Turnpike. We had a brigade of Cavalry guarding the bridge at Sulphur Springs where the Pike crosses the Rappahannock. About four o'clock of Monday the rebels advanced to the bridge at Sulphur Springs drove our Cavalry away & immediately began a rapid advance Northward on the Turnpike. This movement put them on our flank we were obliged to fall back or attack. The former was determined upon.

On Tuesday morning the army was put in motion. The trains on the road East of the Railroad, the 6th 1st & 5th Corps along the railroad, the 3rd & 2nd Corps on the first road west of the Railroad. The rebels you will recollect were on the Warrenton Turnpike. Nothing of moment occurred until the head of our column reached Auburn, the point where the road leading from Warrenton to Catletts crosses the one we were marching along. Here we met two Brigades of rebel Cavalry, immediately attacked them & drove them away — they retreating toward Warrenton. We reached Greenwich about 9 P.M. & camped & the 2nd Corps camped at Auburn.... This morning at daylight we again started forward turning to the Right at Greenwich on the road to Bristow Station. You will observe this would unite the two columns, but I am anticipating. At daylight this morning the 2nd Corps was attacked at Auburn but they repulsed the attacking party after an hours fight. What the loss was I know not. Every thing was quiet again until one o'clock when the rear of our two columns had reached Bristow Station and crossed Broad Run. The rebels again appeared with artillery & made a vigorous attack. The 2nd & 3rd Corps were at this [point] & gave them a handsome reception. I have not learned the particulars but I know that our forces held their ground. The fight continued all afternoon principally with artillery. I do not think the loss on either side was great. Our army is now concentrated at this point, the 6th Corps at Chantilly to prevent a flank movement. The rebel army is in our front. I have no idea what will occur next. The general impression here is that Lee will not fight [a] general battle....

Fairfax Station, Va.
Oct. 16th, 1863

Yesterday our Corps was ordered to this place & Union Mills, the 1st Division being here. Nothing particular has transpired in military matters since day before yesterday except that the rear of our train has come up & we are now out of danger. We will remain here until the intentions of the enemy are made known to us by some further [movement]. It is not expected that he will attack us in our present position. Indeed many think that we were frightened away from the Rappahannock by a small force. The only portion of the rebel army we have yet found is Stuarts Cavalry and Ewells Corps, in all probably 40,000. If any larger army is in pursuit of us it has not yet been discovered....

...I have been up nearly all night & do not feel very bright this morning. I am stationed at the telegraph office to receive dispatches and I find it a very noisy place.... I send you a kiss,

Camp near Fairfax Station, Va.
October 17th, 1863

I am oppressed with a feeling of loneliness. The same I used to have before I was married.... I pass many bitter moments, which might be made happy by your presence. Before I loved I had a consciousness that some thing was wanting to complete my life. How many evenings I have sat at home in solitude and longed for a heart to communicate with mine. At last I found one to whom I could confide all, but a cruel fate tore me away from her.... My life has changed so much since I loved you, it seems as though I am living, before I could hardly say that I knew what life was....

Oct. 18th. All is quiet this morning no indication of a move. Yesterday it was ascertained that the enemy had left our front. Whither he had gone was not definitely ascertained.... Gen. Sickles arrived here day before yesterday he was enthusiastically received by our Division. He reviewed the 2nd Div. yesterday and immediately returned to Washington. Before leaving he reported to Meade for duty, but Meade beg[ged] of him not to insist on doing duty alleging that his health would not permit. Of course there are other reason[s] why Meade did not wish him to take command of the Corps but ill health was a good excuse to set him aside. This transaction will probably create some talk....

October 18th, 1863

I can rejoice with you over the result in Penn.... For curiosity look at Woodwards majorities in Adams York & Fulton counties. One would imagine that having been ravaged by the chivalry they would no long give them support & sympathy. But such is not the case. Their conduct can be explained only in one way namely that they are disloyal. The (our) army after having passed through those counties, said the people were as mean as the Virginians and I was forced to admit the truth of the assertion. In Maryland our army found much sympathy in Pennsylvania none.... It is very evident that Mason & Dixon's line is not the line between loyalty & disloyalty.

Gen. Sickles has not yet taken command of the army, because probably (I know of no other reason) Meade has not been removed. Gen. Sickles is here to-night much to the astonishment of all, he rode into camp on horseback. He says he is going to report to army Hd. Qrs. to-morrow for mounted duty. There is more in this than you imagine.... He reviewed the 2nd Div. today & made a speech in which he threw down the glove to Meade. In the course of his speech he remarked that he would take command of his Corps in a few days. He said that it had been suggested to him that he was too much disabled to take the command at present, but he thought he was the best judge of this matter & should act on his own judgment. This was a direct slap at Meade....

Morning Oct. 19th. We move this morning at 6 o'clock to Bristow Station. This indicates that the enemy has again retreated. Kiss me my Hattie.

9

On the Rapidan

Camp 2 miles South of Greenwich, Va.
Oct. 20th, 1863

This morning at 6 we moved forward [from Bristoe Station] under orders to go to Buckland Mills ... almost due west of Bristoe. Gen. [H.V.] Kilpatrick had reconnoitered the country yesterday & found the enemy at Buckland Mills it was supposed in force & thither we moved to attack him. But long before our column reached there the enemy had left & our column kept on towards Warrenton....

From all the information we have been able to get the rebel army is again beyond the Rappahannock. Their whole army was as far North as Bristoe Station, but left there on Sunday last.... It does not seem to have been their intention to seek a battle but only to drive us back destroy the railroad & gain time by delay for movements in some other portion of the Confederacy. From Bristoe Station to the Rappahannock I presume that they have so effectually destroyed the railroad that it will require at least 2 weeks to build it. They have torn up the track burnt the ties & bent the rails. The road will require new ties new rails & will have to be ballasted anew. The thoroughness with which they destroyed the railroad convinces me that Lee seeks rather to delay our operations than to make campaigns of his own....

Oct. 21st. We are ordered to march to Catletts Station this morning 7 miles from here. This point is 37 miles west of Washington....

Camp (near) Catletts St. Va.
Oct. 22nd, 1863

We arrived here yesterday a little after noon & encamped on the Brentville road a mile from the Station. We are to remain here until the railroad is built and to assist in building it. A detail of 1800 men from the Corps is ordered for to-morrow....

...Gen. Meade is ordered to seek the enemy and give him battle so says to-days Chronicle, and he will move forward as fast as the railroad can be finished. Gen. Meade has lost a great opportunity, one that he will not again have this winter. If he wishes to fight he will have to attack the rebels in their fortifications on the Rapid Ann, and success is doubtful in such an enterprise.

What do you think of the removal of Rosecranz. None here can understand it. Not a word can be said against his actual successor Grant, but the great question why he was removed cannot be answered. I am cruelly disappointed if he has done or omitted anything to merit his removal. I have always considered him Grant's superior, and I am yet unwilling to give up my opinion. The people may have great faith in the military abilities of the administration but when they know as well as I do how miserably this army has been handled they will learn to doubt the policy of some of their appointments.

Duff as a soldier (courtesy Allegheny College).

Oct. 23rd, 1863

There is nothing new in army matters. It is announced in to-days Washington Chronicle that three weeks will be required to finish the railroad and that the army cannot move before it is finished. This is equivalent to saying that the fall campaign is over and that the mission of the army of the Potomac for the next six months is ended. So be it, we can not expect any better from such leaders.

Oct. 24th, 1863

I have not been bothered much to-day; on the other hand, it has required an effort to pass away the time. This morning when I arose & it was late too I was greeted by a cold drizzling rain. In camp such a rain makes every thing dismal. Thus the day began. After breakfast I retired to my tent, picked up the "Atlantic" and read the article entitled a "Letter to Carlyle".... It was a good answer to the many hard things England has been saying about us for the past two years. But the style of the essay appeared to me to be abominable. Such a verbose production.... I wish modern writers would change their style. In this day of peril and struggle we need not wordy but terse vigorous productions. I see very few books in these days that I can bear to read.... I took up her [Hattie's] letter ... then turned to my bible....

The 27th psalm was found and read. I committed to memory a portion of it, but my mind would wander from it. I could not feel an interest in it. I do not realize the immediate presence of the Lord, hence cannot read these verses with any feelings of humility and reverence.... I fancy I can see in it [the Bible] traces of human frailty and error, and this fancy robs the book of all divinity in my hands....

Oct. 25th, 1863

The days work is finished and although it is late I must write you a letter.

This morning the sun rose clear & bright. I took my breakfast late as usual, then sat down & read for a few moments after which I went out and inspected the ambulance train & rode through the camps. By this time lunch was ready for be it known we are fashionable here, we have <u>lunch</u> at 12 o'clock & dinner at 5. Lunch over I rode down towards Bristow Station to take a look at the railroad to see how the work of rebuilding it was progressing. I found that only two miles of the road had been rebuilt, but I was informed that after to-day, they would build it at the rate of a mile per day. At this rate it will require 5 days to complete it to Catletts Station and 20 days to complete it to the Rappahannock. This railroad will cost the U.S. $10,000 per mile or if rebuilt to the Rappahannock river $200,000. Rather a dear price to pay for Meade's out-generaling Lee. The railroad inspected I returned home, read the daily paper, which however contained no news, took dinner & stripped my table for work, for I had a weekly report to make. This has just been completed it is now ten o'clock and my eyes are growing tired. Consequently this letter must soon close.

It was rumored to-day on good authority that ere to-morrow night we will move to Bealton. The rumor I believe came from Corps Hd. Qrs. and is I believe true. I cannot for my part see the propriety of such a move just at present, for it will be two weeks before the

Railroad is completed to Bealton, and to go there now is to increase the distance to haul forage & subsistence without any corresponding gain. The move I am quite certain will be made in a few days if not to-morrow. —

Camp 2 miles East of Catletts Station Va.
Oct. 27th, 1863

Scarcely had I finished my letter of yesterday when we received an order to move. We got under way about 11 o'clock, but moved only two miles to Foulk House on Cedar Run. This morning at day-light we were ordered under arms to be ready to move at a moments notice. The old story of an apprehended attack as the excuse for the order. I am sorry to observe that the army is becoming a good deal demoralized by constant alarms. They are convinced that they are bamboozled day after day and their spirits are wearing out. I do not hope any thing from this army this fall. It will be too late ere we reach to the Rapidann for our strategic generals to do anything. — It was three o'clock before we got the position righted and Hd. Qrs. established. The night was very cold & before I could go to bed I had to warm myself so that by getting up at daylight I did not get more than an hours sleep. In consequence I did not feel bright when I arose this morning. As soon as I had Breakfast the Gen'l sent me to Corps. Hd. Qrs. to report. They were three miles distant and it was nearly noon before I returned. After lunch I lay down and tried to sleep but there was so much noise about that I was frequently disturbed. I slept till dinner, than had my dinner and read the papers. This did not require a long time, for there was nothing in the papers worthy of notice except an extract from a speech of Gen. Rosecranz at Cincinnati. I fear the removal of Rosecranz will prove to be a mistake. As yet I have been unable to discover the cause of his removal. He says in his speech that no such charges as those published in the papers have been made against him. It was immediately surmised after his removal was known here that he would be placed in command of this army. The publication against him of charges by the Washington Chronicle, the acknowledge[d] Administration organ led to the belief that he was removed for some blunder. These charges are not explained away. I await with curiosity the future developments.

Oct. 27th, 1863

This forenoon I did nothing. Gen. Birney asked me to go out riding with him. I did so. He went to visit Gen. Ward commanding the 32 Brigade & Col. [P. Regis] DeTrobiand commanding the 3rd Brigade, & then paid a short visit to the "Jersey Settlement" as it is called, which lies between here and Brentsville. We stopped at a widow Lady's named Kline. She immediately appeared and after apologizing for her appearance began a statement of facts etc. going to show how she had been treated by the soldiers, & closed her speech by asking for a guard which the General promised to send her. The Gen'l then ask[ed] her where the "Jersey Settlement" was, and she replied that he was now in it. He then asked her if she was from New Jersey & she replied that she was adding, that if the General doubted it she had the papers to prove it. The General told her that it was not necessary to produce the papers, that her <u>tongue</u> was sufficient evidence. She was a woman of fifty, I judge, but talked very intelligently and fluently. She said she had two sons both of whom had gone North to get out of the way of the Rebels. She said the soldiers had taken her cattle, sheep, hogs & chicken, and had even entered the house & carried off her knives & forks tin ware etc. Her story was no doubt true for our soldiers are the most shameful marauders that ever lived. The discipline of our army in this respect is sadly deficient. The rebel army never pilaged half so much in Penn. as our army pilages here among people who are undoubtedly loyal. Yet the practice is winked at by almost every General in the army.

All is quiet along the lines. We are so far to the rear that we do not hear of any thing. I believe however that nothing unfortunate has taken place....

Oct. 28th, 1863

To-day was more pleasant than yesterday yet it is still cold and disagreeable. This morning I sat down before a large camp fire after breakfast to read. I had Gibbon's second volume of the Decline and Fall of the Roman Empire. I was reading the description of Constantinople. But I did not read to much profit. Around a general camp fire there are too many loafers, for industriously disposed people to accomplish much. I was interrupted and annoyed and finally had to give over my reading. The tendancy to loaf, and talk nonsense and obscenity is a very strong [one] in the army. I try to keep away from all crowds, but sometimes cannot succeed. If you make a fire outside of your tent you are sure to attract some one to inconvenience you. The only way to avoid these nuisances is to keep close to your tent. This I usually do. I shall get a stove I hope ere long, & then I can have my own domicil and pursue my reading quietly.

Fortunately I am very well suited in a tent-mate. He is several years my junior and is [in] consequence some times a little noisy, but in every other respect his company is very desirable. His habits are fully as good as mine, his tastes are fine, he never makes use of a profane or obscene word, besides he is quite intelligent although not very well educated. He is a son of J. B. Ford one of the firm of Appleton & Co. New York a 1st. Lieut. in the 99th Pa Vols. & Ordnance officer of the Division. At Sulphur Springs when we were compelled to pair off, he & I were assigned to one tent & fortunately were both very well suited. Ours was the only tent at that celebrated camp, that was free from drunkenness and loudness. He expects soon to be made a captain. He richly deserves it for he has been in the service a long while and has done his duty well.

Camp 3 miles South of Warrenton
Junction Va.
Oct. 30th, 1863

I was disturbed this morning at one o'clock by the Adjutant Gen'l, who announced that we had orders to move at 7 in the morning. As I had no particular preparation to make I felt sure that I could take a good sleep and still be ready in time. But there was a good deal of noise outside and my sleep was frequently disturbed. It was scarcely day-light when the bugle blowed and aroused every one.... After some difficulty we got the Division under way.... We halted at one o'clock P.M. After lunch I lay down and slept to make up what I lost last night. When I got through my sleep dinner was ready, this over I went to work on my monthly inspection report....

In military matters in our army I hear of nothing new, except that I was informed to day that it was intended to build the Railroad only to Warrenton Junction. What this may mean I know not except that it be a halt until the crisis is past in the South West. There is a conflict impending there which if decided in our favor will almost close the war. But I fear that it may go against us because, the rebel generals have an opportunity to send off almost the entire Virginia army. However, I have great confidence in both Grant and Burnside....

Oct. 31st, 1863

Yesterday's Herald gave me an inking of the reasons why Rosecranz has been removed. It seems that he has furnished information to some scoundrels to make an attack on the administration. A man named Trusdale [?] has published a book which purports to be a history of the Army of the Cumberland but is in reality an attack on the administration for the manner in which the war has been conducted. Trusdale wrote the book but most of the facts contained in it were furnished by Rosecranz, as is very evident from the character of them. If he is not laboring for his personal advancement by the disparagement of others, he has certainly permitted bad men to make use of his name to further their schemes for the embarrassment of the administration. If this surmise is correct and I can not doubt it, the President has not removed him to soon. As valuable as his services as a soldier may be to us we can afford to dispense with them when they are no longer rendered with cheerfulness & good motives.

Nov. 2nd, 1863

The fact that the Pontoons were brought forward to-day strengthens the belief that an attempt will be made to cross the Rappahannock. The adoption of the route to Richmond by way of Fredricksburg necessarily involves a battle at the very start or some very astute strategy. Of the latter I do not think our generals will be guilty. The former they have no difficulty in finding when they want it. You may soon expect stirring news from this army unless appearances are deceptive. Whether we will have a repetition of the blunders of last fall remains to be seen. I will not predict disaster, but I have no hope in a favorable result. My prayer is that I may be disappointed.

Nov. 4th, 1863

After breakfast I contemplated a ride, but Capt. [James C.] Briscoe informed me that the General contemplated a ride and desired me to remain at Hd. Qrs. I immediately settled myself for the day. I took up my book and began to read. I read until lunch, then took a solitary walk for a long time until the papers arrived.... They chronicle a substantial victory in New York.... The elections are now over and Europe and the South may take notice that we are united....

...Women are generally assigned to the left side because usually that side is the weaker, but with me the contrary is the case since the unfortunate 31st of May. Lately I find myself unconsciously using my left hand for every purpose. I feel that my right arm is weak, so weak that I fear that without some care it may become comparatively useless. I am afraid to attempt any thing with it that requires exertion lest I fail or injure myself. In other words I am now left handed. I do not know how much farther the injury may carry me but I know I shall not soon forget it....

Your heart beats exactly with mine....

Nov. 5th, 1863

The camps are somewhat crowded but look well. In several places I observed conscripts receiving their first lessons in military movements. Their awkwardness, almost makes one laugh. Yet but a short time ago all were like them. Passing along the picket line I observed nothing particular except that the pickets looked lazy and indifferent, the consequence of no enemy being near them....

After my ride I sat down and had a quiet read for a couple of hours then came the papers and ... then came a letter from my Hattie.... I observe by to-days paper that Gen. Butler has been assigned to the Department of the Peninsula & North Carolina to which is added Baltimore. This addition of Baltimore rather disappoints Gen. Birney since I have been informed that he confidently expected to be Seenck's [Robert C. Schenck's] successor. Some of his staff have been talking very fluently about going to the city to winter....

Kelly's Ford, Va.
Nov. 8th, 1863

We crossed the river here yesterday, the enemy making a slight resistance. We took 300 prisoners our loss was slight. The enemy retreated during the night we are now advancing towards Brandy Station. I have not time to write any particulars. Sedgewick made an attack yesterday at Rappahannock Station & took 800 prisoners + 4 Guns.

Brandy Station, Va.
Nov. 9th 8 A.M.

We marched here yesterday....

The army was divided into two wings as I have already told you. Our wing the left, consisting of the 1st 2nd & 3rd Crops, under command of Gen. French, started from their encampment near the junction at daylight on Saturday morning the 3rd Corps having the advance. We reached the river at Kelly's Ford about 12 o'clock with the head of the column, but it was 2 o'clock before we got our forces in hand to make an attack. The enemy appeared on the opposite bank in strong force it was thought. About 2 P.M. the 1st U.S. Sharpshooters advanced to the Ford started into the stream went right across, & flanked the enemy's rifle pits, capturing the men that were in them & clearing the way for the 1st Div to cross, which it did immediately; The 1st Div. once over the pontoons were laid & the other two Divisions of the Corps crossed. By the time they were over it was dark, & it was deemed advisable to advance [no] farther that night. The enemy occupied a wood about a mile from the river.

Early yesterday morning a deserter came in & told Gen. Birney that the enemy had left. Gen. Birney immediately ordered a reconnaissance which developed the fact that they were gone. As soon as it was daylight we moved forward taking the road towards Brandy Station. We found the road clear until we came within a half mile of the station, when we found the enemys cavalry. We were ordered to halt here & wait for Sedgwick's column advancing on our right. We delayed here through some mismanagement until about 3 o'clock when we advanced drove the enemy cavalry away losing three or four men. We then advanced & encamped at the Station where we are at present.

Sedgewick column which advanced on our right on Saturday & attacked at Rappahannock Station. He found a Brigade of the enemy & a battery on the North side of the river. He immediately charged them & captured the whole party. In all I believe we have taken a battery & 2000 prisoners (our Corps has taken (400) prisoners & Sedgewick Corps the rest) & driving the enemy I suppose beyond the Rappahannock. This will restore the prestige we lost by our late retreat.

It is positively asserted that Gen. Lee has left the army of Virginia & gone west and that A. P. Hill is in command in our front....

Brandy Station, Va.
Nov. 10th, 1863

This morning I did not have the courage to get up early. I waited until the sun rose before I left my bed....

It was certainly nine o'clock before I got breakfast this morning. After breakfast I was sent out by Gen. Birney to see that our picket line connected with the line of the 6th Corps. I went with the officer of the day for the 6th Corps found the left of their line then went to hunt up the officer of the day for our Division. As he was about the business of establishing pickets and moving round constantly I had a long and tedious search for him. I found him however about one o'clock, & showed him where the picket line was to be, & then returned to Hd. Qrs. Here I found every one busy making themselves comfortable, by putting chimneys in their tents & flooring them etc. I turned in and helped some with our own and just at dark we completed. And let me say it is just as comfortable a room or tent as one could desire. It is floored, & furnished with a bunk stove table & chairs, so that last night['s] discomfort is compensated for by this night's comfort....

Nov. 11th, 1863

Last night was a very cold night. Notwithstanding we had fire in our tent until a late hour it froze a strong ice on a bucket of water inside the tent. This morning was bright and pleasant, but a strong wind set in from the Southwest about 9 A.M. and continued all day, increasing to quite a gale since dark. I think we will soon have a rain storm.

This forenoon I started out to ride through the camps. After having done so I stopped at the house of John Minor Botts which is just on the left of our line. I am no great admirer of the man, never was a[s] you know but as there has been a great deal of talk about him I wished to see him. We found him at home, were invited into the house where we likewise saw Miss Botts. Before telling you what he said and done I will try to describe him. He is a little taller than I am and stoutly built. His head is not large but round and covered with a thick growth of gray hair. He eye is grey not large his face round & full & he wears the full beard except the mustaches. He stands and walks erect, & has the haughty self important air & demeanor of a Virginia slaveholder. His daughter whom we saw, was rather slender & delicate looking & dressed in mourning. She did not remain long in the room & I had no conversation with her.

The man himself is a great talker. He first gave us a history of his treatment by the rebels since our army left here. Among other things reading us an editorial from the Richmond Examiner wherein they denounced him as a Unionist. Then he read a letter which he had written in reply to it. In this letter he hinted although he did not expressly state it, that he had done nothing against the "peace & dignity" of the Confederate States. He declared that he had taken no part in the war, but had lived and would die a Unionist & such trash. After paying his respects to the rebs. he next turned to our government and to Secretary Stanton in particular. It seems he had written to Stanton when our army was here before, asking permission to go North to purchase dry good & Groceries and to have them transported by sail from Alexandria. Stanton did not see fit to comply with this request, believing no doubt that Botts was not better than any other rebel. Whereupon he gets exceeding wroth and indites an epistle to Abraham, which epistle Abraham did not take the trouble to answer. This slight has evidently offended him & it would not surprise me if he would advise Lincoln's removal.

After this had been gone through with, he invited us into another room to show us a bust of Henry Clay. The bust was very fine, but not valuing very highly the man it represented, I did not care very much for it. I saw many other things however the possession of which I almost envied him. Small & chaste works of art, which make a home beautiful and interesting were there in profusion. Those which I thought finest were "<u>carvings</u>" <u>in</u> <u>cork</u> of landscapes. The ones he had were scenes on the Rhine. He had got them in Europe. The[y] attracted my attention for I had never seen them before. The most prominent picture was John Minor Botts presenting articles of impeachment against President [John] Tyler. Exactly when & where this took place I do not remember but Botts has a large painting representing it. The whole house as well as the man is written over with "John Minor Botts." As for his loyalty, it is not strong enough to hurt the rebels any. He is a man who takes care of himself & cares nothing for his country.

Nov. 12th, 1863

In military affairs all is quiet. Not a hostile sound has been heard for three days. The troops are busy fixing up quarters as though they are to remain here all winter which is not at all probable. The railroad is completed almost to the Rappahannock. The bridge completed and we will be connected with Alexandria by sail. Supplies will then be brought up and the army will again move forward. If we can move with secrecy and dispatch as we did last time great results will be achieved. The army can move if our generals have the brains to conduct it.

Brandy Station, Va.
Nov. 13th, 1863

In to-days papers we received Judge Woodward Lowrie & Thompsons opinions that the Conscript Law is <u>unconstitutional</u>. How far will those contemptible old traitors carry their folly. Their decision is so unreasonable that it sounds to me like treason, which it undoubtedly is. When I contemplate the acts of such men I am always pained to think that oblivion will save them from infamy.

We have also Gen. Meade's official report of the battle of Gettysburg. It excites no comment except when he speaks of Gen. Sickles to whom he gives no credit whatever. The officers of our Corps have always thought the advance of our corps which was done by Sickles, on his own responsibility saved the army from route. Gen. Meade takes a very different view of it. Sickles is able to take care of himself.

There is nothing new in the army: we are lying quietly in camp although every one expects to move soon. We have a campaign to make yet, the Rapid Ann is to be crossed & Lee's army is to be defeated for he will surely contest our crossing. If properly managed I think we can cross the Rapidann as successfully as we crossed the Rappahannock. All these movements depend on generalship. The late movements give me great hope. It is the only time we ever surprised Lee['s] army and the only time we successfully attacked it.

Nov. 14th, 1863

About 4 o'clock this afternoon it began to rain quite hard and has continued ever since. If it rains all night the streams will be swollen and our advance I presume retarded. I hope it may not be retarded long, for in all probability there are only forty days left us for campaigning. We ought to make good use of them and must.

Nov. 18th, 1863

How strange it seems to look back over the last three years. How eventful, yet compared with the present & the hastening future how unimportant they seem. Did you find the date of my first "muster in." I presume not. I have no record of it, although I have a very distinct recollection of it. I think, however, it was about the middle of June 1861. You will remember, however, that we went into camp on the 1st day of May, & that my term of service actually dates from that time. Two years have made some changes with me. Others are just where they were then. I have been fortunate, they have not.

We are preparing for a great move. We are to move with 20 days rations.... I have no doubt that it is Gen. Meade's intention to change his base of operation to the Richmond & Fredricksburg road. To do this we have to cross the Rapid Ann, & more than likely in doing so we will have a general engagement. We are about as well prepared for it now as we can be yet I fear if the movement is postponed much longer we may have Longstreets troops to oppose us again. The latest news we had from Chattanooga informed us that Longstreet was moving.... [His recall to this area] would render our triumph doubtful. <u>Unless</u> Lee is reinforced we will have an easy victory here I think.

Nov. 19th, 1863

I loved you when I was home last, have loved you ever since I first saw you, this you know, but you know not what a change has been wrought in my heart since I last took you in my arms. I may not love you more than I did then but I certainly feel that we are more closely united....

I am afraid I could not write an essay on the subject you mention. The most weighty reason against profane swearing I suppose is that it is a sin.... Profanity is of two kinds, frivolous or light and passionate.... You very frequently hear men use profane language in ordinary conversation. This they do from force of habit without ever thinking of the import of the words or of their sinfulness. Men think it manly to swear because they hear others do it. Besides the sinfulness of language thus used, speaking in a worldly sense it is impolite. Purity of language which is supposed to indicate purity of thought is the first and most important requisite of a gentleman.... The influence which these thoughtless words have upon the individual himself no one can estimate. It fixes upon him a habit of speaking carelessly or without thinking thereby enervating the mind, it renders his language impure & objectless & thusly degrades his thoughts, and if [it] does not corrupt the heart, it makes it to a certain degree insensible to the finer feelings. Profanity in the sense I have just spoken of it is a part of the language of the nation....

But that profanity is most lamentable & ruinous which expresses those fierce passions of the soul cruelty anger and revenge. In this sense it is an outward indication of the wickedness of the heart.... I have observed in the army that the tyrant always precedes an act of tyranny by a volume of oaths.... Profane swearing is the surest indication of heart filled with wickedness.

I need not dwell on the influence of language upon others. Every word idly spoken or spoken in anger, will injure not only the author but every one upon whose ears it falls. The man who uses profane language is guilty of the double crime of degrading himself and corrupting others....

Nov. 21st, 1863

It has rained hard all day. This will no doubt cause delay in our movement. I do not expect that we will move before the 1st of Dec. I am sorry the rain came for there seems to [be] every opportunity for a movement at present. The fate [of] East Tennessee & Burnside's army has been decided ere this. I have confidence that the victory is with us, notwithstanding I have some fears. Certainly nothing can now prevent Gen. Grant from crushing Braggs army, and it may be said that now too is Meade's opportunity.

Nov. 23rd, 1863

To day has given evidence that it is certainly the intention to change the base of operation, to the route via Fredricksburg I have no doubt.... They have sent all surplus baggage to Alexandria, expecting it to be sent to them again by some new route. I do not anticipate a general battle, for I know it is not Gen. Meade's intention to attack the enemy in his entrenchments. He can turn them and after they are turned the enemy will not stand. He can not fight us on the field hence he will fall back to some new defensive position. I do not expect that we will capture Richmond this fall. I do not anticipate that we will more than cross the Rapidann & establish our selves on the new base by way of Aquia Creek & Fredricksburg. After this is done the season for active operations in this country will be over. If the government consults its own interest it will put the army into winter quarters on the 1st of January & not move it again until the 1st of May.

I have just been paid for the months of Oct. & Nov. & will send ... $200.... There is labor. There are trials and dangers ahead of me, but through them all you will go with me never once thinking of yourself but only of your loved husband....

Nov. 24th, 1863

We are still at Brandy.... This morning about seven o'clock an order arrived suspending the move until further orders. It was suspended so we presumed in consequence of a threatened rain storm which was not so heavy as was anticipated.; ...

Portion of a letter from Levi. Duff usually managed a clear hand despite the awkward circumstances in which he often was forced to write (courtesy Allegheny College).

Nov. 24th, 1863

I have a bit of news for you. I have been relieved from duty as Acting Asst. Inspector Genl of the 1st Div. & ordered to take command of the 110th Regt. Pa. Vols. What is the reason of the change I know not but I derive comfort from the knowledge that the duty has been assigned me without my asking it.

I have long felt that here I am not in my place and in many respects the change gives me pleasure. The comforts of the new position will not be so great but the duties will be lighter. I will leave these Hd. Qrs. to-morrow....

Culpepper Ford
Rapid Ann River
M. Nov. 28th, 1863

On the morning of the departure of the army from Brandy Station I took command of the 110th Reg, as I informed you I was ordered to do. The regiment was ordered by Col. Collis com'der of the Brigade to report to Lt. Col. [R.V.W.] Howard Chief Quartermaster of the Corps to guard the wagon train. In command of the Regiment I report to Lt. Col. Howard & has since been with the train. The train moved from Brandy to Richardville on the 26th & yesterday from the latter place to this Ford which is about 8 miles above the mouth of the Rapidann. We do not expect to move to-day.

The army left Brandy the same morning & proceded across the Rapidann river crossing it without resistance....The army advanced yesterday towards Orange C. H. but early in the day the right encountered the enemy & stood still. The left still kept swinging round. Skirmishing was kept up all day until 4 o'clock when quite a heavy battle began & lasted for an hour & a half. At dark the firing ceased altogether and we have not heard any since.... The fight occurred about 6 or 8 miles from here at Robertson Tavern....

I get along very well with my new command. The change of position has had the effect of keeping me out of danger as well. I presume I will remain on guard here until the movement is over.

[addendum to previous letter]   Robertson Tavern Orange County
                                                       4 P.M. Nov. 29th, 1863

The train moved last night & to-day from Culpepper Ford to this point. The army is in position about 4 miles beyond. The enemy in front. Picket firing is kept up constantly but no fighting worthy of mention has occurred since the 27th. The loss in our Corps on that day over 400. The loss in our Div. small. I believe it is not Meade's intention to bring on a general engagement at present. Our line of retreat is now open to Fredricksburg in case we should be compelled to fall back. We are in the North East corner of Orange County on what is called mile run. I presume a general battle will be fought soon but where or when I know not. I just learned that orders have been issued for an attack to-day. The 2nd Corps it is said has gone round the left flank to attack them. They are waiting to hear it fire when a general attack is to be made along the whole line. I am quite well....

Richardville Va.
Dec. 1st 1863

The same day we reached Robertson's Tavern we were ordered back to Culpepper Ford. We got under way again with the train about twelve o'clock & as the roads were rather good we reached the Ford with the rear of the train with which I was the next morning at day light but did not get across the river until near noon. After having a little breakfast I lay down to take a sleep for I had not slept any during the two nights previous. Three or four hours sleep made me feel better. Last night was passed in quiet. Early this morning we got an order to move back to Richardville.... This was soon done as the distance is not over two miles. It is now three o'clock. I have not heard from the front to-day. Day before yesterday nothing was done, yesterday ditto except that a general attack was ordered and our division advanced & drove in the rebel outposts & at this point the order for attack was countermanded. The indications to-day are that our army will fall back without a fight unless the rebels retreat which is not probable. I must confess that I do no[t] understand the movements....

Brandy Station, Va.
Dec. 3rd, 1863

To-day has been quiet. I have busied myself fixing up quarters and am now as comfortable as before the move. The whole army is in its old camp.... I do not know the cause of the failure. The campaigning in Virginia is ended for this year. It was found to be very difficult to manouvre our artillery in the late fight on account of the softness of the ground....

Dec. 4th, 1863

It pleases me to know that my character is becoming known at home. This knowledge will be of great value to me when I return, since every one is suspected and justly so, who returns from the army.... Character which is of so much value at home has no value whatever in the army. Strange as it may seem, my character instead of being an advantage to me here is a disadvantage. At Div. Hd. Qrs. there were fourteen staff officers three of whom did not drink. Two of them were despised on this account and snubbed on every occasion. Maj. Duff the third one, they esteemed somewhat but not so much as they would have done had he been a drunkard....

Camp near Brandy Station, Va.
Dec. 6th, 1863

At 9 o'clock yesterday morning we were ordered to change camp. We soon tore down and got under way. Arriving at our new camp we began to clean off the ground, but before we had been many minutes at work at [sic] order came to pack up and be ready to move at once. The wagons were ordered to be loaded and in readiness to go to the rear. This took from us our tents and nearly all of our comforts. We lay around all day expecting to move at night-fall, but night came and still no movement.

About ten o'clock the order was countermanded & we were ordered to resume work on our camp. I immediately ordered up my wagons & got my blankets supposing that with them I could be comfortable but there came up a furious wind-storm which made it very cold and I was more or less uncomfortable all night. This morning work was resumed. I have my tent up and have it floored, but as it is without chimney it is a dreary uncomfortable place. I think I shall have a chimney before night.

Our wise heads held a counsel of war last night. What course of policy was determined upon I do not know; but I hope they may be able to avoid the frequent alarms of the last few days. The soldiers are getting tired of running out of their comfortable quarters every night....[1]

Dec. 7th, 1863

It is very cold; winter is really upon [us], campaigning is ended at least for the present and I have no doubt for the winter. We still continue to fix our camp. I got a chimney built to-day, but the builder was not very expert & it does not throw out heat enough to warm the tent. I will have it improved to-morrow. I lay very cold last night, & anticipate the same fate to-night.

We have no news of importance. I heard to-day however that Brig. Gen. [John Potts] Slough and several subordinate officers had been arrested in Alexandria for defrauding the government. The sentiment prevalent in the army is that a Quartermaster or a Commissary ought to defraud the government all they can. The sentiment of the army upholds a system of peculation in all of the departments. Indeed it is strange what an army [is]. It is not to be wondered at that we do nothing. There is much talk in Washington I understand concerning Gen. Meade. It is pretty generally believed that he will be relieved. The army has said & thought but little of the matter & cares less. This last campaign over the river has convinced the army that all of our generals are wanting in certain respects. One is just as good as another so there is no need of a change....

Dec. 8th, 1863

There is yet no indication of a desire to give leaves, but since the season for operations is past I have no doubt that an order will soon be issued granting leaves. Gen. Meade can scarcely ignore the custom established by Gen. Hooker last spring....

I have no news to write. Everything is extremely quiet. The army seems to have given over all idea of further movements.... We are all busy building winter quarters but it is scarcely possible that we will remain here all winter for wood is too scarce. We will have to go back to Catletts Station, where wood is abundant....

I am getting along very well with my new command. Very many funny things have happened since I came here, but I have not room for the story.... When I first received the order from Gen. Birney to take command of the regiment I did not think he was complementing me. Although it has done good fighting, the regiment since it came to the Division has always been published as "ratty" which it really was from want of a proper officer, and as Gen. Birney did not ask my pleasure in the matter, I thought it a kind of a soft let down by him. It really was so but is more pleasant than I supposed it would be. There were many things at Hd. Qrs. which I did not like and I many times wished myself away, and now that I have been relieved I hope it is permanent. A staff officer has to be to a certain extent the "tool" of the General (to use a low but expressive term) and I could never be made such hence I was always at variance with the general. Here I am king and can do as I please.

On December 11 Duff told Harriet that he had applied for a ten day leave.

Dec. 12th, 1863

Happening to be at Div. Hd. Qrs. to-day I inquired if my application for leave had been forwarded. I was told that it had not that it had arrived to late to go to-day. The brigade commander had requested me to send it in early last night so that he could forward it early this morning. I performed my part of the engagement but he neglected his. The consequence of this neglect is that my application for leave will not reach the Hd. Qrs. of the Corps before to-morrow afternoon, and as that is Sunday & they do not sign on that day any papers except those of vital importance it will not return to me before Monday evening the 14th the day on which I expected to be home....

This day has seemed very long to me, & to-morrow will I fear seem longer. Every day until I see you will be long and irksome.

Shortly after writing to Harriet on December 15, Levi finally obtained his furlough and traveled home for an all-too-short visit. On his return to the army, Harriet and Levi again took up their pens.

Allegheny City
Dec. 28th 1863

My precious husband

How can I best speak of the varied feelings with which I address you to night. Since my last letter was penned, I have welcomed you home I have again bidden you farewell. The bitterness of that parting I have not yet felt as I know I must. I endeavored to keep my mind employed with only thankful thoughts.... Again and again am I assured that God blessed me on my wedding day.... I wonder now if I could trust my self to say a few words upon the subject of your reenlistment — to tell you [how] much I admire the patriotism which prompts you to the act. I can love my noble husband only the more. Yet when my eyes were on you I feared to speak lest the wild cry of the hungry heart might find utterance instead of what I would you should hear. But our thoughts and feelings are so akin I am sure you know my thoughts although unspoken....

Harriet

Brandy Station, Va.
Dec. 29th, 1863

I am safe at camp. I find everything as I left it....

But I must tell you the troubles of my trip. In the first place the train on which I started from Pittsburg did not make a close connection at Harrisburg for Baltimore, ... and I was obliged to remain at Harrisburg until 7 A.M.... [The train I took for Baltimore] went along very well until we reached Friedlands a station 40 miles north of Baltimore where we ran against a freight train which had run off the track.... [We] arrived at Baltimore at 5 P.M. about the time I should have arrived at the army.... [I got to Brandy Station] a day behind time as usual. However I am more fortunate than I was last year for my absence this time will be unnoticed. Many here were very glad to see me. During my absence Gen.Meade issued a order denying leaves & furloughs to the regiment on account of our inspection report that was forwarded in Nov. giving a very bad account of the condition of the regiment. As the regiment suffered for the want of a head, the men were glad to see me back to take command. Lt. Col. [Isaac] Rodgers is still here. I have not heard whether he has taken any steps towards getting out of the way but presume he has not.

Dec. 30th, 1863

I do not wonder that Englishmen say that we stand on no higher moral ground than the South as touching the question of slavery, for never yet has it been manfully said "Slavery must die." We justify it [the Emancipation Proclamation] as a war measure, we admit that our constitution sanctions it [slavery], & say to ourselves as well as to foreigners "we would save it if we could." Mr. [Henry Ward] Beecher says to an English audience we hate slavery because the slaveholders have rebelled. In all his speeches there is not one word for the down trodden Negro.

I never very much admired such anti–slavery men as Beecher. He never plants himself on the firm ground that slavery is a sin, but is continually seeking some other excuse for fighting it....

Our regiment has just received an order to repost to the state of Penn. with all of its officers. I am going with it. I will be home I think in a week.

Brandy Station, Va.
Jan'ry 1st, 1864

Your words on the subject of re–enlistment meet my hearty concurrence. I could not burden you with another three years anxiety except under the peculiar circumstances of the case. As I informed you when I was home — at the date of my last promotion I was sworn in for three years. This is the case with all of the officers of the regiment for all have been promoted during the last year. The men of the regiment have reenlisted almost unanimously, & the officers have not been asked to re–enlist. The regiment has been ordered to the state of Penn with its officers without asking them whether they wished to go or stay. As no one has a desire to remain behind we have all concluded to go. I presume, however, that before we are ordered back to the army we will be obliged to re–enlist. I think there is no harm in accepting a permit to go home to kiss my wife — do you? ... However, I shall feel myself at liberty to abandon the regiment & I will likely return to the field with it again.[2]

Baltimore, Md.
1 P.M. Jan'y 5th, 1863 [4]

We left the army on Saturday morning, and arrived in Washington at 5 o'clock the same. Here we were delayed until yesterday at noon, when we succeeded in getting a train and after a cold & tedious ride arrived here last night at 10 — .... My time has been occupied as well as that of the other field officers ... in keeping the men together, which under the circumstances has been very difficult.

I have not been very well since we left the army. Coming from Brandy to Washington I was compelled to ride on a platform car, & I got very cold. That night I slept in a good bed & felt tolerably well the next day, but that day & night & the next day I staid in the barracks with the men, & their interminable noise gave me the head ache, which mixed with the cold made me quite sick yesterday.

Head Quarters 1st Division 3rd Corps
Thursday Feby 4th 1864

My dear Major

I was glad to learn that you were enjoying your leave (Oh! Envied man!) and that your prospects of a continued stay "about home parts" in the enjoyments of its luxuries, was so good.

You are so earnest and kindly importunate in your request that I write you all the news. So at the risk of being tedious I will try briefly to narrate some of the events that have transpired during your absence.

First in importance and on the order of occurrence, is our change of camp of our Division some three weeks ago: to a locality where wood and water is abundant and where no John Minor Botts "molest or make us afraid." We are distant some three miles from Brandy Station and two and a half miles from Culpepper. The regiments have constructed for themselves what Genl. Birney considers to be the model camps and quarters of the Army both as regards comfort and appearance. Our Headquarters we flatter ourselves surpass any in the army in quarters and outside decoration. The Genl. is comfortably fixed in the house while "the Staff" occupy log houses 12 feet by 18, which are boarded inside and adorned in the most "palacial style" with wall paper, carpets and all the modern conveniences and improvements. We have with us on a visit four ladies, being Mrs. Genl. and Mrs Major Birney, and Mrs Tobias and "Mother Birney"

I have been acting as Division Qr. Mr for the past month, performing in addition the duties of Ordnance officer and Aid-de Camp. I was fortunately relieved as Ordnance Officer last week by Capt [Franklin] Sweet and as Aid- de Camp by the arrival of a new A. D. C. on the Staff—Capt [Charles] Noble [Jr.] from Col [Peter C.] Ellmakers regiment.

Genl. B. has been in command of the Corps since Wednesday last. Genl. French having "accepted" a leave of absence. I <u>have</u> heard expressed by <u>one</u>(?) or <u>more</u>(!) words to the effect of an expression of an earnest wish "that his leave might never expire." Strange is it not?

The 99th P.V. 20th Ind. and perhaps the 110th will reenlist as regiments of veterans on the return to the Division of some of the absent regiments

Rogers was ordered before the Board of Examiners but Genl. B. informed me, he intends resigning. I spoke to Genl B. as you desired, about the matter. He says that he would be much pleased if the arrangement you refer to, would be made, and recommends that you make such a proposition to Gov Curtin, Genl B. I think will aid you all in his power.

> Truly your Friend
> E. L. Ford
> Capt etc

Harrisburg Pa.
Febr'y 17th, 1864

I am rather pleased that we are still detained in this city....

We are about selling our regiment for $250 a head. Delaware or Chester County will be the purchaser. At the time of re-enlistment no credit was given except to the state, and the men now have the option of chosing their districts. It will be a fine thing for our veterans if they get $250 each.

Febr'y 18th, 1864

We are having some difficulty to credit our regiment as we desire and will I presume fail altogether. You saw published in the Dispatch I presume the correspondence between Capt. Foster & Col. Fay: The tone of this correspondence indicates a reluctance to permit veterans to receive local bounties. But it has been permitted in many instances and the attempt to make fish of one and flesh of another is unjust. Those who were foremost to re-enlist are to be deprived of local bounties.

I enclose you Wendell Phillips late speech at Cooper institute. It is worth a perusal. I never read one of his speeches without feeling that I have been benefited by it. I can see I think as clearly as he can that the war will not be ended until justice is done to the Black race. The nation will never be out of trouble, although actual war may cease until the niger question is permanently settled by giving him his right.

Camp Bullock, Va.
Febr'y 21ˢᵗ, 1864

We arrived about an hour since at camp. Our regiment [has not] yet been assigned a spot on which to erect its habitations but will be this evening. They have very fine camps here and plenty of wood and I think we will be quite comfortable in a few days.

...There is a good deal of stir and talk in the army now, about the proposed consolidation into 3 Corps of which I spoke to you in my letter of Dec. It is said that the order is to be issued in a few days.... It is proposed to form three Corps of four Divisions each — in all 12 Divisions. We have now 5 Corps & 15 Divisions of course some Generals will be slaughtered in the consolidation. It will however make a better army, and I wonder that it was not done long since. If now they would consolidate a great many regiments and send off inefficient officers they would be doing another good thing, and save the government a great amt. of useless expense.

Febr'y 22nd, 1864

This morning about ten o'clock I received an order to report to Lt. Benjamin to take charge of a fatigue party. I road [to] Brandy Station the place designated in the order, but could not find or hear of Lt. Benjamin. I could only hear of a Lt. Buryard, and I could not even find him, so after searching four hours I came home. Army detailing for duty operates some times oddly. For instance when at Yorktown a number of men were required to work on a certain day, the order started at Army Hd Qrs the morning of the day the work was to be done, but would never reach the regiment to which it was directed until evening....

I found on my return that my man "Doctor" [Melton] had taken good care of every thing I left with him. The baggage the regimental officers left in the wagons was nearly all stolen. The only thing belonging to me that is missing is the suit which I purchased at Boobyers for the Doctor. It has never reached here.—

I am feeling weary again this evening. I find two months absence from the sadelle has unfitted me for enduring a long ride. I shall get used to riding again in a short time.

Febr'y 23ʳᵈ, 1864

We have little new in the army. They had a grand ball at 2ⁿᵈ Corps Hd. Qrs. last night. Many ladies were present among the notables Mrs. Gov. Curtin & Mrs. Sprague etc. A number of officers were drunk so I am told. This is not surprising. Such carousals do not benefit our army. There is much talk about the consolidation....

My duty took me to Brandy Station and this time [I] succeeded in finding Lt. Buryard not Lt. Benjamin, and was politely informed that I was not needed to-day but would be to-morrow....

Our camp is going up rapidly, but we field officers have no tents yet. We expect to get some to-morrow.

...I am not yet acclimated to camp life, but the preliminary stages will not go hard with me....

Febr'y 24ᵗʰ, 1864

To day has passed with me as usual nothing for my hand to do except to go through the usual dull daily routine. I went to Brandy Station early this morning, and waited a short time before the men detailed to work came. After they came I had another wait until the tools came, then I had to march the larger portion of the men not less than four miles to the woods to cut timber. When we reached the timber it was noon and I told the men to eat their dinners and gave the officers instructions what to do then rode home having concluded that they could get along without me. I shall go forth again in the morning.

The Division was reviewed to-day by Gen. French. I did not go to the review and consequently cannot tell you what took place. Some of the troops are said to have looked well. Our regiment went out with "big hats" and presented an odd appearance. We gathered the hats from the debris left at Garrison in March 1862.

...We received our tents this evening and have the[m] put up also stoves in them, but our bunks are not made. In a day or two we will have all the necessary arrangements made for living comfortable. I am a little annoyed by my detail to work on the roads. I had hoped to enjoy a season of rest at least until the return of the 110th.

Camp near James City, Va.
Febr'y 28th, 1864

We broke camp this morning at 6 o'clock and started towards Culpepper at 7 o'clock. Passing through the town we turned to the right taking the road to this place, we reached here at 2 P.M. We halted and were told that we would remain all night. I dismounted and lay down & took a "nap" of about an hour and felt much rested. While I was sleeping the regiment was sent on picket under Lt. Col. Greenawalt. I thought I was a straggler for a moment but soon discovered that I had not been required. After eating a little supper I went with Lt. Col. to the picket-line when he said he had a house to quarter in. On reaching the Pickets I entered a small but comfortable deserted house. A bedstead and a cupboard the rest of the furniture has been carried off. As Lt. Platts [Platt] says we are partaking of Virginian hospitality. As I have only a dim wood fire for light. The light is improved & I will not finish the above sentence.

Our march to day was quite pleasant, would have been very pleasant but for some dust. We have not yet been favored with an understanding of the movements of the army.... The main movement is made by the Cavalry and we are supporting it. It is either making a reconnaissance or a raid I presume the latter. The rebel cavalry is now said to be in a very bad condition, and our cavalry may now be able to make a raid with impunity.

What a loss it is that I cannot be with you always. If I were <u>my</u> spirits would never wear out, as it is they some times do....

Febr'y 19th, 1864

To-day has passed mainly in quiet. This afternoon we heard some cannonading in the direction of Gordonsville, but it did not continue long, and was not of very much importance.

...[The cavalry] left Madison C. H. this morning at 2 A.M. One portion, I believe under Gen. [Hugh Judson] Killpatrick going towards Gordonsville and another under Gen.[George A.] Custer going towards Charlottesville.... As Custer left Madison this morning at 2 o'clock, for Charlottesville some 35 miles distant we congratulate ourselves that there is excitement in Charlottesville and all over Virginia rebeldom. Unless something unusual happens we will probably return to camp day after to-morrow.

To-day I paid a visit to Thoroughfare Mountain which is near our camp. We have a signal station on the top of it, which communicates with Gen. Sedgewick at Robertson & sends his dispatches to Gen. French by way of Clark Mountain thence to Gordy [?] Mountain thence to Hd Qrs. of the Army.... I enclose you a small pine twig, which is the only living thing I could find there on. It is too early for flowers.... It is sleeting to-night, the beginning of a great storm which has threatened for several days. I dread marching to-morrow not for my self but for the men who go on foot....

Camp James City, Va.
March 1st, 1864

This has been a rainy dismal day.... Just at dark it began to snow very hard and the ground was soon white. It is still snowing but not so hard. The soldiers many of them have no tents and will pass an uncomfortable night. But the march back will be the hardest thing to accomplish, and the most fatiguing to the men.

A messenger has just arrived, who brings word that Gen. Custer is returning that he went within sight of the railroad near Charlottesville but found the rebels too strongly posted to destroy it. So his part of it has proved a failure. The other party has not been heard from. If it proves successful it will be sufficient for once. The rain has stopped any other movements for the present....

I have been very fortunate during the campaign. I have quartered in a house every night, and I find much comfort in it to-night....

Camp Bullock, Va.
March 6th, 1864

All have about come to the conclusion that Gen. Killpatricks raid is over and that he has not accomplished much. Our principle talk here now is on politics. The Col. and I have just had a "heat." Strange to say although he is an avowed abolishist he takes the very ground that has been taken by the conservatives since the war began, viz that we will conquer the rebels sooner by lenience than by vigor. As things now look this will be the Lincoln platform before the Baltimore Convention. It is needless to tell you that I belong to the radical wing of the party. I believe in striking for the end at once and directly. Presuming that Lincoln holds the views above set forth I am for Butler or Frémont. I cannot ... follow the doctrine of expediency as laid down by you. You assure that Lincoln would be surer of an election because he is somewhat two sided in other words "on the fence," than a man who is outspoken.... [But that would be to admit] our democracy is a failure. Because you assert by your policy of expediency that the people are not intelligent enough to vote what is right, and in order to get them to vote right, you must put up a false light while steering to the true one....

I will not deny that this is the policy which has always been pursued by our politicians, and I can cite you this war as the fruits of such a policy....

With regard to bestowing the right of suffrage upon the negro, I will compromise with you, if you will agree to deprive every white man that cannot read and write of the right of suffrage, then I will only ask you to extend it to such negros as can read and write. But so long as you insist that a dirty Irishman born and reared in the bogs of Ireland without character and without knowledge shall vote so long will I insist that every negro in the land be he descended from a slave or free mother be allowed to vote likewise. I believe that our political liberty is too large, but it is unjust to proscribe one race and admit another.

10

In Camp

The success of Grant in taking Vicksburg and Chattanooga suggested to many that he was the Union's best general. President Lincoln, wearied by the persistent tendency of the Army of the Potomac to avoid engaging the forces of Lee, appointed Grant general-in-chief of all Union armies in March 1964. Henry Halleck willingly accepted the lower post of chief of staff. Grant was not a desk officer and soon made his headquarters with the Army of the Potomac. Meade retained his title as that army's commander, but in fact the army now fell under the direction of Grant.

Camp Bullock, Va.
March 7th, 1864

To-day I spent 2 ½ hours the most tedious and vexatious I ever spent in the army at Court Martial. These courts are necessary adjuncts to the army but I have thus far failed to see the utility of the one of which I am a member. To-day we convicted a Sergeant of calling the officer of the day "sl—d sun [sic] of a bitch" and defying him in the execution of his office—a crime punishable some times with death, one of the most flagrant crimes against the discipline of the army—& then his sentence was made so light as to disgust me, it will certainly bring the Court into contempt. On my way home I queried with myself what was the use of Court Martial. Surely the judgements of ours will encourage rather than prevent crime. So this army runs at all ends.—

I observe by the papers that Gen. Sickles has a[t] last succeeded in striking at Gen. Meade. I knew he would do it. The blow will be a heavy one and if Meade stands up under it, it will be surprising to many. Already Meade['s] special advocates are beginning to cry that he is persecuted. This kind of talk it is to my mind evident, proves that the charges against him are well grounded. The affair may end in giving a new commander to the army of the Potomac. So let it be. I should be sorry to see Meade relieved, although he has treated our Corps shame-fully. If the commander of the 3rd Corps did commit a blunder at Gettysburg, it is unjust to punish the Corps therefore. This Meade has done and is doing.

Gen. Grant is on his way to Washington. Alas that he should be. His day of usefulness is past. In Washington he will sooner or later pay the debt which all men who go there must pay, corruption then degradation.

March 8th, 1864

The Tribune states that the most prominent members of the Committee on the Conduct of the War and many high officials have recommended the removal of Meade. I rather think he will "kick the beam." Gen. [Daniel] Butterfield has been sent for to fix the responsibility of certain orders issued at Gettysburg. Gen. Butterfield will stab Meade if he can.

March 10th, 1864

This morning an order was received from army Hd. Qrs. to send all of the women now in the army out of it. The order stated or rather hinted that the time was near at hand when active operations must begin.... The weather had been very fine here for a month past. But to day has dampened all such thoughts [of operations], for rain has been falling and mud has been rising.... I have no objection to the orders sending the women out of the army. They never should have come here and I am glad to see them going away.

I am very well. The rain storm has not affected our quarters any. We are just as snug as we could be in a house. When we go out however, we go "plout" into the mud.

March 11th, 1864

The Herald of yesterday states that the consolidation of the army into three corps has been finally determined upon, & that the 1st & 3rd Corps are to be consolidated into the 2nd, 5th, & 6th. This may be all very well but I do not think that it treats our Corps justly. It was the third corps formed in the United States, one of the original four into which the Potomac army was divided in the spring of 1862. The 5th & 6th Corps were "bastards" formed on the Peninsula expressly for McClellan's pets Porter and Franklin and I do not think it just to merge our corps into either of them. But Gen. Meade thinks otherwise. Though broken up the name of the 3rd A.C. will not be forgotten. But I must not write more about this.—

March 13th, 1864

We had a Div. review to-day. We got through with it at 3 o'clock. I came home with a very severe head-ache. I laid down put a wet towel on my forehead and tried to cure the ache but I was not successful. It still continues but I think I can sleep it off to-night. The head ache being with me a frequent occurrence I took the trouble to ask the Surgeon about it to-day, & he seemed to think I required a nervous stimulant. I have a horror, however, of medicine and dont think I shall soon take any....

Our review passed off very well. The Div. looked remarkably well. Gen. Birney complimented our Brigade on their good marching.

March 17th, 1864

You smiled upon me lovingly this morning in your letter of the 12th.... This has been a windy cold day, and to make it really disagreeable we had a Corps review. (Just here while I think of it consult the Dictionary on the word "<u>review</u>," and inform me if the noun is accented on the first or second syllable). We left camp at 10 o'clock and marched to the plain between Bott's and Brandy & then the Corps was formed in column of Brigade & soon Gen. French made his appearance. And a fine appearance it was too, for he is a fine looking man, dressed neatly and rides a very fine horse. But all this "show" is deceitful, for he is full of whiskey and stupidity within. He rode along the front and rear of each Brigade, then we were marched in review, & dismissed. The performance was very good, but the cold was intense and I was glad when it was all over.

Military movements are at a stand here.... We expect Gen. Grant here in two or three weeks. The 110th is expected back this week. I will soon know my status in that regiment.

March 17th, 1864

I believe my letter of yesterday evening was dated the 17th....

Last night was the evening of Gen. Birney's weekly reception, and Col. Greenawalt and I determined to see the Gen'l. The receptions have been held weekly during the winter, but since the late move have fallen into disuse. In consequence it happened that only the Lt. Col. & Lt. Paterson [George C. Patterson] of our regiment were present with me. The Generals

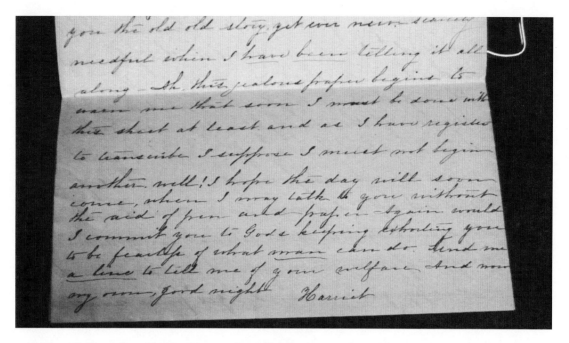

Portion of a letter from Harriet. Her touch was lighter than Levi's, and her nervous condition sometimes required her to use pencil rather than pen. The passage of time has therefore made some of her missives difficult to decipher (courtesy Allegheny College).

wife is here, and we were likewise introduced to her. We had a conversation with them for an hour. The Gen'l is as politic and intriguing as usual. His wife was so so and that is all that can be said. We know the General very well but have not seen his wife. In consequence we had some talk about the latter personage....

March 18th, 1864

We have a little stir in the army this evening. We received a telegram this afternoon stating that the enemy were crossing at Raccoon Ford in force, & were directed to have three days rations on hand and be ready to move. It is not probable that we will move yet we might. At best the enemy is making a demonstration on our lines.... It is supposed that they are making a reconnaissance, but for what purpose I cannot imagine. It cannot be to ascertain whether we are here yet for from their signal station on Black's Mountain they can look into our camp....

The rumors about the reorganization of our army still continue. The appointment of W. F. Smith to be Major Gen'l in the regular army ... gives strength to this rumor that he is to command this army.... This appointment is made with a purpose, & every one here believes that he will be placed in command of this army. The only notable thing he did when in this army was the storming of the rebel fortification at Warwick Creek near Yorktown in April 1862. He failed because he was drunk it is said.... He is a cousin to the present Governor of Vermont.

General Grant's order assuming command of the ... Armies of the United States. Hd Qrs. are to be in the field and until further orders with the army of the Potomac. This indicates that we are expected to do something. He leaves Nashville tomorrow....

March 19th, 1864

The bustle of yesterday evening is all gone. We received an order yesterday evening just after I closed my letter revoke[ing] the order to be ready to move. It is stated that the alarm was false. I could not think my self that Lee was crossing at Raccoon Ford either to make a reconnaissance or an attack, because the one was unnecessary & the other would be foolish, and I have yet to find him guilty of either an unnecessary or foolish move. In a few days Grant will arrive and then I presume we will know our fate. It is altogether probable that he will reorganize the army and put a general in command of it whom he knows. It will not matter much who commands the army if Grant is present in person. He will give the army great confidence, and I hope he may be able to overcome his adversary, but I am conscious that heretofore he has not been fighting generals as Lee. Not understanding his antagonist he may fail in the first encounter. Let us hope for the best.

March 20th, 1864

Do not forget to urge Sardis to continue his schooling. As I wrote him it is too late for him to enter the army. Seriously speaking however, it may be a source of regret to him as long as he lives that he did not take part in this struggle....

I am not surprised to hear of the outcry against Camp Copeland. It was an abominable place when we were there. It must be worse now. We ought to have those officers out here a while to train them. We have had about 60 recruits there for a month and cannot get them to the army. We receive three or four occasionally. The campaign will be far advanced before we receive all of them. There is much talk here of an early move.... It is thought by many that this [present] route [to Richmond] will be abandoned and the Peninsula route again adopted.... I am ready for any thing so it gives us success. The man & the way to lead to victory is what I want....

March 21, 1864

The military situation is unchanged. The man "on horseback" as the Herald calls Grant, has not yet arrived.... I feel quite certain that Grant will reinforce this army a good deal before he moves it. He can reinforce it without weakening any other army by gathering up the scattered regiments. A "Grand Review" is the first immediate prospect....

March 22, 1864

To-day I have indulged some forebodings concerning Grants success at the first trial. In the first place I think he is greatly overrated by the country. I do not consider him the greatest soldier we have. I give that preference to Gen. Rosecranz however strange it may seem to many. Gen. Grant is no doubt a man of quick and powerful execution but I fear he has not the depth of intellect necessary to conceive and arrange the details of great operations.

It is conceded on all hands too that in his front here he has the most sagacious rebel general one whose ability is so much superior to that of generals whom [he] has been fighting that comparison is unnecessary. Besides he is ignorant of Gen. Lee's method of warfare and will have to have at least on[e] tilt with him to learn it. But my greatest apprehension arises from the conviction that the spirit which now controls this army — being manifestly in the interest of McClellan and the West Point clique — will I should not assert betray him — but will not go heartily with him. He should begin to reorganize this army by removing every Corps commander in it. It is necessary for self protection and for the interests of the army. The Democrats well know what a god-send to them a defeat of this army would be. It would almost make the Presidential election sure in McClellan's favor. Hence they will connive at the defeat all they can, and if defeated, they will come forward with the dogma that Grant has been interfered with by President & the War Office, and call upon the people to oust them. I should be sorry to see affairs take this turn. If they do, it will well nigh work our ruin.

March 23rd, 1864

I feel lost without you. As much as I have loved you I was not conscious of the influence of your presence on my sprit. I had got into the habit of idly lounging a good deal from being compelled to do it while on the march, but I find since my return that the habit is gone. I feel like working all the time and working vigorously too. My heart is cheerful yet not buoyant as it would be if you kissed me every morning before the day's work began....

March 24th, 1864

We have our own jokes here about the "man on horseback." I will tell you more about him when I see him....The impression is general [in Washington] that Baldy Smith will command this army.

March 26th, 1864

This is a dark and stormy night.... I am not well....

To-day there has been more re-organization. Our Division has been consolidated into two Brigades: one to be commanded by Brig. Gen. Ward now commanding our 2nd Brigade; and the other to be commanded [by] Alexander Hays who is relieved from the command of the old 3rd Div. 2nd Corps by reason of the reorganization. The consolidation of our Division makes brigades of 10 regiments each, a very unwieldy organization & one I am sure that will not work well in practice. To make the reorganization complete they must consolidate regiments, which I presume will be the upshot of the matter. In that case I will get my discharge, & I care not how soon it comes.

The 110th returned last night, but so far as I have learned I am not to be returned to the command of it. With regard to Gen. Birney I can safely say that he placed me in command of it, in order to displace me from his staff without hurting my feelings.... Subsequent events have proved my judgment correct. As for Col Collis who made application for me to be returned to the Brigade so that he could place me in command of it, he was actuated in part by a desire to improve the condition of the regiment and in part to enhance his own interest in the brigade. I presume he would desire now to return me to the regiment, but the consolidation sets him back and his influence is of no avail. As for the officers of the regiment, many of whom were favorable to me mostly from the conviction that they could do no better now keep shy of me, supposing that Rodgers will be permitted to command now unmolested. There is the true statement of the case as it now stands. By a little intrigue I presume I might succeed in getting it again but my spirit will not brook such a thing so I will keep clear of it. The regiment has received about 200 recruits and will make a good battalion if properly officered, but under its present officers, will never be any thing but a second class organization. To crown all the regiment has been transferred to Ward's brigade and is now in his hands, & if he desires to make any change of commanders he has <u>todies</u> of his own to shove forward so that in any event that I can imagine my prospects are at an end. I feel a little disappointed but I do not think I regret it much. I can still serve where I am.

I have been a good deal disgusted to-day, a natural feeling to one under the circumstances. The spirit of all of our troops is completely broken. The[y] know that they have fought well and no reports made to Washington can ever convince them of the contrary, and they are conscious that their services and sacrifices have been overlooked nay scoffed at by their superiors. Men with these feelings are not likely to endeavor to do much and henceforward not much need be expected of them. Our officers matter not a little, but are quiet as yet. In the 2nd Div. they are more outspoken. Last night at "Dress Parade" [men] in the "Excelsior" Brigade appeared with the 2nd Corps badge on their "unmentionables" in an unmentionable place. This is an index of the bickering that is in store for us. The same feeling pervades the 1st corps. I fear we have fallen into the hands of thieves. Look out for squalls. I no longer look for success in this army this summer; to much re-organization will ruin it. I always desire to be hopeful but I cannot be under the present circumstances.

"Inter nos" — I have been thinking to-day that I would brush up a little in military matters and go before Gen. [Silas] Casey['s] Board and be examined for a Colonelcy of "Colored Troops." I have no doubt that I could pass the required examination and would thereupon get the appointment. I have thought of the subject before but always dismissed it when I thought of my wife because the assuming of such a position would necessarily take me away from home for many years and perhaps consign me to the army for life. I could never make up my mind to such a destiny. No idea of personal comfort or advancement impels me to it now. But I am conscious that many officers are now appointed to the command of "Colored Troops," who have no confidence in or fellow feeling for that unfortunate race and I am sure such officers will fail in their endeavors to make them appear respectable soldiers in the eyes of the world. Having full confidence in their loyalty and their courage and being of opinion that they can only achieve the political privileges to which they are entitled by their own bayonets, and having an anxiety that they should achieve them, I feel it almost a duty to give them the benefit of the talents and knowledge I have been blessed with. I have no desire to remain longer in public life. I am tired of it — disgusted with it. I have no longer patience to associate with men who have no regard for honor decency or integrity. And to be commanded by such is almost enough to ruin me.—

...Your husband needs a kiss to night. Give love to all, and to my wife an earnest kiss for love's sake.

March 27th, 1864

To-day has been a pleasant beautiful spring day. The sun was bright & warm and every thing seems to have new life. A look at the far distant blue Ridge a grand view of which is had from a knoll near our camp reminded us that winter had just gone. The snow still lingered there and they looked cold and forbidding. The more I see of this country the more I admire it. I asked myself to-day "what would have been the condition of Virginia to-day, if instead of the profligates of a profligate reign of an English monarch, the Pilgrims had landed here.["] It would have blossomed with peace and comfort instead of being wasted with hostile [hostility?]. The natural wealth of Virginia cannot help making a prosperous people and its natural beauty must make a noble people. But the curse of all curses is upon it now. When [the] storm passes her fields will again yield their treasures of wealth and beauty to those whose fortune it is to occupy them.—

March 28th, 1864

If people are astonished at the number of letters you receive what must be their astonishment at the number you write.... When I was home just before our marriage ... something was said about sending Maggie [Duff] to school in Pittsburg, & the suggestion that you might take care of her....

[Neither you nor your mother should take over the task of housing Maggie]. The only place that she can be sent is to the College, and that in my judgment is an abominable place. It seems to me more like a house of correction than a school for training. To place a child (like Margaret for child she is) in a straight jacket Methodist College would have the same effect upon her body and mind as Chinese shoes would have upon her feet. Her body would be enervated her mind blunted, her heart hardened. Of all things on God's earth I most abhor monastic discipline. I believe that young women should enjoy freedom more than they now enjoy but not the vicious freedom which society permits or rather enjoins. They should be taught womanhood as young men should be taught manhood, and they should have liberty to look into the world and see what womanhood in its highest acceptation means....

March 29th, 1864

Rain, rain storm is all the news I have to night.... About 8 o'clock we received an order announcing that the Corps would be reviewed to-day by Lt. Gen. Grant, provided it did not rain. This was soon followed by another order to be in line at 9 o'clock. We were in line accordingly, but just at this moment the clouds became heavy and it began to sprinkle rain. Nevertheless we started, and had proceeded a mile in the direction of the review ground near Stevensburg when it became evident that it was going to rain hard, & the troops were marched back to camp, very well satisfied under the circumstances.

With the exception of that short journey I have been in my tent all day. However I did not spend any time profitably for I felt disinclined to do any thing. Nearly all of the time I was thinking of my wife a goodly portion of it looking at her picture and admiring it.

...What is to be done, with the long lonsome summer months in prospect. During these months they give no leaves of absence, must I do without your kisses? I fear I must. I will make up for losses however when I come home....

March 30th, 1864

Gen. Hays has taken command of our Brigade. He says he "has come down a peg" he does not command Division any more. His merits are all summed up when you say he is a good fighter. He is a man of no very large amount of military knowledge and has no discretion at all. He was once a man, I think, of fine intellect but liquor has very much impaired it. He is generally considered a good officer and is no doubt a fair average Brigadier, but more than that I scarcely think he can lay claim to. The men have confidence in him and all seem satisfied.

To-morrow we are to move camp — that is exchange camps with the 3rd Div. which has been transferred to the 6th Corps.... Since our Div. has been transferred to the 2nd Corps & the 3rd Div. to the 6th it comes necessary for those two Div. to exchange camps in order to unite the corps. We are to go into their camps and they are to come into ours. It will be like putting a little man into "big breeches," & a big man into little breeches for our regiments are all small and theirs are all large. The advantage however is on our side, we can be accommodated in their camps, they cannot be in ours.

In camp near Culpepper, Va.
March 31st, 1864

We left our old camp this morning at 8 A.M. and arrived here about 11. We were assigned to the old camp of the 87th P.V. Halting some distance from it the Col. and I rode over to look at it, in expectation of finding a good camp. Imagine our surprise when we arrived at it and found it in a bad location without arrangement, and in a condition that can only be expressed by the adjective "abominable." The Col. got his ire up as he is wont to do frequently, and declared that he would rather encamp in a plain where no huts were to be seen than to live in such a camp. I concluded that such a step would be far better and so we went in search of a locality. We soon found it about 300 yds. in advance of the old camp. After a good deal of parleying & surveying to get the lay of the ground we finally determined how we would build the camp. Having done this we went for the regiment. On arriving there we found that many of the officers and nearly all the men desired to remain in the huts. The Col. hesitated for a few moments, but finally said that they should not and forthwith marched the regiment to the new location selected by us. By this time it was 12 but the men went to work with a will, and to-night finds us well on with a new camp made out of the lumber left by the 87th. If we are favored with good weather to-morrow, by evening our men will be as well housed as they were in the camp we left. How the 87th even lived in their camp is a mystery to us. Certainly they must have rotted. We lose nothing in moving camp, only incur a little labor & trouble. The Col. did a good thing in not allowing the men to go into the old huts. We never could have cleaned away the filth.

I am almost as comfortable to-night as I was last night. My floor is not so good consisting of loose clap-boards but by to-morrow night, I will have no reason to complain....

Apr. 1st, 1864

This to me has been a lonesome dismal day. The forenoon was cloudy and the afternoon was rainy with a fair prospect to continue all night. But what made it most dreary to me was my own thoughts. Feeling an indisposition to study this morning I wandered about camp for a while, & dropping into an officers tent picked up a book, a mere glance at which made me miserable all day. I am ashamed to mention its title to you if nothing else than shame prevented me. It was a book, however, widely known and I suppose widely read for it is a standard of its kind. I have often heard of it but had never seen it. My curiosity tempted me to look at it to find out where it was written, by whom it was written, and the main points in the life of the author. I skimmed over a few pages of it, but it was so thoroughly impregnated that every word & line was full of meaning. You know my weakness, it inflamed my imagination, & all day long I could not get my mind from it. Happily the impression has left me this evening. I longed for your presence not that I desired to bear to you such thoughts but because in your presence such thoughts cannot come. Forgive me, Hattie, for having burdened you with this much. This misfortune was uppermost in my mind and I could not help speaking of it....

There are no indications of a move at present; on the contrary it is evident that it will be postponed some time yet. Grant is again [in] Washington....

April 2nd, 1864

All bad feeling on account of the breaking up of the Corps has left me, if I ever had any. Bad feeling I do not think I was possessed of, I felt sad. No one entering the service made a more solemn vow or more sacredly kept it than I have done in regard to allowing dissatisfaction to influence my performance of duty. Not a word of dissatisfaction at the reorganization of the army has yet escaped [my] lips. I seldom speak of it and then only when it cannot be avoided. In regard to the other matter the least said the better.

Near Culpepper, Va.
April 3rd, 1864

I was guilty of something I know not what last evening, when I read in your letter of the 29th "should feel indeed that your commission to serve thus were my death warrant." For a short time I felt that I had lost you. What gave me the feeling I know not for I had not made up my mind to leave you and enter that service. For once I could not put my arms around you, could not kiss you. It was a strange freak but I hope you will forgive it. This evening it is quite different. You are seated quietly on my knee with your arms about my neck, & your soft cheek pressed close to mine. You are happy, so am I. Listen while I tell you something that will make you happier.

I have come to a conclusion concerning the Negro service, to wit that under the circumstances I cannot enter it. To give you my reasons at length would require too much time. I can only state briefly that I am unwilling to violate the principle upon which I have acted so long and with which I have every reason to be thus far satisfied. It is to quietly do my duty, which I am, and wait until I am called to fill a higher position. I will then feel sure of my ability to fill such higher position, besides having saved my dignity which would be lost by begging it. I am aware that in public life a man will not get along rapidly on this principle, but I long for the day when I can bid adieu to public life. Returning to private life my talents and character will give me my true position, since there intrigue cannot succeed. I will then be relieved from the necessity of obeying the commands of men who are my inferiors in every respect. You will agree with me in this. Yes you will love me the more for being thus independent.

...Likewise I wish to prevail upon you to spend the summer in the country. You can go where you like but go somewhere where you can exercise nearly the whole day in the free air. Do not be afraid of the rain, it will not hurt you. I am so well satisfied that all that is necessary to make you a strong woman is vigorous exercise, that I will not be quiet until the experiment is tried.

April 4th, 1864

Hattie, my Hattie, I would give the world did I possess [it] for one moment of your presence this afternoon....

Last evening I received a notice to attend Court Martial this morning at 10. at Div. Hd. Qrs. I left our camp about 9, having a little business to attend to before the Court met. That little business consisted in looking after the interests of a client. On Saturday I received a note from Col. Collis stating that he had been ordered to Phila. and that in consequence he would not be able to attend to a case which he had undertaken, and which was about to be tried, and asking me to take it and do what I could for the man. As it is a peculiar case I was well enough satisfied that it fell into my hands. A Captain Morgan of Co. F. 3rd Maine Reg't was promoted to be major of the reg't some time last December, and some of his friends at home published the promotion in a paper published at his home with the usual addenda that he was a brave and effective officer etc. Whereupon a Sergeant of his company in writing to a friend remarked that he had seen in the last "Republican" (the name of the paper) a puff of Maj. Morgan. That such stuff would do to tell the folks at home but that the soldiers would not be gulled by it. That Maj. Morgan was a drunkard and cowardly and giving instances of his cowardice at Chancellorsville and Gettysburg. This unfortunately for the Sergeant found its way into the papers, the papers found their way back to the regiment, and created great indignation among Maj. Morgan and his friends. The Major at first endeavored to compel the Sergeant to sign a retraction but the Sergeant refused and there upon he preferred charges against him for conduct prejudicial to good order and military discipline. In regard to the Statements of the Sergeant I have every reason to believe they are true from what I know of the regiment and the parties concerned. Major Morgan is what at home we call a drunkard although he would scarcely be called such here, on account of the great degree of beastliness required to make a drunkard, and as for his courage it [is] likewise doubtful but the proof is not quite so clear as in the other case. I have made up my mind that in defending the man, that if they succeed in proving that he wrote the letter, I will prove the Major a drunkard and try hard to prove him a coward. There are so many things involved in the case that I have not the remotest idea what the result will be. Courts Martial are very capricious in deciding law points and this makes it still more doubtful. I will give you the result when it is known.—

The last sitting of the Court of which Lt. Col Greenawalt was President was a stormy one. A few days before we had tried a man for desertion, and had acquitted him on the ground that he had not been mustered into service, a very necessary preliminary before a man can be found guilty of desertion. The original muster-in roll of this company was produced to the court but the mans name had been erased or marked out in two places, furnishing very strong evidence that he had been rejected. On the other hand it appeared in evidence that he had remained with the regiment about six months after the supposed rejection, had obtained a furlough gone home, returned to the regiment tried to obtain another furlough failed and then left (or as it was alleged deserted) and never returned. As I have remarked the court found him not guilty on the ground that he had never been mustered into the service, all six in number concurring the finding although Lt. Col Greenawalt seemed to be in doubt in regard to it. The case completed was handed to Gen. Birney. Without much consideration he returned with the statement that the court had erred. When up for reconsideration Greenawalt and the Judge Advocate, who was the same Morgan aforementioned, could see the error, mainly in [it] seemed by virtue of Gen. Birney's disapproval & so expressed themselves. It was very evident that they wished to have the court coincide with Birney's views. We talked a long while, Greenawalt insisted that the Court had decided wrong, attempted to "bully rag" as the boy[s] would say, refused to permit a vote to be taken until he saw that it was folly to resist longer. We voted five not guilty and one Greenawalt guilty, and the case was returned unaltered to the General. I have not heard the result of his last review, but no doubt he is wroth. But with the majority of the court this did not make much difference, with Greenawalt and the Judge Advocate it did. How I do despise a man much more I despise a general who must make a "tool" to use a vulgar expression of every man that serves under him. Such a one is Birney; he gives the worst officers in the Div. preference, if they are only subservient to his purposes. These are all the legal matters I have to tell you, except that since my return I have been reading Blackstone a good deal. I find my old habits readily come back. I feel more interest in my law books than I do in the army. After the long vacation I think I can return to my first love with renewed energy. This will be pleasing to you since in this business I can be home every night....

On picket, Pony Mtn. Va.
April 6th, 1864

Yesterday morning it was raining very hard, I got awake at day light, but hearing no stir in camp ... resolved to lay abed a little while.... The Asst. Clerk thrust his head into my tent and handed me an order which read that Maj. Duff was detailed as Field Officer of the Picket for the 2nd Brig. 3rd. Div. to report at Brig. Hd. Qrs. at 8 A.M. I hastily glanced at my watch & it said 7 o'clock 10 minutes. I said to myself the situation is interesting. The tour is for 3 days and I have nothing prepared, neither have I my breakfast. Getting up as quickly as possible I soon got things in shape and gave orders to have my horse ready & breakfast prepared. I was ready for the journey just at 8 o'clock with the exception of eating my breakfast. That being ready I sat down to it but took good care not to get up until I was fully satisfied, surmising that this was probably all I would get during the day. My surmise was nearly correct as the sequel will show. I reported at Brig. Hd. Qrs. The Picket had already been sent to Div. Hd. Qrs., following it I arrived there just in time to report that it was there. In a short time the Div. Officer of the day came up & having received his instructions from the Adjt. Gen'l he told me that my detail was to go to Pony Mountain to relieve a portion of the 4th Div. 2 A.C. A staff officer from Gen. [Joseph B.] Carr's Hd. Qrs. (4th Div.) should have been present to lead us to the Picket line, but he had failed to & the Div. Off. of the Day knowing where the Mt. was and that the Picket line was somewhere near there, started in search of it, & ordered me to follow him with my detail. I did so. It had rained all the night & day previous & was even then raining very hard. I felt very well, the storm sort of braced me, I faced it and seemed to enjoy it, but my mare, noble little animal as she is, could not face it; but fished around & chafed the bit, as though she desired to run away from it. When I looked at the men, however, I felt that my courage was very cheap for they were loaded with gun & cartridge box knapsack & haversack & with all this load had to face the storm & march on foot through the mud. They grumbled not a little of course, but I thought that if they could endure it even with grumbling, I should endure it without. We marched directly across the fields to the North side of the Mountain (which you will recollect is about a mile East of Culpepper C. H.). In taking this route, we had a great many ditches and little streams to cross over some of which the men jumped, but were compelled wade through many sometimes waist deep. Arriving at the North side of the mountain we halted & the Div. officer of the day went to find the Line. By this time my stock of patience was well nigh exhausted. I began to feel that I was not as well prepared for the difficulties to be encountered as I had imagined. My mare too, from jumping too many dicthes [sic] & carryng me over fields which on account of the long continued rain were just like a quicksand, began to be tired, made me sensible that she was so, & this fact added much to my discomfort. However it was time yet to become irritated. Hattie in the storm the men, being wet soon got cold & began to cry out forward march. I could not help them, for I did not know where to go. Imagine how I felt when we remained in this situation 3 hours at least before we could ascertain the portion of the line that was assigned to us. I indulged in the mean time in some I fear very injurious & unnecessary thoughts against negligent staff officers. I wondered too how this army had got along as well as it has, since every time I went on duty I found the same negligence and want of care on the part of officers who had the direction of affairs. It may be that my idea etc. is too nice, but so it is I never see a movement made that could not be accelerated & render[ed] easier, by the exercise of a little foresight & the expenditure of a little labor on the part of the staff. Once more started we arrived at the Picket line on the South side of the Mountain at 2 P.M. After some preliminaries I got my men posted and relieved the 4th Div. Although the line was not formed as I ordered I concluded to leave it alone a little while & endeavored to get something to eat. I went to a house near by together with the Div. Officer [of the] Day, but we met with poor reception. There was nothing in the house, and neither of us had any thing with us but the Col.['s] man had a haversack with some provision in it & he ordered this cooked for us. We had sufficient to make us all a very good meal and this was all we had for the day and considered ourselves fortunate in having this much. This morning I managed to get some breakfast & live in hopes of having a dinner since I have sent to camp for a supply.

We are posted on the South side of Pony Mt. in what I may term a ... wilderness. To be sure I am at a house which is inhabited but there is not a sign of life about it. The ground about the house was once cleared and cultivated but the young pines have been shooting up all round for at least five or six years which gives the whole a deserted forlorn appearance. The inhabitants of this house are a tall coarse slattern woman of perhaps thirty and five small children all her own, the oldest being 8 ½ years old, and her appearance would seem to indicate that before the completion of another half year the 6th child may be added to the number. Her husband is a Commissary Sergeant in Picket's Div. of the rebel army and has been in the service three years. She gets a living by cooking for the officers that stop at her home who pay her & with the money she buys corn meal from a neighboring mill. I asked her how she got along for clothes, & she replied that there is now a store in Culpepper at which they can buy some articles at exceeding high rates, for instance calico at 60 to 70 cents, and every other article in like proportion. She and her children had a miserable life indeed, but judging from her looks & habits & surrounding circumstances it never was any better. I mean to ask her what her husband did for a living before the war broke out.

...Far away from you as I am in the heart of a Va. Wilderness—the light of your love in my heart makes me happy....

Yesterday was a stormy day yet I feel gratified for its experience. I was sorely tempted to

April 6th 1864

From the Hall burying ground. Pony Mountain Va.

Leaves from burying ground near Pony Mountain, Virginia, April 6, 1864 (courtesy Allegheny College).

be impatient but my feelings were calmed by the reflection that my burden was light when compared to those of the most of God's creatures. The noble animal that carried me all day long with very little fretting taught me a lesson of endurance and patience which I needed to learn....

April 6th, 1864
[enclosed in previous letter]

...The day has been rather pleasant, the warm sun in the afternoon drying the mud some. I have spent the day to little profit, being employed nearly all day running along the line. I got it better arranged than it was yesterday, but it does not yet suit me and I will have a good deal of work to-morrow.

I am seated at the table in the house. I occupy one corner of it & three officers playing cards occupy the other corners. These gentlemen are not very proper company for you, but I am not able to crowd them out of the picture....

I can only think of a little gossip that I heard concerning out Div. & its commander. It is rumored that Gen. Birney is to be relieved in which event I have reason to believe Gen. Alex. Hays, who now commands our Brigade will command it. The rumor appears probable to me for many reasons. First Birney is disliked very much by both Hancock & Meade & on this account will be relieved by them if they can accomplish it. Besides he is the senior general in the Corps except Hancock, & in case any thing should happen [to] Hancock the Corps would fall to him. This I know to be contrary to Hancock's wishes, who desires Gen. [John] Gibbon comdg 2nd Div. to be the ranking Div. commander. On the other hand I think under the circumstances Birney would like to be relieved. He no doubt feels that further advancement in the army is impossible unless it changes commanders, & even should the commanders be changed, his chances would be very few, regulars getting the promotions now.—

Camp (near) Culpepper, Va.
April 9th, 1864

The night of the 6th I did not sleep very much because I had the whole responsibility of the Picket Line on my shoulders. I was prepared to get up any moment, and of course any sleep was not sound. In the morning—the 7th I rose at four o'clock, went out and inspected my line and found it all right, returned and had breakfast. After breakfast went out & properly arranged the line, the storms of the previous days preventing. This accomplished it was noon & the Div. Officer of the Day Lt. Col. Warner of the 40th New York made his appearance. He had already seen a portion of the line, it only remained for me to show him the remainder. We rode to the left, and when within 3 posts of that end of the line met the Corps Officer of Day, who was making his daily inspection. He was accompanied by one of Gen.

Hancock's staff. He was a <u>brigade</u> commander in this instance a colonel — Col. Coons of the 14th Ind. He was a rather large red faced ill natured looking man. The two Officers of the Day having the sash over the shoulder and readily recognized each other. Col. Coons remarked that he found our Pickets badly instructed etc. and requested Col. Warner to go along the line with him, so off we all started. The first post we visited we found the corporal seated on a board smoking a pipe, & two men seated near, ... one of them reading, the other one not doing any thing in particular. The sentinel as well as the Corporal failed to give the Col. the proper salute. The Col asked the men if they had not been instructed to salute. They replied that they had not. I was now compelled to say that his officer — a captain — had received proper instruction — whereupon he ordered me to place the officer in arrest. He claimed, however more compliments from the outposts & sentinels than I had instructed them to give, in fact more than my orders called for. It seemed that he had given the order, which was a written one, a much wider interpretation than I had. We continued to move along the line the Col. complaining all the time that our pickets were useless and slovenly. The truth is the men of our Div. have always been instructed not to pay any compliments when on Picket. Gen. Kearney would have cursed the officer to perdition who would have required a picket to salute him. Consequently the men did not fall into the change of system very readily. As we rode along I got into a discussion with Hancocks staff officer concerning the different interpretations put upon the order, he contending that theirs was right and I as stoutly contending that it was unwarranted. This staff officer was a captain of about the same physique as John Culbertson — with the same weak soft whining voice — he looked like the last effort of some aristocratic family whose days & years had been spent in debauchery. He was, however, well educated. He complained that discipline was not severe enough & that soldiers were not respectful enough to the officers. I expressed my opinion that no man should — that is no subordinate officer — ... insist on such strict discipline in the army while its head remained as it is; that the moment an officer did so he was ruined. Our volunteers in consequence of the mild sway of the President and our Generals have to be governed by a sort of moral suasion, which he did not understand. Whenever he is brought into contact with the soldiers he will learn it. — Having gone along the line of outposts, I being the only one that knew the way to the reserves rode forward to conduct the Colonel. Of course I immediately fell into conversation with him or rather he immediately began to talk to me; for I answered him only when compelled to do so by questions. The burden of his story was self congratulation that he belonged to the 2nd Corps that Hancock was a very fine officer etc. and then he insinuated that only Hancocks troops were obedient and respectful — that all others were slovenly negligent. With this valedictory he left us. Lt. Col. Warner and myself immediately returned to Hd. Qrs. and had some dinner. During this time we talked over the visit of the Corps officer of the Day, some remarks were made not very complimentary to the gentleman. —

The day was very pleasant and after dinner the Col. & myself went outside of the house to look around. The first thing that attracted our attention was a family burying ground.... It was a brick wall enclosure ... and contained 19 graves all marked except four. On the outside were 2 graves which the woman of the house told us were colored folks.... The wild and almost uninhabited spot in which it was located made me think that the man who located it had a queer fancy. Yet fifty years ago that spot may have been the dwelling place of a wealthy and powerful family. Who knows fifty years make a great change. The burial place is well taken care of ... flowers are planted along the walls on each side, while to the walls clings the ivy. I send you a couple of ivy leaves the flowers were not in bloom.... The spring is very backward....

I visited the Picket Line once in the afternoon then had supper. After dark I thought of talking with my Harriet but there was too much company so I postponed it. Besides the Lt. Col & myself there were two other officers of a Michigan regiment in the house. The[y] were all from the forests but only one of them is worthy of notice. He was a Lieutenant a man of about my height but much heavier build weighing 183 lbs. — had a deep sonorous & pleasing voice — and altogether was one of those physical perfections which I love to see. His character I judge is just as sturdy as his frame, for although he is not educated, he is possessed of a large amount of common sense. He entertained us during the evening with a description of his life and adventure in the forest which were related I judge without any exaggeration certainly without any ostentation of style. To me who had seen or heard of such things a thousand times these adventures were not so wonderful as they were to the Colonel who was raised and had lived all his life in the city....

...Just ask Firman when you see him if he could send me a horse.... One of my horses which cost me $150 — laid down & died yesterday. I must have another for I cannot get along with one....

April 10th, 1864

Continuing my picket experience I slept soundly during the night of the 7th and awoke at day light the next morning much refreshed. After inspecting the line I took breakfast and then arranged every thing for going home for this being my third day I expected to be relieved. At 11 o'clock I went down to the reserve expecting the relief to come there, it did not come returned again to my own Hd. Qrs. and was there only a few minutes when Lt. Col. Stoughton, the new Div. Off. of the Day made his appearance and announced to me that I was not to be relieved: on the contrary he had brought 400 men with him who were ordered to report to me and with them I was ordered to relieve the 4th Div. thereby extending the line about 2 miles. This my relief was not so pleasant as I had anticipated but I did not stop to grumble. There was not time to be lost. There was a day's work to be done and I must do it. I went with Col Stoughton showed him the line, and then went in search of the officer commanding the 4th Div. Line which we were ordered to take up. We soon found him below Stevensburg a captain of the 16th Mass. An intelligent talkative Yankee. We had not talked with him long before we ascertained that the burden of his grief was the same as ours viz. the Corps officer of the Day. For a short time we had a free interchange of opinion concerning the breaking up of the 3rd Corps and the disposition of the officers of the 2nd manifested towards us. This colloquy ended, I obtained from him the arrangement of his line and immediately returned to my men divided them into squads and sent them off to relieve his men and then returned to him and informed him that in a short time his men would return from the line. Just then it was dinner time and he having dinner ready invited me to dine with him which invitation I accepted gladly for I was hungry. After dinner I wished the Captain good luck bid him good bye and started to a cavalry camp near by to get a shoe put on my mare: she had pulled one off in the mud during the morning. I soon brought up in the 7th Mich. Cavalry and was very kindly informed by a blacksmith in Co. C that he would drive a shoe for me. I asked him if his officers permitted it, he replied they did not care. He got to work and soon put the shoe on. When he had finished I reached my hand in my jacket and pulled out my greenbacks to pay him. I asked him what his work was worth expecting to pay him about $1. Imagine my surprise when he answered me that he had enlisted to shoe horses that he was paid for so doing by "Uncle Sam" & that he could not receive pay from me. I was so much confused by his answer that I forgot to beg the man's pardon for insulting him: but quietly rode away. I was so struck by his unusual conduct that I could not for a long while get it out of mind, and I am sure I shall never forget the feeling with which I received this honest man's answer. I offered him pay because it is the universal practices for an officer or man to charge for any thing he does outside of his strict line of duty.

Leaving the blacksmith I rode to the right of the line and gave directions for my old reserve to go to where we had established a new one just in front of Stevensburg, and remained on the right until almost dark. I then started to go to Yates a house some two miles in rear of the line where the Div. off. of the day was stopping. I lost my way two or three times but finally after my patience was nearly exhausted found the place; after a short talk with that officer I left him to go to the main reserve in front of Stevensburg, where I had proposed to make my new Hd. Qrs. I lost my way again for there are so many roads that even in day time it [is] next to impossible to find the right one. I reached my destination after much vexation at half past nine P.M. I immediately lay down under a blanket with my sturdy Michigan friend expecting to get some rest, but I got but very little for I was so tired I could not be still. Oh how I wished for an opportunity to put my arms around you. My wife is dear to me at all times, but when I am tired and worn out, I feel as though I could not be restored except by a kiss from her. That lone dark night her presence would have been a new life to me. However, I slept some during the night, and felt somewhat restored in the morning. After breakfast the Div. Officer of the Day visited me and asked me to show him the right of the line. I went with him and when we neared the right of the line I was told by one of the officers on duty there, that a Major had come to relieve me was hunting me and had gone to the left of the line. I left Col. Stoughton and immediately went back to the reserve expecting to overtake the Major there. But he had been there & having been informed that I had gone to the right of the line started after me. I could do nothing but wheel about, and follow him again. On arriving at the right again I found him and received from him the much sought for information that he had come relieve me. I wrote him out a statement of the line and then started for camp where I arrived at 11 o'clock in a drenching rain. Dinner was soon prepared & consisted of "Apple Dumpling." Having eaten these I lay down and went to sleep. I awoke about 4 o'clock but lay abed until 5 — when I was called to supper. I took supper, sat down and wrote my wife a letter, washed all over put on clean shirts then went to bed and slept all night....

April 11th, 1864

I have felt unhappy to day and am feeling so to-night. This morning after breakfast when I was making preparation to go to Court Martial and defend Maxwell whose case I have before mentioned to you, I received an order detailing me as Division Inspector and ordering me to report to Maj. Gen. Birney without delay. I scarcely know how I felt after reading the order; my first impulse was to write and ask you if it was proper for me to go. I half thought that I should not go, yet the fact that I had been called without my own solicitation seemed to indicate that I should go. But I resolved to visit the Corps Inspector and state to him that the detail was personally objectionable to me and would ask him to revoke it.

In the mean time I reported at Div. Hd. Qrs. and was told that the Gen. would like to see me. I went in and told him I had come to report in obedience to orders. He said that since the orders required them to have a major at Div. Hd. Qrs. he had preferred me and intimated that he had caused me to be detailed. He did not say that he preferred me in any event. This would have been stretching his policy too far perhaps. He then told me how he desired me to act towards him, for really my action is in a great measure independent of him. In many things I always agreed with him, but often he attempted to control my action entirely because it was his interest to have certain matters suppressed. He could never count on me supporting his interests in such cases hence it was necessary to have me relieved and I was relieved.

It was this relieving that galled me. It is looked upon as an advancement to be detailed as an inspector especially of Div. consequently when I was relieved it was a disgrace although it was done through no demerit of mine. When I was again detailed it seemed to me that if I accepted it, I would only be subjecting myself to a new disgrace. It was this that so much made me desire to see & talk with you on the subject.

This afternoon I visited Corps Hd. Qrs. to see the Corps Inspector but did not find him at home consequently I was disappointed. I am then obliged to make up my mind without advice and I have resolved to go for the present. I have extreme reluctance to seem to evade any duty that is imposed upon me in the service. In order to avoid this I make a point to obey every order without hesitation so I shall do in this case: I will go to Div. Hd. Qrs. tomorrow.... I trust that I may find the situation more pleasant then it was when I left it. There is one advantage now over my former details and that is that I cannot be relieved by Gen. Birney nor by any other Gen. in the Army without the consent of the Inspector General of the Army. His consent I am sure can only be obtained for some direlection of duty in the department — hence I feel safe.

Hd. Qrs. 1 Div., 3 A.C.
April 12th, 1864

This evening finds me at Div. Hd. Qrs. although I do not feel at home yet. The day has passed without the occurrence of any thing unusual. I attended Court Martial this forenoon and afterwards assumed the duties of my new office. I have done nothing as yet for I was kept busy at the Court. We were unable to finish the case of Maxell. It will require another day. The case is still in doubt.

I cannot write you a long letter this evening because as I have said I do not feel at home. I cannot talk. Two gentlemen are seated to my left playing dice. This is not very comfortable to me but I cannot avoid it. Give love to all & accept a kiss from your husband

Near Brandy Station, Va.
April 13th, 1864

We have had a review to-day, by those distinguished Generals Meade and Hancock. It was only a Div. review consequently it was soon over. After the review, these generals accompanied by Gen. Birney and several Brig. too numerous to mention called on Minor Botts, old "connecting link," as I heard a staff officer very facetiously & very aptly call him to-day. They remained there but a short time when the[y] came to our Hd. Qrs. and had lunch. They did not remain long consequently the staff did not get riotous as usual.

After all this had taken place I got something to eat and went out to condemn some property. This done I proceeded towards Corps Hd. Qrs. to see the Assistant Inspector Gen'l, as I had not seen him since assuming my duties here as well as to ask some information of him. When I arrived at Corps Hd. Qrs. I was informed that he was at his dinner. I waited a half hour and then again asked for him and was told that in a very few minutes I could see him. I concluded that I had waited long enough and got on my horse and rode home. I have since been told that he is a very exalted personage, and difficult to see. It is fortunate that I was unable to get an interview [f]or not knowing the style of man I might have made a bad impression. I will know how to take him now. I can reach him with a communication and meet him some time accidentally.

Hd. Qrs. 3 Div. 2 A.C.
April 14th, 1864

You may ask what I have been doing. I can reply that I have been attending Court Martial and condemning property. The case of Maxwell is not yet concluded. I think to-morrow will finish it.

...Everything is very quiet here. Hancock continued his review to-day in the 4th Div. I was too busy to be present.— By the way Greenawalt was Div. Off. of the Day yesterday and Col. Brooke of 53rd P.V. was Corps Officer of the day. I saw Greenawalt this morning, he says that Col Brooke found much fault with our picketing. My successors on the picket seem to face ever worse than I and I thought I was scolded enough.

I do not yet know how we will get along with this terrible 2nd A.C. They seem to me to add insult to injury. Since our Corps has been broken up the[y] have an idea that we are good for nothing. These fellows will be remembered. We may perhaps meet them face to face of one of these days....

Hd. Qrs. 1st Div. 3 A.C.
April 15th, 1864

To-day finished the testimony in the case [of Maxwell] and to-morrow will I suppose finish my part in it....

...Hattie, you are losing nothing by my absence. I feel that my present labor is making me a better man. When I return to you I will be fitted to be your husband....

Hd. Qrs. 3rd Div. 2 A.C.
April 18th, 1864

By the way I do not like the appearance of Col. Brooke. I can scarcely believe in him to the same extent that Charles does. I have often queried why he has not been made a Brigadier. The matter was explained to me a short time ago. He was the major of [John F.] Hartranfts regiment the 6th [4th] I believe (3 mos) which marched away from the 1st battle of "<u>Bull Run</u>" it is presumed that his name is registered in Washington and this black spot set opposite to it....

...If you see father tell him to buy me one [a horse]. I need two horses now more than I did with my regiment. I want a <u>strong</u> <u>active</u> horse. I care nothing for looks it is <u>action</u> and <u>endurance</u> that I want. I make no exception to any color except gray or white.

April 19th, 1864

After breakfast we had a Div. Review Drill, preparatory to the great Corps review which is expected to take place in a day or two. Lately we have had some new instruction on reviewing and all officers have not yet learned them. Our review this morning I thought a very common affair....

After review I went to Corps Hd. Qrs. On the way I passed by where Hancock was reviewing the 1st Div. of the Corps. The review had just ended as I approached, but I had an opportunity to see some of the troops. They looked very well. I am mistaken if they do not look better than our own although even by outsiders our Div. is said to present a fine appearance. Returning from Corps Hd. Qrs. I had dinner and almost immediately thereafter I went out to inspect property. I went to the 17th Maine first and then to the 110th. There I found Lt. Col. Greenawalt in all his glory. It seems to me I have never told you that he was assigned to the command of that regiment immediately after its return. He gets along very well, but they do not like him apparently as well as they do me. Many of the officers as well as the men seemed glad to see me. I took supper with them and did not get back to my quarters until near eight o'clock. Immediately on my return I learned that the Paymaster was paying & I hied me to him and got 2 mos. pay. I send you by express $250.

...Tell him [Firman] not to buy a horse that has been worked in harness, if he can avoid it. Such horses have a fixed habit of leaning forward which makes them unpleasant to ride.

April 20, 1864

After breakfast I signed some papers, attending Court Martial & reading Maxwells defence. The case was concluded to-day I have not learned the decision — then inspected the Provost Guard at these Hd. Qrs. and then it was dinner time. I found the Provost Guard in very good condition, but the guard house in an abominable filthy state. I think I shall have to address a not[e] to Gen. Birney concerning it. It is cruel to keep prisoners the way they are generally kept in the army.— After dinner I inspected 911 boxes of Hard Bread, then went out to my usual labors....

I am again tenting with Capt. Ford....

April 21st, 1864.

I lay abed this morning until half past eight. I certainly was lazy. At that hour I got up and took my breakfast and all forenoon worked in the office. After dinner I went to the 2 Brig. Commissary and worked all afternoon at investigating their sales of whisky. Gen. Bir-ney ordered the investigation in order to discover frauds which he suspects have been com-mitted by some persons. In my investigation of the same subject yesterday, I discovered that Private Geo. R. Hall of Co. F. of my own regiment had drawn 8 Galls. of whisky in the month of March, by signing his orders Geo. R. Hall 1st Lt. Co. F. 105th PV. I suspect that I will dis-cover like forgeries in some of the other regiment[s].[1] Whisky [is] the most terribly [sic] enemy to good order and military discipline we have in the army. I wish they would do away with it entirely. I wonder why the necessity of such a step cannot be seen. Our rulers are blind on the subject.

Things begin to look a little like a move. We have had fine weather now for more than a week and the roads are beginning to dry up....

Hd. Qrs. 3 Div. 2 A.C.

April 23rd 1864....

I rose quite early this morning and signed papers before breakfast. After breakfast packed up my extra private & public furniture preparatory to sending it to Alexandria, then went out to inspect the unserviceable property belonging to the 63 P.V. I went to the regiment but found the officers all out on drill and had to return to Hd. Qrs. I then went to the 126th N.Y. and to 1st Brig. Hd Qrs. on my whisky investigation. Thence returned to Hd. Qrs. had lunch and went forth again to the 63rd P.V. & from thence to the 40th N. Y. and did not return to Hd. Qrs. again until 6 P.M. So you see I have been busy all day. After taking what we call din-ner here at 6 P.M. I returned to my quarters and found yours of the 19th.

We can envy the men at home during the spring months. We have our house cleaning as well in the army as at home. Our cleaning however, is of a different nature. We get up and march and leave our dirt and houses behind. This movement is just as sweeping your house-cleaning at home. Only those who have served in a large army can have any conception of the dirt and filth that accumulates in and about a camp during the winter season. It becomes necessary for health and comfort to leave it whenever the days get warmer.—

Our move is near at hand. All the preparation are nearly completed a few more wagons are needed, which I doubt not to-morrow will bring. Unless it should storm again we will move within 3 days. It is idle to speculate as to the route: I am satisfied with the certainty that we are to move against the army in our immediate front. I care not what line of attack is adopted. Let the work be done in earnest. Then no fears as to the result.

Our Corps was reviewed yesterday by Gen. Grant and it is said looked very fine. I tried to get a good look at the general but failed....

11

Grant Starts to Move

Lincoln hoped Grant would fight, and he did. The new Union chief saw the key to success to be coordination of the several Union armies — a coordination that had scarcely existed heretofore. It would prevent Lee from moving troops from inactive theaters to active ones to offset the superior numbers of Union troops deployed. Despite Grant's planning, the Army of the Potomac gained little help. In the South, Nathaniel Banks was stymied on the Red River and never launched a campaign for either Mobile or Texas. Benjamin Butler in moving from Fort Monroe on Richmond was outmaneuvered and bottled up on the Bermuda Hundred along the James River. Franz Sigel, whose troops were supposed to clear the Shenandoah Valley, suffered defeat at New Market. Grant nevertheless marched the Army of the Potomac forward, crossing the Rapidan and endeavoring to outflank Confederate trenches to force Lee into open combat. The Southern general responded by once again trying to defeat the Northerners in the woods of the Wilderness, where a year earlier he had won at Chancellorsville.

Hd. Qrs. 3rd Div. 2 A.C.
April 28th, 1864

I have some army news which if true is important. The Burnside expedition, it is said landed at Alexandria and left there this morning marching towards this camp. I am inclined to give credence to the report, because I believe that the best disposition that can be made of Burnside['s] force is to add it to this army. I do not suppose that it will come directly here. I think it will enter the Shenandoah valley & turn the left flank of Lee's army. This seems to me to be the only true way of advancing into Virginia. Once possessed of Gordonsville and Charlottesville, we have the state of Virginia Richmond included within our grasp. I have no faith in the McClellan strategy which desires to dig round the edges of the rebellion. Let us assemble an army and march into the heart of the rebellious territory, they will of course march to resist us, let us then fight them, if we are defeated we can retreat and try again, if victorious we scatter their army and occupy their country. We could go to Richmond and dig them out, but what would that avail us. Lee would only retreat to the next town and [we] would be obliged to dig him out of there also, and the digging would go on ad infinitum until our resources would become exhausted. I am glad that a different kind of strategy is to be adopted. Grant is concentrating a large army here with which to crush Lee's army, and this effectually done closes the rebellion. I am feeling more hopeful this evening than I have felt for many days. Minor reverses we have had lately to be sure. These are nothing because they decide [nothing]. But believing as I do that the rebellion body & soul is here in Virginia and confident that Gen. Grant is preparing to crush it, I await without fear the issue.

I did not write you yesterday because my time was occupied all day in moving camp and it was late at night before I got every thing arranged.... I send you a kiss.

April 29th, 1864

The indications are still more marked that we are about to move. The head of Burnsides Column reached here to-night. His whole corps will be here to-morrow. He has a number of negro soldiers with him. How will the chivalrie Virginians like to cross bayonets with these men. Let them measure them if they dare. Justice will ere long overtake these Southern barbarians.

By the way have you read the Presidents letter to Col. Hayes Editor of the Frankfort Commonwealth. It accurately defines the President's position on the slavery question. He is an anti-slavery man believes that slavery is wrong yet he does not permit that belief to influence his conduct of public affairs.

The President seems to have started on his official career with the conviction that the constitution acknowledged and protected slavery. He took an oath to preserve and protect the constitution therefore he must preserve slavery, and he did not feel it his duty to overthrow it until he felt that he could not save the constitution without overthrowing it. Suppose he had saved the constitution and slavery, what would have been the result? We would just have been in the situation we were in before the war and our blood would have been spilt in vain.

I started out on this struggle with very different feelings. I felt that slavery was a crime and that before we could ask the favor of Heaven on our cause we must wash our hands of the crime. So long as we upheld slavery we were committing the crime for which God was punishing us. Was the punishment likely to cease before the crime was repented of. It seems to me that the President made a great mistake in adopting the policy which he pursued and this very mistake has cost us thousands of lives & will cost us thousands more. I am glad that the President has seen that the crime is impolitic.—

April 30th, 1864

This has been a lonely disagreeable day. I have felt badly all the while. Several times I thought of my Hattie and wished her by my side....

Gen. Burnside has relieved the troops of the 3rd Corps which were guarding the railroad. This looks as though Burnside was to have charge of the railroad. To guard it and keep our communication open with Washington at all times seems to be the duty assigned to him. This leaves the whole army of the Potomac free to advance against Lee no longer embarrassed with protecting our base of operation. We should be able to accomplish something. Rumor has it that Lee is being largely reinforced from the South East coast. No doubt this is true and he will still confront us with a large army. I cannot yet make up my mind as to what will be the result but I hope better the last few days.

What do I think of the Plymouth affair?[1] Well, I think first that Gen. [Henry W.] Wessels ought either to [be] cashiered or hung. He certainly did not make such a defence as he ought to have made with 2500. It is about time to hold Brigadiers to a strict accountability and compel them to fight their way out when they get into a tight place. A general says he is overpowered by numbers and the papers take up this stupid declaration and spread it broadcast over the land. Gen. Wessells lost 150 men killed out of 2500.. What is that. He should have lost ¾ of his men at least before surrendering.—The Grand Ecore affair was another stupid thing. Was it not morally certain that Kirby Smith would attack, before he effected a junction with [Frederick] Steele. Why then was he not on his guard. The operations of other armies so frequently appear like childplay when compared with operations in Virginia, that I often feel disgusted on reading of them.

May 1st, 1864

I cannot fill this sheet than by giving you an item of my military experience to day. Some ten days since Gen. Meade issued an order stating what amount of camp & garrison equipage — this is tents etc. — which should be allowed to each Div. Brig. & regiment, and directing all surplus to be turned in. As usual inspectors were directed to report every officer who did not comply with the order. Day before yesterday I rode through the Division and noted all excesses, not omitting Div. Hd. Qrs. because I felt myself as much in duty bound to prevent excesses here as in the regiments. It so happens that Gen. Birney is living in a "Sibley Tent" which is disallowed by Gen. Meade's order, and this tent was reported by me as excess. This evening Maj. Binney ... said to me: "Major, the General directed me to say to you that he has read your <u>report</u> and <u>will turn</u> in <u>his</u> tent," as much as to say the general considers your report as directed to him personally. I answered him not all as it was my duty as well as policy to do. I felt, however that Gen'l Birney had not treated me with proper consideration. He takes my official acts as a personal affront, because he thinks they interfere with his comfort. This situation of affairs makes me feel badly sometimes, but I have determined to be an inspector — to do my duty as it should be done, even though it may offend Gen'l Birney. I have nothing to expect from his friendship and need fear nothing from his enmity. My duties however are unpleasant as you will see. It was this unpleasantness, that made me desire to decline when first appointed but since I am launched forth I shall not turn back.

Every thing is in readiness for a move, but many seem to think that we will not move for a week yet....

...I send you an apple bud from Brandy. Accept a kiss with it. Give love to all.

May 2nd, 1864

There is very little army news afloat now. I hear that the Penn. Reserves are very much dissatisfied and are becoming mutinous. I wish these Reserves were out of this army. They are a standing reproach to Penn. I hang my head every time I hear them mentioned here. I expect to chronicle the running from the next fight, and they will excuse themselves by saying that they have no business to fight since their term of service has expired.

In taking a ride this morning I passed the spot where an old house stood once. I thought of my wife and immediately went to the deserted garden to find her a flower. I send you what I found. Like all Virginia gardens it was devoid of beauty....

May 3rd, 1864

While all is hurry and bustle I will try to write you a short letter....

We are ordered to move to-night at 11 o'clock. From reading the orders I judge that the march is to be continued all day to-morrow. The movement is a repetition of the Mine Run movement of last fall. Every precaution has been taken to make the movement prompt and to keep it secret until the blow is struck. I hope that no one may fail us for much depends on the issue. I have faith in our troops if they are properly led. If Grant is with us then all may go well. I fear Meade is too undecided to win great victories.

With regard to my personal fate I have thought but little, except that I have resolved more firmly than ever to do my duty. I feel that under present circumstances I am called upon to do more than my duty. Where my duty may call me, and what fortune may befall me I cannot know, I only know that with me as with all others and with my country whose destiny is at stake, God will deal justly. It will not matter what disposition he makes of me.—

On the move I will write to you as often as I can. I presume however that this will be [the] last letter I can send to you until the smoke of a great battle has cleared away. If we are successful and are likely to take the rebels at a disadvantage they will fall back and we will not have a fight immediately but should Lee feel disposed to stand then the crash will come soon.—

I cannot say more than bid you good night. It is perhaps a bit of good fortune that you can receive this valediction in writing. Were I with the dangers to which I am about to be exposed might seem much greater.[sic] Remember me to all. Give me a loving kiss....

Chancellorville, Va.
4 p.m. May 4th, 1864

Although up all last night I cannot sleep and have nothing to do. Therefore I must write to you. The day thus far has been very pleasant and we have reason to congratulate ourselves on the success of to-days manouvres.

Last night at half past eleven we took up our line of march going towards Elys Ford on the Rapidan. By marching quite fast we reached there at 10 a.m. and as the 1st & 2nd Div. had crossed in advance of us without meeting any opposition we likewise immediately crossed without interference. After a short halt on the South or rather East side we pushed on to this place arriving here at 2 p.m. having made a march since leaving camp of 18 or 20 miles. Here we have taken up merely for the night of course the same line on which [we] were attacked May 2 1863. The 1st Div. being on the left the 2 next the 3rd next & the 4th on the right connecting with the 5th Corps (which crossed at Germania Hills) near Wilderness Tavern. The 6th Corps likewise crossed at Germania, and this represents to you the movement of the whole army. As for the enemy we know nothing. Not a single shot has been fired to-day, and we have not heard from our cavalry which is in advance of the 5th Corps. We shall rest quietly to night and to-morrow no doubt continue our manouvering going I think towards Spotsylvania C.H. It is Meade['s] intention I think to manouvre around Lee's right, and to compel him to fall back or fight on equal ground. I think that we will have several days manouvering before any fighting takes place although fighting may begin any day.

Nothing of great interest happened during our march to-day. At Ely's Ford I stopped to see the whole Division over the Bridge and waiting took the trouble to pluck a momento of the place for you. I could not find a flower so I broke off a willow & bitter birch twig. I send them both in order that if one should become destroyed you will still have the other.

When we arrived within three miles of Chancellorville we began to see evidences of the fierce struggle that had taken place last May. The first item noted was the earthworks thrown up by us on Monday after our defeat on Sunday. These had all been leveled by the enemy. When we arrived at what is called the Chancellor House, the browned walls of which are still standing we began to examine the ground more closely for here it was that we had been engaged. The first thing noticed was the effect of rebel artillery fire under which we lay for more than an hour. The wonder was how any one escaped from the terrible ordeal uninjured, since it was agreed on all hand that the fire was close enough to take the "hair off." Gen. Hancock made his Hd. Qrs. near the Chancellor House among some trees which still surround the ruins. We are encamped just on the ground where we had the hard fight of May 3rd. Our Hd. Qrs. are at the grave-yard near the Fair-view House. This house has likewise been burned, though I think subsequent to the battle. Nearly all of our dead have been collected and buried in pits, but none of the graves have been marked, consequently no one can now be recognized, and no bodies can be recovered. Perhaps it is well, for some day no doubt the bones of the heroes who are carelessly covered with earth now and unrecognized will be collected and a suitable monument erected to their memory. The[y] fell here fighting for their country it will I trust reclaim their tomb and recognize their martyrdom. In riding over the field I was shown by Col Craig the spot where Col McKnight fell. I dismounted and culled these small purple (4 leaf) flowers which I enclose you. The other flowers which I enclose we collected on the hottest part of the field & are sent to represent the battleground of Chancellorville in your collection. The velvet flowers are very pretty I think.—

Since looking over the ground here, examining the relative positions held by the contending forces, we can see more plainly than ever the bottomless stupidity of our generals. You will recollect that I wrote to you at the time denying to Sickles the right to the credit the papers had give him. I have had the satisfaction to find my censure deemed just by every one who has talked about the fight to-day. The 11th Corps broke, our line on the right was driven in and the 1st & 3rd Div. of Sickles Corps were much exposed by this disaster. Just at this juncture it got dark and the fighting ceased. Of course it was well known that the fighting would be renewed the next morning. It therefore behooved Sickles to get his corps into position. Instead of doing this quietly under cover of darkness as he might have done, he made a night attack upon the enemy to accomplish some purpose I know not what. It is generally supposed to have been done to rescue the 1st & 3rd Div. of his Corps which have always been represented as entirely surrounded. This however is certain. These Divs. were no less surrounded after the night charge than before. The truth is this night charge which has always been called a great thing — was a great farce. It never amounted to any thing, except perhaps half demoralizing our division and unfitting it for the battle of the next day. But this was not the only injury arising out of the night attack. It delayed our getting out of our bad position until after daylight the next morning — and the rebels attacked us at a great disadvantage and threw part of our Div. into confusion. Otherwise the battle of Sunday might have had a different result. I will not pursue this subject further at present —

I am quite well this evening and have felt content all day. The day has been very pleasant to a horseman, but most too warm for the soldiers....

New Spotsylvania C. H. Va.

7 A.M. May 10th, 1864

I last wrote you from Chancellorville in the afternoon of the 4th. Since then we have been so busy marching and fighting that I have not had an opportunity to write, & if I had could not send you a letter, for communication with the rear is cut off.

I write now hoping that by some chance my letter may reach you. We left Chancellorville early in the morning of the 5th, marched to Todd's Tavern about 6 miles South East. Here we halted until 12 o'clock when we about faced, marched towards Chancellorville about 4 miles, then turned to the left on what is called the Brock Turnpike & marched near to the front where this Turnpike crosses the Plank road leading from Fredricksburg to Orange C.H. Here line of battle was formed along the turnpike facing down the Plank road. The rebels on learning that we had crossed the Rapidan moved down the Plank road from Orange C. H. to meet [us] apparently confident that they could drive us back. The fight or rather battle which we had with them took place at the point where the Brock Turnpike crosses the Orange C. H. Plank road thereby forming a cross road. On our arrival there we found the 2 Div. of the 6th Corps holding the cross road. Immediately after we have formed line an attack was ordered and our Div. as usual had the misfortune to be in advance. Hay's Brigade was on the right Ward's on the left. Gen. Birney sent me to Gen. Ward & I remained with him all the afternoon. Hay's Brigade soon became heavily engaged. Ward was ordered to advance but his troops seemed very reluctant to go and it was only after a good deal of labor that we got them started. When they were once started I went to the extreme left, and urged it forward as fast as possible. It went forward very well but unfortunately the right of the Brigade halted and the left swung round until the extreme left got under the fire of the right. Having got this far I was compelled to halt them. I went to the right, but all efforts to get them to advance were vain & thus [the] afternoon was lost. The casualties in the Brigade were few as there was only a skirmish line in front of the Brigade most of the time. Hay's Brigade was more unfortunate.

It fought on the right of the Plank road, and found a heavy force of the enemy in their front. One of the hardest contests of the War took place in which we lost very heavily and the rebels equally as heavy. Gen. Hays was killed and nearly every field officer of his brigade either killed or wounded. In our regiment, the Col [Calvin A. Craig] was wounded in the face, the Lt. Col. [J. W. Greenawalt] (mortally) in the abdomen. Capt. Hamilton was killed & Lts. Kimple, [James] Sylvis & [James] Miller wounded. About 25 men were killed & 100 wounded. No advantage was gained on either side the two armies lying at dark in the same positions in which they had been fighting. Thus we lay during the night of the 5th. At 5 A.M. the morning of the 6th an attack was ordered & began vigorously. Hays Brigade advanced on the right and [Ward's] on the left. We drove them for about two miles when our advance line having exhausted its supply of ammunition being fatigued & meeting fresh troops began to hesitate and finally gave way and we lost about ½ mile. We checked the enemy at this point and after a good deal of firing the line became quiet. Soon a fresh brigade was sent us from Burnsides Corps and another attack was ordered. It was made with vigor & determination, but met with equal vigor & determination & did not succeed, although we lost no ground. Another short quiet ensued which was broken by a heavy fire on our extreme left beyond our Div. & in the 1st it was said. It did not continue long before it was evident that our line had been turned and was falling back in much confusion. The confusion spread until it became a stampede and all efforts to rally the men was vain & we fell clear back to the Brock Turnpike where we had erected works and it was with difficulty that we rallied there. However we succeeded in getting them in shape and as the rebels did not follow us closely we had time to get our troops in shape. We remained quiet until 4 o'clock when a heavy force of Longstreets Corps advanced on the left of the plank road and attacked our works. Our men held them in check for about ¾ of an hour when the first line broke, the break beginning in the 4th Div. our old 2nd, the second line however stood & the rebels not pressing their advantage closely the first line was reoccupied and the enemy repulsed. This ended the fighting of the 6th. The result was like that of the 5th no advantage on either side. The rebels had lost more killed than we and I think we lost a few more prisoners than they. Next morning the lines were quiet for some time when it began to be rumored that the rebels were in full retreat. Our Brigade was sent out to reconnoiter and soon found them posted about 2 miles in our front in strong works. We remained quiet the rest of the day & just after dark our army began to move to the left & next morning at 8 o'clock we moved off to the left & again reach[ed] Todd's Tavern by noon. About dark of the same day we were put into position there & remained so until noon yesterday when we again moved to the left but did not reach our present position until after dark. We have been quiet all night. This morning there is skirmishing the enemy seems to be along our entire front. We are on the South bank of the Po River near Spotsylvania C. H. It is useless for me to attempt to tell you the position held by our army. We have gained no particular advantage yet except in maneuvering our rear is near Fredericksburg.[2]

I am very well and have been ever since leaving camp on the 7th. I was struck on the right heel by a canister ball & received a slight bruise but nothing more. My spur saved [me] from a severe injury.... Accept many kisses from your husband

<u>Levi</u>

The dog-wood posey carries many kisses.

Allegheny City
May 10th 1864

My dear one

How shall I begin to tell you of these sad anxious days— more intense in their suspense than any before. Hope and Faith are still with me. I have sought to hasten the weary night with reading of your letters in less terrible time. They have comforted me. How true my words are, that I had rather be in possession of your most noble letter of the 3rd than have received my husband home with his former comrades who came on Saturday — and this because I love him so well. Still the cloud of war shuts out the view. We dare not be sanguine — and yet Oh. God, let it be not in vain to hope. There is prayer and thanksgiving in every heart for the success already given. My own precious one am I not near you your heart speaks to me — you live to praise God and serve Him.

I will not write more. Oh, if your eyes never look upon what I have written —
God bless and keep you safe

> your own
> Hattie

> Near Spotsylvania C. H.
> May 11th, 1864
> 6 P.M.

We have been fighting here since yesterday morning. The contest has been about equal. I am still safe and well also Charles I saw him to day.[3]

Love to all. I can not write more now much love

> Battlefield (near) Po River Va.
> May 13th, 1864

It is announced that a mail will go out to day noon and I avail myself of the opportunity to let you know that I am still safe. We had a brilliant fight yesterday, capturing at least 20 pieces of artillery & 5 thousand prisoners. This is merely my guessing. I have no official information. I believe I forgot to tell you in my letter that I am now in command of my regiment. Day before yesterday the 63rd P.V. was given into my charge & I had command of both in the fight of yesterday. Our losses were rather slight yesterday considering our success. It is thought this morning that the rebels are retreating. We have now been fighting and manouvring for nine consecutive days & the men are almost worn out.[4]

I am still well but worn out. Charles was safe yesterday after most of the fighting was over. I have not seen him since. Give love to all & send word home.

Do not forget that I love you

> May 14th, 1864

During the short lull which seems now before us I will try to write you a letter. I wrote you a note yesterday morning. I did not have time to write you a letter. At that time I did not expect that to day would find us here.

A reconnaissance made yesterday morning discovered that the enemy instead of retreating was entrenched in our front. Nothing was done yesterday but throw forward the left of our line to follow the left of the enemy which had been withdrawn a short distance. This morning preparation[s] were made for an attack or demonstration of some kind. Gen. Gibbon commanding the 2 Div. was to lead and we were to follow. We got into shape for advancing & then halted. The movement did not begin and we began to wonder why. About eleven o'clock a staff officer came round and informed us that the attack did not take place this morning because the troops were not in position in time. He added that an attack would likely be ordered about 4 P.M. It is now half past 12 and all quiet along the line except occasional shots from sharpshooters. I do not think that an attack will be made to day for I do not think that we are in position. I do not presume that this front will be directly attacked but that it will be attempted to turn one flank most likely their right again. I do not know to what troops this duty will be assigned but I think most likely to Warren's. The enemy seems to contest every inch of the ground with bitter resolution and I do not suppose that we will have an end of the fighting until he is annihilated or we are defeated.

A congratulatory order was issued by Meade yesterday which you will no doubt see before this letter reaches you. Our captures you will observe have been quite large, but the spirit of the enemy is apparently unbroken. All of the artillery and about 5000 of the prisoners were captured by the 1st & 3rd Div. of the 2nd Corps in a charge made yesterday morning. We surprised the enemy and captured nearly a whole division including its commander Edward Johnston. The enemy came well nigh recovering the ground in the afternoon, by the most persistent attack I have ever witnessed during my three years soldering. The rebel dead lay literally in heaps. Our men were slaughtered also but not so fearfully as the enemy.

It was said yesterday that Gen. C. C. Augur had landed at Aquia Creek with a large reinforcement for us. As yet I have not heard of his arrival here. It may be that we are just now waiting for him to come up. Meade says in his congratulatory order that we may expect reinforcements but the enemy none. I hope they may speedily come. Notwithstanding our decided success, I still fear the issue. To be sure we are stronger than the enemy but he is more desperate, and desperation will accomplish many things when strength will fail. I trust our generals will be as cautious during the time that is to come as they were during the last 12 days.

Personally considered I have escaped very well, but how long this immunity will continue is very uncertain. I trust and hope that I am destined to live through it all. Charles is safe & well. I saw him this morning. Their brigade he says has lost about one half its numbers. The loss in our regiment now consists of 2 officers killed, 9 wounded & one missing, 30 men killed 160 wounded and 17 missing. We left camp with 18 officers & 337 men. Another hard fight will almost annihilate the regiment. I have no idea what the loss in the whole army is, but I think it must be very large.

The weather is quite pleasant to-day....

I had the pleasure yesterday of receiving your letters of the 3rd & 5th... they came at an opportune moment. I had just been marching & on duty in front 48 hours with out rest or sleep....

I looked over the battlefield yesterday for some time, hoping to find a flower to send. I could find none. I enclose herewith two or three little yellow flowers that grow near where I write.... Occasionally as I write the whistle of the rebel sharpshooters bullet sounds above my head....

Flower from Battlefield of Po River, Spotsylvania, May 14, 1864 (courtesy Allegheny College).

3 P.M. As it is quite certain that we will have no further fighting here to day I have concluded to finish my letter. Our troops as I surmised have gone to the left.... I have no doubt that about dark we will march in the same direction.

I send you a honey suckle.... Accept much love from your husband

Allegheny City
May 14th 1864

My own dear husband

How thankful, how more than happy, how — but why attempt to tell for words cannot. Your letter of the 10th reached me last evening. I had given up hope — so terrible had been the carnage — and I knew that your Div. had been foremost. There have been fiercer struggles since. I know not that you are still safe, but I hope — nay I <u>believe</u> that you are. Oh, how my heart has yearned to comfort [you] in the weary weary week that is closing. And yet the dreadful work is not ended. We hear cheering news. But fear to believe. May God bless Gen. Grant with wisdom and strength. Most fearfully have the death-messengers stricken down the noble brave. Gen. Hay's funeral occurs at two this afternoon. Pittsburg is doing all honor to fallen hero. The 9th P[ennsylvania] R[eserves] will follow his body. I wonder they are not ashamed to be seen on the streets— some of them I pity — because they are ashamed. But indeed I feel like drawing my drapery aside, as I pass one on the street, by right of my husband's deeds....

Hattie

Battlefied (near) Po River, VA
May 15th, 1864 (night)

To day the army shifted further to the left but no fighting has been done & to night every thing is quiet even picket firing has ceased. All of our army except Burnsides Corps and our Div. is now on the East side of the Ny River, and I suppose that before morning we will like- wise retire across it. The design of this manouvre is to gradually turn the enemy's right flank and to avoid attacking him in his entrenched position. This is a terrible country to campaign in and this is the most laborious campaign ever undertaken by the army of the Potomac. I venture to say that McClellans retreat from White House to Harrison's landing was child's play compared with it. Our men are beginning to look worn and fatigued. Our losses have been very heavy, but how heavy I do not exactly know. The rebel losses have been much heav- ier than our own, and how they can now confront us so boldly I am at a loss to understand. I guess they intend to make this the last ditch and have made preparations to abandon every other portion of the confederacy first. If this surmise is correct we may not expect to get Rich- mond right away. One thing however is certain that if Lee has not actually drawn troops from other points to strengthen his army thereby leaving them exposed, he will be unable to aid any other army, and as their Western army is weak I expect [William T.] Sherman to be suc- cessful.

Battlefield near the Po, Va.
May 16th, 1864

I know your anxiety is very great yet it had not come so vividly before me as it did in your letter....

To-day has been quiet except a little sharp-shooting, but I have not seen any one hurt. Our army is resting, awaiting reinforcements & for the roads to dry up. The recent heavy rains have made them horrible....

I saw a Washington Star of the 14th. It stated that 15000 wounded had reache[d] Wash- ington and that there were still that number in the field here. I can not but believe that this number is exaggerated. I do not think that our total loss will exceed 30000 and we have lost I suppose 5000 prisoners.... [Sheridan] has entirely used up the rebel cavalry it is said. Their cavalry must be in a very bad condition if ... they have no better horses than the artillery which we captured here had. Their horses were good enough but they looked as though they had no grain to feed them. Surely no animals can endure a campaign like the one we have just had without being grain fed.

My candle is about out and I have nothing more to write. Accept much love....

Battlefield (near) Po River, Va.
May 18th, 1864 8 p.m.

My hope and trust is as strong as ever that I will pass safely through that which is to come. We have be[en] comparatively quiet for the last few days. This morning an attack was attempted but it was abandoned on the enemy's works being found very strong.

The fighting did not last long and I think our loss was small. The reinforcements sent from Washington have about all arrived and active operations will be resumed to-morrow.... I have a presentment that the hardest fighting is over. I can not possibly imagine how Lee can withstand our 15000 fresh troops. It is agreed on all hands that he has not received and cannot receive re-inforcements. Our resources must necessarily crush him in a short time, unless they are wasted and I do not think they will be.

I am very well but still fatigued....

Near Spotsylvania C. H. Va
3 p.m. May 20th 1864

Since I last wrote we have moved about 4 miles east of the late battlefield.... We have received the reinforcements ... to the number of 25000 adding a good division to each Corps. With this reinforcement I think we can scatter Lee's army. Yesterday Ewells Corps of the rebel army made a detour around our right and attacked our train in rear. He was promptly met by a portion of the artillery reserve and driven back a mile. Our Division was sent forward to assist but arrived just at dark. We relieved the artillery reserve but it was too late to do any thing. This morning at 3 o'clock we advanced and found that the enemy had left, leaving behind 500 stragglers which we picked up. But for this diversion I believe it was intended to attempt something decisive to-day. It will be done to-morrow. We have orders to be ready to move this evening....

The rebels whom we took this morning seem more despondent than any we had ever before seen, & there was evidence on the field that when they left they were almost panic stricken. The prisoners taken said they were getting very tired, that our army fought better than ever before, and most of them expressed pleasure in reaching our lines & believing that they would not have any more fighting to do.

I am still quite well but very much fatigued. I am willing to go however as long as there is any prospect of success. I am beginning to feel more confident every day. I believe we will soon rout Lee's army and then our work is done.... I am sure success will crown our effort.

Leaves from Milford on the Mattapony, May 21, 1864 (courtesy Allegheny College).

Camp (near) Milford, Va.
May 22nd, 1864

We expected to march early in the evening but it was eleven o'clock before we were ordered up. At that hour we got under way but the march was very slow & tedious until after daylight when the whole column got into the road & moved rapidly.

By noon we had reached Bowling Green in Caroline County 17 miles distant from where we had started. We were the rear of the corps and earlier in the day our advance had reached this point captured the picket and secured a crossing of the river. Milford is 2 ½ miles South of Bowling Green on the North side of the Mattapony [Mattaponi] river. It is a station on the Fredricksburg & Richmond railroad at the point where the railroad crosses the river. Instead of halting in Milford we marched across the river and took up a strong position on the South side. Our whole corps now lies here entrenched. This secures a crossing

Flower from south bank of the Anna River near Taylor's Bridge, May 23, 1864 (courtesy Allegheny College).

of the Mattapony as we are at this place over all of its branches. I believe only our corps moved yesterday. The rest of the army remained to confront Lee. Between 7 o'clock & dark heavy firing in the west in the direction of our army, but what was the cause of it & what was the result I do not know. We are expecting an attack by Lee to-day, as we are thrown out here from the rest of the army in a rather exposed position unless Grant should push Lee very closely on the right. I have no fears as to the result if we are attacked. We have about 25000 men, and in a strong position entrenched and I do not think that the whole of Lee's army can drive us out of it.

The indications are that we will lie still to day unless attacked. We need rest and I hope it may be given to me. Last night was the first night's sleep that our brigade has had since leaving Chancellorville. Every other night of the 17 we have either been lying awake in the front line, or moving. It is hard to imagine how men stand so much, but they are quite strong yet and in good spirits. I am now commanding and have commanded since the 11 both my own regiment & the 63 in all about 350 muskets....

[P.S.] Our present position it is supposed flanks Lee and will compel him to leave the line of the Mattapony. I hope so for it seems to be too strong a line for us to drive him from without great loss.

(Near) Sexton's Junction, Va.
May 25th, 1861

We left Milford early in the morning of the 23rd and marched to the North Anna at the point where the Richmond & Potomac Railroad crosses it. Here we halted and rested nearly all day. The enemy occupied the South bank of the river had had about two regiments entrenched just at the entrance to the bridge on the North side. At six o'clock our brigade was chosen to charge the works on the North side and if possible capture the men that occupied them. We started forward and soon started them on the run but they were too swift footed for us and succeeded in crossing the river before we could reach them. We were so close to them however that we secured the bridge and by a heavy fire of musketry kept them from burning it.

During the night we threw up entrenchments on the North side & the enemy threw up entrenchments on the South side. Early yesterday morning however Gen. Gibbon comdg the 2nd Div of our Corps flanked their works on their right (our left) and crossed the river. Immediately afterwards our Division crossed on the bridge mentioned and then followed the rest of the Corps. Then Gen. Burnside moved in on our right. Late last evening we advance[d] about a mile from the river and threw up works. The rebels are about a mile in our front and have been entrenching all night and are still working this morning. Just above the bridge of which I have spoken their left touched the river and they held it stubbornly all day shelling our men whenever they crossed the river. I think that during the night they withdrew their left, so that I have no doubt our right will cross the river this morning.

...We are slowly driving the enemy before us, but it is terrible work. These are the darkest days this country has seen. Yesterday I felt myself the terrible exhaustion of the struggle and I feel no better this morning. During the past two nights and [days I] have not slept any and my spirits are not so buoyant as they ought to be. I still think however that another month will put us into Richmond. My health continues very good. In the charge night before last our loss was very slight. We had an officer badly wounded yesterday by a sharpshooter.

North Anna River, Va.

7 A.M. May 26th, 1864

Yesterday when I wrote we were on the front line. Last evening we were relieved and now occupy the 2nd line. There has been no fighting except picket firing since day before yesterday. I presume since the delay has been so long that it is not Grant's intention to attack them here but to turn their position as he did on the Po. The rebel position here is a strong one.... They have been fortifying for three or four days and as they have as much artillery as they can use, their position is no doubt by this time impregnable to every attack except a siege, and it would be folly for us to halt here and undertake a siege. I think that as soon as supplies come up which they are bringing from Port Royal on the Rappahannock, another flank movement will be made towards Hanover C. H. and Lee's army will be compelled to fall back to the defenses of Richmond. Once there, he will have only one railroad the Danville road on which to supply his army and our cavalry is certainly enterprising enough to destroy that, reducing him to a state of siege, which he cannot long stand. It seems to be Grants intention to make such a disposition of his forces as to be able to surround Richmond if Lee's army can be driven in from the North side. Gordonsville is I trust by this time ours and with it will fall Charlottsville thereby relieving Washington and the North from all danger of invasion and rendering the presence at Washington of a large force unnecessary. The troops there can then be sent to re-inforce this army and surely with this large addition we can crush Lee's army. My hopes are higher every day. This army has been maneuvered so splendidly since we left the Rapidann that I scarcely think a disaster possible.

...If [rain] continues all day as it bids fair to, it ... [will] suspend military operations for a day or two. The North Anna at this point is a small stream about the size of the Loyalhanna but its banks are high and bluff and the bed of the river sand rendering it almost unfordable....

Camp (near) New Castle, Va

May 29th, 1864

Since my last we have had another long march. We withdrew from our position South of the North Anna during night of the 26th and the next day marched down the left bank of the river to a point opposite the junction of the North & South Anna. Early yesterday morning we moved forward again and arrived here just before dark. This ... is south of the Pamunkey. Our whole army is now over the river and within 12 miles of Richmond. The enemy is not in force in our immediate front. Last night it was not known by any one with whom I talked where Lee's army was, but it is to be presumed that it is in our front, that is between us and Richmond, probably behind the Chickahominy. This latter stream is the only one between us and Richmond. The Richmond papers talked sometime since as though it was impossible for our army to advance from Fredericksburg but the advance has been made without great difficulty. Grant's future plans have not yet been developed, but I should not be surprised if he should move round Richmond and compel Lee to evacuate the place of [or] pen him up and capture his whole army. With the reinforcements we are able to get we will have a force large enough to surround the city. I would like to know what Butler is doing. I have not seen a paper since the 19th. Our army is in good spirits & marches splendidly. We hear no grumbling as we used to. The men believe in Grant & wherever they may be put they think it all right. On the other hand the rebel army is much dejected. All their prisoners express astonishment at the manner in which our army fights, and every private says he is tired of the war and hopes it will end soon. A company of cavalry was captured in our front yesterday. They were from South Carolina. The men were communicative and expressed a desire to see the war ended, but the officers were silent and indignant. I like to capture these South Carolina fellows for they are the only men that fight hard now. The Virginians are beginning to say hard things against them and to charge them with originating this calamitous war. They are about right but they have found it out too late. If they had recognized the fact three years since Virginia would have saved herself from the ruin which the war has brought upon her.—

This is a very fine country and under a good state of cultivation. There is wheat & rye growing here but the soil seems too light for them. Nearly all the cleared land is planted with some kind of grain, showing the rebel government recognizing that the raising of food is a very important object. The absence of stock of every description except a few negroes is a noticeable feature but it may have been driven off before our advance.

I do not think that we will turn back from the rebel capital as we have done heretofore. No army has ever been handled finer than this army has been since we left the Rapidan. Lee has been completely outgeneraled, and as he is outnumbered, I do not imagine that he will give us much trouble.

I am very well. I do [not] know of any one that stands the hard work better than I do. Exposure to the sun has brought <u>freckles</u> out on my face, and I begin to look as I did when a boy. Hot sun dust and loss of sleep are not very good for my eyes, but I scarcely feel the effects of them yet.

I enclose you a rose bud from the residence of Dr. Fox south of the Anna. It was a beautiful place. But being on the battlefield was destroyed....

Camp 3 miles South of Salem Church
May 30th, 1864
I thought we were at New Castle, but ... we were at Salem Church some 6 miles west of New Castle. Yesterday afternoon a reconnaissance was made by [Francis C.] Barlow's Div. and our lines advanced three miles southward where we are at present. We are about 14 miles North of Richmond. There has been no fighting to-day except light skirmishing we are entrenched and the rebels likewise about one thousand yards in our front. No fighting is likely to take place unless we attack which we may do any moment for we know very little about Grant's plans. They have a strong position and of course it would be hard work to take it. When these charges are made on the enemy's works I always tremble for fear they may fail....

I saw a paper to-day of the 25th, and after reading it felt a little down hearted. After all the bloodshed of the month of May, nothing it seems has been gained. Siegel is whipped and is still running. Butler repulsed and put at rest for the present. This gives Lee an opportunity to receive reinforcements which he doubtless has received to the extent of ours. This no doubt is what makes Grant so cautious or possibly he is waiting until reinforcements sent to Butler may enable him to assume the offensive again.

The people of the North can have little idea of the work done by this army since May 3rd. The papers talk about Butlers army needing rest but what has his army done in comparison with ours. Yet we do not need rest. We can go forward to-day as well as we could after lying in camp two months. I am glad that Grant has some of the Bull dog in his nature and I trust he will hang on until he worries the rebels to death. I am getting impatient. I desire to see the war ended and to get home. I was almost homesick to-day. The memory of my wife is at times almost too much for good, and yet at other times the recollection of her love gives me fortitude to endure trials which without it could scarcely be borne.

12

Cold Harbor to Petersburg

Grant continued to press toward Richmond. Trenches and earthworks enabled the smaller Confederate army to resist the Union troops and inflict important casualties. Grant therefore continued to strive to outflank the Confederates by shifting his own troops to the left (eastward). The Southerners had the advantage of shorter distances to travel as the Union forces arced about Richmond. On June 1 it appeared that Grant's men had finally gotten around the Confederates, but the Union forces were too exhausted to attack promptly. A day's wait enabled the Confederates to bolster their lines, and the Union assault at Cold Harbor on June 3 was roughly repulsed with the Northern forces losing about 7,000 killed and wounded compared to Southern losses of 1,500 men.

Near Cold Harbor, Va.
June 3rd, 1864

Since my last we made another flank movement and had some fighting. We have gained ground but met with losses equal if not greater than the enemy.

From the position in which I wrote May 30th we moved forward on the next day about a mile to the South side of the headwaters of the Totapatany [Totopotomy] creek. We took a few prisoners and met with a slight loss. The night following we withdrew to the North side of the creek & the Sixth Corps which was on our right made a detour around the enemy and came in on the left at Cold Harbor and made a junction with Gen. Smith commanding the 28th Corps. They had quite a fight but drove the enemy and captured nearly a thousand prisoners. That night we withdrew from the right and made a detour around the army coming in on the left of the 6th Corps a short distance East of Cold Harbor. We arrived early in the morning but remained quiet all day and night, our Division being in reserve. This morning at day-light Gen. Barlows Div. charged the rebel works on the extreme left of our line, carried their first line, then their second but failed to hold the last. He lost a good number of men and took about 500 prisoners. Between daylight and nine o'clock there was a good deal of fighting along the line but I have not been able to learn the results.... We are constantly receiving reinforcements which more than make up for our losses. Yesterday I got an idea of the loss in our Corps from which the loss of the whole army may be estimated. Our Corps has lost 23000 men. Our corps is one fourth of the army and it is probable that our loss has been heavier than any of the corps but the loss of the army will not fall short of 50000. Of this number probably 5000 are prisoners, the rest are killed and wounded. This fighting of this campaign does not seem to be more than half over. Fifty thousand more will probably be disabled in the month of June. The rebels have lost as heavily if not more heavily than we and can still survive another such a loss. We can fill our ranks they cannot; hence the end must come....

Our army is in good spirits and confident of final success. The confidence of the army is much firmer than that of the people at home, judging from the tone of the papers.... This afternoon our Division was moved up ... to fill a gap.... The position is in an open field under their artillery and could not be taken in day time, consequently we are just waiting for darkness under cover of which we will entrench ourselves....

June 4th, 1864

To-day thus far has been quiet and I suppose will continue so. We have reached the outer defenses of Richmond and will be obliged to bring up our siege train, and begin our parallels. I understand that they are already planting siege guns on the line occupied by the 18th Corps. No more fighting will take place, I suppose until these guns have done their work.

Last night just after dark the rebels attacked our extreme left held by Barlow's & Gibbon's Divisions of our corps. The attack lasted probably a half an hour, and the enemy was repulsed with heavy loss. It is said the rebels were made drunk before the charge was attempted. This must have been the case because with all the moral[e] gained lately it is difficult to get our men to charge. I have heard it stated that some of Barlow's men behaved badly yesterday. Our men fight well enough but discipline is so lax that they require to be carefully handled.

...In addition to what I mentioned first put in [your package] 3 or 4 prs. of socks of the kind I wear. I have had several pairs stolen lately and am well nigh bare-foot. I wish you to send me also a nice red-patch bound with gold. It should be firmer than ... single merino. The one you put on my hat when I was home caught in a branch during the Wilderness fight and was torn nearly off. It has been hanging merely by one corner since and is much faded. I want also a piece of ribbon for my Kearney badge....

...Soon I hope this terrible time will be over and I will be permitted to return to you and stay with. I feel anxious that Grant may continue the campaign and the fighting until we have conquered as I am sure we must. Let us have these terrible days over....

I am very well and have been thinking about you all day....

June 5th, 1864

Yesterday after I wrote we moved to the left and rejoined our corps and are now lying quiet in the 2nd line of rifle-pits. In front of the 2nd Div. of our corps there is a good deal of picket firing, elsewhere every thing is quiet. We have received hints that we may stay here several days. Since we have driven the enemy in effect into Richmond possibly we will now wait a few days for some co-operative movement....

...How inspiring it is to look at your picture and feel that your life is devoted to me. And yet it sometimes occurs to me that ere I see your face again I may be called away. It is impossible to live around death as I have for the last month and not recognize that soon perhaps you may be called away. And still I do not feel anxious, my feelings are very different from yours. Sometimes I find my self reckoning my chances. Of 350 men who crossed the Rapid Ann in my regiment 225 have passed from it by death and wounds. Two out of every three have left us & what are the chances of those remaining? But such speculations are idle. A few days since a Sergeant of our regiment was sitting in his tent writing a letter not dreaming of danger. A stray ball entered the tent and gave him a sever wound in the thigh. Yesterday a captain of artillery was seated by his battery unconscious I presume of the presence of any enemy, a ball entered his head killing him instantly. So Gen'l Sedgewick was killed. I might mention a thousand instances of the same character. Death is appointed unto us all, where when & how we know not. We only know that when we have fulfilled our time we will be called away.

During this whole fearful struggle I have felt hopeful, and still have a consciousness that I will be permitted to return to you in safety. When taking my departure from you on my first visit home last winter, you will recollect that you knelt and prayed for me. You asked that if it was God's will that I might be returned to you in safety. At the moment you uttered the sentence the question occurred to me shall I return? The answer seemed as clear as though it had been spoken that I would return to you. This impression is still upon my mind although I know there are fearful days before me.

The more fearful grows the contest the more certain do I feel that I am needed here and that is my appointed place and fact that another hand and not my own guided me to my present position makes me feel that I am doing my duty. I may be here to fall in some one of our battles or to pass through all danger into peace. I know not which, I only know that God will deal justly with me and under his care I can securely rest.

I sincerely hope that my dear good wife will not be too anxious concerning me....

Near Gaines Mills, Va.

June 6th, 1864

To-day has been thus far (4 P.M) quiet. Last night after dark we vacated the 2nd line in rear of Gibbon and marched to the left of Barlow and took up a position on and protecting the road leading from Mechanicsville to Bottom Bridge. We have thrown up works and are lying very quiet. The two lines are not more than 500 yds. apart and the picket lines are separated only about fifty yds. But there is an agreement to have no picket firing consequently not a shot is fired. At several times during the day the pickets have conversed with each other and exchanged papers etc.

This morning about 7 o'clock a captain of Gen. Lee's staff and a major comdng the picket line appeared on the road with a flag of truce, stating that they were the bearer of dispatches from Gen. Lee. Some delay occurred before the flag was met, but when once met about a dozen of their officers came forward and a like number of ours. The[y] chatted for some time. Very little however was said about the army. The rebel officers expressed a desire that the war might be speedily ended, but did not say how they wished it ended, nor did they make any boast of what they had done or what they were going to do. The acknowledged that Grant was very long-winded and that they were rather surprised at the perseverance of our army. One gave Capt. [Harrison] Nelson of the 57th a Richmond paper of June 4th. The news in it was rather astonishing. It represented that on the morning of the 3rd when Barlow charged their line, that we had made fourteen distinct charges and lost not less than 1000 men. The lie is so preposterous that the men who wrote it must have been conscious that his cause could only be sustained by wholesale lying. It likewise stated that there had been further fighting on the south side of the James, without about equal success. It further stated that Johnston had repulsed Sherman and that the latter was retreating. The latter statement however was expressed in such indefinite terms that I very much doubt its truth. On the contrary I think it false. The paper pretended to be hopeful but it stated that the roar of cannon and musketry could be heard in Richmond. It is too be hoped that ere long they may hear it more distinctly.

Our army is now very much rested: when we get a little clothing we will be in as good condition as we were when we crossed the Rapidann. There is very little sickness in the army — in fact none at all except mild diarrhea resulting in most instances from carelessness.

It is the general impression here that we will continue our flank movement, and finally will establish ourselves on the south side of the James.

In consequence of the moving and working last night I got very little sleep, otherwise I am feeling very well....

June 7th, 1864

We have been favored with another quiet day. Some cannonading is now taking place a mile or two to our right but I presume it is not of much consequence. We were ordered to move last night at dark but the order was subsequently countermanded. The army occupies nearly the same position it occupied several days ago....

The people are ready to believe every move of Grant a retreat. I cannot understand on what foundation this belief rests unless they desire him to retreat. The people of [the] North as a body are either a pack of cowards or traitors. Our army was never in such spirits, never I believe in better fighting trim than at present. In every encounter since the battle of the Wilderness we have driven the enemy, and at the wilderness he was so roughly handled that he was obliged to retreat. Since this campaign began the moral[e] of our army has improved wonderfully while the spirits and dash with which the rebel army has heretofore been possessed has been lost entirely. Two Corps of their Va. Army have well nigh been annihilated Hills & Ewells. Longstreets Corps has suffered much but not to the same extent that the other two have. This campaign may not end for two months yet, but I feel sure that the end will be victory. The tone of [the] rebel press as well as the tone of all the prisoners that have been taken is despondent. They feel that if Grant <u>hangs on</u> that they will be obliged to succumb and I feel sure that Grant is able to and will hang on.

But how shall my dear dear wife get along during these dark days. I know you will never lose sight of me, but then I fear this long continued anxiety may prove too much for you. Always think me safe Hattie when you do not hear from me. The dangers to which I am exposed are much magnified by you, and yet the toil and hardships cannot be <u>imagined</u>. It is indeed a wonder that men can stand what this army has stood for the last months, and still we are ready to endure as much more still cheerful and hopeful.

June 8th, 1864

The military situation has not changed here during the day so far as I know. Our siege-works in front of Gen. Gibbon's line are now very close to the rebel works. It is said that in a few days we can blow them up. Possibly we are awaiting the completion of this work. The rebels have heavy guns in our front. Some say they are 64 pou. But I think they are not quite so large.

...These victories in other portions of Virginia, will no doubt create diversions in our favor and give us an opportunity to do something here notwithstanding their strong works. It is difficult to imagine how they can survive this campaign if we still continue to press them vigorously. We have already gained much in Va. and will ere long gain more although, I fear the siege of Richmond will be a prolonged one. But I am satisfied that our army can and will endure it. We are confident and determined to take Richmond.

I have not seen Charles for some days. Since I am not on the staff I do not go about as much and consequently do not see him so often. I heard to-day that his friend Col. Brooke has been seriously wounded on the 3rd. Charles was not hurt I learned.

To-day has been quite pleasant. Our men have recovered from their fatigue and are getting quite jovial....

June 9th, 1864

To-day has been quiet and pleasant as usual. There is some picket-firing in front of our 2nd Div. but none else-where. As usual I received and read the late Richmond papers.... The paper intimate[s] that we do not hold Cold Harbor. It is possible to blind the people for a while but the truth will out finally. These lies will ere long recoil on their own heads.

The siege goes on, so it would seem to an outsider but not so to us. Grant seems to be resting his army to strike a great blow in some quarter, where it will fall I know not. The general impression with us as well as with the rebels is that he will change his base to the south side of the James River. It is thought that he will turn it on the East but I should not be surprised if he should attempt it on the west. Grant moves with boldness and confidence and an attempt to turn Richmond on the West is just such an undertaking as he would be likely to engage in. A move of this kind would in a few days decide the fate of our army or the confederacy. I believe our army is equal to the task if well led and I be[leive] Grant can lead it. Instead of pressing the siege of Richmond provisioning and clothing his army look out for a big bold movement soon.

June 11th, 1864

To-day has been pleasant and quiet again. Scarcely a shot has been heard in any direction. Both armies are resting I presume for a future trial of strength.

Last night we moved but the movement was very inconsiderable yet it kept us awake all night. The movement consisted simply in moving across the road and building a rifle-pit. We got through with the pit a little after day-light then lay down to rest. Contrary to our expectation the rebels did not fire a shot at us. We were within short range and made a loud noise, but I suppose they did not care how much we worked. To-day we have had inspection for the first time since leaving camp. Of course the men did not look very trim but the inspecting officer thought we looked very well under the circumstances.

We are still without news and without papers.... I can hardly think that the papers are designedly kept out of the army, yet I can not explain our failure to receive them on any other hypothesis. I [am] anxious to hear the result of the Baltimore Convention. I was told to-day, by way of rumor that Lincoln and Andrew Johnson had been nominated. This is undoubtedly a strong ticket, and if not interfered with by the radicals will carry the day by a large majority. The rebels seem to be very afraid of Lincoln and for this reason I have latterly desired his nomination. If he is nominated without any split in the party, the nomination will have great weight on the present struggle. The hopes of many rebels will be crushed.

It is said that our army to-day began to move towards the left with the design of crossing James River.... It is impossible to divine Grant's plans.

I do not feel very well to-day. My cold instead of getting better last night got worse, and my head feels muddier than yesterday....

June 12th, 1864

You seem to have had astonishing news from Grant. You seem to think that he is able to throw shells into the city. Not so at least from the position held by the army. In an air line I believe we are about 7 miles from Richmond, which is two miles further than the "Swamp Angel" would throw a shell. The fighting on June 3rd was more extensive than I at first supposed and was not so successful as reported in the Northern papers. I thought it an inconsiderable affair by a couple of Brigades of our Corps, but it turns out that a general assault was made along the whole line, and repulsed at almost every point. Our corps gained some ground, but at a terrible sacrifice of life. This is the only fighting since the campaign began in which we have been worsted or for which we have not obtained an equivalent. The loss in our army on that day was said to be 6000 but I think this an exaggeration....

Our Chaplain Rev. [John C.] Truesdale preached for us to-day for the first time. He is a clever talker. His text was "When a man dieth where is he?" Job-14-10++— His sermon was short and principally about death with which we are very familiar. He was attentively listened by the whole regiment, which was a surprising circumstance considering their religious habits. He may get along very well while we are campaigning — in camp he will be more severely tried.

It is supposed that we will move to-night or to-morrow night, whereto no one knows....

Northern hopes for a prompt end to the war were high. Lee, with his army depleted, adopted a defensive strategy of attrition. Northern dismay at the elusiveness of definitive victory stimulated Copperheads and others who favored a compromise peace. Seeking to terminate the conflict, Grant moved his troops south from Cold Harbor and across the James River. Their goal was to seize Petersburg and cut off the supply lines to Richmond and Lee's troops. Though the Union forces held a considerable majority, poor leadership, confusion, hesitation, lack of coordination, and veteran reluctance to attack earthworks led to Federal failure. Union losses numbered about 11,000, about twice as many as those suffered by the Confederates. The Confederate defense had gained sufficient time for Lee to send reinforcements to hold Petersburg, and Grant was forced to turn to siege tactics.

Before Petersburg, Va.
June 16th, 1864

My last letter dated 12th inst. was written in the rifle-pits on the Chickahominy. I spoke of our expected movement, & told you that our supposed destination was South of the James River. What was then merely surmised is now accomplished. We left the Chickahominy early Sunday evening the 12th marched till after midnight then lay down & rested till day-light. The march was then resumed. We passed Tunstalls Station on the Richmond & York River Railroad, then took the road to Long Bridge on the Chickahominy which we crossed about noon. Continuing our march across the Peninsula we arrived at Charles City C. H. about dark. Remained there during the night and till next day near noon when we marched to Wilcox's Landing on the James River where we got aboard transports and were ferried across the river. Our regiment crossed on the Helen Getty. On the South side of the river we landed on Windmill Pt. & camped that night near the river on Wilcox's plantation. Yesterday we started a little before noon and reached this place about 12 last night. The 18th A.C. which took transports at the White House preceded us here and yesterday evening surprised the enemy and took their works except a redoubt West of the town. We are about the centre of the line & are not more than a mile from Petersburg our batteries can easily throw shells into the city. Our right rests pretty well down the river, I suppose at Fort Clifton which is said to be 5 miles below. Our left does not yet extend to the river, but I presume it will when our army all gets up. Ours & the 185th Corps being the only ones here at present.

In the fight here yesterday our negro soldiers took an important part. I have heard that [they captured] 16 pieces of artillery but I do not credit the rumor. A very important position was gained however with a very slight loss on our part. Gen. Beauregard's troops are here. I saw one this morning brought in by a colored soldier. He belonged to the 47th N.C. I had not time to asked [sic] him what he thought of the war. The reversed circumstances of the two men as they passed along our lines caused a good many remarks. One Major remarked that when the war first broke out he could not have tolerated such a scene. What a fine thing that this war has compelled [men] to think and act more justly. The negro as he walked along to me looked more manly than did the white man. Several dead rebels have been seen here to-day <u>bayoneted</u>. It is supposed that our colored soldiers remembered their murdered bretheren.

The campaign progresses satisfactorily. I think that we can soon take Petersburg and then I have no doubt we will march directly to Burkesville Junction. Once in possession of that junction we cut all the railroad communications Richmond has on the South. If the rebels are wise they will abandon Richmond before ... Grant can reach that point and thus save their army. If they do not they most certainly will lose it. They may stake the fate of their confederacy on Richmond and hold on to it till the last moment, but if they do their ruin will be the more speedy and complete.

I am quite well to-day although I had been quite unwell for the past three days. A bad cold disturbed my whole system. Three compound cathartic pills taken night before last brought things to right.

The weather is pleasant. The sun is hot but there is a breeze stirring all the time. The nights are cool, sometimes even to discomfort. We had not had a mail since we left the front of Richmond. Our communication will be well established in a day or two & then we can receive & send letters daily. I send you a wild rose from the Long Bridge, & a wild rose-bud from Wind-Mill Pt. many kisses on both. Give love to all. Your husband wishes to be remembered

> New Market near Petersburg, Va.
> June 18th, 1864
> [written but not mailed]

After my letter was written on the 16th, our brigade was ordered to attack the rebel lines. The attack was made at about six in the evening, & did not amount to much. In advancing our men came upon some old rebel huts & immediately gathered in groups behind them and they could not be got forward. We suffered but very slight loss. A new regiment from Mass suffered some because the men did not take the precaution to shelter themselves. Something was expected from the attack and its failure was very mortifying to Gen. Birney. There are many reasons for its failure, which are too numerous to give in a letter.

After dark we were relieved from the front line & laid in the second during the night. Yesterday morning we moved to the front line again just to the right of the Suffolk road. In the evening we were relieved from that position & moved farther to the right & during the night my command occupied the 2nd Line. This morning another attack was ordered on the enemy's lines, by our Div. supported by Gibbon. We started forward at 5 P.M. but only moved a short distance before it was discovered that the works in our immediate front had been abandoned. We moved forward about a half mile where the rebels were found entrenched along the Suffolk Railroad in a line at right angles with the position formerly occupied by them. We wheeled our line and formed it along the Suffolk Turnpike where we are at present. There is a good deal of sharpshooting going on even some shelling on our left with these exceptions the lines are quiet. I presume another advance will be ordered this evening. I can not describe to you the present position of affairs. We are about a mile from Petersburg. The enemy is either retreating from here or shortening his lines I know not which. A very few days will serve to determine the fate of Petersburg. Once in possession of this town I think Richmond virtually in our possession.

I am quite well but very sleepy in consequence of being knocked about during the last two nights. The weather is still quite pleasant. Give love to all & accept many kisses....

> Near Petersburg
> June 18. 1864

Dear Madam,

Your husband is doing well — I regret that that I have to write you that he was wounded to day, and that his right leg was amputated — He is in good spirits and received the very best attention. I would not advise you to attempt to come here — but it would be better to come to Baltimore & remain there until the Major reaches Fortress Monroe — The Major was wounded with the colors of his Regiment in his hands, a few yards in front of the rebel works —

> Very respy yrs
> Charles H. T. Collis
> Col.

Near Petersburg, Virginia
June 20th, 1864

Mrs. Duff;

This is monday noon. Your husband has just been sent to the boat — six miles distant. Fearing that the ambulance would be too rough for him. They are carrying him there on a stretcher. Since I wrote you on the 18th, stating the nature of the wound, he has been doing very well — when he started to day he seemed in good sprits. He will reach Washington tomorrow (the 21st). He says he will telegraph you from Fortress Monroe, or else at Washington. The surgeon here seems to have no doubt about his recovery — I think a month from now he will be able to come to Pittsburgh and probably sooner. He has been well cared for here and General Birney is sending our regimental surgeon along to take charge of him to Washington or whatever place he is to be taken to— our regiment has suffered quite severely — in the late engagements— Col Craig returned to reg last evening his face is nearly well — Trusting that my strong expectations of your husband's recovery may be fully realized

I subscribe my self your friend,

John C. Truesdale,
Chaplain, 105th Reg. Pa. Vols.

Allegheny City
June 21st 1864

My own dear husband:

It is high noon — not by any means the time for letter writing. I have been thinking — oh, how many thoughts of you as I tried to busy <u>myself</u> as well as my hands with the morning work. How could I hope that you were still unharmed, when so <u>many</u> among the veteran <u>few</u> have fallen? The details of your fight at Petersburg have just reached us. But just a moment since like an inspiration came the sure <u>belief</u> that you were unharmed. I could not help rising up to my feet with the impetus the feeling gave me. And now I am seated to tell you — or rather to talk with you, so sure am I that you will hear. How critical the days are for [the] nation — and how will it end? I have nothing of moment to say, now that <u>I am near you</u>....

Hattie

Telegraph

Washington 22 1863

Mrs. H. Duff
Allegheny

My Right Leg is Amputated above Knee Come to Washington without delay to Avenue House Bring Trunk and Linin with you Am doing well

Capt. L. B. Duff

Scott, in her History of the One Hundred and Fifth Regiment of Pennsylvania Volunteers, *111–12, uses Duff's words to describe the action in which Duff was wounded. It began at half-past noon on June 18:*

"'I was ordered to take the front advance with my regiment, which now formed the right of the second line. In taking the advance I had to go over some heavy artillery regiments which occupied the front line. The men seemed very reluctant to do this; but, upon my peremptory order, the One Hundred and Fifth went over, but a large portion of the Sixty-third remained behind. We advanced into an open field boldly, with flags flying, and the rebels immediately opened upon us with musketry and artillery, throwing canister. For some distance we advanced under a murderous fire, and, on looking around, I found that no portion of the line but my small regiment had moved. Having arrived at a point where the ground took a sudden rise, and where, by lying down, we could in a great measure shield ourselves from the enemy's fire, I halted and ordered the men to lie down. I then went back to the road and informed the brigade commander, Colonel McCallish, that an attempt to charge by my small regiment would be foolish, and asked him to move the troops up on my left. His only answer was that he could not get them started. Disgusted, I went forward to my own line, and was just getting it started when I was shot down.'"

Washington D. C.
June 23rd 1864

Mother dear

This day finds my sad journey ended, for which I thank God. The Doctors say the limb is doing <u>splendidly</u>—but indeed if you saw it you would think it a terrible sight. I shall endeavor to be cheerful although I feel that my critical days are yet to come. The limb is off about 3 inches below the joint. Levi is cool and calm but very weak. Every one is so kind—we shall need for nothing—the wound is dressed every day—three surgeons were present this morning. Dr. Voss came with him from the battlefield—will remain some days. Col. Collis kindly sent six men all the way from Petersburg to City Pt. to carry Levi on a stretcher thus avoiding the ambulance. I will write no more. I am very well....

Harriet

Washington City
June 29th 1864

Dear ones

Would that I could tell you of the happy change in my feelings since this time yesterday. I had realized from the moment I saw the wound that it was a miracle if life could master this cruel stroke of death. But yet I was unprepared to hear as I did on <u>Monday</u> <u>night</u> that mortification <u>had</u> <u>begun</u> and that in a few hours all that remained to me would be the mangled body. Oh the certainty was terrible to bear—if God had not sustained me I should have died. Soon the <u>agony</u> gave place to calm trust in God. I felt that my <u>Father's</u> hand had brought all for his own good purpose. I had not spent a moment alone with Levi since the moments were so critical I feared to be left without [help]. However I felt that now I must tell him of his danger and hear of his hopes for eternity. Can you realize my joy—nay indeed I was happy despite the dark shadow which loomed every where on the horizon. Can you take some of the joy to your own hearts when I tell you that I found him calmly resting in Jesus' arms with all the humility and trust of a little child. O how willingly now would I give him up to God since he was His through the blood of Jesus. Our words were few for Levi was too weak to speak many. What a night of watching it was. I feared that each pulsation but wore away the silver cord and that the golden bowl would break to fragments. In the early morning I discovered that some faint traces of healthy suppuration could be seen. When Dr. McCormack came to dress it, he found that the life principle was the stronger—the sloughing of clotted blood was giving place to healthy matter. It was like expecting life from the dead—but I think there is no mistake God has heard and answered our prayers. The system seems to have rallied again—his appetite returned—just now I have fed him almost one half a young stewed chicken—we give him a drink of beef essence every half hour and procure him every thing his appetite craves. We still dread the hemorrhage. But they have placed a tourniquet on the limb and some one watches all the time. I pray God may prevent and that He will bless the means so skillfully applied. The danger is not all past—but <u>some</u> of it is. I do not allow myself to think yet that I <u>am sure</u> to bring you home a living hero. Oh, pray continually that the precious life may be spared that our darling may be a valiant soldier of the Cross as he has been for his Country.... Levi thinks he cannot spare me many moments from his side, however he told me this morning to sit down and write you that he was better — he sends much love to you all....

Epilogue

The physical stamina, determination, self-discipline, and bond of love between Levi and Harriet so evident in their wartime correspondence stood Duff in good stead. With the care of Harriet and "Doctor" Melton and good medical attention by September he could travel to Allegheny City where he celebrated his twenty-seventh birthday. In October he returned to Washington, where his offer to resume military duty was rejected. Informed he would have to report to Camp Convalescent at Annapolis, Levi resigned and was officially discharged on October 25, 1864. His rank was lieutenant-colonel. He had been awarded this commission in May 1864, but had not received it until after his wounding. The fight that caused him to lose his right leg was remembered by the remnants of the two regiments he commanded, the 105th and 63rd P. V. C., as "The Hare's House Slaughter."

Duff procured a wooden prosthesis, with articulated knee and ankle joints controlled by springs, which he secured with straps over his shoulders. Every morning for the rest of his life a half-hour was consumed in fitting the leg to the stump. He learned to stride the hills of Pittsburgh at a good pace and could easily mount and descend from buggies and street cars. As he grew older and gained weight, he made use of a cane.

Duff resumed his law practice in January 1865. He and Harriet had been living with her mother, but Levi soon bought a two-story brick house on Beaver Street within walking distance of the Allegheny County Court House, not far from the Nixon home. Hailed as a war hero of the victorious Union, he enjoyed considerable status in Pittsburgh. His law practice thrived, thanks in part to this and to the business connections of his father.

As his letters show, Levi was a radical Republican in his political views but did not have high regard for politicians. In Allegheny County, where the Republicans were known as the Union Party, politics at this time were controlled by powerful bosses such as Robert W. Mackey. The party itself was divided over how the secession states should be readmitted to the Union and over the future political and economic status of former slaves. A candidate for the leading local office of District Attorney who was free of party quarrels and publicly viewed as a war hero suited the party leaders' purposes well. They persuaded Duff to accept the nomination they procured for him, though Levi did little or no campaigning.

Duff was elected, but the gold ring turned to brass. No more willing to be influenced in his legal activities by the opinions of the political bosses than he was by the views of General Birney, tensions soon arose. According to his son: "Finding they could not control the young soldier the bosses set out to reduce his authority and fees. This they did so thoroughly that Colonel Duff, forewarned of the personal annoyance, the participation in or compliance with shiftiness, double dealing and dishonesty inevitably required of those holding public offices, resolved henceforth to devote himself to the practice of civil law."[1]

He did so and quite successfully. By nature critical of power and privilege, he accepted numerous cases as counsel against large corporations. His contact with criminals during his three-year term as District Attorney — and an attempt to bribe him in connection with one case (he threw the man offering the bribe out of his house)—caused him to have such dislike for criminal cases that in private practice he refused to take them on.

Duff's disavowal of politics was not complete, however. The economic travails of the country under the Grant administration caused him to support the Greenback-Labor Party in 1872. He was even more outraged by the blatant spoils-system run by the Republican party chief of Pennsylvania, Don Cameron. Duff therefore allowed himself in 1882 to become the nominee for lieutenant-governor on the ticket of the Independent Republican party created by leading reform-minded citizens. The rift in the Republican party permitted Democrats to win the key state offices. Disgusted with the Republicans, Duff thereafter supported the Democrats but eschewed running for office.

Until 1893. An expansion of the number of Allegheny County judges offered opportunity for new faces to

Duff in late 1864. One-legged and weak, Duff nevertheless hoped to continue to serve the cause (courtesy Allegheny College).

reach the bench. Duff ignored invitations to run yet was nominated by the Citizen's Industrial Alliance. This was one of many reform-minded political groups; however, it claimed to represent the concerns of the laboring lower classes and the Negro. Always a supporter of the underdog, Duff was swayed. He accepted the nomination of the Democratic party, did almost no campaigning, and came in last among the four candidates.

The success of his legal career and the regard in which he was held by reformers in Pittsburgh no doubt was gratifying to Duff. But what nourished his life most centrally was his marriage to Harriet. Alas, they were to experience tragedies.

Their first child born in 1866, a boy named after his father, lived only fifteen weeks. No food could be found that would support him. Harriet grieved deeply, but she showed no signs of the nervous disease that had plagued her during the war years. A second son was born in 1867, Samuel Eckerberger Duff. He, too, failed to thrive until goat's milk was tried. Daughter Helen Grant Duff, named in honor of the general and president, was born in 1869 and was healthy. But soon Harriet began to experience severe headaches and dizzy spells.

A believer in fresh air and exercise, Duff had a house built on Williams Street in the suburbs, away from the manufacturing plants beginning to crowd their neighborhood. Harriet's mother, Roseanna Nixon, came to live with them. Still, Harriet's health did not improve, and so Levi sent her for total rest at a sanatorium in Danville, New York. Once again their correspondence resumed through much of 1871 and 1872. Upon return, Harriet seemed well and lively. In 1874, a new baby named Edgar succumbed, unable to thrive on any food. Two years later, Hezekiah Nixon Duff was born and flourished. The household rejoiced. Sixteen months later, suddenly and unexpectedly, Harriet Nixon Duff died of "congestion of the brain."

Levi squared his shoulders and carried on, aided in looking after the household and children by Grandmother Nixon and "Doctor" Melton. It was fortunate that shortly before Harriet's death on July 13, 1877, the household was expanded by the arrival of Livi Bird Duff Reese, then about twenty-two years of age. Reese, the son of Levi's sister Sarah, had come to Pittsburgh to study law in Levi's office. The young man proved a good student and soon played a key role in mentoring the Colonel's children. Melton, however, became insane and had to be sent to an asylum.

Helpful, too, was a good friend of Harriet, Agnes Feree Kaufman. Also a school teacher and member of their United Presbyterian Church congregation, Agnes was about eight years younger than the Duffs. She did much for the young family. Friendship grew, and Levi and Agnes married on January 16, 1882.

It was awkward for the elderly Roseanna Nixon to stay in the household with her son-in-law's second wife, so she moved to live with her daughter in Tacoma, Washington. Duff himself purchased a new residence on Taylor Avenue in a nice section of Allegheny City. Reese continued to live with the family for another ten years. Young Samuel headed for the West Coast as soon as he graduated from Western University (later the University of Pittsburgh) in 1886. He would marry in 1890 and name his first son Levi Bird Duff III.

Tragedy came again in 1877, when young Helen Grant Duff died of typhoid fever and anemia. This loss on top of all the others seemed finally to effect a toll on Levi's characteristic optimism. Nevertheless, he remained active in his law practice and energetically participated in reunions of his regiment and of the Grand Army of the Republic, saving banners and pins just as he had saved Harriet's letters. He took particular pleasure in the late 1880s in speaking at a dedication of a monument to the 105th Pa. V.C. at Gettysburg (see Appendix B).

Agnes Feree Kaufman Duff died in July 1913 of pneumonia. Levi, then seventy-six and in good health, decided it was time to close his law practice. He moved to Lansing, Michigan, to live with Hezekiah's family. There he took pleasure in his grandchildren and the clean air and fishing. He died January 18, 1916, of a stroke that rendered him unconscious in his sleep two nights previous. His grave is in Uniondale Cemetery, Pittsburgh, between those of his two wives.

The war and the love that grew during it and helped Levi endure the boredom and bloodshed were the defining experiences of his life. The war maimed both him and Harriet. Ironically, though twice wounded so as to be considered mortally so, Levi lived more than seventy-eight years. Harriet, her condition permanently weakened by nervous anxiety, did not live to be forty.

The war was indeed the defining experience for many Americans of the era, and especially for those who served in the opposing armies. Duff was like his comrades, but he also differed from them in significant ways. He was close to the median age of Union enlistees, white, and native-born (less than a quarter of the wearers of the blue were immigrants). Yet he had far more education than most and was already a professional man (only about three percent of Union soldiers had previously held peacetime professional posts).[2] Even more distinctive were his personal habits: no use of profanity or tobacco and almost none of liquor, reading of serious literature, abjuration of the company of "camp women" and gambling, preference for solitude rather than convivial gatherings, reliable and regular correspondence.

Many soldiers became discouraged, and Levi was not immune to this emotion. But he kept his optimism better than most. Above all must be noted his sense of duty and strong self-discipline.

Youths often entered the ranks in a surge of enthusiasm and excitement to undertake a great venture. Many others, and Levi was among these, took up arms because they saw the war as a crusade to preserve the country and liberty. Preservation of the Union was a key rallying point in the North. Duff was concerned for his country, but not so much for the concept of Union. His motivational cause was more than the abolition of slavery, it was justice for the Black race and for racial equality. Indeed, he was convinced that the war was a cathartic punishment laid upon the country by whatever Providential power there was to force a cleansing of its sins regarding the Black race. He always termed the conflict "The Slaveholder's Rebellion." Such a strong sentiment on this issue was shared by only a tiny number of Union troops.[3] The Emancipation Proclamation actually brought a brief decline of morale among numbers of Union troops and supporters. Not so for Levi, whose spirits rallied.

All this is not to say that Levi did not feel an initial sense of excitement and a desire to experience battle. But he quickly shifted to a more measured approach, studying and analyzing geography, troop movements, strategy, tactics, weather effects and tendencies, and above all, quality of leadership. In battle, some soldiers were moved to a combat rage by surges of adrenalin. Others repressed their fear of physical harm by focusing on the need to maintain their reputations and not be considered cowards by their fellows or in their home towns. Duff seems not to have been consumed with desire to hold the esteem of his companions but rather kept moving forward in battle out of a sense of duty, responsibility, and, yes, pride in being that sort of man. Even as a member of the Society of Seven at Allegheny College, he seemed to share with others of that group a sense that they should act and perform in a manner superior to that of most individuals. Superior how? Through performance of duty and self-discipline that repressed undesirable characteristics and promoted those that benefited the individual and society.

Levi envisioned the war as a crucible for the nation, disciplining it, and giving it a meaningful history and a true identity. He also recognized that the conflict was a shaping and refining fire for himself as a person. Despite loneliness, despite the waste and horrors he continually saw around him, he therefore could write to Harriet that the army experience was making him a better man. It forced him to develop his self-discipline, to understand himself and others better, and thus to be an improved mate to Harriet in their hoped-for future. Early in their separation, Harriet expressed a similar thought, writing: "If years should separate us in presence, they cannot in thought — the discipline will benefit us both — when the cup of happiness does reach our lips we will not grasp it with eager, careless hands, but with a sure and well tried power, which will not suffer one drop to escape...."[4]

Though Levi might tell Harriet he cared little what others thought of him, he took pride in his reputation and stories of good character that filtered back to his love. He was quick to obtain the accouterments of each rank he achieved, regardless of the cost. Levi, like many other officers, nourished hope of advancement, advancement that might enhance his prestige and perhaps move him to a safer post. A sense of propriety and dignity, however, prevented him from indulging in the political maneuvers so often required for promotion in the reserves.

Five things above all did Levi scorn, even though they reflected significant portions of daily life in his times. In ascending order they were profanity, petty injustices and favoritisms, drunkenness, politicians, and poor leadership. His perception of the foibles of generals and officious colonels was acute. Those officers who chose appearance over substance, advanced through political connections, threw their weight around, or failed to note the subtle differences in commanding volunteers compared with draftees he openly scorned. In particular, he criticized leaders who lacked the courage to advance or the knowledge of how to manage troops and devise strategy. Those he admired included Lee and Stonewall Jackson (at least as far as tactics went, though Duff could not praise any man who served the slaveholders' rebellion), Grant, Frémont, Rosecrans (if the rumors surrounding his dismissal be discounted), and especially Kearny. He soon found he had no use for, among others, Halleck, C. F. Jackson, McClellan, McCall, and Robinson; he was disappointed by Hooker and rapidly lost faith in Meade.

Duff's judgments at times, as for example his view of General David B. Birney, may have been unduly harsh.[5] Surely his impatience with Lincoln, who was so carefully juggling a coalition of political camps, was unwarranted. Levi believed that presidents and generals should be held to high standards. Was there hidden arrogance in this? Not really. Duff was a realist and took no delight in spelling out what he considered to be plain fact. Perhaps later in life, when he failed to campaign for offices to which he was nominated, relying on his reputation to gain him votes, there may have been a touch of arrogance — or was it naivety? The opinions on strategy and troop movements revealed in Levi's letters were not always prescient. Yet many of them stand well the tests of time and hindsight.

Duff did not appear to believe in an afterlife, a heaven, or a personal savior. But he did feel that he was in the hands of a benevolent Providence. He witnessed a great amount of death and unbelievable horrors, yet he seldom wrote of them and seemed to accept them as the price to be paid for the cleansing of the nation. Or at least he did not dwell on them. Nor did he talk of himself killing men. Fatalism some might call his posture; others might term it stoicism. Harriet was overjoyed to consider it faith. Whatever it was, it afforded Levi perspective, confidence, and calmness in the face of tragedy. It, his love of country, his dedication to racial justice, and mutual love for and with Harriet and later Agnes sustained his life. When at last it ebbed, he asked that the stone box enclosing his casket carry a bronze plate with his name, birth and death dates, and the words that he saw as defining his life: "A LOYAL SOLDIER OF THE UNITED STATES IN THE SLAVEHOLDER'S REBELLION 1861–1865."[6]

Appendix A:
*Chans des Confédéres**

Chans des Confédéres	**Song of the Confederates**
1er	1st
C'est la Louisiane qu'appelle cest enfants	Louisiana calls her children
C'est à nous d'aller à son secour	We must go to her rescue
A nous jeune creôle de St. Landry	We young Creoles of St. Landry
C'est à nous de prendre les armes.	Must take up arms
Encor	Chorus
Mourir pour la Louisiane 2 fois	To die for Louisiana 2 times
C'est le sort d'un Creôle "	Is the fate of a Creole "
C'est la vie d'un Louisianais "	It is the life of a Louisianan "
C'est le sort le plus beau "	A most beautiful fate "
Le plus dignes d'envie "	The most enviable "
2ieme	2nd
Adieu ma mére. Adieux mon pére	Farewell, Mother. Farewell, Father.
Je vous quitte pour batter l'ennemie	I leave you to combat the enemy
C'est la Louisiane qui mappelle sous les armes	Louisiana calls me to arms
Car je dois dèfendre ma patrie	I must defend my fatherland
Encor	Chorus
Mourir pour la Louisiane 2 fois	To die for Louisiana 2 times
C'est le sort d'un creôle "	Is the fate of a Creole "
3	3
C'est les dames des Oppeloussas	The ladies of Oppeloussas
Qui nous ont donnez notre drapeau	Gave us our flag
En nous disons jeune soldatts	Telling us young soldiers
Il faut vaincre ou mourir	You must vanquish or die
Encor	Chorus
Mourir pour la Louisiane	To die for Louisiana
....	....
4	4
Nous quittons la Louisiane	We leave Louisiana
Pour aller batter l'ennemie	To confront the enemy
Nous avons la capitain Spencer	We have Captain Spencer

Verses found in papers collected by Levi Bird Duff at Fort Magruder May 6, 1862.

Qui nous crie en event Marche	Who calls "Forward March"
Encor	Chorus
Mourir pour la Lousiane	To die for Louisiana
C'est le sort d'un creôle	Is the fate of a Creole
....	....

5eme	5th
Quand l'ennemie avance sur nos pas	When the enemy advances on us
La capaine Spencer a tient en tête	Captain Spencer takes the lead
L'epé en main nous crié charger la bayonnette	His sword in hand, he cries "Mount bayonets
Et frappe l'ennemie au coeur	And strike the enemy to the heart"
Encor	Chorus
Mourir pour la Lousiane	To die for Louisiana
C'est le sort d'un creôle	Is the fate of a Creole
....	....

6eme	6th
Nous avançons sur l'ennemie	We advance on the enemy
Nous les fessons tomber à chaque pas	We make them fall at each step
Nous leurs donnons la poudre et le plom	We give them powder and lead
Et les frappons tous aux coeurs	And strike them all to their hearts
Encor	Chorus
Mourir pour la Lousiane	To die for Louisiana
C'est le sort d'un creôle	Is the fate of a Creole
....	....

7	7
Quand nous sortons du champ de bataille	When we leave the field of battle
Le capaine Spencer nous crie aux armes	Captain Spencer cries "To arms"
Nous avont remportez la Victoire	We have won Victory
C'est á nous la Liberté	We shall have Liberty
Encor	Chorus
Mourir pour la Lousiane	To die for Louisiana
C'est le sort d'un creôle	Is the fate of a Creole
....	....

8eme	8th
Nous revenons dans nos campagnes	We shall return to our lands
Avec la liberté sur nos front	With liberty on our brow
Grace-à-Dieu nous avont la victoire	Thanks to God we have victory
C'est à lui que nous devons la liberté	We owe our liberty to Him
Encor	Chorus
Mourir pour la Lousiane	To die for Louisiana
C'est le sort d'un creôle	Is the fate of a Creole
....	....

9eme	9th
Quand nous rentrons dans nos foyer	When we return to our hearths
Nous voyons tous et changer	We see that all has changed
Les amis sont tous dispercer	Friends will have dispersed
Et les filles sont toute aporties	And the girls will all be taken away
Encor	Chorus

Mourir pour la Lousiane	To die for Louisiana
C'est le sort d'un creôle	Is the fate of a Creole
C'est ls vie d'un Louisianais	It is the life of a Louisianan
C'est le sort le plus beau	A most beautiful fate
Le plus digne d'envie	The most enviable
— Fin —	— End —
Fait le 26 Septembre 1861 au camp Lee	Written September 226, 1861 at
E. Linder Tombour	Camp Lee [trans. J. E. Helmreich]

Appendix B:
Gettysburg Memorial Address

Duff's papers include an announcement of a reunion of the 105th Regiment of the Pennsylvania Volunteers and a dedication of a monument at Gettysburg scheduled for July 2, 1888. Present also is an announcement of another gathering for the same purpose at the same place on September 11, 1889. Perhaps one was for the ground breaking, the other for the completion of the monument. In both instances, Levi Bird Duff was listed as offering a short address. Next to these announcements in his papers lay the following notes of the comments he apparently delivered at the second gathering.

The 105th P. V. C. monument at Gettysburg. Located near the Sherfy House on the Emmetsburg Road, the monument displays the face of a wildcat. Its presence in western Pennsylvania in the early nineteenth century gave the regiment its nickname (photograph by the editor).

Comrades of the 105 Regiment:

We have met perhaps for the last time on this battlefield. A long time has elapsed since we fought here. The great struggle of which this battle was a part is ended. Its dangers have been braved, its toils have been endured, its sacrifices have been made, its fruits have been gathered. Our country is at peace and we assemble to-day not as soldiers, but as citizens of a united and free country.

How changed the scene since 26 years ago. The 105 regiment arrived upon this field at sun down of July 1 1863. The Army of the Potomac was concentrating for a decisive conflict. The first days fight was over and our army had suffered severe loss and had been forced back through the town & had made a stand on Cemetery Ridge. As we approached the field we knew we came to certain battle. We were already warned that victory was doubtful, but we came resolved to face the enemy, to fight, and if need be to die, in defense of our country. It was a moment of great peril. The Army of the Potomac alone, stood between the government and chaos. We felt the agony of the burden that was laid upon us and we knew that the country stood behind us waiting, listening, hoping for victory but trembling for the result.

The second day brought a fierce & bloody fight, which ended as did the first with the loss of ground by our army, but when darkness closed the contest, the enemy lay upon the field baffled, beaten. The flower of his army lay dead and he was still confronted ... [by] a brave determined foe. Whatever may be the thoughts of others, whatever may have been the opinion of the enemy, the soldiers of the Army of the Potomac felt at the close of the second day, that the victory had been won. At dark of that day, he sank to rest beside his dead comrades in the full conviction that his country was safe. The third day came and with it another stubborn conflict — the enemy in forlorn hope made an assault upon our centre. It failed, but gave a brilliant and bloody close to a disastrous defeat. Hence forward the wave of rebellion gradually receded and the rebel army sank slowly sullenly, but hopelessly into the grave.

In the battle fought here the 105 regiment bore its part, and bore it nobly. We are not here to boast of its achievements or to tell the story of its valor. The one is unnecessary the other we may safely leave to history. We are assembled to dedicate a monument erected to mark its position in the battle. It is not a monument reared to the memory of an individual — it marks no conquests — on it are no words of vaunting triumph. It is a plain enduring memorial of the 105 regiment. Upon it is inscribed briefly the story of the regiment — its enlistment, its muster out, the battles in which it was engaged and the number who fell in battle. This stone impartially records the service and perpetuates the memory of every man that belonged to the regiment, whether he fell in this battle, or some other whether he died by the way or is living yet. And when we are all dead and our names are forgotten, this monument will remain as an enduring memorial of our services.

And what was the 105 regiment. It was a regiment of volunteers not mercenaries — it was not composed of soldiers of fortune, but of citizens, who in the hour [of] danger, came to the rescue of an imperiled government. When the country called, theirs was not to make reply, theirs was but to do and die. In 1861 under the first call for volunteers for three years or during the war, the 105 regiment enlisted. It took its place in the Army of the Potomac and shared its defeats and its victories. But the war lingered and at the end of its first enlistment it enlisted for another term of three years. The regiment volunteered for the war — it took up arms when the rebellion began, it laid down its arms only when the rebellion was crushed. It put its hand to the plow and looked not back. It faced the rebels until the last one had died on the field of battle or surrendered. Its actual battle service began with the war it ended at Appomattox. When the history of the great conflict — the slaveholder's rebellion — is made up — when there is meted out to each regiment its just share in the noble work which saved this government & established liberty throughout the land — the 105 regiment will be found among the faithful and brave, among those which answered the first call to arms and among those which served loyally to the end. Nor must we forget the cause in which the regiment served. Action is ennobled only by a noble cause. The conflict between freedom and slavery is an old one. It has convulsed all governments and all peoples since the earliest dawn of history. It still lingers in many lands to blight and destroy, but happily it is ended forever among English speaking people. It was once the boast of an English judge that the air of England was so free that a slave could not live in it. To our shame be it said such a boast could not be made of our country before the slaveholders rebellion. It is one of the anomalies of history that slavery found its final resting place and made its last stand under the freest government on earth. But so it was. The fathers who founded this government on the principle that all men are free and equal and transmitted it unimpaired to their children left untouched negro slavery as it then existed. It was believed that the humane and enlightened sentiment which then prevailed, would soon abolish it. But by toleration it grew and spread, until the spirit of slavery over-ran the whole nation. It savaged the halls of legislation — it poisoned the fountain of justice — it made religion a mockery — it destroyed the sanctity of the home.

It oppressed the negro—it enslaved the white man. Its deadly virus blighted alike the manhood of the South and the humanity of the North. The whole nation was benumbed and stood dumb under the influence of this great iniquity. The hour of deliverance came, but it came not without sacrifice. Among those who stepped out from the North to offer themselves as a sacrifice were the men of the 105 regiment. You can trace the marches of the regiment by the graves of its dead. Its work is done, its rests from its labors. The nation lives—the oppressed are free.

Comrades, in the times yet to come and long after we have passed away, many pilgrims will visit this battlefield. They will pause before this stone & when they read the list of battles & turn to the other face & read the number of the killed & wounded they will be filled with admiration at the heroism the loyalty & devotion of the 105 regiment. There can be no more eloquent eulogy of the dead, there can be no higher praise of the living than to say of them: they belonged to 105 regiment Pa. Vol.

Chapter Notes

Introduction

1. James M. McPherson, *This Mighty Scourge* (New York: Oxford University Press, 2007), 155–66, a reprint of his article "Spend Much Time in Reading the Daily Papers," originally published in *Atlanta History: A Journal of Georgia and the South* (Spring 1998).

2. Information regarding Levi Bird Duff's youth and later life may be found in a "Family History" written by Levi's son Samuel Eckerberger Duff about 1934, unpublished typescript, Papers of Levi Bird Duff, Special Collections, Pelletier Library, Allegheny College, Meadville, PA.

3. Letter of May 3, 1858, quoted in S. E. Duff, "Family History."

4. James M. McPherson, *For Cause and Comrades: Why Men Fought in the Civil War* (New York: Oxford University Press, 1997), viii.

5. Harriet Nixon letter of September 13, 1861. The letters of Levi, Harriet, and others reproduced in this account are all from the Papers of Levi Bird Duff, unless otherwise indicated.

6. S. E. Duff, "Family History."

7. Kate M. Scott, *History of the One Hundred and Fifth Regiment of Pennsylvania Volunteers. A Complete History of the Organization, Marches, Battles, Toils, and Dangers Participated in by the Regiment from the Beginning to the Close of the War, 1861–1865.* Philadelphia: New World Publishing Co., 1877.

Chapter 1

1. Journal of Harriet Howard Nixon, Papers of Levi Bird Duff, Special Collections, Pelletier Library, Allegheny College, Meadville, PA.

2. Harriet and Levi frequently referred to individuals other than close friends and family members by their last names only. Where possible, first names or initials are editorially supplied at the initial mention. Helpful in this connection is Samuel P. Bates, *History of Pennsylvania Volunteers, 1861–5; Prepared in Compliance with Acts of the Legislature*, 14 vols. (Wilmington, NC: Broadfoot, 1993–94 republication of 1869–71 edition). Full identification cannot be achieved in all cases. The same last name may appear multiple times, records were not always complete, and Duff's spelling proves occasionally errant.

3. This man was either Joshua or William K. Bai-

ley. Both survived to be mustered out of service in May 1864.

4. Conrad F. Jackson became colonel of the 38th P. V. in May 1861. He became a brigadier general July 15, 1862, and was killed at Fredericksburg, December 13, 1862.

5. L. W. Smith. Appointed captain of Company A May 1, 1861, he resigned in June 1862, but was commissioned colonel of the 169th P. V. in November 1862.

6. Union General Benjamin F. Butler first made a name for himself in Massachusetts politics. Upon the outbreak of war he gained the rank of brigadier general in the Massachusetts militia. He was the sort of politician-militaire that Duff resented. Butler won notice by restoring order in fractious Baltimore and for refusing to return escaped slaves to their owners. For a short while he held command of Fort Monroe and the department of eastern Virginia. After being relieved of this command, he led volunteer forces in capturing Fort Hatteras and Fort Clark, to which expeditions Duff here refers. He went on to a noted and controversial career in the military, especially in New Orleans in 1862, and in politics.

7. It may be presumed that Duff here refers to Brig. General Nathaniel Lyon.

8. Frémont at the time commanded Union forces in the West.

9. Breckinridge, senator from Kentucky and vice president from 1857 to 1861, was the nominee for president of the southern branch of the Democratic Party in the election of 1860. He remained active in Washington, D.C., until expelled by the Senate's resolution December 4, 1861, requiring support of the union. He soon became a general in the Confederate Army and served as Secretary of War for the Confederate States.

10. This poorly drained camp was located near Langley, Virginia; another Camp Pierpoint was located along the Ohio River near Ceredo, Virginia (now West Virginia). The names seem to have been assigned to honor Francis H. Pierpont, governor of "restored" Virginia — the part of the state which remained loyal to the Union. At the time Pierpont's name was frequently spelled "Pierpoint," although when he graduated from Allegheny College eighteen years before Duff, and again in later life, he employed the "Pierpont" spelling.

Chapter 2

1. Either Moses or Robert.
2. Pvt. Eliakim or Sergeant William C.
3. Smith died of his wounds on January 14, 1862.
4. Chadwick also studied at Allegheny College, four years behind Duff. A copy of a collection of his letters to his parents is in Special Collections, Pelletier Library, Allegheny College, Meadville, PA. See Jonathan E. Helmreich, *The Flag of the Allegheny College Volunteers* (Meadville, PA: Allegheny College, 2002).
5. Duff quotes the penultimate stanza of John Greenleaf Whittier's "At Port Royal," first published in 1862. The first line in the original begins with the word "That" rather than the word "The." Also, "and" is used rather than an ampersand.
6. Amor A. McKnight, a Brookville, Pennsylvania, printer turned lawyer as early as the winter of 1860 had begun recruiting a company he entitled the Brookville Rifles. After the attack on Fort Sumter, McKnight offered the services of this militia to Governor of Pennsylvania Andrew Curtin. It was assigned to the Eighth Regiment of the Pennsylvania Volunteers. After the regiment completed its three months' service, McKnight was authorized by the War Department to raise a full regiment for service for three years or the duration of the war. The former Brookfield Rifles became the core of the 105th Regiment Pennsylvania Volunteers (known as the Wild Cat Regiment), of which McKnight served as colonel. His emphasis on the manual of arms and on discipline was at first resented by his troops but later appreciated.
7. Steadman was a member of the same literary society at the college as Duff.
8. Half-brother to the colonel, the approximately fifteen-year-old youth was not officially part of the regiment.
9. Hays was a member of the Allegheny College class of 1840. He did not graduate, transferring to West Point to pursue a military career.

Chapter 3

1. James M. McPherson, *Ordeal by Fire: The Civil War and Reconstruction* 2nd ed. (New York: McGraw-Hill, 1992), 243.
2. Quoted from Samuel E. Duff, "Family History."
3. Ibid. Col. A. McKnight's June 2, 1862, report of the battle contained the following paragraph:
"Lieutenant Cummiskey, of Company D, had his head blown off by a cannon ball while gallantly leading his men forward to repulse a charge of the enemy. As an officer he was unsurpassed. He had every qualification of a gentleman, and was brave and chivalrous to a fault. Captains Kirk, [Albert C.] Thompson, Duff, and Greenawalt, with Lieutenants [James P.] Geggie, [Ezra B.] Baird, McLaughlin, [Cassius C.] Markle, and [Albert J.] Shipley, were wounded in the midst of the combat and whilst urging their men on." *The War of the Rebellion: A Compilation of the Official Records of the Union and Confederate Armies.* Series I—Volume XI—in three parts—Part 1—Reports (Washington: Government Printing Office,

1884), 851. Some weeks later, Duff received a note from Cummiskey's father.

> Sept 15ᵗʰ 1862
> North Mahoning twp.

Dear Sir: After my Best and Kind respects to you I wish to inform you that I understood that you ware Seriously wounded in the Battle of Fair Oaks on the 31 day of May 1862 in that Same Battle you lost your first Lieut J. P. R. Cummiskey I have oft times wished to hear of you and to get a letter from you

You may be able to give me some particulars as respects the Deceased he ws my Son a dutiful Child a Studious Student A Splendid Schollar an eminent Teacher and according to report a Brave man in the Army of the United States Co. D. 105 Regt PA

My Dear friend Captain Duff you will write to me and let know Some of the particulars about my Son J P R Cummiskey in all of his letters to me he spoke highly of you I Now Address you as his Capt and friend yours with respect E M Cummiskey

Levi's reply is not known. Surely it must have been difficult to write.

Chapter 4

1. Edward and Charles Smith were the brothers of Sarah Smith, one of Harriet's closest friends. Their homestead, near Beatty, Pennsylvania, was known as Springfield Farm. Harriet often visited there.
2. McKnight had fallen ill and was medically advised to rest at home. Unable to receive a furlough, McKnight resigned. He returned to service in March 1863.
3. Scott, *History of the One Hundred and Fifth Regiment*, 62.
4. Duff's recollection of calendar dates here appears to be one day off, for Second Bull Run was fought on August 29 and 30, not the 30th and 31st.
5. The capture of Longstreet proved to be just a rumor.
6. Philip Kearny, killed at the Second Battle of Bull Run, was greatly admired by the men of the 105th Regiment, P.V.C. He was one of the few Union military leaders that Duff truly respected.
7. At the close of October Lincoln did dismiss Buell, an open critic of emancipation, from leadership of the Army of the Ohio following the general's failure vigorously to pursue retreating Confederates in Tennessee.

Chapter 5

1. Duff usually applied the Hedgeman River name only to the North Fork of the Rappahannock, but many others in the nineteenth century applied it to the entire river.
2. Edward J. Allen, colonel of the 155th Regiment, P.V., was arrested and imprisoned for a period by army superiors for seizing a room in the house of a noted rebel to serve as a hospital for sick soldiers of his regiment. Bates, *History*, VIII, 800.
3. Owston survived to be mustered out with the company in May 1864.

Chapter 7

1. Watkins survived this wound, though he was captured. He later returned to the Union lines and was killed at Petersburg June 18, 1864.

2. Many Union supporters and some rival newspapers considered the *New York Herald* as harboring sympathies for the South and inclined to support Copperhead views. See Brayton Harris, *Blue & Gray in Black & White: Newspapers in the Civil War* (Washington: Batford Brassey, 1999), 41–46.

3. Duff here may be referring to the Polish Revolution of 1863, quashed by Russian troops, which stirred possibility of intervention by other European powers, or more likely to the growing tension between Denmark and Prussia over the Schleswig-Holstein question. British interests were involved in both cases.

Chapter 8

1. Scott, *History of the One Hundred and Fifth Regiment*, 86. Scott indicates that the regiment reached White Sulphur Springs on July 27, but Duff's letters indicate that his unit did not reach that location until July 31. He considered their chase after Lee to have begun on June 11.

2. Sickles was severely wounded in the second day of battle at Gettysburg; his leg was amputated.

3. The manservant was a fugitive field hand from Georgia, declared a contraband of war in 1862. He was the paid personal servant of Duff in 1863 and 1864 during the war. Duff's leatherbound notebook carries the following memorandum:

HdQrs. 105th P.V.C.
June 4th, 1864

"Memorandum"

Gave "Doctor" Melton "Due Bill" to pay for $110.15 for services to date.

Melton continued to serve Duff in the years after the war and was the Duff family coachman and gardener from 1870 to 1878. "Doctor" Melton fell insane, apparently violently so, in the latter year and was placed in an asylum by Duff. Melton died in 1879.

Chapter 9

1. *The War of the Rebellion: A Compilation of the Official Records of the Union and Confederate Armies.* Series I—Volume XXIX—in two parts—Part 1—Reports, 756 (Washington: Government Printing Office, 1890) contains Duff's report of his first days in charge of the 110th Pennsylvania Volunteers in the Mine Run, Virginia, campaign:

Report of Maj. Levi B. Duff, One hundred and fifth Pennsylvania Infantry, commanding One hundred and tenth Pennsylvania Infantry

Headquarters 110th
Pennsylvania Volunteers,
Camp near Brandy Station, Va.,
December 6, 1863

Sir: I have the honor to report that on the 26th day of November, 1863, the day of the commencement of the recent operations, the One hundred and tenth

Pennsylvania Volunteers was ordered to report to Lieutenant-Colonel Howard, chief quartermaster, Third Corps.

It so reported and was assigned by him to the duty of guarding the trains of the corps. On the 26th, it marched with the trains from Brandy Station to Richardsville, arriving at the latter place at 2 A.M. of the 27th. On the 27th, at 9 A.M., left Richardsville and arrived at Culpeper Mine Ford, on the Rapidan River, at 3 P.M. Remained in camp at the ford until 9 P.M. of the 28th, when the trains started for Robertson's Tavern. The regiment marched with the trains all night, and arrived at Robertson's Tavern at 2 P.M. of the 29th. The same evening, at 9 P.M., started back to the ford with the trains, and arrived there at 11 A.M., the 30th. On December 1, the regiment moved with the trains from the ford to Richardsville. Left Richardsville again at 12 m. on the 2nd of December, and arrived at Brandy Station at 3 A.M. the morning of the 3d instant. At 9 A.M. of the 3d, was relieved by Colonel Howard and report to Colonel Collis, commanding brigade.

The marching, though severe and continuous, was borne manfully by the officers and men of the regiment.

I am, sir, very respectfully, your obedient servant.
LEVI BIRD DUFF
Major 105th Pa. Vols., Commanding 110th Pa. Vols.

2. With close of the three-year term of enlistment of the bulk of the Union's veteran soldiers approaching, the government launched a major effort to persuade soldiers to re-enlist. A $300 federal bonus, in addition to state and local bounties, was offered. Those Pennsylvania regiments that signed up a sufficient numbers of returnees were promised continuation. The veterans were also offered a thirty-day veteran furlough. Two hundred and forty members of the 105th Pennsylvania Volunteers, Duff's original regiment, reenlisted, and therefore the unit was ordered home as a group for its leave. Levi went with it.

Chapter 10

1. Hall's highest rank was that of corporal. He was discharged on surgeon's certificate in October 1864.

Chapter 11

1. Reference is made here to the Confederate naval and military attack launched at Plymouth, North Carolina, on April 17, 1864. Union troops under the command of H. Wessels abandoned Fort Comfort, concentrated at Fort William, and surrendered its garrison on April 20.

2. Scott, *History of the One Hundred and Fifth Regiment of Pennsylvania Volunteers*, 97 provides Duff's description of events on Friday, May 6 (the day after Gen. Hays was killed). The 105th undertook a successful charge but then had to retreat as it ran out of ammunition and the rebels gained reinforcements. "Major L. B. Duff, who was serving on General Birney's staff says:

'Suddenly a heavy fire broke out on our left, about a quarter of a mile to the left of the plank-road, and soon our line there gave way and got into one of those unaccountable panics which happen in the best of armies, and began to fall back rapidly. The infection spread to the rest of our line, and the whole advance line fell back pell-mell to the Brock turnpike. Here we had thrown up works, and with much difficulty we succeeded in rallying the men behind them. The rebels followed us, and we had only got fairly settled when they attacked us. Owing to the fact that the line of breastworks was made of timber, and that it took fire just to the left of the Orange Court-House road, our men were obliged to abandon it. The rebels came close up to it and then our second line gave way, and for a while it was thought that everything would go; but two regiments of our division, the Twentieth Indiana and the Ninety-ninth Pennsylvania, and the section of a battery, held firm just on the left of the Orange Court-House plank-road. Upon these our line rallied, the rebels were hurled back, and quiet restored. At the time the break occurred the One Hundred and Fifth was in the second line of breastworks, charged forward and occupied a position in the front line. In doing so, Captain [William J.] Clyde and some others mounted the front line of breastworks and urged the men forward.'"

3. Among Duff's papers is a leather notebook that contains the following, apparently a draft of a report.

Hd Qrs. 105th P.V.

May 19th, 1864

Capt. F. E. Marble

Actg. Asst. Adj. Gen'l

Sir:

I have the honor to submit the following report of the part taken by the 105th Regt. P.V. in the recent operation after I assumed command of the regiment.

In the afternoon of the 7th of May, when I took command I found the regiment lying in reserve with the rest of the Brigade on the Wilderness battle ground in rear of the Cross Roads. About 4 o'clock it was moved forward and occupied the works on the right of the Plank Road. Remained there but a short time & then marched Eastward along the Plank Road about 2 miles, about faced & marched back & occupied the 2nd line of works on the left of the Plank Road. Lay in the works all night, next morning (8th) moved on the Brock Turnpike towards Todd's Tavern, arrived at the Tavern about noon amassed south of it about ? of a mile about four o'clock moved West of the Tavern to the right of the road leading to Orange C. H. built works & lay behind them until the afternoon the 9th. Leaving the works the regiment moved a short distance on the Spottsylvania C. H. road then turning to the right & after a short delay crossed Corbins Branch of the Po River & turning down the river halted after dark near the junction of Corbins branch & Glady Run. On the 10th recrossed Corbins Branch & moved to the left to support troops of the 5th Corps, while making an attack on the enemy works. The 105th Reg't formed the left of the 2nd Line, the Brigade being in two lines. Remained some time but did not become engaged, then march[ed] towards the right about half mile turned to the left & went within a short distance of Po River. I was here ordered to form the regiment on a knoll near the river on the left of the 5th Mich. While doing so the regiment was opened on by a bat-

tery from the opposite side of the river. The fire was murderous, but the men stood their ground until ordered to fall back, which they did & formed in line without delay in rear of the knoll. Under the fire of this battery 2 officer[s] were wounded & 1 enlisted man killed & 10 wounded. Moved from this position back to the support of Warrens Troops, remained there a short time then moved back to the right to support Gen. [Francis C.] Barlow. Formed 2nd line of Gen. Barlow's left and lay there all night. On the 11th moved into the advanced Rifle pit occupying the extreme right on the right of the 17th Maine. Vacated the rifle pits in the afternoon and massed in the woods in rear. On 10 P.M. same night were ordered to march, going towards the left. The march was slow and tedious and just at dawn we arrived and took position for the charge which followed. The Brigade was in two lines the 105th Reg't the right of the 2 Line. The line moved forward promptly when the order to charge was given. On reaching the edge of the woods near the Landon House, ... [here the narrative breaks off]

4. Duff's leather notebook also contains two drafts similar in wording written on May 13, 1864; the following is the more complete]

Hd. Qrs. 105th P.V.

May 13th, 1864

Capt. F. E. Marble

Ast. Adjt. Gen'l

I have the honor to report that in the charge of yesterday morning my command, composed of the 105th and 63rd P. V., struck the rebel works at the point where the works begin to retire to the right, taking battery posted there & passed on over the Jefferson Davis battery 100 yds. further to the right & thence to the extreme right across a swamp capturing on the other side of the swamp 2 rifled pieces these were subsequently lost & the Jeff. Davis battery before it was hauled off fell between the lines.

I have the honor like wise to report that Gen. Stuart was captured by Capt. Daniel Dougherty of the 63rd P.V. & the flag of the 18th North Carolina reg't by Lt. A. H. Mitchel Co. A 105th P.V. & the flag of the 24th North Carolina was captured by Corporal [John M.] Kindig of the 63 P.V.

Respectfully Submitted

Confederate General J. E. B. Stuart was mortally wounded at Yellow Tavern on May 11, 1864. According to his biographers, the general was taken to Richmond where he died. There is no mention of any, even brief, capture of Stuart by Union troops. Duff's reference here, therefore, appears to be due to incorrect information and may not have been included in his final, formal, report—or is a mystery. Captain Dougherty lost his life in this battle.

On November 1, 1865, writing from Annapolis, Maryland, Brig. Gen. John R. Brooke wrote an extensive report of the activities of his command, the Fourth Brigade, First Division, Army of the Potomac from May 3 through June 3, 1864. In it he makes reference to L. B. Duff's performance on May 12:

"After proceeding about 500 yards, I encountered a second line of works with a marsh in its front. Owing to the disorganization of my command I could not make a determined attack on this line. The enemy came out in strong force, when I retired, fighting to the line already captured, where I found a large number of the Third Division, who seemed to be engaged in gathering spoils, and could not be made available for the defense of this line, though there were many gallant men among them who did their duty bravely, conspicuous among whom was Major Duff, One hundred and fifth Pennsylvania Volunteers, who, with a portion of his regiment, did good service at this time." — *The War of the Rebellion: A Compilation of the Official Records of the Union and Confederate Armies*, Series I, vol. 36, Part I — Reports, (Washington: Government Printing Office, 1891), 410.

Epilogue

1. S. E. Duff, "Family History."

2. James M. McPherson, *Ordeal by Fire: The Civil War and Reconstruction* 2nd. Ed. (New York, McGraw-Hill, 1992), 356.

3. James M. McPherson, *For Cause and Comrades: Why Men Fought in the Civil War* (New York: Oxford University Press, 1997), 117.

4. Her letter to Levi of September 21, 1861.

5. That he was not alone in being critical of Birney, an officer who achieved his first positions through political connections, is evident from this note sent to Harriet by Levi.

Washington D.C.

Oct. 19th, 1864

General Birney died yesterday in Philadelphia. There is a fulsome eulogy of him in this mornings Inquirer. Res contra, I met a former Captain of the 86th N. Y. belonging to our Division. I told him that Gen' Birney was dead. "That's in answer to the prayers of his old Division" said he & added "he ought to have died five years ago." Doctors differ.—

6. S. E. Duff, "Family History."

Select Bibliography

Primary Sources

Chadwick, James D. Letters (copy of originals). Papers of James D. Chadwick, Special Collections, Pelletier Library, Allegheny College, Meadville, PA.

Duff, Harriet Nixon. Civil War letters. Papers of Levi Bird Duff, Special Collections, Pelletier Library, Allegheny College, Meadville, PA.

Duff, Levi Bird. Civil War letters. Papers of Levi Bird Duff, Special Collections, Pelletier Library, Allegheny College, Meadville, PA.

Duff, Samuel Eckerberger. "Family History." Unpublished typescript, c. 1934. Papers of Levi Bird Duff, Special Collections, Pelletier Library, Allegheny College, Meadville, PA.

Nixon, Harriet Howard. Journal and letters. Papers of Levi Bird Duff, Special Collections, Pelletier Library, Allegheny College, Meadville, PA.

The War of the Rebellion: A Compilation of the Official Records of the Union and Confederate Armies. Prepared under the direction of the Secretary of War by Robert N. Scott. Washington: Government Printing Office, 1880–1900.

Secondary Sources

Bates, Samuel P. *History of Pennsylvania Volunteers, 1861–5; Prepared in Compliance with Acts of the Legislature*, 14 vols. Wilmington, NC: Broadfoot, 1993–94 (Republication of 1869–71 edition).

Battles and Leaders of the Civil War. Being for the Most Part Contributions by Union and Confederate Officers. Based upon "The Century War Series" edited by Robert U. Johnson and Clarence C. Buel. 4 vols. New York: Yoseloff, 1956.

Catton, Bruce. *This Hallowed Ground: The Story of the Union Side of the Civil War*. Garden City, NY: Doubleday, 1956.

Harris, Brayton. *Blue & Gray in Black & White: Newspapers in the Civil War*. Washington: Batford Brassey, 1999.

Helmreich, Jonathan E. *The Flag of the Allegheny College Volunteers*. Meadville, PA: Allegheny College, 2002.

McPherson, James. M. *Battle Cry of Freedom: The Civil War Era*. New York: Oxford University Press, 1988.

_____. *For Cause and Comrades: Why Men Fought in the Civil War*. New York: Oxford University Press, 1997.

_____. *Ordeal by Fire: The Civil War and Reconstruction* 2nd ed. New York: McGraw-Hill, 1992.

_____. *This Mighty Scourge*. New York: Oxford University Press, 2007.

Scott, Kate M. *History of the One Hundred and Fifth Regiment of Pennsylvania Volunteers. A Complete History of the Organization, Marches, Battles, Toils, and Dangers Participated in by the Regiment from the Beginning to the Close of the War, 1861–1865*. Philadelphia: New World Publishing Co., 1877.

Index

Numbers in **bold italics** indicate pages with photographs.